ECONOMIC RESTRUCTURING
AND
FAMILY WELL-BEING IN RURAL AMERICA

ECONOMIC RESTRUCTURING
AND
FAMILY WELL-BEING IN RURAL AMERICA

Edited by

KRISTIN E. SMITH AND ANN R. TICKAMYER

Published in cooperation with the Rural Sociological Society

The Pennsylvania State University Press
University Park, Pennsylvania

Library of Congress Cataloging-in-Publication Data

Economic restructuring and family well-being in rural America /
edited by Kristin E. Smith and Ann Tickamyer ; published in
cooperation with the Rural Sociological Society.
p.   cm.
Includes bibliographical references and index.
Summary: "A compilation of policy-relevant research by a multidisciplinary
group of scholars on the state of families in rural America in the twenty-first
century. Examines the impact of economic restructuring on rural Americans and
provides policy recommendations for addressing the challenges
they face"—Provided by publisher.
ISBN 978-0-271-04861-1 (cloth : alk. paper)
1. Rural families—United States.
2. United States—Rural conditions.
3. Manpower policy, Rural—United States.
I. Smith, Kristin E.
II. Tickamyer, Ann R.
III. Rural Sociological Society.

HQ536.E326 2011
330.973´0091734—dc22
2011005692

Contents

Foreword

CYNTHIA "MIL" DUNCAN

We often think of rural communities as places where time stands still, whether we are living in a small rural town or just passing through familiar landscapes. The same pasture stretches out beyond the rock wall, the same farmhouse sits off on the hill overlooking the soybean fields, the same road twists up the hollow along the creek past the old coal tipple, the bayou has the same blue-green tint to it where small boys are still fishing. Mrs. Johnson is still postmistress, the Haleys still run the hardware store, though it's young Tim and his wife, Ellen, now. One of the Red Hats is still on tribal council. It still takes forever to get to the store. The kids still go up to the lake to party. That family at the end of the road is still struggling. The school is still having trouble attracting teachers; the hospital can't keep doctors and nurses any better than it used to.

But for all these images of time standing still, we know rural America has always been changing, economically and demographically. For the most part this has meant population and economic decline, but the process has been uneven and has varied over time and place. As Kenneth Johnson and Calvin Beale wrote in a 1998 *Wilson Quarterly* piece, rural America lost population for most of the twentieth century, as young people moved to cities for jobs and other opportunities. Of course, America's natural resources and low-skill manufacturing have long provided fodder for a rural economy, but over the years jobs in these areas have steadily declined while opportunities in cities have expanded. Indeed, as Johnson and Beale note, urban population growth has outstripped rural growth since 1860, with notable big population declines like the 1950s and '60s migration from the rural South and the coalfields of Appalachia following mechanization.

The fundamental economic restructuring that is causing so much adjustment in rural America today has been unfolding for many years. There has been considerable scholarly attention paid to the economic transformation that rural America has been witnessing since the mid-1980s. Many scholars, including some of the authors in this edited collection, have tracked and analyzed that change.

But to date there has not been a detailed, comprehensive look at how these changes have impacted children and families. In this volume, *Economic Restructuring and Family Well-Being in Rural America,* Kristin E. Smith and Ann R. Tickamyer have assembled a wide-ranging collection of analyses of how rural families have adapted to economic restructuring and what it has meant for them and their children. This family focus is invaluable for policy makers, researchers and their students, and those who care about America's rural communities.

This volume contributes to ongoing Carsey Institute efforts to understand the challenges that face rural America. Through Carsey Institute research, we have learned a lot about how rural America is changing and the importance of place-based research. One piece of research that has been particularly enlightening in understanding the diversity within rural America is a publication called *Place Matters.* Larry Hamilton and his colleagues illustrate that today there are four rural Americas, and economic and demographic changes unfold differently in each. Since 2007 the Carsey Institute has interviewed almost twenty thousand people in the Community and Environment in Rural America (CERA) survey, comparing their different backgrounds, communities, and economic experiences and trying to understand their perspectives on changes in their communities and on environmental issues.

We have found, for example, that there are areas rich in natural amenities like lakes and forests, mountains, and seashores that have been attracting second-home owners and retirees, growing and changing with the newcomers. With three out of five baby boomers saying they want to live in a small town or rural community when they retire, these naturally beautiful Amenity-Rich Areas are likely to see increased growth in the years ahead. Some families are struggling to adjust to economic changes in these places, but their odds of making it are much better than those for folks in places that have seen steady population decline and out-migration of young people.

Areas that have long relied on extracting or processing natural resources continue to lose population as industries move overseas or achieve productivity increases with existing or declining workforces. Some have the potential to steward their natural resources and become attractive to retirees and footloose professionals, but old habits and systems die hard, and the path to amenity-based growth is uncertain. We at the Carsey Institute call these places Transitioning

Areas with Amenities. They fall in the middle on many of our measures, somewhere between the booming Amenity-Rich Areas and the others. They are fascinating places to examine the contemporary impact of economic change on families, organizations, and communities as they struggle to chart a new course. Families in these areas feel the brunt of economic restructuring, at both the household and the community levels, as resources shrink and jobs change and disappear.

Rural America also includes areas with few natural amenities and limited recreation opportunities. Here economic decline has been reflected in protracted population decline, with little prospect for growth. Large areas of the agricultural heartland of the Midwest and Great Plains, together with remote timber- and mining-dependent areas of New England, the upper Great Lakes, and the Northwest, fit in this Declining Resource-Dependent Areas category. Such counties cut a broad swath through the heart of the country, with widespread population loss and an aging population. Yet Carsey surveys document that in many of these areas, social capital is off the charts—high trust, everyone across the spectrum attends meetings and belongs to organizations. Even with their futures in jeopardy, many of these communities reflect the rural ideal of small-town America where people know and look after one another—even as they struggle with widespread and protracted population decline, with deaths outnumbering births and young people leaving in droves. It is likely that challenged families find social support in these areas both from their communities and from their extended families. Yet they will likely face continuing economic challenges even when the national economy recovers.

Finally, significant parts of rural America continue to be plagued by chronic poverty. Sadly, this is not a new story for rural America. Recent Carsey research documents the large concentration of persistently poor counties in many parts of rural America. In these areas, adequate resources have never been invested in education or community infrastructure and now whole communities are broken. These Chronically Poor Areas have much in common with inner-city neighborhoods, where poor people are concentrated and community institutions are weak and lack resources. Trust is lowest in these places, even though roots are deep, and education lags at all levels. High school graduation rates are dismally low, and unemployment and disability high. Families struggle in these communities, and many of those who could leave did so long ago, leaving remaining residents with even fewer social, economic, and human resources but more personal, family, and community problems to cope with.

Despite the differences between the "four rurals," Carsey's CERA surveys identified some interesting common threads woven throughout: everywhere people express serious concerns about the number and quality of jobs; in each of our community types many people would advise their own children to leave for opportunity elsewhere; core patriotic values run deep in all of our community types, with nearly everyone knowing local people who are serving in Iraq or Afghanistan. In many cases, these young people serve both to support their country and in the hope that military service will enhance their own opportunities for the future. So the impact of economic changes on families in rural America that this volume explores is an enduring concern of many living in a broad cross-section of rural communities. In the face of the significant economic transformations now under way in rural America, many of our respondents express concern for both the future of their children and the future of their communities. That such concerns are so widespread, whether the communities see their population growing, declining, or stagnant, underscores the timeliness of the topic.

Change continues in rural America as larger forces sweep across the country. With a grounded, empirical understanding of those changes, policy makers and community leaders can make better decisions. Smart policies and proven programs can affect how these transformations unfold and impact families; when we understand the circumstances families face and how they are trying to adjust to change, we can make better policy and improve programs to ensure that rural families can realize a good life for themselves and their communities. This book goes a long way in both analyzing the changes and their impacts and documenting policies and programs that can make a difference.

Acknowledgments

We are grateful to Cynthia "Mil" Duncan for her support and encouragement, which was critical at several junctions in this project. Thanks also to colleagues at the Carsey Institute, including Kenneth Johnson, Marybeth Mattingly, Barbara Wauchope, Curt Grimm, and Amy Sterndale, whose genuine interest in the manuscript inspired a will to continue. We appreciate the work done by Jared Bernstein at the initial stage of this project. We are especially thankful to the Annie E. Casey Foundation, the W. K. Kellogg Foundation, and the Carsey Institute for financial support.

We also thank Steven Sapp and the Rural Studies Series for supporting this project and external reviewers for their comments and suggestions. Special thanks to Clare Hinrichs, Diane McLaughlin, and Leif Jensen for their ongoing backing of this project.

Kristin is especially grateful to her research assistants, Katherine Seabury, Michelle Stransky, Siobhan Whalen, and Jessica Bean, whose ongoing assistance over the years with logistical, administrative, and research support was crucial to the successful completion of this project. Thanks also to Melanie Higgins Dostie and Susan Colucci for administrative support.

Ann appreciates the assistance of Ann Bennett at Ohio University and Linda Kline and Linda Mace at Penn State University. Numerous students in graduate seminars have contributed to the thinking that went into this work.

We also want to thank all the contributing authors for their attention to detail, prompt responsiveness to our requests, and patience as we navigated the process of turning an idea into a reality. The editors also want to thank each other for inspiration and a "can do" attitude, which made this project a pleasure.

INTRODUCTION

KRISTIN E. SMITH AND ANN R. TICKAMYER

This book documents how family economic change has influenced family well-being in rural America. Rural areas have been hit hard by economic restructuring. Well-paying, traditionally male jobs with benefits (such as in manufacturing) have declined dramatically, only to be replaced with low-paying, service-oriented jobs—jobs that do not offer benefits or wages sufficient to raise a family. Even this type of employment is scarce in many remote rural areas, and with the advent of welfare reform, the safety net has also become frayed. The nature of rural economies and their dependence on a less diverse industrial structure make them particularly vulnerable to the negative economic and social consequences of economic restructuring, such as job loss, underemployment, and lowered earnings. Concurrently, rural areas have experienced changes in family life, including an increase in women's labor force participation, a decline in married-couple families, and a rise in cohabitation and single-parent families. Now more than ever, social scientists need to provide context for the current economic troubles facing rural America and suggest policies for assisting rural people during these troubles.

Based on original research commissioned explicitly for this volume, each chapter sheds light on the neglected topic of how rural families fare in the face of economic turmoil and job loss, with a focus on policy. This volume is not an examination of economic change per se but of the *consequences* of this change for the men, women, and children who make up rural populations. A mix of quantitative and qualitative research methods, representing both large national data sets and regional and local case studies, it brings together different components of an underexplored but complex story of change, loss, and survival in rural America. It takes a comparative approach by analyzing rural-urban differences, while emphasizing rural people and places with in-depth analyses of uniquely rural issues and populations. It also looks at change over time, exploring ways that rural and urban areas have converged, or have not, and exploring the reasons why or why not. Written by a multidisciplinary group of leading experts in economics, demography, sociology, and policy analysis, and drawing on both quantitative and qualitative research methodologies, the essays in this volume inform policy in rural areas and set the stage for future research.

This volume brings together original, policy-relevant research on the state of families and their members in rural America at the end of the first decade of the twenty-first century. Like the rest of the nation, rural areas have witnessed major social and economic upheavals over the past several decades that have had significant effects on the lives and livelihoods of their residents. Yet how these changes affect rural families and children, in contrast to those in urban and national settings, has received relatively little systematic analysis.

Our undergirding assumption is that economic conditions have a large effect on family well-being, coping strategies, and ultimately demographic change, and that these in turn shape and are shaped by policy responses. This book provides an understanding of how economic restructuring has affected rural families. Therefore, to lay the foundation for the more focused examination of effects, outcomes, and policies that follows in the subsequent chapters, we begin with an introduction to rural life and an overview of what restructuring has looked like in rural compared to urban America.

Next, in a general overview of the changes in the rural economy and concomitant changes in family life, we document how rural places have transitioned over the years. In the second and third sections, we examine the responses of men, women, and families to these changes. Chapters in the second section focus on men's employment hardship in rural areas, the rise in women's employment and breadwinner status, and the different responses from men as they are not able to live up to the male breadwinner role. This section not only underscores gender differences and pays specific attention to women's economic role in families, but also scrutinizes what economic restructuring and the concomitant changes it brings for family breadwinning roles mean for men. Chapters in the third section investigate the intersection of family change and economic hardship and the adaptive strategies families use to help make ends

meet. The fourth section turns to characteristics of rural low-wage employment, including the work schedules of low-wage work and demographic and
regional variations in low-wage rural workers, drawing connections to their
implications for family and child well-being. A final section describes what
policies and programs are available in rural areas and their efficacy in alleviating the detrimental effects of economic restructuring. The conclusion integrates the findings from these studies to provide a research and policy agenda
for advancing the well-being of rural families and their members.

The Rural Labor Market

Understanding the changes in employment patterns due to economic restructuring in rural America is fundamental as it lays the foundation that the
subsequent chapters build upon.[1] The following analyses of Current Population Survey data from 1979 to 2007 consider changes in the rural, urban, and
suburban job markets in three dimensions: (1) how jobs compare across the
three geographic areas; (2) how jobs have changed over time in these three
areas; and (3) whether rural job markets are relatively or absolutely worse off
than the other areas.

Table I.1 shows changes in unemployment and employment rates by place
for 1979 to 2007. Unemployment rates are highest in the central cities, followed
closely by rural areas, and lowest in the suburban areas. Unemployment trends
are fairly similar across place. Employment rates, however, reveal less of a trend
in rural areas relative to the other areas, as they hover between 58 and 61 percent. This finding suggests that there is less robust labor market demand in
rural relative to urban places.

Tables I.2 and I.3 examine the changing share of jobs held by workers by
industry and occupation. Across the board, the share of workers in manufacturing jobs has declined and the share in services has increased. Table I.2 shows
that differences in the shares of workers by industry are not very large, nor have
they changed in particularly different ways. In rural, central city, and suburban areas, we see the shift from manufacturing jobs to services, though that
shift has been somewhat attenuated in rural areas. For example, in suburban
labor markets, manufacturing went from 27 percent of the workforce in 1979 to
about 12 percent in 2007. That change represents a decline of about 15 percentage points, two-thirds of which occurred among durable (heavy equipment)
manufacturers (we separate out the two components because there exists a
wage premium for durable relative to nondurable manufacturing). In rural

markets, the shift was smaller, a 12-percentage-point shift from 29 percent to 17 percent.

Occupational shifts (table I.3) were of similar magnitudes across the three areas, as the share of blue-collar jobs fell and that of service and white-collar jobs rose. As with industry, there are notable level differences, reflecting the industry-level differences above. Specifically, there are still more manufacturing jobs, and thus more blue-collar workers, in rural places relative to urban or suburban.

Table I.4 shows hourly wage levels in 2007 dollars for workers age eighteen to sixty-four by location and by education level from 1979 to 2007. Average real wages, shown in the top panel, were flat for the "all" group (note that this group includes workers whose location is not identified) over the 1980s, rose fairly solidly in the 1990s, and rose considerably less so in the 2000s.

The major difference by place regarding these overall averages is that rural wages fell in real terms fairly steeply, by 7.7 percent, over the 1980s. As the last line of the first panel shows, urban workers earned, on average, 11 percent more than rural workers in 1979 and 22 percent more in 2007, a doubling of the relative urban advantage. For suburban workers, the average premium rose from 23 percent to 33 percent.[2] The earnings of rural workers are generally lower in both trend and level than those of urban or suburban workers.

This analysis suggests that the lower wages in rural areas relate to unfavorable levels and shifts in job structure (industries and occupation) relative to the other areas, and differences in educational attainment by place.

What effect do differences in industry composition by place have on wage levels and trends? A simple shift-share exercise as shown in table I.5 shows that regarding industry, these share differences have little effect on wage levels. The table uses information on industry shares and wage levels for 2007 to answer the questions (a) how would rural wages differ if the industry structure were different in rural areas, that is, were the same as in central cities or suburbs, and (b) how would urban and suburban wages differ if their wage levels were paired with the rural industry job structure?

The results show that rural wages would only be slightly higher (less than 1 percent) if the industry job structure were the same as that found in central city and suburban areas, and (lower panel) urban/suburban wages would be about equal or very slightly lower if those workers faced the rural industry structure. These results suggest that the lower rural wage is more a "within-cell," or rural, phenomenon than one driven by a particularly downgraded industrial job structure.

Turning to differences due to education, the 1980s is widely recognized as a period when educational wage differentials—specifically, the wage premium for college relative to high school workers—grew sharply. As the last line in each section reveals in table I.4, this trend occurred in rural areas also, as the college/high school premium rose from 42 percent to 66 percent over these years. But the increase in the premium was much larger in urban and suburban areas, growing around 50 percentage points in both.

This result is partly driven by some surprising trend differences in rural versus other area wage trends. Over the 1980s, when real wage gains accrued exclusively to college workers, rural workers with college degrees experienced zero real gains. The college premium rose significantly for them nevertheless, since high school wages fell 12 percent. In the 1990s, a uniquely positive period for rural workers (and one we examine more closely below), gains for non–college-educated workers were particularly strong. Thus, the rural education differential did not grow as much as that of other places, for two reasons. First, college workers did not do as well in rural areas in the 1980s as they did in the other places, and second, non–college-educated workers did much better in rural areas in the 1990s.

Another way of stating this latter point is to note that wage inequality grew much less quickly among rural workers in the 1990s than among nonrural workers. Other research in the 1990s, such as Bernstein and Baker (2003), shows that the full-employment job market that prevailed in the latter years of that cycle was particularly helpful to the least advantaged workers. Previously, minority workers have been the focus of this work, but the 1989–2000 results reveal that rural workers also get a disproportionate boost from the job market in these years.

Table I.6 reveals an interesting difference between these three places regarding the education levels of the workforce. Overall, the rural workforce has a lower level of education than central city or suburban workforces. Over the past three decades, there has been a large shift from high school or less to some college or more, but the pattern of the shift has been somewhat unique in rural settings. In rural relative to central city and suburban places, there are many fewer high school dropouts—15 percentage points, compared to 8–9 points in the other areas—but there are also smaller gains among college graduates. The reason for this is a larger gain in the share of workers with some college but not a large gain for those receiving a four-year degree. In central city and suburban places the large gains were found among those receiving a college degree.

The difference in education level may also explain some of the unique challenges facing rural workers in today's job market. Research has shown that in the 1990s and 2000s, employment and wage growth has been more robust at the low and high end of the educational distribution, with less favorable results for workers in the middle (see, for example, Autor, Katz, and Kearney 2006).

The main conclusion from this analysis of the changes in rural, central city, and suburban labor markets due to economic restructuring is that labor markets are just relatively less favorable in rural economies. Yes, there are somewhat more low-wage agriculture jobs in rural communities, but that is a small share of employment. The industry and occupational structures are more similar than different in rural, central city, and suburban places.

And yes, the educational distribution is less favorable—rural places have lower levels of college graduates and a slower trend in educational upgrading compared with other places. One could make an argument that prices are lower in rural areas, but this is likely to be canceled out by higher energy consumption in terms of variations in the cost of living. One important distinction, however, is that there is some evidence that employment growth has not been as strong in rural places, which can depress wages.

This analysis suggests that the quality of jobs, ceteris paribus, is lower in rural communities. Another issue is the quantity of jobs available in rural areas—wages did relatively well in rural areas during the 1990s boom. These findings do not point to a structural deficit or other problem with the rural labor market, but rather to wages being depressed by the number and the quality of jobs. One avenue to help raise wages in rural areas is investing in public infrastructure, with a strong rural component. Rural areas need good jobs and good multipliers from the earnings of workers in those jobs. Economic restructuring and globalization have decreased the quality of jobs in rural areas and in America altogether, and raising the demand for labor with good-quality jobs would go a long way in raising wages in rural America.

Continued educational upgrading in rural areas would also help to raise wages, but a concern here is that the workforce would be "all dressed up with nowhere to go." This analysis does not indicate that there is a strong labor demand for skilled workers in rural places relative to urban and suburban places. The large relative share of workers with some college education in rural areas may suggest that jobs that require high education levels are not abundant in rural places.

With this understanding of the implications of economic restructuring in mind, we now turn to a discussion of the sections included in this book and the major findings from the chapters. This book explains how families have coped with these fundamental economic changes in how family economic life is organized. It documents a story of rural families rising above the adversity of economic restructuring in America.

How Has Family Life Changed in Rural America?

This volume begins with a look at rural families in a changing society. Rural families are coping with economic, social, and cultural change. A shift from agricultural and extractive production to lower-wage industries has occurred, with the result being that today "rural" is no longer equivalent to "farm." In fact, only 10 percent of rural people live on farms. In chapter 1, Daniel Lichter and Deborah Roempke Graefe set the stage by painting a picture of rural America today—economic restructuring continues to place pressure on the economic well-being of families; increased divorce, nonmarital childbearing, and co-habitation place rural children at a higher risk of poverty; and although an influx of immigrants and minorities has revitalized many small towns and rural places, it has raised concerns about racial relations, immigrant assimilation, and spending on new infrastructure.

Changing Economic Opportunities and Changing Roles

In chapter 2, Leif Jensen and Eric Jensen examine several indicators of employment hardship, including unemployment, underemployment, contingent work, and worker displacement. They compare these factors by place and gender from 1980 to 2006 and show that the picture is complex but that on balance the employment circumstances for rural men are less favorable than those of urban men, but more favorable than those of rural women. Rural men have lower labor force participation, higher unemployment, and higher underemployment than urban men. Worker displacement has declined to a larger extent for rural than urban men, such that from 1992 onward displacement rates were lower for rural men. Contingent work, a relatively uncommon form of employment hardship, was slightly lower among rural men. Jensen and Jensen show that rural women are disadvantaged compared with rural men, but that over time their circumstances have improved while the circumstances for rural men have worsened, resulting in a reduction in rural gender disparities.

A key question addressed is how families have responded to economic change. The restructuring of the rural economy has had lasting ramifications on how families organize their work and family lives. Economic restructuring has both pushed and pulled women into the paid labor market. As men's jobs in traditional rural industries such as agriculture, natural resource extraction, and manufacturing declined, service sectors expanded, creating opportunities for women at the same time that households needed an additional wage earner. In chapter 3, Kristin Smith documents the rise in women's employment and the narrowing of the gender gap in employment in both rural and urban areas. Large employment gains occurred among married women, single mothers, and women with higher levels of education in rural areas. Not only are rural married mothers more apt to work outside the home, their earnings have increased since 1969. This is noteworthy because rural married fathers' earnings declined over the same time period, resulting in a larger economic provider role for married mothers. Even so, the earnings of rural families are lower than those of urban families, and growing at a slower pace, underscoring the rising inequality between rural and urban families. Given the growing number of families that depend on the earnings of women, Smith calls for policies that facilitate work and family (such as paid sick leave, family medical leave, and flexible work schedules) and increase earnings or supplement wages (such as raising the minimum wage or expanding the Earned Income Tax Credit).

In chapter 4, Jennifer Sherman digs deeper into how families cope with changing roles due to economic restructuring. Using ethnographic and interview data, she explores how structural and labor market transformations produce changes in gender norms and identities in a rural community that has historically been tied to a single industry, logging. Sherman finds that flexibility with regard to gender norms is key to creating stable relationships in a context of rapid and catastrophic economic collapse. For couples tied rigidly to traditional husband as breadwinner / wife as homemaker gender norms, when men cannot fulfill the economic provider role, they struggle with their inabilities to be the sole providers, creating tensions that often lead to relational instability. On the other hand, couples in which men are able to refocus their conceptions of masculinity on more attainable goals, such as active parenting, experience less strife and more personal and marital satisfaction. In light of these findings, Sherman argues that rural men are more flexible with regard to masculine identity than found by previous researchers, and that flexibility with regard to gender identities, as well as gender roles, is vital to sustaining stable families under conditions of rapid structural change.

Economic Hardship, Family Change, and Family Adaptive Strategies

The chapters in the next section address two main questions: how has economic restructuring contributed to family change, and what strategies do families employ to rise above the difficulties caused by economic restructuring? Economic restructuring has altered men's and women's roles in the economy, and in turn influenced family formation and stability across the United States. Economic downturns and job loss can make family life difficult and stressful, and these conditions may promote family instability or encourage marriage, or both. While Sherman's chapter examines how economic restructuring and job loss among men lead couples to adapt their gender roles, chapters 5 through 8 examine the intersection of economic hardship and family change and the adaptive strategies families use to help make ends meet.

In chapter 5, Diane McLaughlin and Alisha Coleman-Jensen examine the relationship between economic restructuring and the change in prevalence of female-headed households with children from 1980 to 2000. To assess the influence of economic restructuring on the change in prevalence in single motherhood, they estimate weighted least squares regression models of change at the county level. They find that measures of economic restructuring are associated with a rise in single motherhood. Counties with economic restructuring that created poor-quality jobs and part-time work for men had larger growth in single motherhood. However, increases in part-time work for women were associated with slower growth in single-mother families. Growth in full-time jobs (which are more likely to offer better wages and benefits) contributed to more traditional family formation and stability. Further, counties with the highest prevalence of single-mother families also had the fastest growth in single-mother families, underscoring the need for improved or expanded services and programs in high-prevalence counties. They conclude that as U.S. policy makers consider ways to alleviate the negative ramifications of economic restructuring, they must consider men's and women's employment separately and craft policies that create good-quality, livable-wage jobs.

While McLaughlin and Coleman-Jensen show the link between economic restructuring and the destabilization of families on the county level, Anastasia Snyder in chapter 6 probes further by analyzing individual-level data and focusing on rural women's divorce and remarriage patterns to critically examine the role of marriage in rural women's lives. Rural women are less likely to divorce, and they are more likely to remarry after divorce and to remarry quicker. The end result is that rural women spend more of their lives married than women in central cities or suburbs. Snyder argues that rural women may have a preference for marriage in part because of the challenging economic context in which they reside and in part because of the tendency to hold more traditional family values. Rural single mothers face significant challenges providing for their families, thus the preference for marriage among rural women may be a family adaptive strategy to provide greater economic stability for themselves and their children while enabling the fulfillment of traditional family values.

One of the side effects of economic restructuring is that families have to adapt to the tougher economic times; garner their resources, and piece together elaborate and multifaceted survival strategies. In chapter 7, Margaret Nelson explores the survival strategies of low-income families in a rural county in Vermont as these are shaped by economic restructuring and marital status. Economic restructuring has resulted in a dichotomy between families in which at least one member holds a good job (defined as year-round, full-time employment in a firm that offers benefits) and families that rely exclusively on bad jobs. Nelson demonstrates that the relationship to the formal economy has consequences for the survival strategy of the family and for the capacity of parents to provide predictable lives for their children. Namely, families with a good job have higher wages, tend to rely on a dual-earner strategy, engage in self-provisioning, and barter with other households. They can do this in part because the good job is stable, has predictable hours, and has paid vacation or sick leave. Families with bad jobs are disadvantaged because the bad jobs impede the families' collective ability to respond to family needs and to support a second worker. Further, differences exist between the survival strategies of single-parent and married-couple families, with varying consequences for children. Nelson concludes that increasing wages is important but not sufficient to self-sufficiency among low-income families. Increased access to workplace benefits and job flexibility—indeed, paid time off to respond to family needs—and continued state support are necessary as basic supports for working families.

In chapter 8, Katherine Jewsbury Conger addresses how economic hardship affects the health, well-being, and long-term marital outcomes of families who lived in the upper Midwest during the agricultural depression of the 1980s. Using the Family Stress Model, one of the primary theoretical models proposed to explain the connection between family economic circumstances and developmental changes in parents and their children, Conger shows how conditions of economic hardship, such as losing a job, affect parents' psychological distress, contribute to cutting back on spending for household needs, and produce emotional distress. She argues that the dynamics of the romantic relationship predict whether a married couple will experience marital disruption when economic pressure and emotional distress combine. Husbands and wives who pull together and demonstrate high levels of social support and those who have effective couple problem solving had less marital conflict. In addition, economic pressure in families creates risk for adolescents. Conger concludes that by understanding the effect of economic hardship on marriages, parents, and their children, policies and programs can adequately address the multifaceted challenges families face when economic hardship hits.

Low-Wage Employment

A growing number of the jobs in rural America are low-wage, and a large proportion of the low-wage jobs are held by women. We learn from Nelson's analysis in the previous section that some of the low-wage jobs are "good" jobs and some are not. In this section, attention turns to the characteristics of rural low-wage employment, including the work schedules of low-wage workers, and then more specifically to variations by race and ethnicity and region in low-wage rural female workers, drawing connections to their implications for family and child well-being.

Another side effect of economic restructuring is that more workers work in "bad" jobs where they do not have control over their work schedules and that their schedules vary from day to day and week to week. As employers in several industries embark on aggressive strategies to cut costs and maximize revenue, just-in-time practices that match employees' work hours to customers' hours become more common. These changes in strategy typically mean that the work schedule is erratic and is not controlled by the employee. In chapter 9, Elaine McCrate takes a hard look at the work schedules of rural residents, examining the variability of work hours, and the flexibility and the amount of worker control over work schedules. Rural parents are more likely than urban parents to have schedules with starting and stopping times they do not control, including both jobs with rigid hours and jobs with variable hours. Single parents, who likely have the greatest need for job flexibility, are the least likely to have control over their work schedules, and rural single parents are less likely than their urban counterparts to have schedules that they control. This pattern of less control over work schedules is especially prominent among black and Hispanic single parents living in rural areas. Since 1997, the number of jobs with erratic hours beyond the control of the worker has grown and is now widespread, traversing most industries. McCrate calls for a two-pronged approach so workers can accommodate their family demands without negative ramifications on their work: first, increased child care options for parents, with an emphasis on backup plans, coupled with policies that give workers more flexibility and control, such as paid sick leave and vacation time; and second, policies that provide tax relief for employers who create good jobs and encourage employers to create jobs with stable hours through higher wages for jobs with irregular schedules or cross-training.

For the nation as a whole, race does not seem to be correlated with low-wage employment among women. However, in rural America, race and ethnicity are significant factors in women's low-wage employment. Marlene Lee shows in chapter 10 that black and Hispanic women are more likely than white women to be employed in low-wage work in rural areas. Lee uses regression coefficients and decomposition techniques to attribute about one-third of the difference between rural and urban rates of low-wage employment to differences in education levels and rates of full-time, year-round employment (i.e., structural differences in returns to individuals and job characteristics between rural and urban populations). However, structural differences in returns to individuals and job characteristics account for most of the gap between rural and urban low-wage employment rates within race and ethnic groups. When considering racial and ethnic differences in rates of low-wage employment in rural areas, differences in population characteristics account for most of the differential: living in the South is a large contributor for rural black women, and low education levels are a large contributor for rural Hispanic women. Lee concludes that narrowing the gap between rates of low-wage employment requires improvements in education and job quality in rural areas, but attention must also be paid to the structural differences in returns to education and full-time, year-round employment.

A disproportionate number of rural poor are women who are gainfully employed but earn near poverty-level wages. In part, the rise and persistence of women in low-wage employment is a result of economic restructuring. Using county-level data, Cynthia Anderson and Chih-Yuan Weng compare indicators of low-wage work across place in chapter 11, paying specific attention to variations in region and occupation. Rates of low-wage work tend to be higher in rural areas and vary by region, with the South typically having the highest rates and the Northeast the lowest. Female low-wage workers in rural areas tend to be single mothers, minorities, and workers with low education levels. Rates of rural low-wage work are higher for certain occupations, including food preparation, health care support, building and ground cleaning, personal care, and farming, fishing, and forestry. Because movement up and out of these occupations is not common, workers may be trapped in "job ghettos." These results suggest that raising the minimum wage may not be sufficient for improving the lives of rural low-wage workers, since even twelve dollars per hour is not enough to sustain families. Instead, Anderson and Weng argue that increased access to good jobs is needed, which may require increased education and training to ensure that rural low-wage workers are not trapped in job ghettos but rather experience avenues of job mobility.

Work and Family Policy

This volume concludes with a focus on the programs and policies that might alleviate the detrimental effects of economic restructuring and their efficacy in rural areas. Chapters 12 through 16 examine key policy areas that either have or would make a material difference for rural families. A concluding chapter integrates the findings from these studies to provide a research and policy agenda for advancing the well-being of rural families and their members.

Economic restructuring has had substantial effects on the economic prospects of rural families, with particularly negative consequences for young people. In chapter 12, Liliokanaio Peaslee and Andrew Hahn critically review the literature on the state of rural youth development, with an emphasis on approaches that work to promote economic self-sufficiency among rural youth. They contend that successful rural economic renewal rests on strengthening opportunities for young people, and to revitalize rural communities, youth education, employment, and training programs must be linked with rural economic development plans.

Balancing the demands of work and family is difficult for any family, but rural low-income families face distinctive barriers due to the lack of resources available in many rural areas and financial constraints to accessing services. In chapter 13, Nicole Forry and Susan Walker review the research and identify the unique assets and challenges experienced by low-income rural families in securing care that supports both children's development and parental employment, using federal and state policies as examples. Expanding child care subsidies and the Child and Dependent Care tax credit would further alleviate the burden of the high cost of child care for rural low-income families and facilitate maternal employment. Increasing Head Start and pre-kindergarten programs would ease the lack of access to formal child care in rural areas.

Economic restructuring puts rural families at risk of churning in and out of health care coverage or of losing health insurance altogether. In chapter 14, Deborah Roempke Graefe examines the trends in insurance coverage over the past ten years, comparing rural and urban families by race and ethnicity and poverty status, and considers how economic restructuring has played a role in the loss of health insurance coverage in rural areas. The prevalence of small businesses in rural areas, coupled with the high employee share of insurance premiums, contributes to the lower rates of private health insurance coverage in rural places. Since 2000, the loss of manufacturing jobs concurrent with the increase in service sector jobs has resulted in a larger share of rural Americans going without health insurance coverage. Rural minorities and low-income rural families are particularly disadvantaged as they are at high risk of experiencing a coverage gap. Graefe calls for a comprehensive approach that includes both health care market strategies and legislated health coverage policy.

A major impetus for welfare reform was to move welfare recipients into paid employment. Yet detailed studies of livelihood practices prior to welfare reform find that low-wage workers were often worse off than those on cash assistance or who combined income sources. This may be especially the case in poor rural areas where work is scarce and additional obstacles to employment, such as lack of transportation and child care, are endemic, but there is little research in these settings. In chapter 15, Ann Tickamyer and Debra Henderson track employed and nonemployed human service agency participants in communities with different levels of capacity to implement welfare-to-work policies from 1999 to 2005 and assess whether workers are better or worse off. While county differences are minimal, workers are better off than nonworkers and more so by the third survey year. They employ a wide variety of livelihood strategies beyond work for wages. Nevertheless, they remain poor and vulnerable to numerous hardships. Tickamyer and Henderson conclude that the safety net is frayed and does not provide adequate assistance for those seeking employment or working in low-wage jobs.

While Tickamyer and Henderson focus on county differences in their ability to implement welfare-to-work policies, in chapter 16 Domenico Parisi, Steven Michael Grice, Guangqing Chi, and Jed Pressgrove address whether welfare reform has affected the use of the Earned Income Tax Credit (EITC) in rural counties where the conditions to obtain, retain, and develop a job do not exist. They find that TANF and EITC pay off differently depending on the conditions in the local environment. The work-first philosophy of welfare reform results in uneven policy that exacerbates the disadvantages of single-mother families when no jobs exist in the local community. The EITC has contributed to improving the quality of life of the working poor in rural areas, and helped them to remain attached to the labor market. However, the benefits to EITC are not uniform, with fewer rural workers rising out of poverty due to the EITC and fewer benefits accruing to black workers in rural areas. They conclude that one-size-fits-all policies do not afford equal opportunities to all, and that the welfare-and-work debate should shift focus onto how local environments differentially

shape opportunity and impede individuals' efforts to attain personal responsibility and economic self-sufficiency.

What Is to Be Done About the Challenges Facing Rural Families in Light of Continued Economic Restructuring?

Several primary lessons emerge from these chapters that lead us to identify
policy options that we think provide the most promise for improving the lives
of rural families. This book illustrates the wide variety of ways that the lives
of rural families have changed and adapted to the consequences of economic
restructuring. As a whole, it documents the resiliency and adaptability of rural
communities and families in the face of adverse economic circumstances. By
studying the effects of economic restructuring on rural families and communities and how families are coping in light of continued economic hardship, we
can recommend policies and programs that can assist them.

Our policy recommendations fall into several broad categories. First, rural
areas need better employment options—stable jobs that pay a livable wage with
benefits and predictable and controllable schedules. New and creative ways to
create rural jobs should be considered. Mindful that rural areas are diverse,
opportunities to bring in new technologies, especially energy and green technologies, may be fruitful endeavors and look different in various rural communities.
Second, rural areas have dire service and amenity needs, such as improvements
in schools, health care, day care, transportation, recreation, and social services,
that, once addressed, will lead to viable and sustainable rural families and communities. Third, rural areas are in need of investment in infrastructure for new
information technologies, such as broadband Internet access, public transportation, and other public services that will ultimately support employment and
services. Fourth, rural areas need policies directed at rural places, but it is important to note that policies directed at all distressed families, including rural
residents, remain an important priority but need to be further targeted for
specific populations. Thus, tax credits, such as the Earned Income Tax Credit,
have a major role in assisting rural families, but greater efforts need to be made
to make sure that rural families understand and make use of these programs.
Finally, this book demonstrates that even though we know what specific policies and programs can be of assistance to rural families, the bigger issue is how
to make them happen. This book is a first step toward understanding the complexities and challenges facing rural families and communities and garnering
the political will to support their efforts as part of the larger policy agenda.

Table I.1   Unemployment and employment rates, by place, 1979–2007

	1979	1989	2000	2007
Unemployment rates				
All	5.9%	5.3%	4.0%	4.6%
Rural	5.8%	5.7%	4.4%	4.9%
Central city	7.3%	6.8%	5.0%	5.4%
Suburban	5.0%	4.2%	3.3%	4.1%
Employment rates				
All	60.1%	63.0%	64.4%	63.0%
Rural	58.0%	59.5%	60.7%	59.3%
Central city	58.0%	60.4%	63.2%	62.5%
Suburban	63.2%	66.5%	66.8%	64.7%

SOURCE: Jared Bernstein's analysis of CPS data.

Table I.2 Industry shares, by place, 1979–2007

	1979	1989	2000	2007	Percentage point change 1979–2007
Rural					
Agriculture	3.0%	3.1%	2.6%	2.3%	−0.7%
Mining	2.1%	1.4%	1.1%	1.5%	−0.6%
Construction	6.7%	6.1%	7.0%	7.4%	0.7%
Manufacturing	29.3%	25.6%	21.5%	17.4%	−11.9%
Nondurable	13.4%	12.1%	8.6%	6.4%	−7.0%
Durable	15.9%	13.6%	12.9%	10.9%	−5.0%
Transportation, utilities, communication	7.6%	6.6%	7.0%	7.2%	−0.4%
Wholesale trade	2.7%	3.3%	2.6%	2.6%	−0.1%
Retail trade	13.8%	15.6%	11.8%	11.5%	−2.3%
FIRE	3.9%	4.0%	3.9%	4.4%	0.5%
Services	26.2%	29.2%	37.1%	39.9%	13.7%
Public administration	4.6%	5.0%	5.6%	5.9%	1.1%
Central city					
Agriculture	0.5%	0.8%	0.4%	0.3%	−0.2%
Mining	0.6%	0.4%	0.1%	0.2%	−0.4%
Construction	4.8%	4.8%	5.6%	6.9%	2.1%
Manufacturing	23.4%	17.4%	12.8%	9.6%	−13.8%
Nondurable	9.0%	7.5%	4.8%	3.5%	−5.5%
Durable	14.5%	9.9%	8.0%	6.1%	−8.4%
Transportation, utilities, communication	8.4%	8.1%	9.6%	8.5%	0.1%
Wholesale trade	4.0%	3.6%	2.7%	3.0%	−1.0%
Retail trade	14.6%	15.8%	10.6%	10.5%	−4.1%
FIRE	7.6%	8.2%	7.9%	8.0%	0.4%
Services	30.3%	35.1%	45.4%	48.2%	17.8%
Public administration	5.7%	5.8%	4.9%	4.8%	−0.9%
Suburban					
Agriculture	1.1%	1.1%	0.7%	0.5%	−0.6%
Mining	0.5%	0.5%	0.2%	0.3%	−0.2%
Construction	5.5%	6.1%	6.5%	7.2%	1.7%
Manufacturing	27.0%	20.7%	15.7%	11.7%	−15.3%
Nondurable	9.3%	7.3%	5.1%	4.0%	−5.3%
Durable	17.7%	13.4%	10.6%	7.6%	−10.1%
Transportation, utilities, communication	8.4%	8.1%	9.5%	8.6%	0.2%
Wholesale trade	4.5%	4.5%	3.5%	3.4%	−1.0%
Retail trade	14.5%	15.1%	11.0%	11.3%	−3.2%
FIRE	6.5%	7.9%	7.5%	7.8%	1.3%
Services	26.8%	30.9%	40.5%	43.9%	17.1%
Public administration	5.2%	5.1%	4.7%	5.3%	0.1%

SOURCE: Jared Bernstein's analysis of CPS data.

Table I.3 Occupational shares, by place, 1979–2007

	1979	1989	2000	2007	Percentage point change 1979–2007
Rural					
White collar	43.2%	45.7%	49.4%	50.2%	7.0%
Blue collar	43.6%	39.3%	35.2%	33.2%	−10.4%
Services	13.2%	15.0%	15.4%	16.6%	3.4%
Central city					
White collar	54.0%	58.1%	60.3%	61.2%	7.2%
Blue collar	31.6%	25.8%	22.7%	20.6%	−11.0%
Services	14.4%	16.1%	17.0%	18.3%	3.9%
Suburban					
White collar	57.2%	62.7%	64.2%	63.6%	6.4%
Blue collar	31.9%	25.6%	23.0%	21.7%	−10.2%
Services	11.0%	11.7%	12.9%	14.7%	3.7%

SOURCE: Jared Bernstein's analysis of CPS data.

Table I.4 Real hourly wages, by place and education, 1979–2007, 2007

	Real hourly wages by year				Change in real hourly wages		
	1979	1989	2000	2007	1979–1989	1989–2000	2000–2007
All	$16.66	$16.74	$18.63	$19.50	0.5%	11.3%	4.7%
Central city	$16.44	$16.61	$18.39	$19.36	1.1%	10.7%	5.3%
Suburban	$18.19	$18.61	$20.42	$21.16	2.3%	9.8%	3.6%
Rural	$14.77	$13.64	$15.43	$15.87	−7.7%	13.1%	2.9%
Central city / rural	$1.11	$1.22	$1.19	$1.22	9.5%	−2.1%	2.3%
Suburban/rural	$1.23	$1.36	$1.32	$1.33	10.8%	−3.0%	0.7%
Rural							
Less than high school	$12.46	$10.66	$10.75	$11.10	−14.5%	0.9%	3.2%
High school	$14.24	$12.55	$13.80	$13.99	−11.9%	10.0%	1.3%
Some college	$15.02	413.74	$15.10	$15.23	−8.5%	9.8%	0.9%
College graduate	$20.16	$20.18	$22.94	$23.25	0.1%	13.7%	1.4%
College / high school	$1.42	$1.61	$1.66	$1.66	13.6%	3.3%	0.0%
Central city							
Less than high school	$13.61	$11.54	$10.84	$11.04	−15.2%	−6.0%	1.8%
High school	$15.32	$14.11	$14.38	$14.55	−7.9%	2.0%	1.2%
Some college	$16.21	$15.71	$16.28	$16.39	−3.1%	3.7%	0.6%
College graduate	$21.96	$24.01	$27.56	$28.30	9.3%	14.8%	2.7%
College / high school	$1.43	$1.70	$1.92	$1.94	18.7%	12.6%	1.5%
Suburban							
Less than high school	$15.01	$12.70	$11.34	$11.82	−15.4%	−10.7%	4.3%
High school	$16.25	$15.52	$15.74	$15.83	−4.5%	1.4%	0.6%
Some college	$17.49	$17.41	$18.07	$18.00	−0.4%	3.8%	−0.4%
College graduate	$24.90	$26.24	$29.95	$30.68	5.4%	14.1%	2.5%
College / high school	$1.53	$1.69	$1.90	$1.94	10.4%	12.5%	1.9%

SOURCE: Jared Bernstein's analysis of CPS data.

Table I.5   Job structure and wages, by place, 2007

	Industry shares			Hourly wages		
	Rural	Central city	Suburban	Rural	Central city	Suburban
Agriculture	2.3%	0.3%	0.5%	$11.97	$13.82	$12.15
Mining	1.5%	0.2%	0.3%	$19.69	$34.33	$22.92
Construction	7.4%	6.9%	7.2%	$17.13	$17.32	$20.50
Manufacturing (nondurable)	6.4%	3.5%	4.0%	$15.44	$18.25	$23.12
Manufacturing (durable)	10.9%	6.1%	7.6%	$16.45	$21.94	$23.42
Transportation, utilities, communication	7.2%	8.5%	8.6%	$18.02	$20.28	$22.75
Wholesale trade	2.6%	3.0%	3.4%	$15.96	$20.51	$23.10
Retail trade	11.5%	10.5%	11.3%	$12.89	$14.91	$16.17
FIRE	4.4%	8.0%	7.8%	$17.98	$24.03	$25.80
Services	39.9%	48.2%	43.9%	$15.48	$18.87	$20.30
Public administration	5.9%	4.8%	5.3%	$18.53	$23.91	$25.10
Total	100.0%	100.0%	100.0%	$15.87	$19.36	$21.16

Shift share exercise:	Central city	Suburban
Using rural wages with central city or suburban industry share	$15.96	$15.97
Using central city or suburban wages with rural industry shares	$19.37	$20.99

SOURCE: Jared Bernstein's analysis of CPS data.

Table I.6 Education levels by place, 1979–2007

	Less than high school	High school	Some college	College graduate
Rural				
1979	25.2%	42.0%	18.8%	14.1%
1989	18.0%	44.7%	22.0%	15.3%
2000	12.7%	40.5%	28.9%	17.9%
2007	10.1%	39.1%	31.5%	19.3%
1979–2007	−15.0%	−2.9%	12.7%	5.2%
Central city				
1979	21.8%	35.4%	23.5%	19.3%
1989	16.0%	32.1%	26.8%	25.1%
2000	13.7%	27.9%	28.4%	30.0%
2007	12.5%	25.7%	27.2%	34.5%
1979–2007	−9.2%	−9.7%	3.7%	15.2%
Suburban				
1979	16.1%	38.1%	24.5%	21.2%
1989	10.6%	35.3%	27.4%	26.7%
2000	9.1%	29.9%	30.2%	30.8%
2007	8.3%	28.3%	29.7%	33.8%
1979–2007	−7.8%	−9.9%	5.2%	12.5%

Source: Jared Bernstein's analysis of CPS data.

Notes

1. The analysis and interpretation of the data in this section were conducted by Jared Bernstein, who at the time was with the Economic Policy Institute and currently is chief economist and economic policy advisor to Vice President Joe Biden.

2. Bernstein also regression-adjusted these differentials, and the same pattern holds.

SECTION 1

CHANGING ECONOMIC OPPORTUNITIES AND CHANGING ROLES

RURAL ECONOMIC RESTRUCTURING

Implications for Children, Youth, and Families

DANIEL T. LICHTER AND DEBORAH ROEMPKE GRAEFE

Under cover of the "myth of rural stability" (Logan 1996), rural America has been rocked by rapid and ongoing economic, social, and cultural change over the past century or more. Americans often think of rural places as the "antithesis of the modern urban world—more moral, virtuous, and simple" than the rest of America (Brown and Kandel 2006). Urbanization and the blurring of cultural and economic boundaries, however, have threatened the pastoral symbolism of rural life. Rural areas today are not immune from urban influences. "Rural" is no longer or perhaps never was equivalent to "farm." Indeed, only 14 percent of rural people work on farms today, only 10 percent actually live on farms, and many farm families depend on nonfarm employment to make ends meet (Whitener and Parker 2007).

Concise but accurate generalizations about rural communities and family life today are nearly impossible to draw. Rural communities are extraordinarily diverse. Indeed, it is difficult to find common ground among communities that range from upscale rural retirement communities, to high-amenity small towns in close proximity to big cities, to growing rural settlements composed of foreign-born Hispanics, to disproportionately poor and minority communities in the South and elsewhere, where opportunities for good jobs and upward mobility are limited. Most Americans living today were born in cities or have lived most or all of their adult lives in them. Their exposure to rural people and places is mostly limited to "rural consumption"—rural vacation resorts, outdoor camping, hiking, fishing, and skiing. Such experiences are hardly representative of the approximately 50 million people—20 percent of the U.S. population—who make rural America their home.

Our fundamental objective here is to highlight economic changes in rural America and the putative impacts on family life. First, we describe recent economic changes in rural America, while emphasizing ongoing patterns of economic and industrial restructuring that have transformed many parts of the country. Second, we outline the implications of economic restructuring for rural families and children. We emphasize the link between ongoing economic change, including the "great recession" of 2008–10, and the stability of rural family life. Third, we outline several avenues for policy intervention. More importantly, we emphasize the need to move beyond common stereotypes, such as the erroneous but long-held belief that rural families and children have been largely immune to economic transformations in American society. In many ways, rural families have been on the forefront of America's family revolution.

Economic Restructuring in Rural America

Agriculture and extractive industries today account for only a small share of all nonmetropolitan (nonmetro) county employment (Brown and Kandel 2006; Lobao and Meyer 2001). Federal farm policies have been a boon to corporate farming, often at the expense of small family farms and the rural communities that serve them. America's transition to fewer but larger farms has been driven by America's market-based economy, the globalization of farm commodity markets, and a U.S. farm policy that often favors corporate agriculture (Goldman and Watts 1994). Even though farm-related activities employ almost one-fifth of all Americans, less than 2 percent of the U.S. population lives on farms, and almost all (90 percent) of family farmers (as opposed to corporate farmers) rely on some household income from nonfarm sources. Not surprisingly, income inequality is higher among farm families than among U.S. households as a whole (Ahearn, Perry, and El-Osta 1993).

In many of America's small towns and rural areas, sectoral shifts from agricultural and extractive jobs to low-wage manufacturing and service industries have undercut the economic stability and well-being of rural families, while leading to persistent out-migration of its young people. Rural America is "aging in place." Indeed, large shares of rural areas—especially in the upper Midwest—are experiencing population decline; deaths now exceed births in over eight hundred nonmetro counties (Johnson 2011). Immigrants, drawn by the demand for low-skill labor in agriculture and nondurable manufacturing (e.g., food processing), have sometimes filled the vacuum, bringing new cultural challenges to the community (e.g., language differences) and placing unfamiliar demands on health services and schools (Kandel and Cromartie 2004; Crowley and Lichter 2009).

For example, Gouveia and Stull (1995) documented the economic impacts of a new meat-processing plant in a small Kansas community. They showed that new growth—mostly of Hispanics—brought temporary shelters and mobile home parks, social problems, and soaring school enrollments that pushed dropout rates to the highest in the state. Student turnover was very high (about one-third per year), and absenteeism became chronic. Both violent and property crimes increased dramatically. Child abuse tripled and surpassed the state rate by half. Increased demands for social services could not easily be met with the community's tax base. But single-community case studies are hardly representative of all fast-growing rural communities (Crowley and Lichter 2009).

Rural communities also are often hit hard by the loss of manufacturing jobs because of economic restructuring and globalization. Plant closings in single-industry rural communities can be especially devastating, with economic impacts that reverberate throughout the entire community. To be sure, some of the rural jobs lost in manufacturing have been replaced by job growth in the service sector (McGranahan 1999). But service sector jobs typically pay low wages and have less potential to stimulate economic growth than the extractive and manufacturing employment they replace (Vias and Nelson 2006). The shift to service sector jobs over the past decade or two has brought falling wages in many parts of rural America.

Not surprisingly, many families in rural and small-town America have fallen behind economically, especially in comparison with their counterparts in metropolitan (metro) areas. This is not simply a matter of the lower "cost of living" in rural areas (Nord 2000). In 2005, rural workers earned only seventy-two cents for each dollar earned (per capita) in urban places. Moreover, income inequality has increased more rapidly in rural than in urban counties over the past two decades (McLaughlin 2002; Parrado and Kandel 2010), as rural poor families have fallen further and further behind the living standards that have typified the average American. Poverty and inequality, family disruption, and residential instability have become all too common in many rural communities (Brown and Lichter 2004; Snyder, McLaughlin, and Findeis 2006). Economic change and family change are inextricably linked.

Since the 1970s, rates of poverty in rural areas nevertheless have declined faster than in other areas (Weber, Duncan, and Whitener 2002), even as the average incomes of the poor have lagged incomes of the middle class. More recently—at least since 2001—rural poverty rates have ticked upward. The late 2000s recession brought rapidly increasing unemployment rates in rural areas, from 5 percent in mid-2008 to 9 percent in mid-2009 (Kusmin 2009). As a result, the nonmetro poverty rate in 2007 was 15 percent, compared with a national rate of 13 percent. Poverty rates were even higher in 2009 (16.6 percent), better reflecting family incomes at the height of the recession (U.S. Census Bureau 2010). Changing national and rural poverty rates also may increasingly mask large and persistent geographic and racial/ethnic disparities in economic well-being. Indeed, even as many "rural pockets of poverty" have dried up, rural minorities are both disproportionately poor and remain concentrated in high-poverty areas. The concentration of poverty among minority children is often extreme (Lichter and Johnson 2007; Lichter, Parisi, Taquino, et al. 2008). Historically, nonmetro poverty has been highly concentrated and persistent in regions with large minority populations (Beale and Gibbs 2006).

The Changing Rural Family

Marriage is on the public policy agenda—for obvious reasons (Nock 2005; Cherlin 2009). Poverty rates are roughly one-fifth as large in married-couple families as in single-parent families. Today, fewer people are getting married, and those who marry are marrying at later ages (Lichter and Qian 2004). Divorce rates have remained at historically high levels over the past two decades (Teachman 2002). And a recently released report by the National Center for Health Statistics now indicates that nearly 40 percent of all U.S. births are to unmarried women (Hamilton, Martin, and Ventura 2009). The number of out-of-wedlock births hit an all-time high of 1.7 million in 2007. Moreover, cohabitation has transformed recent patterns of partnering and parenting in United States (Cherlin 2009; Seltzer 2000). The share of women who have ever cohabited increased from 45 percent to 54 percent between 1995 and 2002 (Kennedy and Bumpass 2008). In 2008, roughly 25 percent of all families with children were headed by single mothers (U.S. Census Bureau 2009a). Only 62.7 percent of U.S. children lived with both biological parents (U.S. Census Bureau 2009b). These recent changes in family structure have placed upward demographic pressure on poverty rates nationally (Martin 2006; McLanahan and

Percheski 2008) and represent a behavioral mechanism that sometimes links poverty between parental and filial generations (Ludwig and Mayer 2006; McLanahan 2009).

This revolution in American family life has not bypassed rural America. Rural families have nevertheless been largely ignored in current policy debates. Rural and small-town America is no safe haven from family change (Lichter and Jensen 2002). Indeed, rural patterns of marriage, divorce, cohabitation, and nonmarital fertility are now remarkable similar to patterns found in large cities. Economic restructuring and the shortages of good jobs in rural communities have been linked to increases in single mother–headed families through rising unwed childbearing and divorce (Snyder and McLaughlin 2004; McLaughlin, Gardner, and Lichter 1999). Rural family change both reflects and reinforces economic hardship and growing inequality (Brown and Lichter 2004).

RURAL LIVELIHOOD STRATEGIES

The share of families with minor children that are headed by a single parent is remarkably similar in rural and urban areas (O'Hare and Churilla 2008; Brown and Lichter 2004). From 1990 to 2008, the percentage of rural children living with both parents declined from 76 to 68 percent (see fig. 1.1). In rural married-couple families, both spouses often work outside the home. Rural couples have

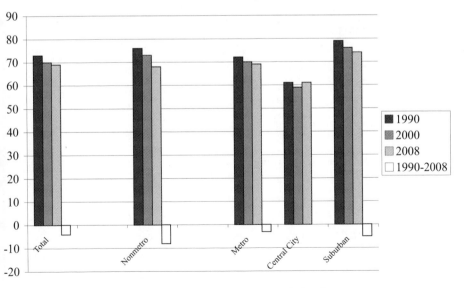

FIG. 1.1   Percentage of children living in married-couple families, 1990–2008 (SOURCE: O'Hare and Churilla 2008)

adopted a dual-worker strategy to make ends meet. Moreover, during the late 2000s recession, rural women were more likely than urban women to enter the labor force, especially if they were poor (Smith 2009). Higher rates of under-employment also characterize rural workers; they are more likely to be working part-time involuntarily or to be working full-time at poverty-level wages (Jensen, McLaughlin, and Slack 2003).

The livelihood strategies of rural single mothers also are comparable to those of urban single mothers, but for rural mothers full-time work often pays poorly (Brown and Lichter 2004). Among full-time working single mothers, rural women are much more likely to use food stamps (29 percent compared with 19 percent of urban single mothers), but are less likely to rely on welfare benefits (15 versus 29 percent). Even among single mothers receiving food stamps, rural women are less likely to be on the welfare rolls (Brown and Lichter 2004). The social stigma associated with welfare participation is an important barrier to receipt among rural mothers. Even when the stigma can be overcome, rural women have a hard time getting good and affordable child care that enables them to work or to meet the new work requirements to receive government cash assistance (Lichter and Jensen 2001). Consequently, rural mothers have the triple disadvantage of higher poverty, more barriers to the work, and lower economic incentives to return to work.

Rural families tend to rely more heavily on the informal economy for second jobs to make ends meet (Nelson 1999b). But rural single mothers often lack the financial resources to start their own businesses, leaving them to odd jobs that provide unreliable sources of steady income. Many must rely on extended families or on live-in boyfriends. Figure 1.2 compares rural and urban women's use of these livelihood strategies. Differences in the percent-ages of women who cohabit and who double up with other families are small. These data provide little indication that strong rural family and kinship networks provide a large and supportive informal "safety net" that big-city mothers lack.

To be sure, marriage also can be an important route from poverty for poor rural women. In one study, however, rural single mothers were less likely than their urban counterparts to marry (Porterfield 2001). The strong link between family economic distress and divorce and separation (Conger et al. 1994) has clearly disrupted traditional expectations of rural family life (Struthers and Bokemeier 2000). The "great recession" of the late 2000s has likely undercut the economic basis for marriage and family stability in many parts of rural America. There is little indication that the current retreat from marriage has run its course in rural America.

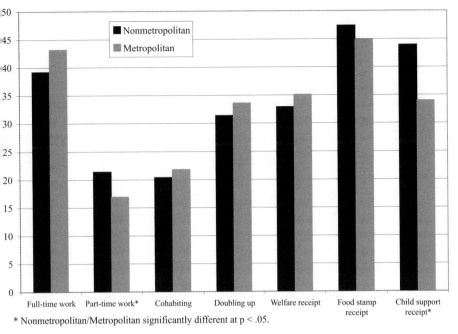

* Nonmetropolitan/Metropolitan significantly different at p < .05.

FIG. 1.2   Percentage of single mothers utilizing economic survival strategies, by non-metropolitan and metropolitan residence (SOURCE: Brown and Lichter 2004, table 1)

WELFARE DEPENDENCE

Welfare dependency is highly stigmatized in rural America (Rank and Hirschl 1993). A disproportionately small share of eligible recipients in rural areas makes use of government cash assistance programs or food stamps. The least populated and largely rural states generally (especially in the South) provide many fewer cash and in-kind benefits to the poor. Although recent studies of the 1996 welfare reform bill have shown few rural-urban differences in employment take-up rates, some state-level studies indicate fewer positive effects of the welfare overhaul on rural employment and earnings (Whitener, Weber, and Duncan 2001). Work-first welfare reform does not address the limited job opportunities available in rural areas, improve the human capital and job skills of rural workers (e.g., low educational attainment), or fully address the chronic lack of rural work supports (Gibbs 2001). For example, lack of public transportation, child care, and job training is sometimes cited as an important barrier to successful welfare-to-work transitions in rural areas (Henry and Lewis 2001).

While many poor welfare-recipient mothers in general have been able to increase their incomes and earnings since the 1996 welfare reform bill was passed, rural welfare-recipient mothers have continued to have higher poverty rates than their urban counterparts, and more of them can be counted among the "working poor" (Lichter and Jensen 2001a). Rural women have shorter spells of welfare use compared with urban women (Lichter and Crowley 2002; Porterfield 1998), even though the wages of rural women leaving welfare tend to be lower than the wages of those leaving welfare in urban locations (Meyer and Cancian 1998). Indeed, for rural workers in a low-wage or part-time job, underemployment and the likelihood of remaining "stuck" in poor jobs are high (Findeis and Jensen 1998). Rural job growth and earnings growth lag their urban counterparts. For rural women, successful welfare-to-work transitions are made difficult by low educational attainment and few good jobs (Gibbs 2001). The implication is clear: the "safety net" available to rural families is often inadequate in addressing the economic dislocations associated with rural industrial restructuring and globalization.

RURAL CHILDREN AT RISK

Recent studies of rural families have shown that economic and employment circumstances influence trajectories of child development through parents' emotional status and parenting behaviors (R. Conger, K. Conger, et al. 1992; Conger and Elder 1994b). Financial stress undermines psychological well-being and compromises mental health, which in turn are linked to harsh parenting (Elder et al. 1995). Unemployment and financial stresses also are related to maternal depression, which is associated with punitive disciplinary strategies (McLoyd et al. 1994). Economic distress and unemployment are also linked with greater aggression and family violence (Murata 1994). Abusive mothers are more likely than other mothers to be socially isolated and under personal strain (Daniel, Hampton, and Newberger 1983).

Children's living arrangements have changed dramatically with increased divorce, nonmarital childbearing and cohabitation, and single parenting (Lichter and Eggebeen 1994). Perhaps surprisingly, rural children today are less likely than urban children to live in married-couple families, and a larger percentage live with cohabiting parents. Indeed, the share of rural children living with a cohabiting parent more than doubled after 2000 (O'Hare and Churilla 2008; O'Hare et al. 2009). These children are "at risk" of high poverty rates (Manning and Brown 2006). Especially at the lower end of the income distribution, cohabiting relationships increasingly end in dissolution rather than marriage (Lichter, Qian, and Mellott 2006; Graefe and Lichter 1999). Previous studies show that family transitions, born of cohabitation and divorce, have negative implications for children's developmental trajectories and early adult achievement.

Rates of single motherhood are especially high among rural minorities. Wiley, Warren, and Montanelli (2002) found that rural African American mothers living in two economically struggling Midwest communities were dealing with unemployment of the household head, a loss of public assistance benefits or income, high debt levels, and, in a third of cases, problems maintaining independent housing. While their sample included volunteers answering local ads (thus potentially biasing the sample toward economic disadvantage), they found that financial, health, and substance abuse problems were associated with reactive, aggressive, and lax parenting. Religious involvement provided a buffer against stressful life events, a finding that reinforces the importance of social support and community involvement.

Not surprisingly, low-income rural children face a larger array of physical and psychosocial stressors than middle-income children. They also experience higher levels of psychological and physical distress and exhibit lower levels of self-regulation (Evans and English 2002). Typical stressors include substandard housing and crowding, family turmoil, community violence, and childhood separation. These conditions are likely to contribute to child and adolescent behaviors that compromise successful developmental trajectories and self-sufficiency in young adulthood. For example, juvenile violence tends to be highest in rural communities with disproportionate shares of children living in single-parent homes, greater residential instability, and higher ethnic diversity. As shown in figure 1.3, single parenting is the strongest correlate of juvenile delinquency in rural communities, although ethnic diversity and residential instability also affect higher delinquency rates (Osgood and Chambers 2003). Rural children have higher dropout rates and lower educational attainment and standardized test scores than suburban children (Roscigno, Tomaskovic-Devey, and Crowley 2006).

ADOLESCENT CHILDBEARING

Rural adolescents often lack access to reproductive health services, including family planning services and abortion providers (Lichter, McLaughlin, and Ribar 2002). Sexually active rural adolescents face privacy concerns about acquiring or purchasing effective contraceptives (from the family doctor or local drug or convenience store), which limits their use. Religious fundamentalism and an

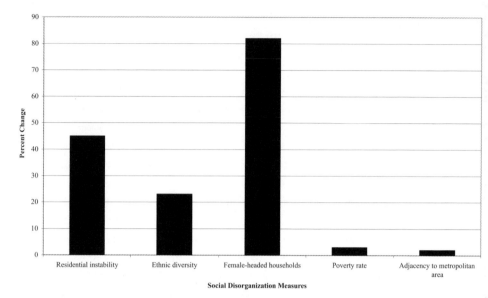

FIG. 1.3   Difference in the juvenile violent crime index associated with a 10 percent increase in measures of social disorganization in rural counties of Florida, Georgia, Nebraska, and South Carolina, 1989–1993 (SOURCE: Osgood and Chambers 2003, table 2)

active churchgoing population in many small rural communities may also impose strong moral proscriptions against nonmarital sexual activity. Many rural adolescents may be ill-prepared emotionally or lack the knowledge to effectively prevent an unintended pregnancy if they become sexually active.

In many rural states, unintended pregnancies are resolved by out-of-wedlock births or shotgun marriages; abortion is often not an option for financial, moral, or other reasons (Lichter, McLaughlin, and Ribar 2002). Youth in disadvantaged rural communities are more likely to drop out of school and engage in risk-taking behaviors such as alcohol abuse, which heightens the risk of out-of-wedlock pregnancy. Unwed mothers are less likely to marry, stay married, or marry an "economically attractive" partner (Graefe and Lichter 2002). This exacerbates the intergenerational transmission of poverty and income inequality.

Teenagers living in counties with low per capita income and high income inequality tend to have very high birthrates—more than 5 percent of teens give birth each year, compared with only 2 percent in middle-class communities (Gold et al. 2001). Social stress and the lack of access to reproductive health services may compromise young women's sense of self-worth and adversely impact their reproductive decision making. Importantly, having high self-esteem, being raised by highly educated parents, growing up without being poor, and avoiding substance use are protective factors against adolescent motherhood (Berry et al. 2000). Indeed, rural adolescents and young adults lacking good educational and job opportunities may regard the "costs" of out-of-wedlock childbearing to be both minimal and acceptable. Shortages of economically attractive potential marriage partners may also change the calculus of reproductive decision making (South and Baumer 2001).

EDUCATIONAL ACHIEVEMENT

The nation's most poorly performing schools (as defined by achievement on standardized tests) tend to be found in the most impoverished areas of the country, including poor rural school districts (Lichter 1993). The school and family resource disadvantages of rural children mean they face dramatic educational investment inequalities. Socioeconomic status influences trajectories of academic achievement (Alexander et al. 1987), partly because family income is linked to early cognitive growth (Moore and Snyder 1991), and partly because the nonpoor spend more time and money in developing skills that contribute to educational attainment (Laureau 2002).

Children in single-parent households perform less well academically compared with children in two-parent families (McLanahan and Sandefur 1994). Children in single-parent families receive less supervision, live more chaotic lives, and face greater financial constraints than children living with both biological parents (Sandefur, McLanahan, and Wojtkiewicz 1992; Thompson, Entwisle, and Alexander 1988; Zill 1996). In rural areas, disproportionately rapid increases in nonmarital childbearing and marital dissolution (Lichter, Kephart, et al. 1992) are expected to exacerbate rural/suburban differences in school outcomes. Parental investment in children's education may also be negatively affected by perceptions (often rooted in reality) that the benefits or economic returns to education in poor rural communities are low (Roscigno, Tomaskovic-Devey, and Crowley 2006). The lack of good jobs affects investments in schooling, which in turn limits upward socioeconomic mobility. It also impedes the development of human resource and local capacity building that is necessary to attract new businesses to the community.

CHANGING FAMILIES AND CHANGING POPULATIONS

Economic dislocations are associated with delayed marriage, higher divorce rates, more out-of-wedlock childbearing, and the rise in single-parent families, which affects the developmental trajectories of rural children and diminishes positive early adult economic outcomes. But rural families are also changing through population succession; the massive influx of Hispanic families in rural communities, especially in the Midwest and South, has offset declines among white families (Johnson and Lichter 2010). The rural economy and workforce are more diverse than ever. The new rural influx of Hispanics, many of whom are immigrants, reflects a fundamental transformation of America's food system from agriculture to food processing and distribution and the accelerated growth of low-wage, low-skilled work in some sectors of the rural economy (Kandel and Parrado 2005). Indeed, more than two hundred rural counties—twice as many as in the 1990s—would have experienced population decline after 2000 if not for the heavy influx of Hispanics (Johnson and Lichter 2008).

Hispanics have higher than average fertility levels. Hispanic women begin childbearing at younger ages, and age-specific fertility levels are higher for Hispanic women at every age from fifteen to twenty-nine. In the 1990s there were 5.4 births for every Hispanic death in rural areas; that ratio rose to 6.4 after 2000 (Johnson and Lichter 2010). Women of childbearing age are overrepresented in the Hispanic population. Fertility rates among rural white women are below replacement levels (Lichter, Johnson, et al. 2010). In this respect, rural economic restructuring has reinforced traditional family structures (e.g., more marriage and less divorce) and higher fertility through racial and ethnic change. Cultural explanations of high fertility typically emphasize familialism as a "core element of Hispanic culture" (Landale and Oropesa 2007, 396). Familialism—as measured by fertility and family formation—is arguably the linchpin of changing cultural patterns and assimilation among most Hispanic groups, including Mexicans.

A growing rural Hispanic population has transformed many small towns, but has also raised new concerns about racial relations, immigrant assimilation, and the putative burden on local taxpayers of bilingual education and social services. Higher fertility rates bring increased demand for culturally sensitive educational and family-related services. Existing barriers to educational attainment (e.g., English-language ability), combined with poor physical health and lack of health coverage, impede upward generational mobility among Latino immigrant children (Hernandez and Charney 1998). Many small rural school districts are simply unprepared to accommodate the special needs of immigrant children (Crowley, Lichter, and Qian 2006).

Some rural communities today are at risk of becoming new immigrant enclaves—rural ghettos—that impede rather than promote incorporation into American society (Lichter, Johnson, et al. 2010). Clearly, the fate of the nation's rural families is intimately linked to the economic and social trajectories of America's new rural immigrant populations.

Implications for Rural Family Policy

Rural economic restructuring continued apace in the post-2000 period. Moreover, current economic conditions in rural America have been aggravated by the ongoing financial crisis, high unemployment (around 10 percent), and job losses in high-wage jobs. The housing market in rural areas also has suffered, although the rural housing market has never had much of a "housing bubble" to burst. Under the circumstances, it is hardly surprising that the 2000s were marked by a continuing retreat from marriage in rural America. As we have argued in this chapter, economics and family life are highly intertwined (Burstein 2007). And, unfortunately, rising unemployment and underemployment portend continuing increases in family instability and divorce, more family violence and abuse, and higher poverty rates. Out-of-wedlock childbearing and cohabitation increasingly typify America's rural families. With the rapidly changing racial and ethnic composition of many rural communities, efforts to strengthen vulnerable families and promote upward socioeconomic mobility have taken on new urgency.

Rural families and children clearly are on the frontline of economic restructuring. For rural America, the policy options are twofold: (1) increase efforts to strengthen the rural economy and improve work opportunities and the number of well-paying jobs; and/or (2) mitigate the family destabilizing effects of economic restructuring and employment dislocations (i.e., treat families directly). We consider each approach in turn.

Rural economic development strategies—the focus of other chapters in this volume—rarely emphasize the beneficial effects of economic growth on family stability and healthy families. The emphasis instead often centers on a singular important goal: fostering a strong rural economy that promotes job opportunity, higher earnings, and positive income trajectories. As an example, the Council of Economic Advisors released a report in April 2010 on "Strengthening the Rural Economy." Much of the report focused on how to grow rural businesses and expand employment opportunities by providing additional monies for small business loans, encouraging the development of clean energy and biofuels, and promoting rural tourism and recreation. The Obama administration also acknowledges the need for additional investments in rural infrastructure (e.g., roads and bridges, water projects, and broadband Internet) to increase productivity, promote local and regional food systems (e.g., locally grown foods), and improve access to rural education and health care. Age-adjusted mortality rates between metro and nonmetro areas have diverged significantly since 1990 (Cosby et al. 2008), even though rural families spend more of their incomes than urban families on health insurance. The current situation calls for improvements in the quality of rural health care and a more educated rural workforce (with jobs having health insurance benefits).

Interesting enough, the Council of Economic Advisors gives little attention to the rural family, either as a beneficiary of rural economic development or as a resource for "strengthening the rural economy." To be sure, the best marriage-promotion policies may be those that create new and better jobs for rural people and places. Public policy clearly can—and must—focus on the economic sources of rural family change. But it can also treat the symptoms rather than the source of the problem by seeking to mitigate the perverse consequences (including family instability) of continuing economic dislocations and restructuring. Indeed, one of the goals of the 1996 welfare reform legislation (the Personal Responsibility and Work Opportunity Reconciliation Act) was to end dependence on government benefits by "promoting job preparation, work and *marriage*" (emphasis added). Until recently, most states emphasized work rather than marriage. In 2005, the U.S. Congress passed the 2006 FY budget (i.e., the Deficit Reduction Act of 2005), which, among other things, established a program of grants to encourage "healthy marriages." The legislation provides roughly $1.5 billion for training to help couples develop skills that sustain marriages (e.g., counseling and mentoring programs), including unmarried couples with children. Healthy marriage programs in rural areas, however, have been limited. Most of the public policy debate and monies have focused instead on big-city and minority populations. We know surprisingly little about how to promote good marriages and family stability in rural areas.

In the end, promoting strong families goes hand in hand with human resource development and a strong rural economy. Whether current policies focus on the economic sources of family change or on efforts to support marriages and families directly (e.g., through family supports and healthy marriage initiatives), positive changes in rural family life are unlikely to happen quickly. Recent trends in marriage, divorce, and cohabitation and other aspects of family life (e.g., family violence and abuse) are not rooted entirely in changing economic conditions. The historical record is clear: family income levels were lower and poverty rates were much higher two or three generations ago (e.g., in 1950), yet marriage rates at the time were much higher and divorce was uncommon (at least by contemporary standards). Most children were born into married-couple families rather than to cohabiting couples or single women. A strong rural economy will help rural families but will not by itself "solve" all of its problems or reverse trends anytime soon. This is why efforts to strengthen families directly through the "Healthy Marriage Initiative" or related family-strengthening activities are an important albeit controversial and largely untested attempt to build strong families and promote positive developmental outcomes among growing children.

Other policies may also strengthen families and build social and human capital and a better future for rural people and communities. For example, Wolfe and Tefft (2006) outline several early intervention programs that help sever the intergenerational transmission of family instability and poverty. Nurse-family partnerships for the infants and toddlers of young, unmarried, and low-SES mothers have been found to reduce children's risk-taking behaviors in adolescence. Educational support, health, and family services in early childhood improve academic achievement and school completion, and reduce later risk taking among low-income children and the parent involvement of their mothers and fathers. Older children in single-parent families who were mentored through Big Brothers and Big Sisters of America perform better in school and are less likely to engage in substance use and aggressive behaviors. Job Corps provides free education and training programs that help young people learn a career, find and keep a job, and learn to be self-sufficient, which may have the indirect benefit of promoting marriage and stable families, especially in communities impacted by economic restructuring and persistent poverty. Most of these programs, not surprisingly, have targeted big-city populations rather than sparsely populated rural communities, where economic dislocations have contributed to unprecedented family changes over the past few decades.

The past decade has brought large and unprecedented changes in rural family life. Conventional stereotypes about strong rural families and supportive kin networks are no longer consistent with demographic reality. Indeed, rural families and households today look more similar to than different from their counterparts in urban areas (O'Hare and Churilla 2008). Rural family patterns are rapidly converging with rather than diverging from national patterns. At the same time, the extraordinary diversity of rural America and family life gives reason to be cautious about easy generalizations. If the past is prologue, the continuing transformation in American family life will proceed unevenly across geography, racial and ethnic groups, and social classes (i.e., rich and poor).

EMPLOYMENT HARDSHIP AMONG RURAL MEN

LEIF JENSEN AND ERIC B. JENSEN

At first blush, the employment circumstances of men in rural America would hardly seem a subject worthy of concern. Given the employment challenges women have faced, particularly in rural areas, where barriers to employment are arguably more severe, they would seem the ones whose changing circumstances it is critical to understand. Women, after all, have entered the workforce in very large numbers over the past half century. In 1950, 29 percent of the workforce consisted of women, compared to 46 percent today (Bureau of Labor Statistics 2003). The rise in labor force participation has been particularly sharp among married mothers, who have accounted for the majority of the increase in total labor force participation since World War II (Cohany and Sok 2007). And it is women—rural women in particular—who continue to face persisting and significant employment disadvantages; notably, their average earnings and wages lag considerably behind those of rural men or urban women (Cotter et al. 1996). And when arguably the most momentous piece of social legislation of recent times, the 1996 Welfare Reform Act, sought to reduce welfare dependency through gainful employment, the target population was overwhelmingly women (Lichter and Jensen 2002).[1]

In a bygone time when the image of the male as family "breadwinner" had some legitimacy, a focus on male employment as sufficient for understanding family economic well-being ostensibly made sense. Indeed, early studies of

intragenerational status attainment and intergenerational social mobility analyzed data on men only, since historically so few women were part of the paid
labor force (Blau and Duncan 1967).[2] Lewis (2001) notes that the breadwinner
ideal type may never have existed in its pure form, since married women have
always worked to some degree. But she acknowledges that "there were historical periods in some countries and for some social classes for which the model
more accurately described the social reality than others; for people of the mid-
dling sort in the United Kingdom and the United States in the late nineteenth
century and large tracts of the middle and respectable working classes in the
years following World War II in many western countries." However, in both
rural and urban America, that model has been rendered largely anachronistic
by the rise in single-female family headship, owing to the rise in both divorce
and nonmarital childbearing (Davanzo and Rahman 1993), and in female labor
supply and dual-earner couples (McLaughlin, Gardner, and Lichter 1999).

So why study the employment circumstances of rural men? There are several reasons. First, among married couples with children in both rural[3] and
urban areas, the husband's earnings still contribute tremendously to family
well-being. Data from the 2006 Current Population Survey (CPS) suggest that
among married couples with children, the husband's wage and salary income
contributed 70 percent of total family income on average, which compares to
30 percent for the contribution from the wife's earnings. The corresponding percentages for rural couples are 66 percent and 34 percent, respectively.
Second, structural changes to the rural economy have taken a toll on traditionally male lucrative and secure job opportunities (Glasmeier and Salant
2006). To be sure, rural women have been adversely affected by job loss due
to global industrial restructuring, notably in the textile and apparel sectors
(Hamrick 2005), but the effect on rural men has been more severe. Third, there
is evidence that rural men—particularly those who are less well educated and
thus more vulnerable to employment hardship—may have been bypassed by
the beneficial effects of the "hot economy" of the 1990s. Davis and Bosley (2007)
analyze nationally representative panel data from this decade and find that
while low unemployment and job growth had predictably beneficial effects
on wages overall and for rural women, they did *not* register for rural men.
Finally, the marriage promotion provisions of the 1996 welfare reform sought
to reduce reliance on public assistance by helping recipients benefit from the
well-documented economic benefits of marriage (Lichter, Batson, and Brown
2004). While the feminist literature compellingly argues that these provisions
implicitly rely on the viability of a breadwinner model that inherently sub-
ordinates women (Curran and Abrams 2000),[4] to the extent that marriage is a

viable economic strategy and to the extent that welfare reform brought father-hood to biological fathers who might otherwise have stayed away, it is impor-tant to examine their employment circumstances, whether rural or urban.

In this study, through an analysis of multiple years of data from the CPS, from the closing decades of the twentieth century up to the present, we assess several key dimensions of employment disadvantage: underemployment, job displacement, and contingent work.[5] To our knowledge, this is the first attempt to bring all three dimensions into one analysis. In the following section we describe these dimensions conceptually and as operationalized in our analy-sis. We then give a descriptive portrait of employment hardship among rural men, with emphasis on those who are married, and married with children, in comparison to their female counterparts. In the concluding section we discuss policy implications.

Dimensions of Employment Hardship

The entire analysis is based on data drawn from the Current Population Sur-vey (CPS), the official source of unemployment statistics and the nation's prin-cipal source of data on trends in employment. Conducted by the U.S. Census Bureau on behalf of the Bureau of Labor Statistics, the CPS is a monthly sur-vey based on a nationally representative sample of roughly fifty thousand U.S. households. The surveys gather data on a wide range of employment indica-tors used to operationalize the forms of employment hardship we examine here. The data files contain information about households and all families and individuals residing within them. While a core set of survey items are asked each month, the monthly surveys feature various blocks of questions that allow for in-depth exploration of particular issues on a yearly basis. For example, the March CPS, or Annual Social and Economic Supplement, contains ample socioeconomic and demographic variables not included in the survey during other months of the year, making it a rich source of data not only on workers, but also on their households. As described below, we use the March CPS to measure underemployment. Other months add supplemental questions (or "supplements") to the core questionnaire, which we take advantage of here to measure job displacement and contingent work.

We measure rural residence as living in a county that is defined as non-metropolitan (nonmetro). Metropolitan (metro) areas consist essentially of core counties with one or more cities of fifty thousand or more people, plus sur-rounding counties tied economically to the core county through commuting patterns. The counties defined as metro and nonmetro are updated decennially based on results from the U.S. Census and have undergone other adjustments over the years, particularly in 2003 (USDA Economic Research Service 2007a). Thus, the set of counties identified as nonmetro changes over the time period we consider in this analysis. Because the CPS public-use files do not contain county identifiers, we, like other researchers, have to use a floating definition. The pool of nonmetro counties has declined in number, reflecting the empirical reality of the steady urbanization of America. To take account of the significant variation that exists between cities and suburbs, we show data for metro areas as a whole and within them, and for residents of central cities versus non-central cities separately. We now turn to our measures of employment hardship.

UNDEREMPLOYMENT

For the vast majority of households, adequate employment is a key element for ensuring economic well-being. One way to conceptualize employment adequacy is the degree to which workers are employed full-time, or for the number of hours they desire, at jobs that pay a livable wage. Those who fall short of this threshold can be regarded as underemployed. Originating in the Labor Utilization Framework (LUF) developed by Hauser (1974) and later refined by Clogg and associates (Clogg 1979; Clogg and Sullivan 1983; Sullivan 1978), a standard definition of underemployment is made up of four mutually exclusive employment conditions: sub-unemployed ("discouraged workers" who would like to be employed but are out of work and did not seek a job in the previous four weeks because they believed none were available); unemployed (those who are not employed but are looking for work or are on layoff with the expectation of being called back); involuntary part-time (workers who are employed less than thirty-five hours per week but would opt for full-time work were it available); and low-wage work (the "working poor," who are working full-time but for earnings that, when adjusted for weeks and hours worked, fall below 125 percent of the official poverty threshold). All other employed adults are defined as adequately employed. Research on underemployment has consistently shown a higher prevalence of underemployment in rural than in urban areas (Lichter and Costanzo 1987; Slack and Jensen 2002). Adequately employed rural workers also have a greater chance than urban workers of becoming underemployed and have a more difficult time moving out of underemployment (Jensen et al. 1999). While factors on the demand side (e.g., industrial structure) and supply side (e.g., lower education) offer partial explanations for rural under-employment (Jensen et al. 1999; Slack and Jensen 2002, 2004), the nonmetro

disadvantage has not been fully accounted for in research to date. Also noteworthy is that rural women suffer "double jeopardy" in terms of underemployment prevalence, owing largely to their high rates of working poverty. While our
focus in this study is on rural men, we will be attentive to gender differences.

JOB DISPLACEMENT

Economies are always evolving in response to emerging technologies, production processes, comparative advantages, consumer preferences, and a host of
other factors that together determine the nature of labor demand within places.
As the industrial mix and skill requirements of economies inevitably change,
some workers will lose their jobs as their skill sets come to be in lower demand.
When these workers have established work histories otherwise, have lost their
jobs because the positions have been eliminated or moved away, and are apt to
have a difficult time finding the same kind of work, they are said to have been
"displaced" (Hamrick 2001; Glasmeier and Salant 2006). This displacement is
not temporary—the result, for example, of cyclical downturns in the economy—but more permanent, a structural unemployment rooted in secular
trends in industrial structure. While the United States has always been part
of a world economy and globalization is not a recent development, a cause of
worker displacement that has captured the concern of policy makers and labor
force scholars in recent decades is outsourcing. This occurs when production
once performed domestically—particularly in manufacturing, but also in services and other sectors—is moved offshore to places where the cost of production (chiefly wages and benefits) is much lower.

Workers who are laid off because of a company's closing, relocation, or
downsizing are considered displaced workers.[6] Using the Displaced Workers
Supplement from the CPS, we calculate three-year displacement rates from
1984 to 2004. The CPS classifies workers as displaced if in the past three calendar years they lost or left a job because their plant or company closed or moved,
because their position or shift was abolished, because there was insufficient
work, or for other similar reasons. The displaced worker rate is then calculated
as the proportion of all workers who have been displaced within the past three
years.

As it is a concept that has gained attention only in recent decades, the literature on displacement is still emerging. Only a modest amount has focused on
displacement in rural areas, which is somewhat surprising given the structural
disadvantages and lack of diversity characterizing many rural labor markets that
would seem to place rural workers at greater risk of displacement. In a helpful

review, Hamrick (2001) describes research indicating that rates of displacement during the 1980s were greater in nonmetro than metro areas, and that rural displaced workers endured longer stretches of subsequent unemployment and lower earnings when they finally *did* find work, in comparison to those in metro areas (Swaim 1990). In the early 1990s, these rural disadvantages apparently disappeared (Torgerson and Hamrick 1999). Hamrick (2001) finds that in the later 1990s nonmetro workers were not more likely to be displaced than their metro counterparts (if anything, they were less likely), yet did have a lower likelihood of finding a job thereafter. More recently, Glasmeier and Salant (2006) report increasing displacement rates from the late 1990s into the 2000s, and that displacement from manufacturing was a greater problem in rural than urban areas as we entered the new century. With respect to gender differences, Garner (1995) shows a clear male disadvantage, with higher displacement rates among men than women consistently over the 1980s. Hamrick (2001) likewise reports higher displacement among nonmetro men than women in the mid-1990s (though in metro areas it was women who were at a disadvantage in this regard). In the analysis below, we will be attentive to whether men, and rural men in particular, are especially vulnerable to displacement.

CONTINGENT WORK

Job displacement is a function, in part, of increased exogenous labor market competition. That is, to the extent that they can, firms lower production costs by simply moving operations to locations where those costs are lower. As an alternative strategy to minimize labor costs, contingent work arrangements have risen to national prominence. The terms "contingent worker" and "contingent workforce" can be traced to labor economist Audrey Freedman (1985), who described emerging employment relationships that were conditional or transitory and afforded firms significant flexibility in meeting fluctuating demand (Barker and Christensen 1998). The term has included a variety of different specific employment circumstances, such as part-time, on-call, temporary, and/or contract or outsourced employees (Horne, Williamson, and Herman 2005).[7] While some argue that contingent work arrangements might actually enhance the leverage that workers—especially skilled workers—can bring to the labor market (Barker and Christensen 1998), the detrimental implications for earners in terms of uncertain futures, income instability, and a frequent lack of health care and other benefits are glaring. While contingent work may be perfectly suited to some workers' situations, for many others it represents an inferior alternative to regular and stable employment.

For our purposes, contingent work describes employment that is temporary and unstable. The prevalence of contingent work by gender and residence was measured using data from the February Supplement of the CPS for the years 1995, 1997, 1999, 2003, and 2005. The CPS defines contingent workers as wage and salary workers who, for nonpersonal reasons, are in temporary jobs that cannot last as long as they wish and self-employed workers and independent contractors who have been employed less than a year and do not expect their self-employment or contract work to last more than one year. The prevalence of contingent work was operationalized as the percentage of all workers who fall into this category.

Research on the prevalence and nature of contingent work in rural America is scant. This is surprising since, as usefully reviewed by McLaughlin and Coleman-Jensen (2008), the literature suggests ample reasons why contingent work and other forms of nonstandard work might be particularly apparent in the countryside. For example, industrial structure (e.g., dependence on extraction), firm size, lower-skilled and more routinized production processes, vulnerability to global labor market forces, and employer-employee power relations that favor the former all suggest that contingent work arrangements may be more apparent in rural areas. McLaughlin and Coleman-Jensen (2008) confirm a higher prevalence of contingent work in nonmetro than metro areas (higher even than in central cities with other covariates controlled). With regard to gender, their findings suggest that women workers are more likely than their male counterparts to be in contingent work arrangements. Here we focus on gender differences by place of residence, with an eye toward establishing the circumstances of rural men vis-à-vis rural women and urban men in their likelihood of being contingent workers.

Research Findings

We begin by considering the most basic workforce indicators, including labor force participation and unemployment. Table 2.1 shows labor force participation rates among adults age eighteen to sixty-four in the United States from 1980 through 2006. In this and subsequent tables, rates are shown for men and women and, within each, for those who are married or married with own children present. These data are shown for those residing in nonmetro and metro counties and, within the latter, for those within and without the central cities of metro areas. Our focus in each table will be magnitudes and trends in employment indicators among nonmetro men, with emphasis on the comparison to metro men and to nonmetro women.

Labor force participation is defined as being employed or unemployed (on layoff or out of work but looking). The percentages in table 2.1 indicate that since 1980 there has been a slight decline in labor force participation for males in all residence categories; however, the greatest declines were registered for males in nonmetro areas. In 1980, 88 percent of nonmetro males over the age of eighteen were included in the labor force, but by 2006 only 82 percent were. As a result of the steeper decline in rural areas, by 2006 nonmetro males had lower labor force participation rates than men living in metro areas generally or central cities in particular.

It is noteworthy that, while already high, the labor force participation rate of rural men is even higher among those who are married (87 percent in 2006), and is higher still among rural married men with children (94 percent). This underscores the importance of the father's employment for the economic well-being of children in married-couple families. While less steep, the decline in rural men's labor force participation is seen also among those who are married and married with children.

Countervailing the decline in men's labor force participation is a dramatic increase in the employment of women. While women's labor force participation rates are lower than those of men in any year, residence, or family status category, the rise in women's labor supply also is universal. Focusing on nonmetro women, labor force participation rose from 60 percent in 1980 to over 70 percent by 2006. Also, while being married and married with children were associated with lower labor force participation among women in 1980, by the new century these women actually had *higher* labor force participation than women overall. In sum, women—nonmetro women in particular—went a long way toward closing the gap with men in labor force participation. While the focus here is on men, this striking trend in women's labor supply cannot be ignored.

A conventional indicator of employment status is the unemployment rate, where unemployment is defined as being out of work and actively looking for work (including those who are on layoff). The unemployment rate is the number of individuals unemployed divided by the number in the labor force (i.e., employed or unemployed) multiplied by 100. While unemployment is a component of underemployment to be described below, its ubiquity in the national media as a fundamental indicator of macroeconomic health calls for a separate treatment here.

Unemployment rates by gender and geographic location are presented in table 2.2. Immediately noticeable is the countercyclical nature of unemployment, falling amidst economic expansion and rising when the economy slumps. For example, the unemployment rate among rural men was relatively high (7 percent) during the somewhat weak economy of the early 1990s, and low (only 5 percent) in 2000 amidst the tail end of the economic expansion during the Clinton administration. It rose again by 2006 (to 6 percent), presaging the deep recession to follow. With regard to residential differences, unemployment rates are uniformly higher among nonmetro than metro men and are on par with those in central cities. Being married is associated with lower unemployment among rural men, although there is no discernible difference between those with and without children. With respect to differences by gender, although unemployment is highly countercyclical, there appears to be a secular trend toward lower unemployment among rural women, especially among women who are married (overall or with children). Indeed, since 1980 rural men have consistently had higher unemployment rates than their female counterparts.

Next we turn to underemployment. As noted, underemployment goes beyond unemployment to include performing involuntary part-time work, being a discouraged worker, and being in working poverty as three additional states of employment hardship. Underemployment is also a countercyclical condition, as evidenced by the fact that among males in all residence categories, the pattern was one of increasing prevalence in the 1980s, a sharp decline in the 1990s, and then a gradual increase since 2000 (table 2.3). With respect to residential differences, nonmetro men are at a decided disadvantage relative to their metro counterparts and have underemployment rates similar to those in central cities of metro areas. Underemployment rates are much lower among married men than men overall, although among them the rural disadvantage continues to be apparent.

Perhaps most striking are differences by gender. Women are certainly affected by the same cyclical forces as men, but noteworthy among rural women is the steady decline in underemployment prevalence even amidst periods of recession. To be sure, rural women always have higher rates of underemployment than rural men; in 2006, for example, about one in four rural women were underemployed, which compares to a rate of one in five rural men. However, the steady improvement among rural women in underemployment served to appreciably reduce the gender gap in this regard. The circumstances of urban women did not improve to the same degree. A picture that seems to be emerging is one of rural men marking time in terms of employment hardship, while rural women are gaining ground.

As a form of underemployment, working poverty (i.e., underemployed by low income) captures public attention and concern because those in this category are working and thus "playing by the rules," but they are doing so at wages that do not allow them to makes ends meet. For this reason, and because research suggests that this form of underemployment is especially prevalent in rural areas, we spotlight working poverty in table 2.4.

Underemployment by low income for males in all residence categories follows the same pattern as underemployment generally—increasing during the 1980s, declining in the 1990s, and gradually increasing again since 2000. This pattern indicates that real wages also are sensitive to business cycles. Again, nonmetro males have higher rates of working poverty than their metro counterparts, and are on par with central city men in this regard. And as was seen for underemployment generally, compared to all rural men, those who are married and, even more so, married with children have lower rates of working poverty.

The contrasts by gender are again striking. The comparison between men and women in nonmetro areas suggests that working poverty is a far greater problem among rural women than men. However, the prevalence of working poverty among rural women declined steadily (from 23 to 18 percent between 1980 and 2006), while that for rural men showed only a mild countercyclical trend. As a result, rural women gained ground on rural men and narrowed the gap in working poverty. Another interesting gender difference does not bode as well for women, at least as breadwinners. As noted, rural married men—those with children especially—had a lower prevalence of working poverty than rural men overall. Among rural women, however, there was almost no difference in this regard. Married rural women were only slightly less likely to be in working poverty compared to rural women overall.

For many companies to stay competitive in a "just-in-time" economy, they must maintain a flexible workforce. Companies have come to rely increasingly on "contingent" workers to fill this need. Workers who are temporarily employed, self-employed for less than one year, or employed on a short-term contractual basis are classified as contingent workers. The prevalence of contingent work by gender, residence, and year is presented in table 2.5. The rates of contingent work are relatively low, and the trends and patterns haphazard. This is partly because contingent work items were added recently, so we only have data for 1995–2005. Moreover, as an emerging phenomenon that is more structural, contingent work is not likely to be especially cyclical.

Still, there are a few differences worth noting. First, among men, to the extent that there is a residential difference, it would seem to slightly favor rural men, who have slightly lower rates of contingent work than their metro counterparts. Second, married rural men, those with children especially, have a somewhat lower prevalence of contingent work than rural men overall. Third, while the gender differences are unremarkable, rural married males have somewhat lower rates of contingent work than rural married women. In sum, contingent work—as measured here—is a relatively uncommon form of employment hardship that seems to burden workers equally by gender or residence.

The restructuring of the U.S. economy has shifted the focus of production from one of manufacturing and industry to one of service and information. In part, this reflects the movement of traditional manufacturing jobs overseas. An inevitable result has been the displacement of some workers from their jobs permanently. How have rural men fared in this regard over the years?

Three-year displaced worker rates by gender and residence are reported in table 2.6. Several results stand out. First, displacement rates for rural men were particularly high during the 1980s and have generally declined since. In 1986, for example, the three-year displacement rate for rural men stood at 6 percent. While the rate generally declined thereafter, there is some evidence of countercyclicality, with rates being especially low in the late 1990s but ticking upwards as the new century unfolded. Second, during the 1980s displacement was a greater problem among rural than urban men, but this rural disadvantage reversed. Urban men show higher displacement rates almost every year since 1992. Third, compared to rural women, rural men have been significantly more vulnerable to displacement. While this male disadvantage has attenuated over the years owing to sharper declines among rural men than women, it persists in every year of observation. Rural men are simply more vulnerable to displacement than their female counterparts. This may reflect employment volatility found in many historically male-dominated industries, such as mining, forestry, and construction. Finally, it is noteworthy that married men (including those with children) are *more* vulnerable to displacement than are men generally. This finding may reflect the fact that older men are more likely to be both married and in occupations and industries at greater risk of structural adjustment.

To round out this descriptive portrait and place the spotlight more on rural men, table 2.7 shows how the prevalence of all these basic dimensions of employment hardship varies across key sociodemographic stratifiers. The data are from the most recent CPS with data available for an employment hardship measure. The table is restricted to rural married men with children. We find that there is a strong educational gradient in the risk of employment hardship. Not surprisingly, those who only have a high school degree or less are far more likely to be unemployed, underemployed, in working poverty, displaced, or holding contingent employment positions than are those who hold college degrees.[8] Similar disadvantages are registered for racial and ethnic minorities relative to non-Hispanic whites. Interestingly, with the exception of working poverty ("low-income"), Hispanics are advantaged relative to non-Hispanic blacks. There is a curvilinear relationship between age and employment hardship, with the youngest rural married males with children being highly vulnerable compared to their middle-aged counterparts, and those in their preretirement years facing increased risk. A stark exception is the linear relationship between age and displacement, with the oldest group showing the lowest risk of permanent job loss. This result is surprising if one assumes that it is older workers whose skills are most apt to become outmoded. Finally, regional differences suggest that different forms of employment hardship may be more common in different regions. Unemployment rates are higher in the Midwest, underemployment and working poverty are most common in the South, displacement rates are highest in the Northeast, while contingent work is more common in the Northeast and West.

Summary and Discussion

This chapter has explored the employment circumstances of rural men, beginning by calling into question the sense in doing so. Why care about rural men if it is women—rural and urban—who have flooded the labor force, face notorious labor market disadvantages, contribute increasingly to family economic well-being (and more often on their own), and were the targets of the 1996 welfare reform? Perhaps a focus on rural men is needed precisely because they have been largely ignored in research and policy debates. The employment of rural men is still critical for the economic well-being of rural families (even if it is less important than it used to be), and yet rural men also are subject to the same economic forces facing rural workers generally. And while the notion of the male breadwinner has become all the more anachronistic, a lot is still riding on how they fare in the labor market.

So how are rural men doing in terms of employment? We examined this issue by bringing together, for the first time, a set of indicators of employment hardship available on various supplements of the Current Population Survey of the U.S. Census Bureau. These include unemployment, underemployment, working poverty, contingent work, and displacement. The picture that emerges is rather complex. Relative to urban men and rural women, rural men are advantaged in some ways and disadvantaged in others. Here we highlight some of the most salient results.

The labor force participation rate for rural men declined in recent decades—much more so than did that among urban men. Rural women, on the other hand, showed steady increases in labor force participation. The result was a significant narrowing of the rural gender gap in labor supply, with women approaching (if not fully achieving) parity with men in this regard. A decidedly rural male disadvantage is seen in unemployment. Historically and today, rural men have higher unemployment rates than either urban men or rural women. Indeed, rural women seem to have enjoyed a decline in unemployment over time. Rural men are also disadvantaged relative to their urban counterparts in terms of underemployment (which conceptually bundles unemployment, working poverty, involuntary part-time work, and discouraged workers into measure of employment hardship). While rural men are always less likely to be underemployed than are rural women, steady improvement among rural women, combined with merely countercyclical movement among men, has caused a significant narrowing of the gender gap in rural underemployment. Precisely the same pattern holds for the prevalence of working poverty; rural men are disadvantaged relative to urban men and advantaged relative to rural women, and steady improvement among rural women, combined with stagnation among rural men, has resulted in a narrowing of the rural gender gap in working poverty. The results for the prevalence of contingent work are not striking, but do suggest a rare advantage of rural men over their urban male counterparts. Finally, worker displacement was more common during the 1980s compared to later years, and rural men enjoyed a steady decline in this regard. Indeed, after 1992 they had lower displacement rates than urban men. Rural men have been far more subject to displacement than rural women, a disadvantage that has abated but persists. In sum, the employment circumstances of rural men (including those who are married, and married with children) are not as bright as those of men in urban areas. And, while rural women suffer unacceptable disadvantages in employment relative to rural men, over time their circumstances have improved markedly while those of rural men have worsened.

Because the forms of employment hardship explored here are diverse, a range of policies needs to be considered to help workers cope with this hardship or avoid it altogether. Increased minimum wages and Earned Income Tax Credit (EITC) benefits would reduce the prevalence of working poverty. Increasing and extending unemployment benefits would help workers bridge periods when, through no fault of their own, they are between jobs, and may also keep some from being so discouraged that they quit looking. Job retraining is critical for those who have been displaced, and these programs could be more proactive by anticipating and targeting occupations and industries whose positions are at greater risk of displacement. The rise in contingent work is welcomed by some temp workers not interested in a long-term commitment. But for those who are reluctantly settling for the uncertainty and negligible benefit packages of contingent work, greater support is needed. They, too, should enjoy unemployment insurance coverage, and a universal health care system would at least allow them to cope without having to worry about sickness or injury. Policies to reduce barriers to labor organizing and increase the leverage of workers also are needed. Finally, employment generation policies and programs, including those promoting entrepreneurship, need to be strengthened in order to increase labor demand and reduce, among other things, involuntary part-time employment.

These policy ideas are not new, yet several are politically unpopular. In this regard it is useful to recall that the social insurance programs of the New Deal era evolved from an economic depression that laid bare the structural roots of deprivation. This recognition faded over time, such that the closing decades of the twentieth century witnessed erosion in government responsibility for the disadvantaged and the ascendancy of individualist and neoliberal social and economic policies. At the same time, the ongoing forces of globalization have given rise to further industrial restructuring, underemployment, permanent job losses, a rise in contingent work, and other forms of employment hardship among rural and urban workers that are quite obviously structural in origin. These structural roots will need to be more widely recognized if meaningful positive change is to be politically feasible.

Table 2.1 Labor force participation rate by gender and residence, 1980, 1990, 2000, and 2006

	Nonmetro				Metro				Central city				Other metro			
	1980	1990	2000	2006	1980	1990	2000	2006	1980	1990	2000	2006	1980	1990	2000	2006
Males	88.1	86.6	84.6	81.7	88.7	88.3	86.8	85.5	86.3	85.3	83.9	83.1	90.2	90.0	88.3	86.8
Married	92.1	90.6	89.3	87.3	93.8	93.0	91.9	91.3	92.3	91.6	90.0	90.0	94.8	93.9	92.8	91.9
Married with children	95.2	94.7	94.2	93.5	96.4	96.1	95.8	95.4	95.4	94.4	94.1	93.5	97.1	96.9	96.6	96.2
Females	59.6	68.0	73.1	71.2	62.3	70.2	73.8	71.6	62.5	67.9	72.3	70.3	62.2	71.4	74.2	72.0
Married	56.9	66.4	72.6	72.3	56.4	66.9	71.0	69.7	56.8	64.8	68.6	67.5	56.1	67.5	71.4	69.9
Married with children	56.0	69.2	74.1	73.5	53.4	65.4	69.9	67.5	54.5	61.8	67.7	63.9	52.8	65.8	69.2	68.1

SOURCE: 1980, 1990, 2000, and 2006 March CPS.

Table 2.2 Unemployment rate by gender and residence, 1980, 1990, 2000, and 2006

	Nonmetro				Metro				Central city				Other metro			
	1980	1990	2000	2006	1980	1990	2000	2006	1980	1990	2000	2006	1980	1990	2000	2006
Males	6.6	6.9	4.8	5.8	6.3	5.4	4.0	5.1	7.8	6.7	5.1	5.9	5.4	4.6	3.3	4.4
Married	4.5	4.5	3.0	3.2	4.1	3.5	2.1	2.7	4.9	4.1	2.5	3.1	3.6	3.0	1.9	2.4
Married with children	4.7	4.2	3.2	3.2	4.3	3.7	2.1	2.8	5.1	5.0	2.1	3.0	4.0	2.8	2.0	2.5
Females	7.0	5.6	4.1	4.3	6.0	4.7	4.1	4.6	7.1	6.3	5.2	5.6	5.3	3.7	3.4	3.9
Married	5.7	4.2	2.8	2.4	5.0	3.4	2.8	3.0	5.7	4.2	3.4	3.9	4.6	2.9	2.4	2.5
Married with children	5.8	4.8	3.1	2.9	5.7	4.1	3.0	3.4	7.3	5.3	3.6	4.3	4.9	3.6	2.6	3.0

SOURCE: 1980, 1990, 2000, 2006 March CPS.

Table 2.3 Total underemployment rate by gender and residence, 1980, 1990, 2000, and 2006

	Nonmetro				Metro				Central city				Other metro			
	1980	1990	2000	2006	1980	1990	2000	2006	1980	1990	2000	2006	1980	1990	2000	2006
Males	20.3	23.9	17.8	20.8	16.3	17.5	15.2	17.6	20.0	21.8	18.4	21.0	13.9	14.8	13.1	15.3
Married	14.4	17.1	11.4	12.9	9.6	10.8	9.1	10.2	12.2	14.2	11.8	12.9	8.2	8.8	7.7	8.5
Married with children	13.7	16.2	11.5	12.8	9.3	10.7	8.9	10.1	12.0	15.0	12.3	12.8	7.9	8.3	7.2	8.6
Females	37.2	36.5	27.2	25.6	27.6	24.3	19.9	21.4	30.0	27.8	22.8	24.8	25.6	20.9	17.4	19.0
Married	35.0	32.7	22.9	21.1	25.7	21.1	15.8	16.5	27.6	24.4	17.8	19.4	24.4	18.1	13.9	14.9
Married with children	34.6	33.5	23.9	22.7	27.5	22.9	16.8	17.5	30.1	27.0	19.8	20.4	25.9	19.6	14.4	16.1

SOURCE: 1980, 1990, 2000, 2006 March CPS.

Table 2.4 Low-income underemployment rate by gender and residence, 1980, 1990, 2000, and 2006

	Nonmetro				Metro				Central city				Other metro			
	1980	1990	2000	2006	1980	1990	2000	2006	1980	1990	2000	2006	1980	1990	2000	2006
Males	10.2	12.3	9.8	10.7	6.9	8.3	8.5	9.3	8.2	10.1	9.8	11.1	5.9	7.2	7.4	8.2
Married	7.2	9.4	6.5	7.2	3.5	4.9	5.2	5.5	4.7	6.8	6.8	7.1	2.8	3.8	4.4	4.5
Married with children	6.4	9.1	6.3	6.9	3.1	4.7	5.0	5.4	4.3	6.6	7.2	7.4	2.5	3.6	3.9	4.5
Females	23.4	23.5	19.2	17.5	16.3	14.8	12.8	13.3	17.0	16.4	14.1	14.9	15.6	12.8	11.6	12.0
Married	23.2	22.3	16.9	15.7	15.9	13.6	10.7	10.7	16.8	16.0	11.9	12.0	15.2	11.5	9.6	10.0
Married with children	22.4	22.4	17.3	16.5	16.1	14.2	11.4	11.2	17.1	16.8	13.3	12.2	15.4	11.9	9.7	10.5

SOURCE: 1980, 1990, 2000, 2006 March CPS.

Table 2.5 Prevalence of contingent work by gender and residence, 1995, 1997, 1999, 2001, and 2005

	Nonmetro					Metro					Central city					Other metro				
	1995	1997	1999	2001	2005	1995	1997	1999	2001	2005	1995	1997	1999	2001	2005	1995	1997	1999	2001	2005
Males	4.1	3.6	4.1	3.5	3.7	4.5	3.9	3.7	3.7	3.9	5.0	4.6	4.4	4.5	5.1	4.1	3.7	3.3	3.2	3.4
Married	2.7	2.0	2.3	2.6	2.4	3.2	2.7	2.5	2.7	2.9	3.6	3.1	3.2	3.3	4.6	3.1	2.6	2.1	2.4	2.3
Married with children	2.5	2.0	2.0	2.3	1.7	3.1	2.6	2.3	2.8	2.6	3.6	2.8	2.9	3.6	4.0	2.9	2.5	1.9	2.6	2.1
Females	4.2	4.2	4.0	4.5	3.4	5.4	4.8	4.7	4.0	4.3	5.9	5.1	5.3	4.2	4.9	5.4	4.7	4.4	4.1	4.0
Married	3.5	3.3	3.3	4.6	2.9	4.2	3.9	3.4	3.1	3.4	4.3	4.1	3.9	3.0	4.4	4.2	3.7	3.2	3.2	3.1
Married with children	3.7	3.5	3.6	5.1	2.4	4.3	4.2	3.5	3.6	3.6	4.3	4.4	3.6	3.7	5.8	4.3	3.9	3.3	3.7	3.3

SOURCE: 1995, 1997, 1999, 2001, 2005 CPS.

Table 2.6 Three-year displaced worker rates by gender and residence, 1984–2004

| | Nonmetro | | | | | | | | | |
	1984	1986	1988	1992	1994	1996	1998	2000	2002	2004
Males	5.0	6.4	4.4	4.2	3.3	3.5	2.2	2.7	2.7	2.9
Married	5.4	7.0	4.7	4.4	3.8	3.9	3.1	3.0	2.9	3.1
Married with children	5.4	7.0	4.7	4.3	3.8	3.9	2.2	2.7	2.7	3.6
Females	2.3	3.2	2.0	2.0	2.1	2.4	1.5	1.8	1.8	2.5
Married	2.2	2.9	2.0	2.1	2.0	2.3	1.3	1.6	1.6	2.4
Married with children	2.2	2.9	2.0	2.1	2.1	2.5	1.3	1.7	1.4	2.5

| | Metro | | | | | | | | | |
	1984	1986	1988	1992	1994	1996	1998	2000	2002	2004
Males	5.0	5.1	3.7	5.2	4.2	3.5	2.7	2.3	3.04	4.1
Married	5.3	5.8	4.2	5.5	4.7	4.0	2.1	2.5	3.37	4.5
Married with children	5.3	5.8	4.2	5.5	4.6	4.0	3.1	2.5	3.61	4.6
Females	2.4	2.7	1.9	2.9	2.6	2.5	2.3	1.9	2.35	2.8
Married	2.2	2.5	1.8	2.8	2.4	2.4	2.3	1.8	2.0	2.8
Married with children	2.2	2.5	1.8	2.8	2.2	2.4	2.2	1.9	2.0	2.5

| | Central city | | | | | | | | | |
	1984	1986	1988	1992	1994	1996	1998	2000	2002	2004
Males	4.9	5.1	4.0	5.3	3.6	3.2	2.8	1.9	3.0	4.2
Married	5.3	5.7	4.6	5.6	4.0	3.6	3.3	2.0	3.3	4.8
Married with children	5.3	5.8	4.8	5.5	3.8	3.8	3.2	2.2	4.2	5.1
Females	2.6	2.8	2.1	3.4	2.4	2.5	2.2	1.8	2.6	2.9
Married	2.4	2.6	1.9	3.2	2.1	2.6	2.2	1.8	2.3	3.0
Married with children	2.4	2.6	1.9	3.2	2.0	2.4	2.0	2.0	2.8	2.5

| | Other metro | | | | | | | | | |
	1984	1986	1988	1992	1994	1996	1998	2000	2002	2004
Males	5.1	4.9	3.8	5.3	4.8	3.7	2.6	2.3	3.2	4.3
Married	5.3	5.7	4.2	5.7	5.3	4.2	3.0	2.6	3.4	4.8
Married with children	5.3	5.7	4.2	5.8	5.0	4.4	3.1	2.5	3.6	4.8
Females	2.3	2.7	1.8	2.8	3.0	2.6	2.3	2.0	2.2	2.9
Married	2.0	2.6	1.8	2.7	2.7	2.4	2.3	1.9	1.9	2.8
Married with children	2.0	2.6	1.8	2.7	2.4	2.5	2.2	1.9	1.6	2.6

SOURCE: 1984, 1986, 1988, 1992, 1994, 1996, 1998, 2000, 2002, 2004 CPS.

Table 2.7 Employment hardship among nonmetro married males with children, 2004, 2005, and 2006

	Unemployment	Underemployment	Low income	Displacement	Contingent work
Education					
Less than high school	6.1	27.2	14.6	3.2	5.7
High school	4.1	14.5	7.3	4.5	0.7
Some college	1.7	10.2	5.6	3.0	1.5
College	1.5	6.5	4.2	3.0	1.6
Race/Ethnicity					
Non-Hispanic white	2.9	10.7	5.3	3.7	1.1
Non-Hispanic black	6.9	29.7	15.8	4.8	—
Hispanic	3.2	25.2	18.5	2.9	7.9
Other	6.0	15.4	8.1	1.9	2.5
Age					
Less than 30	5.5	21.8	10.7	5.0	3.3
30 to 49	2.8	11.1	6.0	3.7	1.4
Over 50	2.8	13.6	8.5	0.8	2.1
Region					
Northeast	2.5	8.0	3.1	4.2	3.0
Midwest	4.1	11.8	5.7	3.7	0.8
South	2.9	15.4	9.3	3.4	1.6
West	2.1	12.4	6.8	3.4	3.3

SOURCE: 2004 (displacement), 2005 (contingent work), and 2006 CPS.

Notes

1. In chapter 3 of this volume, Kristin Smith explores women and work in rural America.

2. Researchers have begun to examine social mobility between mothers and daughters (see, e.g., Musick and Mare 2006).

3. We use the terms "rural" and "nonmetropolitan" (nonmetro) interchangeably. In referring to results from the Current Population Surveys, rural is measured as nonmetro—residing outside of a metropolitan area.

4. Interestingly, evidence suggests that the decline in breadwinner status among men has promoted a more egalitarian ideology among them and has led them to perceive their spouses' material contributions not as a threat but as a benefit (Zhou and Tang 2000).

5. This chapter was completed on the eve of a deep recession beginning in the late 2000s and so does not empirically capture the fallout from this steep downturn. The employment circumstances we describe here for the mid-2000s would be much worse had we been able to carry the analysis forward by a few years.

6. The ways in which displacement and other manifestations of structural change are experienced and confronted on the ground capture the attention of Margaret K. Nelson in chapter 7 of this volume.

7. In chapter 9 Elaine McCrate addresses the related issue of the rise in haphazard and undependable work schedules that workers are forced to endure and the challenge this trend poses for parents trying to care for their children.

8. Given small sample size, the results for contingent work are somewhat volatile.

CHANGING ROLES

Women and Work in Rural America

KRISTIN E. SMITH

The widespread entry of women into paid employment has played a major role in the transformation of the family, from the agrarian family that dominated American life until the middle of the nineteenth century to the dual employment and partial specialization that we see today (Gornick and Meyers 2003). Women in rural and urban areas alike traditionally specialized in unpaid labor in the home, but with each passing decade both spent more of their time working for pay in the marketplace.

Several societal shifts have contributed to the change in how women allocate their time and negotiate their work and family roles. Social change and shifting family structure, exemplified in delays in marriage, declines in fertility, and the rise in cohabitation and divorce, result in women spending less time married and raising children, leaving more time for paid market work (Casper and Bianchi 2002). The rise in single-mother families, stagnant and in some cases declining men's wages, and job loss in industries that traditionally employ men (such as manufacturing and agriculture) have increased the need for women to work for pay (Levy 1998). The rise in educational attainment among women, coupled with an increase in typically female jobs in the service sector, increased opportunities for women to secure employment in the paid labor market (Blau, Ferber, and Winkler 2002; Falk and Lobao 2003; Sayer, Cohen, and Casper 2004). Furthermore, gender roles have become less rigid, and today it is more common for couples to share responsibility for both work and family spheres (Shelton and John 1996). Public attitudes have become more accepting of women working outside the home for pay (Thornton and Young-DeMarco 2001), even women with young children, and policy makers have introduced legislation to ease work and family conflicts (such as the Family Medical Leave Act) and mandate paid work for single mothers who otherwise might seek welfare (Williams and Cooper 2004).

Many rural communities lack stable employment, opportunities for mobility, community investment and development, and diversity in the economy and other social institutions (Tickamyer and Duncan 1990). However, rural areas have not been immune to the social changes—including the changes in women's employment—that have swept the nation over the past several decades. Rural communities, often perceived as wholesome, traditionally minded, family-friendly enclaves (Seebach 1992) are keeping pace with their urban neighbors in many of these social changes. Even though rural people may prefer a "rural way of life"—where children are raised in intact families surrounded by supportive kin and community networks—the structure of rural families resembles that of urban families, due in part to rising divorce rates and increased cohabitation (MacTavish and Salamon 2003b). Rural households, historically larger than urban households, are now smaller, reflecting the aging population and lower birthrates.

Economic restructuring has both pushed and pulled women into the paid labor market. As men's jobs declined in traditional rural industries such as agriculture, natural resource extraction, and manufacturing, the service sector expanded, creating opportunities for women just as households needed additional wage earners to make ends meet (Falk and Lobao 2003). This was particularly common among farm families in the Midwest during the farm crisis of the 1980s, when women were more likely than men to move into off-farm work and more likely than in the past to contribute needed economic support to their families (Lobao and Meyer 1995, 2001). This trend was not confined to the Midwest, however. From the paper mill communities in northern New England to the coalfield communities of rural Appalachia (Oberhauser and Turnage 1999) to the logging areas of the Pacific Northwest (Carroll 1995; Tickamyer and Henderson 2003), rural women were entering the workforce to help sustain families. Even among communities that adhere to patriarchal norms and strict gender roles, women often have become the primary wage earner as men's jobs have disappeared (Tickamyer and Henderson 2003).

Mindful of these changes that have transpired in rural and urban life since the 1950s, which set the stage for the profound changes in the work and family roles of women and men, this chapter begins with an examination of women's employment patterns from 1970 to 2007, paying close attention to rural-urban variation across family status and education level. To assess trends in women's time commitment to paid market work, measures of women's work effort are presented, again with variation by family status and education level noted. Changes in men's work effort are also considered. Because characteristics that determine whether a woman works for pay or not and how many hours she works are correlated, I present a multivariate model examining the factors that explain women's labor supply to sort out which factors are most important in explaining the changes seen in women's employment. Next, trends in earnings of married mothers and fathers are examined by residence, and changes in couples' economic contribution to family income are analyzed. The chapter ends with a discussion of policy implications.

This chapter relies on data from the U.S. Census Bureau's Current Population Survey (CPS) March Supplements from 1970, 1980, 1990, and 2000, and Annual Social and Economic Surveys (ASEC) from 2007. The CPS provides a nationally representative sample of households and the individuals within those households and collects demographic, economic, and employment information, as well as data on participation in select government assistance programs. Employment rates are calculated for civilians age sixteen to sixty-four who, during the previous year, were gainfully employed. Comparisons presented in the text are statistically significant at the 0.05 level.

Changes in Paid Employment

One important change in American family life is the large rise in women's employment. The majority of the growth in women's paid work occurred in the second half of the twentieth century, nationally and in both rural and urban America.[1]

Figure 3.1 shows employment rates of women and men age sixteen to sixty-four by residence from 1970 to 2007.[2] The proportion of employed rural women grew sharply in the 1970s and 1980s, slowed in the 1990s, and decreased after 2000.[3]

Trends in employment rates of rural and urban women virtually mirror each other, increasing steadily from 1970 to 2000 and decreasing slightly since then.[4] Rural women's employment peaked at 74 percent in 2001 before decreasing to 71 percent by 2005. Similarly, urban women's employment reached a high of 75 percent in 2000 but then also decreased to 71 percent by 2007. However, after decades of slightly higher employment rates among urban women, employment rates of rural and urban women age sixteen to sixty-four converged in 2003 and remained steady, owing to a larger decline in employment among urban women since 2000.

Men's employment, in contrast, has been slowly declining during the same time span, from 92 percent in 1970 to 82 percent by 2007. The proportion of employed rural men decreased from 92 percent in 1970 to 80 percent by 2007, with the steepest declines occurring from 2000 to 2007. Similarly, urban men's employment rates declined by 9 percent, and they had slightly higher employment rates than rural men over the years.

Men's employment historically has been higher than women's in both rural and urban America. However, because of these diverging trends, the gender gap in employment has narrowed significantly in recent decades, driven primarily by the large increase in women's paid employment during the 1970s and 1980s. In 1970, sixty-two rural women were employed in the previous year for every one hundred rural men age sixteen to sixty-four, but by 2007 the ratio climbed to eighty-nine rural women per one hundred rural men. The gender gap in employment has also narrowed in urban areas, from sixty-three urban

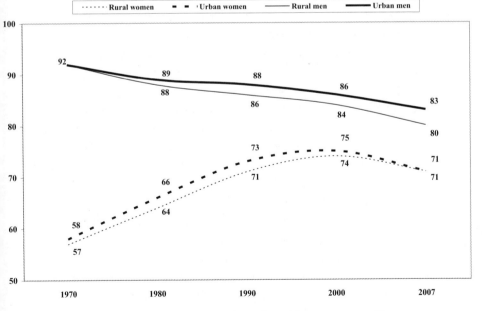

FIG. 3.1   Employment rates of women and men by residence, 1970–2007 (SOURCE: 1970, 1980, 1990, 2000, and 2007 March CPS)

women per one hundred urban men in 1970 to eighty-six in 2007. From 1970 to 2000, the rural and urban gender gap in employment decreased, but because both women and men experienced declines in employment at similar rates from 2000 to 2007, the gender gap in employment remained steady over that time period.

To better understand the changes in women's employment rates over the past four decades, it is important to examine how employment rates have varied across different groups of women. In particular, viewing employment trends by family status and education level illuminates which groups of women experienced gains in employment during the 1970s and 1980s and losses in employment since 2000.

WOMEN'S EMPLOYMENT BY FAMILY STATUS

The gains in women's employment over the past four decades have largely been driven by the changes in work patterns among married women. Historically, rural married women had lower employment rates than rural single women. However, employment rates of married women climbed 20 percent between 1970 and 2000. In 1970, approximately one-half of married women worked for pay, while by 2000, over three-fourths were employed. The majority of the increase occurred during the 1970s and 1980s (see table 3.1).

In contrast, the share of rural single employed women increased only modestly between 1970 and 2000, before returning to rates last seen in the 1970s and 1980s. Employment rates of rural single women did not rise to the same extent as those of their married counterparts, such that rural married women caught up and then surpassed their single peers in the workforce.

Urban married women also experienced large gains in employment from 1970 to 2000. In contrast to their rural peers, employment rates of urban single women steadily increased from 1970 to 2000. Differing from the experience seen in rural areas, urban married women never surpassed single women in the workforce, although by 2007, single and married urban women were equally likely to be employed.[5]

Rural married women consistently have higher employment rates than urban married women over time; however, rural single women consistently have lower rates of employment than urban single women.

Historically, having young children has deterred women's employment because of the concurrent demands work and family place on a mother's time. Over the past four decades, women with children under 6 have had lower employment rates than women without children under 6 in both rural and urban areas (see table 3.1). For example, in 2007, rural married mothers of young children were less likely to have worked for pay in the previous year than married women without young children (70 percent compared with 73 percent), although a majority were employed. Likewise, rural single mothers of young children had lower employment rates than rural single women without children under 6 (67 percent compared to 68 percent). Single women without young children tend to have the highest employment rates.

While employment rates among married women with young children increased steeply over the 1970s and 1980s, employment rates among single women with young children rose largely in the 1990s, particularly in urban areas. Employment rates of urban single mothers jumped from 58 percent in 1990 to 73 percent in 2000, a 25 percent increase in a ten-year span. Over the same time period, rural single mothers' employment rates also rose substantially, from 62 percent to 72 percent. The increase in single mothers' employment has been attributed to a combination of two factors: the 1996 welfare reform bill with its emphasis on moving welfare mothers into paid employment, and the economic boom of the late 1990s, which created a demand for low-wage female employment (Blank 2002).

Across time, rural married mothers with young children were consistently more likely to be employed than urban married mothers with young children. This relationship is not visible among the other three family types shown in table 3.1. This finding may come as a surprise for some because of the perception that rural people hold more traditional values than urban residents, and because of the greater obstacles to mothers' employment in rural areas relative to urban areas, such as less access to good-quality child care and the lack of transportation (Smith 2006; Tickamyer and Henderson 2003). But rural families, suffering from economic contraction and restructuring and the loss of well-paying, traditionally male jobs with benefits, are turning to women's wage labor to bolster the economic security of their families. During the Great Recession the share of family earnings contributed by employed wives increased markedly (Smith 2009).

WOMEN'S EMPLOYMENT BY EDUCATION LEVEL

One pattern that has held fast since the 1970s is rising employment rates at higher levels of education for both rural and urban women. Highly educated women are more likely to work for pay than are less educated women. For example, in 2007, 84 percent of rural women age sixteen to sixty-four with a college degree were employed in the previous year, while 70 percent of rural women with a high school degree were employed. In contrast, only 43 percent of rural women who had not completed high school were working for pay (data not shown). This same pattern is true for urban women as well. While employment rates for rural and urban women with less than a high school degree have remained relatively constant over time, women with a high school or college degree had higher rates of employment in 2007 than they did in 1970. For instance, employment rates among rural women with college degrees grew by 14 percent, from 74 percent in 1970 to 84 percent by 2007.

Changes in Women's Work Effort

Another way to measure women's commitment to the labor force is to consider the amount of time spent on the job (Sayer, Cohen, and Casper 2004). One measure of the level of commitment to paid work is the average annual hours spent in paid employment.[6] Table 3.2 presents this measure of work time commitment (the average annual number of hours) by family status for all rural and urban women and for rural and urban women who were employed in the previous year. Across all family types, both rural and urban women spent more time working for pay in 2007 than they did in 1980.

WOMEN'S WORK EFFORT BY FAMILY TYPE

The same pattern seen above when looking at employment rates is evident when considering the amount of time women spend engaged in paid work. The average annual number of hours women worked for pay in the previous year increased steadily from 1980 to 2000, and then decreased by 2007. But there was one exception: rural married women with young children. This group of women did not reduce their time commitment to paid employment over the 2000 to 2007 time period, but rather increased it. From 1980 to 2007, rural married women with children under 6 increased the number of annual hours worked from 702 to 1,126, an increase of 424 hours annually, or 8 hours per week. Urban married mothers with young children also experienced large gains in annual hours spent working from 1980 to 2007 (a total increase of 373, or a gain of 7 hours per week), but the total gain was less than the gain seen among rural married women with young children due to their decline in hours worked from 2000 to 2007. Although rural married women with young children showed a greater time commitment to paid work from 1980 to 2007 than urban married women with young children, the gap in time spent working for pay between these two groups of women narrowed over the 1980s and 1990s, but then grew quite large from 2000 to 2007. For example, in 1980 urban married women with young children worked 94 hours for every 100 hours rural women did and worked 97 hours for every 100 hours in 2000, but by 2007 they only worked 92 hours per 100 hours rural married women with young children worked.

Table 3.2 also shows that the increase from 2000 to 2007 in average annual hours among rural married mothers of young children is due to an increase in the number of hours working women spent on their jobs each week. Recall that employment rates among rural married mothers of young children dropped slightly from 2000 to 2007 from 72 percent to 70 percent (see table 3.1), which would depress the average annual hours. But average hours among employed married mothers increased by 100 hours in those same seven years, or roughly 2 hours per week, reflecting the increase in work hours among the employed.

Among rural employed women, married women without young children have the greatest work time commitment over the years. Employed rural married women without children under 6 spent, on average, 1,808 hours in paid employment in 2007. This translates into 396 more hours annually, or over 7 hours more per week, than the group with the lowest work time commitment in rural areas (single women with young children).

WOMEN'S WORK EFFORT BY EDUCATION LEVEL

The general trend across all education groups is one of increasing work time commitment to paid employment since the 1980s (data not shown). Rural women with a high school diploma increased their work effort by 172 hours annually from 1980 to 2000 (from 1,514 hours to 1,686 hours), and then decreased it by 11 hours by 2007. This drop in time spent in paid employment among high school graduates was due to a smaller proportion of these women working for pay since the annual hours spent working among employed women with high school degrees increased from 2000 to 2007. Annual hours spent in paid employment among college-educated rural women increased from 1980 to 2000 (from 1,660 to 1,796 hours) and then remained steady, reflecting a rise in the hours employed rural college-educated women spent in paid employment.

Women with higher education levels are not only more likely to work for pay, but when they do, they spend more time annually in paid employment than women with lower levels of education. In 2007, employed rural women with a college degree spent 1,874 hours working at their job in the previous year—a striking 604 more hours annually (or 12 hours per week) than rural women with less than a high school degree and 177 more hours than rural high school graduates. A similar trend exists among urban women by education level.

Men's work effort has remained fairly constant since the 1980s. Among all rural men, time spent in paid employment declined by a total of 97 hours (or 2 hours per week) from 1980 to 2007 (data not shown). But this decline in work effort is due to declining labor force participation (as shown in fig. 3.1), because rural employed men spent more time in paid employment in 1980 than in 2007 (an increase of 81 hours, from 1,942 annual hours in 1980 to 2,023 annual hours in 2007, representing an average increase of 2 hours per week). Rural married men spend more time at work than single men, but the hours rural single men commit to paid work increased by 16 percent from 1980 to 2007, while the hours rural married men commit to paid work increased by just 3 percent over the same time period. Even so, rural married men spend 10 more hours per week working for pay than rural single men (an average of 43 hours compared with 33 hours per week, respectively).

Because characteristics predicting the number of hours a woman will work for pay or not are closely related to each other—for example, lower-educated women also tend to have lower earnings—multivariate regression analysis was used to ascertain the independent effects of several key characteristics on the number of hours a woman worked. In addition, these regression models help us to understand whether the changes over time represent compositional shifts or changes in the forces that affect women's labor force participation directly. Table 3.3 shows the results of tobit regressions for annual hours of employment on women's family status, educational attainment, and the presence of other family income.[7] Age and race or ethnicity are also included in the models as controls. Tobit regressions are appropriate for this analysis because of censoring, as many women in the sample did not work any hours and thus are assigned zero hours on the continuous dependent variable (MacDonald and Moffitt 1980).

In the 1980s in rural America, both married mothers and single mothers worked fewer hours annually relative to unmarried women without children (the reference category in the regression models shown in table 3.3). However, by 2007 the differential for married mothers with young children was no longer significant, suggesting that marriage and the presence of children no longer diminish the number of hours in paid employment for these rural women. Urban married and single mothers consistently worked significantly fewer hours than unmarried women without children, but the differential declined steadily since 1980. In both rural and urban areas, married women without young children worked significantly more hours annually than single women without young children.[8] Taken altogether, these models show a diminishing effect of marriage and children on women's commitment to market work since the 1980s.

The models also show that the effect of education and other family income on women's commitment to market work has changed over time. Relative to women without a high school degree, women with high school and college degrees have increased their commitment to market work since the 1980s, after controlling for the effects of the other factors in the model (family status, other income, age, and race or ethnicity). Education can be considered a proxy for wage elasticity, or the effect of potential wages on women's employment decisions. As the return on women's education in terms of earnings has increased dramatically since the 1970s (Blau 1998; Goldin 1990), it is not surprising to see that the effect of higher education on women's commitment to market work has increased and shows a very large effect for both rural and urban women.

The effect of other family income on women's commitment to market work has declined since 1980 for both rural and urban women, but remains a significant factor depressing the number of hours women spend in paid employment. As other family income rises, women are less likely to work more hours.

Changes in Earnings

To examine the changing economic contribution of mothers relative to their husbands, this section examines trends in earnings among married women with children and their husbands (married men with children). Analyzing national data, research has shown that gains in earnings among women and men differ depending on family status and education level. Previous research has established that children have a direct negative effect on women's pay, even after controlling for work experience and other demographic factors (Waldfogel 1997; Budig and England 2001), and that marriage (and children) seems to have a positive effect on men's wages (Korenman and Newmark 1991; Glauber 2008). Furthermore, the wages of less educated men have declined, but the wages of higher-educated men have risen since the 1980s (Juhn, Murphy, and Pierce 1993; Blank and Shierholz 2006; Waldfogel and Mayer 1999). The wages of less educated women have been flat, while the wages of highly educated women have increased (Blank and Shierholz 2006), resulting in greater inequality in earnings among women. Although there has been substantial work on the gender gap in pay and trends in earnings on a national level by family status and skill level, there has been little work that analyzes these trends by place.

MARRIED MOTHERS' AND FATHERS' EARNINGS

Not only are more married mothers with young children working in the paid labor market, but their earnings have increased significantly since 1970. Undoubtedly, some of this increase in earnings is due to the increase in time spent working for pay among married mothers. Table 3.4 shows median annual earnings for employed married mothers and employed married fathers in 2006 dollars to account for inflation. Rural married mothers earned $11,206 (in 2006 dollars) in 1969, but by 2006 they earned $21,600—an increase of over $10,000 or 93 percent.[9] Over the same time period, the annual earnings of urban married mothers more than doubled, from $12,854 to $27,000 (a gain of more than $14,000). The average earnings of both rural and urban married mothers have increased steadily, yet an earnings gap exists between the two, with higher earnings evident among urban married mothers, and the gap has widened since the 1970s. Rural married mothers earned 87 cents for every dollar urban married mothers earned in 1969, but by 2006 this ratio dropped to 80 cents.

The trend in annual earnings of married fathers, on the other hand, is in the opposite direction. Rural married fathers' median annual earnings declined in the 1970s and 1980s, only to rise slightly in the 1990s and 2000s. Thus, over the past four decades, rural married fathers' earnings lost substantial ground (nearly $2,512), especially noteworthy when compared to the gains in earnings by their wives. Urban married fathers did not fare much better. Their average annual earnings also rose modestly over the 1970s and declined in the 1980s and 1990s to rise again by 2006, but again the overall gains over the past four decades were substantially less than the gains in earnings experienced by their wives—urban married mothers—over the same time period. The gap in earnings between rural and urban married fathers also widened since 1969. The $38,000 earned by rural married fathers in 2006 is only 76 percent of the $50,000 earned by urban married fathers (a larger gap than seen in 1969). Economic restructuring, among other things, has played a role in the decline in men's earnings.

Despite women's remarkable gains in earnings since 1969, men still outearn women by a substantial amount. Even when comparing earnings of married mothers and fathers who work full-time, year-round (thirty-five or more hours per week for fifty or more weeks a year), rural married mothers earned seventy cents for every dollar their husbands earned in 2006, up from fifty-seven cents in 1969. Urban married mothers fare only slightly better, as they earned seventy-two cents for every dollar their husbands earned, despite the similar time commitment to the paid labor force. Both the rural and urban gender gaps in earnings have narrowed over time, primarily due to declining and stagnant men's earnings, but also because of the rise in women's earnings.

MARRIED MOTHERS' ECONOMIC CONTRIBUTION TO FAMILY INCOME

Wives' greater propensity for employment, longer work hours, and increased earnings translate into higher total family earnings among rural and urban families with children. However, the higher earnings among urban women and men help boost their total family earnings above rural families. Figures 3.2 and 3.3 show husbands' and wives' combined earnings in the previous year in 2006 dollars from 1969 to 2006. In each year shown, combined couple earnings of urban families outpace those of rural families. For example, urban husbands and wives together earned $77,000 in 1969 while rural married couples earned $64,000 (a $13,000 difference). By 2006, urban married couples with children earned an annual average of $17,000 more than rural married couples ($75,000 compared with $58,000, respectively). This underscores a rising inequality between rural and urban families and an increased disadvantage for rural children. Despite a greater work effort among rural mothers relative to urban mothers, they are not able to compensate for the rural pay disadvantage.

Figures 3.2 and 3.3 also highlight the growing economic role women are playing in their families. Although fathers contribute more to family earnings than mothers in both rural and urban areas, mothers' increased earnings have bolstered total family earnings, particularly in rural areas when fathers' earnings stagnated or declined.

Women's increased employment and earnings, coupled with men's declining wages and employment, translate into a larger provider role for women. Among rural married-couple families in 1969, it was common for the husband to be the sole provider and the wife to stay home (see table 3.5).[10] By 2006,

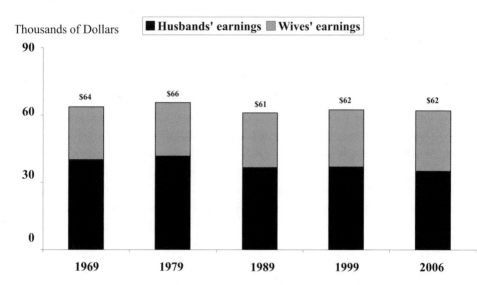

FIG. 3.2   Total family earnings, rural married couples with children, 1969–2006.
Median family earnings are calculated by adding together the wives' and husbands'
median annual personal earnings. Inflation-adjusted to 2006 dollars (SOURCE: 1970,
1980, 1990, 2000, and 2007 March CPS).

the incidence of husbands as sole providers had dropped dramatically, from
48 percent to 22 percent. The decline was also apparent in urban areas. Some
of this decline can be attributed to changes in wives' breadwinning roles.
Couples in which the wife contributed 60 percent or more of the combined
couple's earnings (wife primary and wife sole provider couples) grew from
4 percent to 12 percent in rural families and from 3 percent to 12 percent in
urban families from 1969 to 2006.[11] The proportion of couples who shared
equally in economic provisioning grew steadily among both rural and urban
families (from 10 percent to 25 percent and from 7 percent to 22 percent, respectively). Families with wives as secondary providers grew over the 1970s and
1980s, but then declined. Even so, by 2006 this family type constituted a large
group of rural and urban couples (both around 40 percent). In sum, large
transformations in breadwinning patterns have occurred among married
couples with children, such that by 2006 a large majority of rural and urban
couples were dual providers.

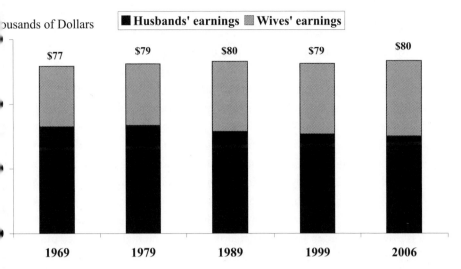

Fɪɢ. 3.3   Total family earnings, urban married couples with children, 1969–2006. Median family earnings are calculated by adding together the wives' and husbands' median annual personal earnings. Inflation-adjusted to 2006 dollars (Sᴏᴜʀᴄᴇ: 1970, 1980, 1990, 2000, and 2007 March CPS).

Policy Implications

Women's work and family roles have changed dramatically since the 1970s. With increasing numbers of women, particularly married mothers, entering the labor force, one of the most pressing challenges facing families today is how to balance work and family responsibilities. Rural areas are no longer immune to these challenges. Given their similarities today, rural families may benefit equally from organizational and government policies tailored to the majority of the populace in the urban areas. Most families depend on earnings to support their living standards, so as earnings lag behind inflation, families feel the squeeze as they try to make ends meet, particularly those families that rely on men's or poor single mothers' earnings.

Policies that support the dual demands of caring for family members while working to meet basic needs are necessary in rural and urban America. Paid sick leave, family medical leave to care for sick family members or a new child, flexible work schedules, and quality part-time jobs are all areas where policies can be expanded to reduce the conflict between work and family.

Rural married mothers with young children are consistently more likely to be employed than their urban counterparts. This finding may come as a surprise for some because the perception is that rural families hold more traditional values than urban residents, and because of the greater obstacles to mothers' employment in rural areas, such as less access to quality child care and the lack of transportation (Smith 2006; Tickamyer and Henderson 2003). But rural families, suffering from economic contraction and restructuring and the loss of well-paying, traditionally male jobs with benefits, are turning to women's wage labor to sustain themselves (Falk and Lobao 2003). Further, Smith (2008) found that rural women are less inclined to "opt out" of the labor force than their urban peers, particularly mothers and highly educated mothers, suggesting that rural women have different pressures and options than urban women. Rural mothers with a college degree have less of a cushion than urban women because of their husbands' lower earnings, and thus may be unable to opt out. This may mean that rural mothers encounter more of the work and family stressors and imbalance.

Rural mothers face serious challenges in finding and securing high-quality child care. Rural mothers rely on home-based care arrangements to a greater extent than urban mothers (Smith 2006), and rural families have fewer child care choices than urban families, particularly center-based care (Gordon and Chase-Lansdale 2001). High-quality early child care and early education programs for preschoolers could help reverse the fact that rural children enter kindergarten with fewer key early literacy skills than urban children (Grace et al. 2006).

State and federal policies that increase earnings or supplement wages will help rural families financially. The vast majority of rural men and women are already working for pay, but often at jobs that do not pay sufficient wages or provide benefits. In 2005, 1.9 million rural workers earned less than $7.25 an hour (O'Hare 2007). Rural low-income families would benefit from raising the minimum wage, and setting the wage to keep pace with inflation. Expanding the Earned Income Tax Credit (EITC) could also help bolster rural families as they struggle with stagnant wages, job loss, and economic turmoil. Twenty percent of rural households relied on the EITC and received an average of $1,850 in 2004 (O'Hare and Kneebone 2007), a big help to families living on the brink of economic instability.

That wages among rural women are consistently lower than those of urban women, particularly among college graduates, makes it harder for rural areas to attract and keep these workers. Developing higher-paying jobs in rural America and increasing occupational diversity for women could benefit the increasing number of families that rely on women's earnings as the primary or sole provider.

Despite the greater reliance on women's earnings among families, industries that typically employ women, such as in the service, health, and education sectors, are increasingly offering wages and benefits that cannot support a family. State and federal policies that encourage better benefits, such as health insurance, and worker flexibility for low-wage or part-time workers, and workers in small businesses (a prevalent employer in rural areas) could make a substantial difference in the lives of rural families.

American families were hit hard by the 2001 economic recession and the jobless recovery. Now American families are challenged in unprecedented ways due to the Great Recession that began in December 2007, with job loss topping 8 million and unemployment peaking at over 10 percent (Bureau of Labor Statistics 2009). With about three-quarters of the job loss among men, families are relying to a greater extent on the earnings of wives. Smith (2009) finds that rural and urban wives' contribution to total family earnings rose in the first year of the recession, from 44 percent in 2007 to 45 percent in 2008—the largest single-year increase in the decade. Family earnings have taken a hit as many families lost their primary breadwinner (the husband) and are trying to get by on the often lower earnings of the wife. Creating policies that support working families should be a strong focus of state and federal policy.

Table 3.1 Employment rates of women by family status, 1970–2007

Family status	Rural					Urban				
	1970	1980	1990	2000	2007	1970	1980	1990	2000	2007
Married	52.6	61.7	70.9	74.5	72.4	50.7	61.4	70.3	73.3	71.2
Married, child under 6	NA	58.8	70.6	71.5	70.0	NA	55.5	65.7	67.9	64.5
Married, no child under 6	NA	62.7	71.0	75.3	73.0	NA	63.5	72.0	75.1	73.5
Single	66.8	67.8	72.1	73.5	68.2	71.0	73.2	75.9	77.2	71.4
Single, child under 6	NA	60.5	62.4	71.8	66.6	NA	58.1	58.4	72.9	65.6
Single, no child under 6	NA	68.7	73.6	73.8	68.4	NA	75.0	78.6	77.8	72.2

NOTE: Employment rates calculated for women age 16–64. Data for children under 6 are not available for 1970.
SOURCE: 1970, 1980, 1990, 2000, 2007 March CPS.

Table 3.2 Average annual hours worked by women by family status and residence, 1980–2007

	Rural				Urban				Change 1980–2007	
	1980	1990	2000	2007	1980	1990	2000	2007	Rural	Urban
Average annual hours										
Married, child under 6	702	973	1078	1126	662	928	1043	1035	424	373
Married, no child under 6	996	1174	1337	1330	999	1235	1356	1354	334	355
Single, child under 6	795	870	1047	941	732	792	1089	1046	146	314
Single, no child under 6	928	1109	1155	1098	1120	1274	1321	1225	170	105
Among employed women										
Married, child under 6	1170	1359	1497	1597	1179	1404	1526	1602	427	423
Married, no child under 6	1539	1619	1754	1808	1545	1697	1798	1835	269	290
Single, child under 6	1310	1395	1459	1412	1259	1357	1494	1592	102	333
Single, no child under 6	1340	1500	1562	1600	1491	1619	1695	1695	260	204

NOTE: Calculated for women age 16–64.
SOURCE: 1980, 1990, 2000, 2007 March CPS.

Table 3.3 Parameter estimates of Tobit equations predicting annual hours of paid work for women age sixteen to sixty-four, by residence, 1980–2007

Year	Intercept	Married, child under 6	Married, no child under 6	Single, child under 6	High school graduate	College graduate	Other family income (ln)	Age	Black	Hispanic	Other
Rural											
1980	1550.4	−334.0	253.1	−276.5	703.5	1059.6	−119.8	−10.1	−115.8	−350.6	−380.9
1990	1447.6	−76.9	329.7	−478.6	757.1	1138.1	−107.0	−8.1	−148.2	−205.8	−329.7
2000	1005.9	−125.6	273.5	−231.2	905.3	1271.0	−67.9	−5.3	89.3	−221.2	−288.6
2007	698.1	(68.7)	383.6	−233.7	965.5	1357.0	−66.6	−2.7	(−0.6)	−147.3	−274.9
Urban											
1980	1500.3	−537.0	77.4	−531.0	758.6	1056.2	−114.9	−7.8	(−38.4)	−149.6	(−46.6)
1990	1334.4	−276.1	219.2	−632.0	854.6	1213.5	−99.5	−6.2	(−26.5)	−183.9	(−91.7)
2000	912.3	−278.7	130.9	−233.2	910.7	1262.2	−68.0	(−0.5)	40.9	−131.9	−212.9
2007	654.5	−139.7	261.5	−209.6	915.5	1273.8	−75.6	3.3	(12.1)	−42.1	−137.0

NOTE: Single with no children under 6 is the excluded marital status category; less than high school is the excluded education level category; and white, non-Hispanic is the excluded racial and ethnic category. All parameters are significant at $p < .05$ except those in parentheses, which are not significant.
SOURCE: 1980, 1990, 2000, 2007 March CPS.

Table 3.4 Median annual earnings for employed married mothers and employed married fathers by residence, 1969–2006

	Rural	Urban
Employed mothers		
1969	$11,206	$12,854
1979	$13,884	$15,273
1989	$14,632	$19,510
1999	$18,151	$24,202
2006	$21,600	$27,000
Employed fathers		
1969	$40,512	$49,593
1979	$41,372	$51,647
1989	$35,768	$48,774
1999	$37,513	$48,403
2006	$38,000	$50,000

NOTE: Includes married mothers and their husbands with children under 18 years old. Inflation-adjusted to 2006 dollars.
SOURCE: 1970, 1980, 1990, 2000, 2007 March CPS.

Table 3.5 Percent distribution of couples' earnings contributions among married-couple families with children, 1969–2006

	Rural					Urban				
	1969	1979	1989	1999	2006	1969	1979	1989	1999	2006
Married couples with children										
Husband sole provider	47.8	35.4	21.9	21.2	21.9	52.5	38.1	28.2	25.4	28.3
Husband primary	38.5	45.9	49.9	46.4	40.8	37.6	45.5	45.8	42.7	37.9
Equal earners	9.7	13.2	18.8	22.0	25.0	7.3	11.7	18.7	22.1	22.3
Wife primary	1.9	2.9	6.2	6.2	7.2	1.2	2.7	5.3	6.8	8.1
Wife sole provider	2.1	2.6	3.3	4.3	5.1	1.5	2.1	2.0	3.0	3.4

NOTE: Includes married mothers age 16–64 with children under 18. Excludes married-couple families where neither spouse is employed.
SOURCE: 1970, 1980, 1990, 2000, 2007 March CPS.

Notes

1. Employment rates in this chapter refer to whether women (and men) from the ages of sixteen to sixty-four were gainfully employed at any time in the previous year. Employment includes wage and salary jobs, and farm and nonfarm self-employment.

2. Refer to Smith (2008) for a discussion of the various ways to measure employment.

3. This stalling of gains in employment among women in the 1990s has been documented elsewhere for the nation as a whole (see Sayer, Cohen, and Casper 2004; Cotter, Hermsen, and Vanneman 2004; Casper and Bianchi 2000) and the decline in employment since 2000 (see Reimers and Stone 2007).

4. The term "rural" here refers to persons living outside the officially designated metropolitan areas. "Urban" refers to persons living within metropolitan areas. Metropolitan residence is based on Office of Management and Budget delineation at the time of data collection.

5. Employment rates of urban married and single women converged in 2006 at 71 percent and held steady in 2007.

6. Some other measures of work commitment include average hours in paid employment, percent working part-time (less than thirty-five hours per week), and percent working full-time, full year (thirty-five or more hours per week for fifty or more weeks in the year). These measures can be seen for rural and urban workers in Smith (2008).

7. This analysis replicates research conducted by Cohen and Bianchi (1999) but expands the sample to include all women sixteen to sixty-four and presents results for rural and urban women.

8. This finding differs from Cohen and Bianchi's results because of the different samples. Cohen and Bianchi show results for all U.S. women twenty-five to fifty-four only.

9. The Census Bureau collects data about last year's earnings; thus the 1970 Current Population Survey data yields estimates for 1969 earnings, the 1980 data for 1979 earnings, etc.

10. According to Nock's (2001) classification of marriages of equally dependent spouses (MEDS), equal providers are dual-income couples where wives contribute at least 40 percent but less than 60 percent of the total couple earnings; wife primary providers are dual-income couples where the wife contributes 60 percent or more of the total couple earnings; and husband primary providers are dual-income couples where the wife contributes less than 40 percent of the total couple earnings. Husband sole providers are couples where the husband reports positive income and employment and the wife reports nonemployment. Similarly, wife sole providers are couples where the wife reports positive income and employment and the husband reports nonemployment.

11. For comparability across years in the CPS, earnings from self-employment in farm work are not included, which in 1969 may explain the large proportion of wife primary and sole provider couples in rural areas.

MEN WITHOUT SAWMILLS

Job Loss and Gender Identity in Rural America

JENNIFER SHERMAN

In 1996, the last of the sawmills in Golden Valley, California,[1] shut down. The Northwest Timber mill was a final victim of changing environmental regulations and industrial downsizing that affected all aspects of Golden Valley's forest sector during the 1990s. The small, isolated community of less than two thousand people was devastated. Mill work, along with the logging jobs that had mostly dried up in the early 1990s, was the mainstay of the community's economic and cultural life. Generations of Golden Valley's men had counted on work in the woods and mills as stable and steady sources of income. The money they earned in these jobs might not have been impressive, but it was enough to afford a modest house and to support a family in Golden Valley. Without the mill, residents feared that "this town is going to dry up and blow away" (Howard 1996). Golden Valley did not blow away, but it did change considerably in the years that followed. These changes included job loss among men, higher workforce participation by women, population loss, and family instability.

In 1990 single-parent households with children made up just 9 percent of total family households there, considerably less than the state average of 12 percent. By 2000, their presence had nearly doubled to 17 percent, now higher than the state average of 14 percent (U.S. Census Bureau 1990, 2000). As Golden Valley declined on the outside, with businesses closing and buildings falling into disrepair, its families began to deteriorate from the inside. Unlike in the poor urban setting, where single parenting is mainly attributed to unplanned pregnancies, in Golden Valley the rising rates of single parenting reflect increases in divorce and separation rates as well as nonmarital childbearing over the period. During this time, California's divorce and nonmarriage rates remained stable. However, nonmarriage occurred at a much higher rate across the state in both 1990 and 2000, while divorce rates in Golden Valley began higher and continued to rise (U.S. Census Bureau 1990, 2000).

Although Golden Valley's families are under high amounts of social and cultural pressure to remain intact, the recent structural changes have resulted in a number of challenges, including threats to existing family and gender norms. In particular, Golden Valley's "traditional" family structure, in which the man is the main breadwinner and the woman is focused on child care and homemaking, is now much more difficult to sustain. The struggles families encounter in reconciling their cultural norms with their economic and labor market realities are creating multiple stresses in Golden Valley. The destabilization of gender norms and the loss of traditional paths to the hegemonic form of masculinity (Connell 1995)[2] have influenced marital and family relationships in both positive and negative ways. While some families have adapted to the

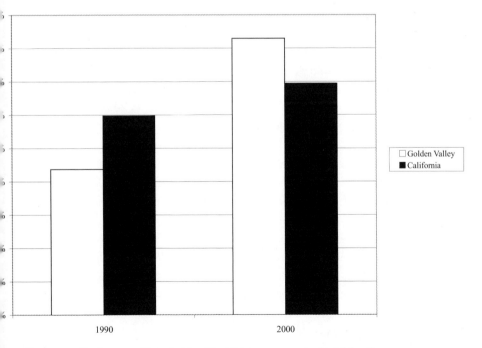

FIG. 4.1   Single-parent households with children as percent of total family households (SOURCE: U.S. Census Bureau 2000)

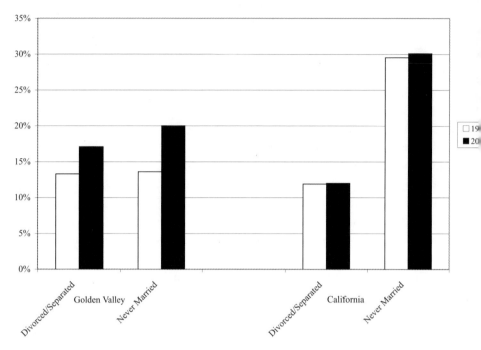

FIG. 4.2   Divorce/separation and nonmarriage rates for adults fifteen and older
(SOURCE: U.S. Census Bureau 2000)

changing conditions, others have fought the changes, often simultaneously creating new tensions and challenges for themselves.

Academic research has long found that poverty can affect family life and
family structure (Bane 1986; Cancian and Reed 2000; Eggebeen and Lichter
1991; Lichter and McLaughlin 1995; McLanahan, Garfinkel, and Mincy 2001;
McLaughlin, Gardner, and Lichter 1999; Testa et al. 1989; W. Wilson 1987).
Golden Valley residents have their own anecdotal evidence to link economic
decline with family struggles, and many believe that men's job loss negatively
affects family life in many ways beyond simply financial strain. For example,
thirty-year-old Allison Butters, whose common-law husband is out of work,
gave this explanation for the breakdown of many relationships since the mill
closure: "I would say that I'm pretty lucky and that lots of people who've been
infected [sic] by the timber industry are not so lucky. I do believe that when
their husbands lose jobs things become very hard. They don't know how to
cope with it or to train themselves in something else. So drugs and alcohol
becomes [sic] a very big deal."

While both rural and urban America have experienced industrial decline
and job loss, these processes have been more concentrated in rural areas, which

are often reliant on single industries. The effects of industrial change in rural areas include high poverty rates and men's job loss, as well as increasing work-force participation by women (Albrecht, Albrecht, and Albrecht 2000). Research on rural families and economic stress suggests that men's experiences with poverty and unemployment in rural communities produce very different out-comes than they do in inner cities (Conger et al. 1994; Davis 1993, 2000; Marotz-Baden et al. 1988; Mederer 1999; Skaptadottir 2000; S. Smith et al. 2003). In urban settings different types of "protest masculinity" often develop in reac-tion to economic decline, allowing men to reconstruct masculine identity around aggression, violence, success in illegal activities, and antagonistic atti-tudes toward women (Anderson 1990; Bourgois 1995; Connell 1995; Venkatesh 2000). Such protest forms of masculinity appear to be largely missing from white, rural areas, where traditional gender and cultural norms frequently remain dominant even in the wake of significant structural change. In Golden Valley, masculine identity remains strongly tied to work and provision, creat-ing increasing amounts of stress for men who are unable to find jobs or make sufficient incomes.

In the face of severe structural upheaval, traditional gender identities are difficult to sustain, and flexibility in gender norms appears to allow men and their families to navigate the changes more easily. The importance of flexible gender ideologies has been noted by previous researchers who examine rural economic change. In diverse rural settings, scholars have found that the degree to which a family is able to survive economic transitions intact depends on role flexibility within the family (Mederer 1999; Norem and Blundall 1988). In Golden Valley, it appears that this type of adaptive ability allows families to traverse shifting economic and labor market terrain with fewer stresses and tensions.

This chapter looks in depth at how the rural context impacts the ways in which families respond to structural and economic changes. It focuses on the interplay between structural forces and gender identities, and illustrates the ways in which families either retrench or remake gender norms to adjust to changing circumstances. For men in particular, the struggle with unemploy-ment and underemployment often creates dissonance between their gender identities and current realities. Some men and their families struggle to retain their gender identities despite the growing conflict, often creating new tensions both internally and within the family. Yet, on the other hand, a number of men and families are adopting new gender understandings that allow them greater access to self-esteem, as well as marital and family satisfaction. This research finds that the ways in which individuals and families react to threatened gender identity can ultimately either facilitate or hinder their adaptations to structural upheaval, unemployment, and poverty.

Field Site and Methodology

This research took place in the small, rural community of Golden Valley, located in a forested mountain region of Northern California. The community has been dependent on the timber industry for nearly a century, and its economic and social life has been devastated by job loss and restructuring in this industry caused by the spotted owl ruling in the early 1990s.[3] This left a large sector of the population with a choice between leaving the area to follow work in the industry and staying put with little prospect for employment, particularly anything that paid comparably to the jobs lost. There was a large out-migration at that time, and although many people later returned, the population has still not recovered fully.

Although it is undeniably unique in many ways, Golden Valley has much in common with rural communities throughout the United States, be they formally dependent on logging, farming, or extractive industries. Throughout rural America, the latter half of the twentieth century was characterized by a trend toward rapid deindustrialization and catastrophic job loss. The trend includes the loss of manufacturing jobs in the rural Northeast and Midwest (Duncan 1999; Fitchen 1991; Knapp 1995), declines in farm ownership and employment in the Midwest, West, and South (Duncan 1999; Elder, Robertson, and Ardelt 1994; Elder, Robertson, and Foster 1994; Fitchen 1991; Norem and Blundall 1988), declines in extractive industries throughout Appalachia and the Midwest (Duncan 1999; England and Brown 2003), and declines in fishing (Binkley 2000; Mederer 1999; S. Smith et al. 2003) and forestry (Daniels, Gobeli, and Findley 2000; Danks 2000; Kusel and Fortmann 1991) along the nation's coastlines. These changes have been accompanied by a shift toward what Nelson and Smith (1999) refer to as "bad jobs"—meaning the replacement of full-time, well-paid work by part-time, low-wage, and often feminized work. Industrial restructuring throughout rural America has resulted in poverty, underemployment, and changing workforce demographics, as well as changing social, family, and gender relations (Bokemeier and Garkovich 1991; DeHaan and Deal 2001; Tickamyer and Henderson 2003). Because it exemplifies so many of these trends, Golden Valley was chosen as an ideal location in which to study the effects of poverty, industrial restructuring, and rapid job loss on a mostly white, rural U.S. community.

This research was conducted in Golden Valley from 2003 to 2004, and consisted of fifty-five tape-recorded, open-ended, in-depth interviews with native and longtime members of the community, as well as a year of ethnographic fieldwork done in Golden Valley and the surrounding smaller communities. About equal numbers of men and women were interviewed (twenty-five women and thirty men), singly and in couples, depending on the subjects' preferences. The subjects ranged in age from twenty-three to sixty years old, and the average age of the sample was about thirty-nine. The original subjects were recruited through contacts in the community, including several people who worked in organizations that focused on job creation and retraining, and a snowball sampling technique was used to find subsequent interviewees. Ethnographic methods were also used to enhance and build upon the understanding gleaned through the interviews, to identify inconsistencies, and to observe social practices in their natural environments.

Those Who Remain

Golden Valley's population is mostly white. However, many of the long-established families there have Native American ancestries as well, and about 8 percent of residents self-identified as Native American in the 2000 Census. A growing number of Hispanics reside in Golden Valley as well (nearly 5 percent in 2000) (U.S. Census Bureau 2000), but this minority group, along with the few African or Asian Americans who have settled there, is not well received in Golden Valley.

Living in Golden Valley presents a challenge to almost everyone there. Table 4.1 compares Golden Valley with the state of California on several quality-of-life measures. In 2000, poverty rates for Golden Valley were more than one and a half times the state average. Unemployment was more than twice the state average, with only 45 percent of the population actively in the labor force. Sixteen percent of occupied residences in Golden Valley lacked telephones in 2000, compared to just 2 percent across the state as a whole. The 1990s, with the closure of the forests and of the last sawmill, were not easy years for Golden Valley's families. Jobs are now scarcer than ever before, with the local schools and the few remaining retail establishments being the main sources of employment. This represents a large change not only in the number of jobs available, but also in the type of available work, as jobs have shifted dramatically from the male-dominated forest sector toward more feminized retail and educational services.

Table 4.2 provides a comparison between 1990 and 2000 on several economic indices for Golden Valley. Interestingly, individual poverty rates decreased slightly over the decade. This is not necessarily due to many people moving out of poverty, but is likely the result of a combination of the out-migration of people who could not find work, as well as women's increased workforce participation and some in-migration by wealthier retirees. Poverty has long been endemic to the community. The percentage of households receiving public assistance also dropped by almost half over the decade,[4] although this significant decrease is likely due more to welfare reform and growing stigma than to a lack of need.

Unemployment, on the other hand, nearly doubled over the ten-year period. This increase was mostly in men's unemployment, which more than doubled, while women's unemployment rose only slightly. As the employment population ratios and workforce participation rates suggest, women's rising unemployment is related to an increased proportion of the female population looking for work compared with the past. For men the opposite is true; their workforce participation rate dropped slightly, suggesting that more men are dropping out of the workforce entirely when they are unable to find work. Table 4.2 also shows that women's employment has risen slightly over the decade, while men's has fallen dramatically. Women and men of working age are now employed in about equal proportions in Golden Valley, which is a significant change from 1990. Even in 1990 the effects of the forest industry's decline were becoming visible. In 2000, however, the collapse was complete, as is clear in the men's employment trends.

While there seems to be a growing acceptance of women in the workforce and female breadwinners, there has been little change in men's attitudes toward what have long been considered women's jobs. Men will stay at home with the children for much of the year, but they generally will not take on paid child care jobs in the formal or informal sector. Nor do they tend to work in the schools except as janitors or teachers, mostly in the sciences and industrial arts. Thus, Golden Valley's men compete with one another for an ever-shrinking set of logging, woodworking, and construction jobs in the area. For those men who are not the hardest workers or the most able, work is increasingly difficult to find.

Golden Valley provides an example of some of the worst economic hardships faced by many rural communities, be they formerly natural resource, farming, or manufacturing dependent. Unfortunately, scenarios like this one can be found throughout rural areas, especially when their lives and livelihoods are tied to a single industry. As in communities throughout rural America (Conger et al. 1994; Mederer 1999; Norem and Blundall 1988; S. Smith et al.

2003), in Golden Valley the decline of the forest industry resulted not only in severe job loss and unemployment, but also in the loss of a "way of life" that its residents held dear.

Results: Job Loss and Gender Identity

Considering all of the challenges that Golden Valley currently faces, it is not surprising that families are struggling. Scholars have long linked poverty and job loss with a number of destructive outcomes, including drug and alcohol abuse, depression, marital and family tensions, and domestic violence (Conger et al. 1994; Cottle 2001; Davis 1993; Elder, Robertson, and Foster 1994; Larson, Wilson, and Beley 1994; Liem and Liem 1990; McLanahan, Garfinkel, and Mincy 2001; Robertson, Elder, and Skinner 1991; Rubin 1976). Generally these outcomes are assumed to be directly linked to the stresses of economic hardship. There is no doubt that economic hardship and job loss create enough stress to devastate family relationships. However, the evidence from Golden Valley suggests that these effects are filtered through the lens of gender roles and identities. More importantly, the gender strategy chosen, and the degree of a family's flexibility or rigidity with regard to gender identities, can mitigate or exacerbate the effects of structural changes like those that Golden Valley has undergone.

This chapter looks in depth at two ideal typical gender strategies employed by families faced with circumstances that challenge their abilities to achieve success according to their own norms. The majority of Golden Valley's families were formed with the expectation of separate, gendered provider and nurturer roles. Men expected to be the breadwinners, while women generally anticipated being mothers first and workers second (if at all). This ideal is now unachievable for most families. The ways in which they react to and address this unattainability have important consequences for them. While some families cling *rigidly* to their cultural norms in the face of great change, others have exhibited surprising *flexibility* with regard to gender roles, norms, and identities. Flexible families, which are able to remake their own visions of fatherhood, providing, and masculinity, appear to navigate the structural changes and economic stresses with decreased amounts of tension and conflict.

While both members of a couple generally adopt that family's gender strategy, subjects' testimonies suggest that it is typically the men whose ideologies ultimately direct the family's overall gender strategy. Women, for the most part, follow their partners' leads and are often left only with the choice of whether or not to leave men whose behaviors are frustrating to them. Women tend to be more flexible than men with regard to changing gender roles or ideologies, in part because they employ a number of strategies that allow them to portray their work activities as consistent with mothering and traditional feminine ideals. Additionally, entering the workforce often allows them greater power within the family, as well as the opportunity to empower themselves as individuals outside of the family setting. For men, who are often leaving the workforce or seeing declining incomes, the changes represent a loss of power and self-worth.

Rigid Masculinity and the Fight to Retain Gender Roles

I have to work. And that's the way I look at it, is I have to work. Whatever she wants to do, then that's what she does. We were both, though, when our kids were babies, said that she's gonna stay home with the kids until they get old enough to where we feel comfortable.

—Craig Layton, thirty-two-year-old hardware store employee and married father of two

The loss of jobs has been particularly difficult for Golden Valley's men, who are now being confronted by circumstances that preclude them from being masculine according to their own cultural traditions. These threats to masculinity are felt and expressed most profoundly within the family context. Demie Kurz (1995, 21) argues that "as wages decline, and as good jobs become more scarce . . . men may increasingly resent the loss of family privilege." Additionally, while for women adapting to the new labor market conditions has required a change in gender norms, but not necessarily major changes in gender identities or the ideals of femininity, for men both norms and identities have been profoundly affected. It is hard enough for men to take on family and household chores that their own fathers avoided; it is a completely different task to rework the expectations of masculinity away from its focus on breadwinning and providing for the family. Not surprisingly, some men refuse to accept this combination of power loss, changing gender norms, and changing gender identities. However, for men who are unwilling to let go of it, traditional masculine identity can carry a high price tag in Golden Valley, often creating struggles for them personally, as well as for their families. In a situation where work that allows a man to be the main breadwinner is hard to come by, breadwinner masculinity is an elusive and hard-won ideal whose pursuit often causes more tension than it relieves.

Many families in Golden Valley are still uncomfortable with the concept of working wives, despite how common they have become there. About a third of the individuals in my sample hold tightly to traditional conceptions of gender roles, fatherhood, and masculinity, despite circumstances that challenge their abilities to achieve these standards. For these families, gender roles are still defined along breadwinner/homemaker lines. For example, in response to the question "What makes someone a good father?" their answers tended to focus on material provision:

My goal, when I was planning to be a dad . . . was they'll have life better than I had it. They won't have to worry about nothin'. So that's what I do. . . . Whatever I can give to them, they've got.
—Rod Mitchell, thirty-year-old sawmill worker and married father of four

I'd say a good dad provides well for your children.
—Kim Clark, thirty-two-year-old married stay-at-home mother of two

To be there. Uh, you know, through whatever, you know. To be his dad, you know, to be there financially, emotionally, the whole thing.
—Kevin Young, twenty-four-year-old unemployed single father of one

Most of these "rigid" respondents (more than 85 percent) were raised in two-parent families, with mothers who did not work outside the home, and they carried these expectations into their adult lives. Many families simply make do with less for the women to remain at home, while the men work seasonally in the woods or with the Forest Service, doing odd jobs or hunting while receiving unemployment insurance during the slow months. Often their work takes husbands far from home for extended periods of time, or in some cases entails lengthy daily commutes over the mountains. In many of these rigid homes, men employ multiple strategies to retain power over their wives, including refusing to do housework and limiting women's access to money.

The struggle to keep women out of the workforce often has a number of personal and financial repercussions, particularly for men who are truly unable to work. Randy Taylor is a thirty-five-year-old married father of two with a debilitating work-related back injury that keeps him from doing physical labor. He was already married with children when his accident occurred while working in the mill. His employers there lied to Randy regarding the extent of his injury, and as a result he did not receive proper treatment. After going untreated for nearly five years, he could barely stand upright, and he subsequently had a series of surgeries over the next five years just to retain minimal ability to stand and get around. His dedication to the masculine ideal of being the sole provider kept him working for those first five years despite the pain.

> Well, you know, when I was working I just, the way I dealt with it was, you know, I didn't have a choice because they said it was nothin' serious in the first place. And then when the mill shut down and whatnot, you know, it was like, at that time I was about ready to take care of it. But then when I went to logging I didn't have no insurance or nothin' like that, so it's, you know, just try to block it out the best I can and try to do what I have to, 'cause, you know, I gotta provide for my family.

Randy has been on disability since 1999, and this has been the sole source of income for his family of four for the entire period. He described the experience of being out of work as personally difficult. "It's been pretty frustrating. Especially at first, it's real hard to be—you know, you were workin' and now you're not workin', and you're not gettin' the money that you're used to and everything, all the responsibilities, you know, I believe it's the man's. I took 'em, you know. I told my wife I'd take care of her and whatnot, so it's pretty frustrating."

For Randy, self-esteem and masculine identity are tied to providing, even in the wake of his accident. He grew up in a two-parent family with a stay-at-home mother and a father whose philosophy boiled down to "Men earn their things, and girls—everything is handed to 'em." Randy feels that his inability to work has been a major source of stress and frustration in his marriage, and that the lack of money is their most urgent problem. "The hardest challenge we face is making it from one payday to the next. You know, just to have enough food and enough kerosene to stay warm, enough food for our kids to eat, that's what our biggest challenge is." Their main strategies for survival include caretaking a trailer for very low rent, borrowing money from relatives, and "eatin' fish and deer" that he kills himself, thus allowing him to still be the main provider for his family. His daily activities as he described them center mostly around hunting, fishing, and spending time with friends.

Although Randy asserted repeatedly that their main sources of marital stress were financial, his wife Christine told a different story. She was often frustrated and on the verge of tears at the Family Empowerment Alliance (FEA), a local support center where she worked part-time as a volunteer. She was frequently unreliable, as Randy often took their one working car during the day without telling her where he was going or when he'd be back, leaving her stranded in their small trailer miles from town. Christine wanted to take on paid work, but Randy forbade it. She complained repeatedly that he was controlling, as well as depressed and angry. Friends of the couple also spoke of their past problems with drug abuse, and speculated about current use. Four months after my interview with Randy, Christine left him and filed for divorce, plunging herself into the ranks of Golden Valley's poor single mothers. Randy said nothing to me that foreshadowed these problems, however, and claimed to have a relatively happy marriage. He told me that he had always wanted a wife and family, and that he was very grateful to have one. He felt lucky to have started his family back when he still had a job, and said that he probably wouldn't have had the confidence to ask Christine to marry him if he had been out of work then: "I wouldn't have had nothin' to offer. Yeah, it would've been a lot harder." When asked if he thought he was a good husband, Randy replied, "Yeah. I'd be a lot better if I had a lot of money, though." For Randy, being a husband and father meant being the provider and head of household, at whatever cost. Without that status, he was unsure whether he could have become either.

While men like Randy often portrayed themselves as self-sacrificing providers, the situation generally appeared different for wives like Christine, who tended to find these situations oppressive and frustrating. Kim Clark is thirty-two years old and married to Al, a man who works seasonally as a logger several hours away. Kim does not work outside the home, although she did before she married Al. During the off season from work, Al is habitually away on hunting trips, and thus still mainly absent from the home. He does little housework or child care even when he is present. As Kim explained with some irritation: "He can't seem to pick his stuff up or, um, clean up his own dishes. Oh, but he's real good at telling me to do it, and having me [do it]." In casual settings, Kim tends to come across as negative and angry, and spends a lot of time complaining about Al. One of her most common complaints concerns his absolute control over their finances. She explained in her interview, "We don't have, um, like a bank account together. All finances are in his name. And, um, we just pay bills as they come. When I need money, I get money, he provides. I don't know, I'd say he gives me whatever I want or need—we don't really fight over that. Sometimes I buck up over it because it's just the damn principle of having a damn checking account! It's just the principle. I'm thirty-two years old and I'm not *allowed* to have a checking account?"

In households like the ones described above, both men and women cited financial responsibility as a father's main task, often regardless of whether the women expressed a desire to be working outside the home. In most of these families money was a major source of stress and tension, yet most did not seriously consider either moving away or having the women take on full-time jobs to ease the stress. But as the repeated complaints of Kim, Christine, and many women like them illustrated, these tensions frequently cause frustration and unhappiness among the women, despite the fact that they tend to be complicit in the arrangements. These women's ideologies have begun to change despite their own and their husbands' reluctance to adapt their lifestyles. Although many have not fully adopted the gender discourses of their working peers, they do appear to be influenced by them. Thus, they find themselves mired in a conflict between old and new ways of thinking about women's roles, freedoms, and financial responsibilities.

Although most families in Golden Valley expressed a desire for "traditional" two-parent families in which the wife stays at home, only a handful were actually able to attain this goal. For them life was generally more difficult than for those who worked, and most stay-at-home mothers expressed a desire for a more flexible family structure, wishing either that their husbands would allow them to work outside the home or that they would treat them more as equals with regard to housework, child care, and access to money. While working women generally either took household chores less seriously or received help from their husbands, most who stayed home did not receive any help from their husbands at all. Thus, they struggled on the brink of the uneven gender revolution (Goldscheider and Waite 1991; Hochschild and Machung 1989). Most were dedicated to remaining married despite their mounting frustrations, and felt that they had no real reason to leave a man who did not drink, use drugs, or physically abuse them. But often this pattern of male control and female submission was linked to underlying self-esteem issues for out-of-work men, who were not only controlling but also depressed, angry, and eventually abusive. As these stories illustrate, families who cling to traditional ideas of masculinity but are unable to achieve them frequently encounter personal difficulty and internal and external conflict, and family units are wrought with tensions. Over the long term, this friction and strain can contribute to many families falling apart.

Flexible Masculinity and Active Fathers

I don't know really what kind of father I am. I just try and just love 'em, and try and spend time with 'em, and make the time I do spend with 'em fun. Playing games, and doin' things, and takin' 'em out. Takin' 'em out to the creek is really fun for me. I like doin' that, even though it's a little bit more work.

—Brian Goodman, twenty-six-year-old hardware store employee and married father of two

Not all the families in my sample struggle so intensely with their self-images and their relationships with masculinity. As Ray (2000) found among male domestic servants in Calcutta, and Waller (2002) found among poor urban males in the United States, I discovered in Golden Valley that many men who cannot achieve a traditional form of masculinity are reconstructing the masculine ideal to make it more attainable for themselves. According to Nonn (2004), the development of versatile masculinities can allow men to resist a sense of failure and build self-worth. About two-thirds of male respondents have a somewhat more flexible understanding of the masculine ideal and acceptable gender norms within the family. Although they draw heavily from Golden Valley's dominant gender discourse, they prioritize different aspects of male identity. Most commonly, flexibility takes the form of rewriting the expectations of fatherhood in a way that allows them to focus on their strengths and abilities. Since men in Golden Valley now often have large amounts of free time but only limited amounts of money to contribute to the family, their strength lies in being active parts of their children's lives and imparting to them masculine skills, values, and work ethic through shared activities. Most of the flexible male respondents focused on involved parenting as the most important part of a father's job, and downplayed the importance of financial support. They discussed how they enjoyed it when their own fathers had spent time with them, or how they felt deprived because their fathers had not been involved with their lives. Thus, by their own standards they are good fathers because they help with homework, attend sports matches, and teach their children to hunt, fish, camp, and understand the value of hard work.

Like their rigid counterparts, the flexible men often were working to some degree, but frequently struggled to find or keep jobs. They were not always happy with the work they did. Several of the older men had taken early retirement to remain in Golden Valley after the mill left, while a number of the younger men were seasonally unemployed. Most openly acknowledged that their families could not survive without their wives' paychecks and health benefits, and showed little shame in admitting this. They also tended to claim that the household work was divided up equally, although the women's testimonies and my own observations suggested that housework still tended to be divided along the inside/outside line (Hochschild and Machung 1989), with women taking on a greater share of daily cleaning and cooking chores and men more likely to engage in more sporadic chores like taking out garbage or cutting wood. More than half of "flexible" respondents grew up with mothers who worked, in contrast to the more rigid respondents, who mostly had stay-at-home mothers. This difference raises the question of the degree to which background influences an adult's gender flexibility.

Ideologically at least, the "flexible" men did not focus on being the head of household in either economic or power terms. Instead, they found self-esteem through masculine parenting and through being what they considered to be "good fathers." Among this group, good fathering was almost always conceived of in noneconomic terms. The following comments were expressed by flexible parents in answer to the question "What makes someone a good father?":

> Support. I just have to say support. You know, just making sure you set a good example, support everything they want to do. If he wants to go play football, then I want to make sure I get him there. Whether it's to play a real game, or whether it's just to come down and play with some of the kids. Just supporting them in everything they do, you know? A pat on the back and a "hey, you're doing great." You know? "I like the way you do that."
> —Andy Richards, forty-year-old small-scale mill worker and married father of two

> You know, he is tired when he gets home from work, but he always finds time. Um, and he does, like, guy stuff. Mom just can't fill that void. It's hard to explain. I just, uh, I think that he does a good job.
> —Liza Wright, twenty-six-year-old grocery store clerk and cohabiting mother of one

> For me it would be to give your kids lots of love. Give them love more than anything. Because to me there's no greater thing in the world than love. I instill it by being able to spend more time with them, and I know that if I were in the city, they'd be alone. I'd be working more, and being in that rat race you're not able to spend that quality time with them.
> —Bill Prader, forty-five-year-old married father of two, sporadically employed as a carpenter

These quotes illustrate the focus on supportive, involved parenting and the purveyance of masculine skills, rather than economic support, as the father's main job.

For many of the families who have successfully survived the mill's closing, this focus on family togetherness and involvement allows men to feel fulfilled and proud of their lives. Their morphing of masculine identity draws heavily upon discourse around equality and involved fathering, yet is strongly rooted in local cultural images of masculinity. As Waller (2002, 40) contends, this new model of involved fatherhood has become more mainstream since the feminist movement of the 1970s, and has encouraged fathers to make emotional connections with their children and share in the work of caring for them. The parenting ideas that the men in Golden Valley borrowed from the larger U.S. culture permitted them to sustain healthy family lives and stable households, despite living in a community in which prefeminist notions of breadwinning and fatherhood are still prevalent.

Jake Robbins, a fifty-two-year-old married father of two, is an example of a man who adjusted his gender ideals to accommodate his changing circumstances. Jake did not expect to have anything less than a traditional family when he got married. Both his mother and his wife Barbara's mother had been full-time homemakers. Jake and Barbara met in high school and got married at age twenty. He went first to work in the woods like his own father, and later switched to the sawmill, where he made enough money to support the family. Barbara stayed home with their young children, going to work part-time at the local preschool only once both kids were in school. Both Jake and Barbara described her original decision to work as one made out of boredom, not financial necessity. She described the job at first as one that was consistent with full child rearing responsibilities: "My kids were old enough that I got tired of staring at the wall. And you can only do so much cleaning, so that was a job that I would be home when they were. You know, and I had their vacations, and everything worked out great." For Jake, it was not easy to see his wife go to work: "Well, I didn't want her to work. But then she finally told me, 'I'm bored, I gotta go get a job.'"

As Jake's work life became less stable, however, he came to appreciate having a working wife, and to recognize the importance of her work to the family's financial survival. When the mill left Golden Valley, Jake moved with it to a suburb of Sacramento, more than five hours away. Barbara and the children stayed behind in Golden Valley, where the Robbinses owned their home and their children were in high school. They described the separation as "stressful" and "miserable." After several years apart, Jake gave up the well-paid job that he found challenging and interesting to return to his wife's side in Golden Valley. It took him nearly a year to find another job, at greatly reduced pay and no benefits, and with no stability. The money he makes now is about equal to what his wife makes, and they rely on her job's health benefits. He easily acknowledged, "Yeah, I wouldn't have been able to do what I've done had it not been for her." Unlike couples in which the men struggled to hold power over the women, Jake and Barbara both described their current state as a partnership. Jake added jokingly, "It's a partnership? What are you talking about? I get the same allowance now as I ever got"—in reference to the fact that it is Barbara, not him, who handles their finances.

For couples like Jake and Barbara, the transition to flexible gender roles seemed relatively natural. For others it was more of a struggle, but ultimately still yielded stronger relationships that were less fraught with the tensions that characterized the rigid families. Brian and Nicole Goodman went through a similar change in gender expectations to keep the family afloat. This young, devoutly Christian couple have both always wanted to create the traditional breadwinner/homemaker family in which neither of them actually grew up. When asked what her goals in life had been, Nicole replied, "Kids were my goal. My biggest thing I always wanted to do was be a housewife." Both Brian and Nicole maintain that breadwinning is his responsibility, and his source of self-esteem, while for her it is a secondary duty. Brian said, "That's my job, I feel like. It's my job to go work for so many hours a day, as long as I can. That's what makes me feel good anyway, is going to work. I'd go crazy if I had to be in the house all the time. It can get really hard on guys that are like that up here." Yet despite their desire to be a more "traditional" family, they both accept that for now there is no way he can earn enough to support their family of four on his own, and her workforce participation is necessary. Although she works several part-time jobs and makes nearly as much income as her husband, Nicole justified her work as secondary, and thus they both still conceived of Brian as the main breadwinner. She explained, "I don't mind doing the part-time to supplement the income, but I don't wanna be the one that does the main income." Nicole made it clear throughout her testimony that she considered her work to be only supplemental and secondary to her husband's job. This downplaying of the importance of women's work has been noted by a number of scholars of gender relations in rural as well as urban areas (Davis 1993, 2000; Gringeri 1994; Hochschild and Machung 1989; Nelson and Smith 1998, 1999).

While Nicole has had to bend her expectations to enter the workforce, Brian has responded with flexibility in fathering and homemaking as well. Nicole described his willingness to help with household chores and child rearing: "He's pretty willing to babysit and stuff, and change diapers, and bathe them and feed them. You know, he doesn't have one of those 'it's women's work' attitudes. 'Cause like, even his dad says like, 'Diapers is women's work'—that old-school kind of attitude. Brian doesn't have that." It is clear from this comment that childrearing is still conceived of as Nicole's job, while for Brian it is supplemental "babysitting." Yet, unlike more rigid men, he is willing to do this type of housework and child care work, and together they have adopted a set of gender discourses that allow them to bridge the gap between their expectations and realities, while still invoking traditional gender ideologies. Nonetheless, it was the letting go of some of their "old-school" gender expectations that allowed Brian and Nicole to maintain a decent standard of living, as well as a strong partnership.

For many of the couples in which gender norms were defined less rigidly, there has been a slow transition from a more traditional idea of marriage and family. In almost all of these flexible couples the wives were in the workforce, and in many instances they were the main breadwinners or significant contributors to the family income. When interviewed together, these couples commonly held much less tension between them, whether they were older couples who had weathered difficult pasts or young couples who had only recently taken on grown-up roles and responsibilities. Most are still haunted by financial struggles, but generally they remain confident that they will survive well enough by relying on both partners' salaries and benefits, as well as whatever help family and community can provide. The wives of these men generally take pride in their own jobs, and accept their roles as cosupporters of the households whether or not they had originally aspired to be working versus at home. For those men who are able to let go of the breadwinning-centered ideologies of their youths, there seems to be considerably less internal turmoil, and a stronger sense of satisfaction with their marriages, their roles as fathers, and themselves as men. Because of their ability to adapt to Golden Valley's changing circumstances, these men's families appear to have a much better chance of long-term stability than do their more traditional and less flexible counterparts.

Conclusion: Family Life and the Masculine Ideal

Many of the stories presented above reflect themes found throughout the literature on both urban and rural poverty and unemployment, including the tendency for job loss and poverty to be correlated with physical abuse, substance abuse, depression, and marital and family tensions (Conger et al. 1994; Cottle 2001; Larson et al. 1994; Liem and Liem 1990; Robertson, Elder, and Skinner 1991). The interview and ethnographic data begin to shed some light on the processes that link these problems together in a rural community like Golden Valley. In particular, the Golden Valley subjects commonly brought up gender roles and expectations as a source of tension and conflict that exacerbated economic and job-related stresses in many of their marriages and relationships.

For men, job loss affects marital and family life in important ways in Golden Valley. Both unemployment and poverty have been linked to domestic violence and substance abuse (Cottle 2001; Davis 1993; Elder, Robertson, and Ardelt 1994; McLanahan, Garfinkel, and Mincy 2001; Rubin 1976), which was the most common cause cited by Golden Valley women for their previous breakups. Additionally, for those poor, unemployed men who cling to traditional masculine ideals, these economic and labor market struggles create an intense dissonance between their goals and their realities. This conflict creates tense situations in which they feel the need to compensate for their lack of economic success by exerting control over their wives, as well as struggling with long commutes, seasonal work, or severe poverty—all of which take their toll on marriages.

Yet the results from Golden Valley suggest that there is more flexibility possible in rural gender roles than was found by previous researchers, such as Nelson and Smith (1998). Many families have managed to remake masculinity in a way that focuses more heavily on realistic goals such as active fathering. These families seem to be able to navigate employment and economic struggles with fewer tensions and with less need for men to exert control over women. In Golden Valley two-parent families are still the majority, and many of them have successfully refocused masculine identity around engaging with their children in such activities as hunting, fishing, and team sports, while wives contribute substantially to the family finances. For these families, borrowing of feminist concepts helps men to retain self-esteem and masculine identity despite their nontraditional gender roles.

Goldscheider and Waite (1991) argue that changes in family structure, including lower marriage rates and higher divorce rates, are due to more than economic conditions, and in particular reflect the working out of the "sex-role revolution" that resulted from women's greater workforce participation. Golden Valley is not entirely cut off from the larger United States. Thus newer ideas about masculinity and fatherhood, such as those introduced by the feminist movement (Hochschild and Machung 1989; Waller 2002), have become part of the larger cultural "toolkit" (Swidler 1986) that Golden Valley residents have at their disposal. As Waller (2002, 55) found in the urban setting, in Golden Valley as well, a new model of fatherhood has begun to emerge as the traditional breadwinning model has rapidly become less attainable. For those men and women who are flexible with regard to their cultural ideals, adopting this more realistic model appears to help them navigate economic and structural changes with less anxiety.

My findings support previous findings on the importance of role flexibility to rural families (Mederer 1999; Norem and Blundall 1988), while further exploring the relationship of gender ideologies to marital and family stress. Without flexible ideologies and discourses that allow individuals to make sense of and justify new roles, gender role flexibility is less attainable and sustainable. This research suggests that the adoption of flexible ideologies can facilitate the transition to new gender roles as required by structural changes, and help minimize the tensions that can threaten families' long-term chances of stability.[5]

Table 4.1   Quality of life measures

	Golden Valley	California
Individual poverty	24%	14%
Family poverty	18%	11%
Child poverty	31%	20%
Unemployment	9%	4%
In workforce	45%	62%
Lack telephones	16%	2%

SOURCE: U.S. Census Bureau 2000.

Table 4.2   Economic changes in Golden Valley, 1990 and 2000

	1990	2000
Poverty	27%	24%
Public assistance	19%	10%
Unemployment	11%	21%
Men's unemployment	10%	26%
Women's unemployment	11%	15%
Men's employment population ratio	50%	36%
Women's employment population ratio	32%	35%
Men in labor force	56%	48%
Women in labor force	36%	41%

SOURCE: U.S. Census Bureau 1990, 2000.

Notes

1. All identifying details, including names of people and places, have been changed.

2. According to Connell (1995, 77), "Hegemonic masculinity can be defined as the configuration of gender practice which embodies the currently accepted answer to the problem of the legitimacy of patriarchy, which guarantees (or is taken to guarantee) the dominant position of men and the subordinate position of women." She further explains, "Hegemonic masculinity is not a fixed character type, always and everywhere the same. It is, rather, the masculinity that occupies the hegemonic position in a given pattern of gender relations, a position always contestable" (76).

3. The 1990 listing of the northern spotted owl as threatened under the Endangered Species Act led to federally enforced reductions of timber harvesting through much of the Pacific Northwest, to preserve the owl's habitat. Federal timber harvests in the region dropped by 80 percent between 1989 and 1994 as a result (Daniels and Brehm 2003).

4. "Public assistance income includes general assistance and Temporary Assistance to Needy Families (TANF). Separate payments received for hospital or other medical care (vendor payments) are excluded. This does not include Supplemental Security Income (SSI)" (U.S. Census Bureau 2000).

5. The research for this chapter was made possible through the generous support of the Rural Poverty Research Center, the University of California Labor and Employment Research Fund, and the Sociology Department of the University of California, Berkeley.

SECTION 2

FAMILY CHANGE, ECONOMIC HARDSHIP, AND
FAMILY ADAPTIVE STRATEGIES

ECONOMIC RESTRUCTURING AND
FAMILY STRUCTURE CHANGE, 1980 TO 2000

A Focus on Female-Headed Families with Children

DIANE K. MCLAUGHLIN AND ALISHA J. COLEMAN-JENSEN

Economic restructuring since the 1980s has altered men's and women's roles in the economy, in turn influencing family formation and stability, which has led to increases in female-headed families with children. Female-headed families with children have become a larger share of households with children overall, and the gap between metropolitan (metro) and nonmetropolitan (nonmetro) areas is closing, so the prevalence of female-headed families with children in nonmetro areas is increasing and becoming more similar to that in metro areas. This trend should garner attention because female-headed families with children have the highest poverty rates of all families with children, placing these women and their children at risk. Very high poverty rates among nonmetro female-headed families with children (Snyder, McLaughlin, and Findeis 2006) and fewer support services for families combine to make single mother–headed families particularly difficult to sustain in nonmetro areas (Brown and Lichter 2004; Lichter and Jensen 2001; Ward and Turner 2007). Economic restructuring, particularly the growth of poor-quality jobs for men, may be contributing to the increase in female-headed families with children (McLaughlin and Coleman-Jensen 2008; McLaughlin, Gardner, and Lichter 1999). This chapter examines

The views expressed here are those of the authors and not necessarily those of the Economic Research Service or the U.S. Department of Agriculture.

the relationship between economic restructuring and the change in prevalence of female-headed families with children across U.S. counties for the 1980 to 2000 period.

We begin by briefly describing the processes by which female-headed families with children are formed and dissolve. The description focuses on individual-level explanations influenced by characteristics of places—the quality of jobs and job opportunities for men and women, the availability of partners, and the acceptance of nonmarital births, cohabitation, and divorce. We do not consider the interpersonal explanations for marriage and divorce—love, companionship, procreation, marital problems. We consider what is known about how female-headed family formation and dissolution differ in nonmetro and metro places. We then provide information on the prevalence of female-headed families across all counties and nonmetro counties in 1980, 1990, and 2000, and we then assess the relationship between economic restructuring and changes in prevalence of this family type. Finally, we discuss the policy implications of our findings.

Pathways by Which Female-Headed Families with Children Begin and End

Female-headed families with children begin through four main pathways: a birth outside of marriage, the death of a spouse, divorce, or the breakup of cohabitating relationships where children are present. Female-headed families with children end through two main pathways. The single mom marries or she cohabits, and the male becomes the head of the household, or the children in the family all reach age eighteen without any change in the relationship status of the mother. Some of these individual-level processes are influenced by the characteristics of the local area in which individuals live. We focus on pathways likely to be most affected by local economic restructuring.

Explanations for the Formation and Dissolution of Female-Headed Families with Children

Decisions to marry, cohabitate, or to end a marriage or cohabiting relationship are affected by the economic circumstances of women and men. Women's economic independence (Cherlin 1992; Oppenheimer 1997; White and Rogers 2000), the availability of attractive partners in local "marriage markets" (Lichter,

Kephart, et al. 1992; W. Wilson 1987), and differences in the acceptance of divorce, nonmarriage, and childbearing outside of marriage (Thornton and Young-DeMarco 2001) have been offered as explanations for local area variations in the prevalence of female-headed families with children. Changes in these conditions will influence whether and how fast the prevalence of female-headed families with children rises or falls.

WOMEN'S ECONOMIC INDEPENDENCE

Increases in women's educational attainment and labor force participation have resulted in women becoming less reliant on men for economic support, thus increasing women's economic independence (Cherlin 1992; Oppenheimer 1997). When women's employment provides adequate income to establish a household, marriage and cohabitation are less likely to be economic survival strategies for women and their children. Adequate income also enables women to leave unhappy or abusive relationships (Nock 2001). Alternatively, women with higher education and earnings have been found to marry later, to have more stable marriages, and to be less likely to have nonmarital births (Rogers and DeBoer 2001; White and Rogers 2000).

Unfortunately, employment has not provided economic independence for women with lower educational attainment or fewer job skills or who are employed in low-wage or part-time jobs. Women in jobs that do not allow them to support their families on their own may be less likely to divorce (Ono 1998) and more likely to form a cohabiting relationship or to marry (Clarkberg 1999). Their contributions to family income may increase family stability by reducing economic distress, especially where men's earnings have declined (Ono 1998; Oppenheimer 1997). Alternatively, discord and distress over finances are linked to divorce (Cherlin 1992; White and Rogers 2000).

MEN'S AVAILABILITY AND ATTRACTIVENESS AS MARITAL PARTNERS

Places with too few men for the number of women have fewer marriages and more female-headed families with children (Lichter, Kephart, et al. 1992; South 1991; W. Wilson 1987). The decline in men's employment and the loss of good jobs (e.g., construction or manufacturing jobs) traditionally held by men with moderate or low education levels (Bluestone and Harrison 1982; Davis and Bosley 2007) have reduced the availability of economically attractive male partners (Edin 2000). As men's economic opportunities in an area decline, divorce is expected to increase. Areas with decreases in men's jobs overall or increasing shares of poor-quality jobs with low earnings for men are likely to see greater marital instability, lower marriage rates, and faster growth in female-headed families with children.

SOCIETAL ACCEPTANCE AND SUPPORT FOR SINGLE-PARENT FAMILIES

Acceptance of female-headed families with children, and conditions that ease the difficulties faced by single-parent families with children (e.g., secure employment, health care benefits, child care availability, transportation, social support from friends and family), can improve viability and well-being in these families (Ward and Turner 2007), possibly reducing the economic need to find a partner. Less acceptance of divorce and nonmarital childbearing associated with fundamental religions (Ono 1999) and nonmetro or farm areas (Albrecht 1998; D. Albrecht and S. Albrecht 1997) suggests that these areas will have fewer services for these families and slower growth in female-headed families with children.

What Do We Know About Formation and Dissolution of Female-Headed Families with Children in Nonmetro Areas?

Patterns of family formation of nonmetro women are more traditional than those of women in metro areas. Nonmetro women marry at younger ages and are less likely to have nonmarital births than metro women (D. Albrecht and C. Albrecht 2004; Heaton, Lichter, and Amoeteng 1989; McLaughlin, Lichter, and Johnston 1993; Snyder, Brown, and Condo 2004; Snyder and McLaughlin 2004). Nonmetro women also are more likely to choose marriage over cohabitation (Snyder et al. 2004b; Snyder and McLaughlin 2004). Marital dissolution is less likely in nonmetro areas or areas with smaller populations (Shelton 1987), possibly due to less acceptance of divorce (D. Albrecht and C. Albrecht 2004; Coward and Smith 1982). Nonmetro are more likely than metro single mothers to have been married or cohabited prior to forming their own family (Brown and Lichter 2004; Brown and Snyder 2006). Nonmetro divorced women and those in cohabiting relationships are more likely than metro women to marry (Brown and Snyder 2006; Snyder and McLaughlin 2006).

SUMMARY

Women's economic independence and men's availability and attractiveness as partners each offer explanations for the relationship between economic restructuring and the formation and dissolution of female-headed families with children. Increasing incomes and labor force participation of women both improve marital stability and make it possible for women to leave unhappy marriages and establish their own families through economic independence. In areas where women's earnings tend to be low and men's earnings are declining, increases in women's earnings and employment may increase family economic stability, thus decreasing the formation of female-headed families with children. Improvements in men's availability and economic attractiveness as mates (through more good jobs for men) are expected to be associated with increased marriage rates and greater marital stability, suggesting slower growth in female-headed families with children. Finally, economic restructuring affects both men and women, sometimes in differing directions. Opportunities for women may improve while men's decline. The consequences of economic restructuring are likely to play out differently across counties depending on the nature of local economic restructuring.

Data and Methods

We use data from the 1980, 1990, and 2000 Summary Tape Files from the U.S. Censuses of Population and Housing, combined with other secondary data sources, to answer the following questions. First, how much variation is there in the prevalence of female-headed families with children across counties in the United States and from 1980 to 2000? In what areas of the United States is the fastest growth in female-headed families occurring? Second, does the underlying economic base of counties influence change in the prevalence of female-headed families with children? Third, how is economic restructuring associated with growth in female headship, and have these relationships changed from 1980 to 1990 to the more economically prosperous 1990 to 2000 period?

These questions will be answered using the following three strategies. First, the percentage of female-headed families with children and change in the percentage of these families across counties in the United States are mapped for counties across the contiguous United States. Second, prevalence and change in the percentage of female-headed families with children under eighteen will be compared for counties with different economic dominance. To address the final question, weighted least squares regression models of change in female-headed families from 1980 to 1990 and 1990 to 2000 are estimated.

Results

PREVALENCE OF FEMALE-HEADED FAMILIES
WITH CHILDREN UNDER EIGHTEEN

Female-headed families with children under age eighteen increased in the United States from 16 percent of families with children in 1980 to 21 percent by 2000. The growth in female-headed families was faster in nonmetro than metro areas (using a 1980 designation of metro; see table 5.1). The metro-nonmetro gap declined by just over 60 percent in two decades, from 5.4 percentage points in 1980 to 3.4 in 1990 to 2 in 2000. Metro areas still had a larger share of female-headed families, but in both areas roughly one-fifth of families with children were female-headed.

The variation in female-headed families across counties is substantial. In 1980 some counties had no female-headed families, while the largest share was 44 percent in the District of Columbia. Map 5.1 shows the spatial distribution of the percentage of female-headed families with children by quartiles in 1980. The quartiles were constructed based on the population distribution of female-headed families with children. Because of this, 81 percent of counties

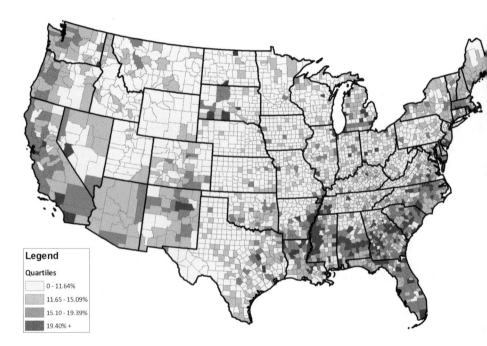

Map 5.1   Percentage of female-headed families with children, 1980 (Penn State University—PRI GIA core—October 2007; data sources: U.S. Census, ESRI)

were below the median of female-headed families with children (15 percent). Counties with smaller populations generally had percentages of female-headed families in 1980 that were below the median.

By 2000 (see map 5.2), the distribution of counties across the quartiles was more even. Just over 69 percent of counties had shares of female-headed families that were below the median for the United States (20 percent). Comparing the two maps, we see an increase in the presence of counties with percentages of female-headed families above the median scattered in the Midwest and in the South and particularly in areas with traditionally high poverty rates, such as Native American reservation areas of the Southwest (especially New Mexico and Arizona), and scattered through upstate New York and Appalachia.

CHANGE IN THE PREVALENCE OF FEMALE-HEADED FAMILIES WITH CHILDREN

The change in the percentage of female-headed families with children also varied substantially. The average percentage-point difference in female-headed families was 3 from 1980 to 1990 (1990 percentage minus 1980 percentage) and

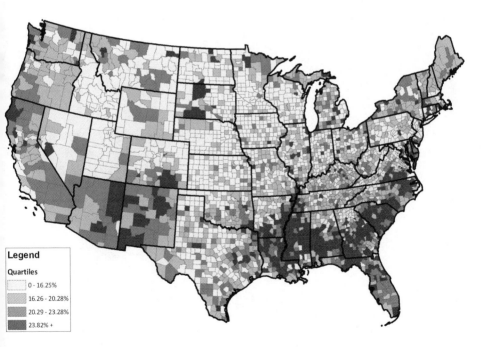

Legend

Quartiles
- 0 - 16.25%
- 16.26 - 20.28%
- 20.29 - 23.28%
- 23.82% +

Map 5.2   Percentage of female-headed families with children, 2000 (Penn State University—PRI GIA core—October 2007; data sources: U.S. Census, ESRI)

2.5 from 1990 to 2000 (2000 percentage minus 1990 percentage). The largest percentage-point increases in female-headed families with children in both decades were spread across the United States (see maps 5.3 and 5.4), including large swaths of nonmetro counties, consistent with the narrowing metro-nonmetro gap.

One question the variation in change raises is whether the counties that experienced the largest increases (or declines) in female-headed families from 1980 to 1990 also did so from 1990 to 2000. The percentage-point differences in female headed families from 1980 to 1990 and 1990 to 2000 were significantly positively correlated, but the correlation coefficient was only 0.18. This suggests that the counties with the largest changes from 1980 to 1990 were not likely to be those with the largest changes from 1990 to 2000. A comparison of counties by quartiles of change in female-headed families revealed that 23 percent of counties were in the same quartile of change in both 1980 to 1990 and 1990 to 2000, while 10 percent had shifted from the highest quartile in 1980 to 1990 to the lowest quartile of change from 1990 to 2000. There was no significant correlation between the percentage of female-headed families with children in 1980 and the 1980 to 1990 percentage-point change. Counties with higher

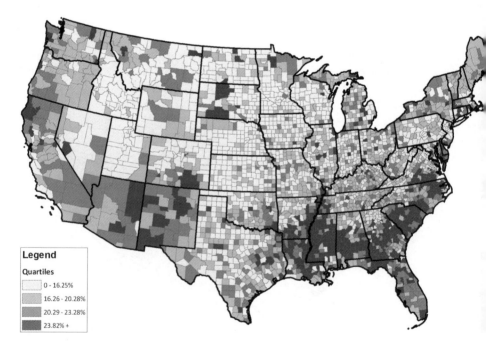

Map 5.3   Difference in percentage of female-headed families with children, 1990 minus 1980 (Penn State University—PRI GIA core—October 2007; data sources: U.S. Census, ESRI)

percentages of female-headed families with children in 1990 were slightly more likely to have slower growth in female-headed families from 1990 to 2000.

These descriptions of change in female-headed families with children indicate that the patterns of change were not consistent across the two decades—counties with larger increases or decreases in one decade were not those experiencing the larger changes in the other decade. This finding suggests that different processes were operating in the two decades or that economic restructuring and other changes occurred at different times in the counties. Next, we examine whether the prevalence and change in female-headed families with children vary by the economic base of the counties.

How Is Economic Structure in 1980 Related to Levels and Change in Female-Headed Family Prevalence from 1980 to 2000?

We examine the prevalence of female-headed families with children across counties in 1980, 1990, and 2000, classified using the Economic Research Service's County Typology (http://www.ers.usda.gov/data/TypologyCodes/1979_1986/type

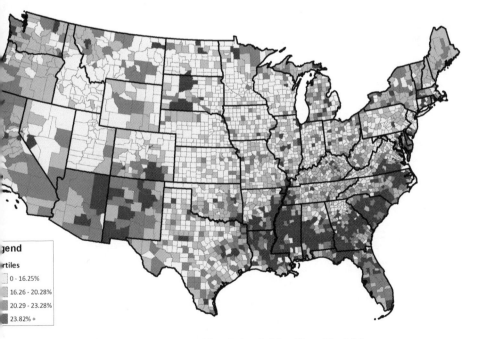

Legend

rtiles

0 - 16.25%
16.26 - 20.28%
20.29 - 23.28%
23.82% +

Map 5.4   Difference in percentage of female-headed families with children, 2000 minus 1990 (Penn State University—PRI GIA core—October 2007; data sources: U.S. Census, ESRI)

s83.xls) of predominant industry in a county in 1979 (see fig. 5.1). Mining and farming counties had the lowest prevalence of female-headed families with children in 1980, with 10 percent. Government counties had the highest prevalence in 1980, with 13.3 percent. By 2000, 17 percent of families with children in farm-dependent counties were female-headed, still the lowest among the nonmetro county types. Government counties still had the highest prevalence in 2000, with 20.7 percent. Mining counties had the largest increase in the percentage of female-headed families with children from 1980 to 2000—8.5 percentage points.

To assess whether the differences in prevalence and change in female-headed families with children were statistically significant across the nonmetro county types, regression models were estimated using the county types as explanatory variables. In 1980, farming- and mining-dependent counties had percentages of female-headed families with children that were significantly lower than in

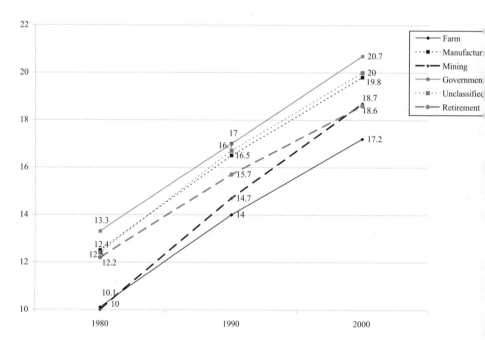

FIG. 5.1   Percentage of female-headed families with children by USDA ERS 1979 typology of counties, 1980, 1990, and 2000. Data are weighted by the number of families with children in each county in each year (SOURCE: U.S. Census of Population and Housing 1980, 1990, and 2000).

"other" nonmetro counties, while government counties had significantly higher percentages of these families. By 2000, the mining counties no longer had significantly lower shares of female-headed families than "other" nonmetro counties. The economic base of nonmetro counties was significantly associated with the percentage of female-headed families with children, particularly differentiating extractive industry-based counties.

Next, we determine if the percentage-point change in female-headed families with children differs across counties using the ERS typology for 1979. Regression models using the ERS typology to predict change in female-headed families with children from 1980 to 1990 and 1990 to 2000 showed that the economic type of counties was unrelated to the change in female-headed families with children.

Which Aspects of Economic Restructuring Are Associated with Increases in Female-Headed Families with Children?

One explanation for the lack of relationship between the ERS typology and change in the prevalence of female-headed families with children is that different patterns of economic restructuring occurred among the counties within the typology categories. To assess the influence of economic restructuring, we estimated weighted least squares regression models of change in female-headed families with children in each decade. The models were estimated for all counties and then separately for nonmetro (2,353 counties) and metro counties in 1980 (708 counties).

Measures of economic restructuring used reflect the gain in employment overall and for all workers and women in each of seven industry categories in each decade.[1] The industry categories are manufacturing; professional services; construction; public administration; wholesale trade; finance, insurance, and real estate; and poor jobs (includes retail trade, business services, personal services, and entertainment and recreation). As shown in table 5.2, the models also included other factors identified as important for the formation and dissolution of female-headed families with children. We focus on the economic restructuring measures and their relationship with change in female-headed families in nonmetro counties. A superscript b beside a coefficient indicates that the estimated coefficients are statistically different over the two decades within residence area.

Only three of the restructuring measures had statistically significant and similar effects in both models for nonmetro counties. An increase in total employment in a county was associated with slower growth in female-headed families with children, as were a total gain in construction employment and an increase in the percentage of women employed part-time. An increase in the percentage of men employed part-time in a county was associated with faster growth in female-headed families with children in both decades, but the effect was stronger from 1990 to 2000. Increases in the availability of men relative to women were associated with slower growth in female-headed families with children in both decades, although the effect was weaker in 1990 to 2000.

Three measures were statistically significant in the 1980 to 1990 decade, but not in the 1990 to 2000 model. Gains in women's employment overall and total gain in poor jobs (suggesting an increase in poor jobs among men) were associated with faster growth in female-headed families with children from 1980 to 1990. During the 1980s, a period of relative economic distress, single mothers may have been entering the labor force to support their families following a divorce or nonmarital birth. The increase in poor jobs for men (relative to women) may have encouraged marital dissolution due to economic stress or deterred marriage or cohabitation for economic reasons. Gains in professional services jobs for women in a county were associated with slower growth in female-headed families from 1980 to 1990, but not 1990 to 2000, perhaps contributing to increased family stability during the 1980s, a time of economic stress.

In the 1990 to 2000 decade, economic conditions had improved in the economy, compared to the prior decade. In this decade of relative economic growth, changes in women's industry of employment were unrelated to changes in the percentage of female-headed families with children. The quality of jobs did matter, however. An increase in the median income for women employed full-time, full-year was associated with faster growth in the percentage of female-headed families with children. An increase in the percentage of women employed part-time continued to be associated with slower growth in female-headed families with children. These findings suggest that women's part-time employment contributes to stability of married-couple families, and higher earnings for women provide the resources necessary to leave unhappy unions or for single mothers to establish their own households.

These results suggest consistency in some of the influences of economic restructuring on the change in female-headed families with children, but also change between the two decades. Generally, these findings indicate that growth in employment overall, and in construction jobs in counties, contributes to family stability, as does an increase in the percentage of women employed part-time. Stronger local economies seem to deter the formation and encourage the end of female-headed families. An increase in the percentage of men employed part-time, an indicator of poorer job prospects for men, seems to encourage the formation of female-headed families.

The findings from these multivariate models indicate that changes in county economies are associated with patterns of change in female-headed families with children. It is important to recall that counties experience economic restructuring differently. Some nonmetro counties, especially those near metro areas, grew during both decades. Some experienced economic decline in both decades, while others followed the national pattern of economic stress in the 1980s and relative prosperity during the 1990s.

The differences in the models for each decade suggest that in periods of economic decline and when women do well relative to men, local economic gains for women are important for female-headed family formation and dissolution. In both decades, growth in employment overall may improve the stability of existing relationships as the number of jobs increases for men and women. The caveat is that these jobs need to be good jobs. Counties with increases in men's part-time employment experienced faster growth in female-headed families with children in both decades.

Discussion and Conclusions

The prevalence of female-headed families with children grew and the gap between metro and nonmetro areas in female-headship declined from 1980 to 2000. By 2000, 19 percent of nonmetro families with children were female-headed, a 7-percentage-point increase from 1980. However, there was substantial variation across counties in the prevalence of female-headed families with children. The model results suggest that economic restructuring has combined with an increasing acceptance of less traditional family forms to reduce the metro-nonmetro difference in prevalence of female-headed families with children.

The economic decline in the late 2000s is likely to affect family formation decisions as economic changes did in past years. The recession beginning in 2008 appears to have affected men's employment more than women's, resulting in proportionally more job losses and higher unemployment for men than women (see Bureau of Labor Statistics 2010), which may contribute to the growth in female-headed families with children. Future research should continue to investigate the influence of economic restructuring during the 2000s and beyond. At this writing, the Census 2010 enumeration is just beginning. These and other data will continue to inform our understanding of the complex interplay between economic restructuring and changes in family structure across the United States.

If the relationships identified in our analysis persist, economic restructuring will continue to be associated with the pace of growth in female-headed families with children. In particular, growth in poor jobs and part-time work for men will be associated with faster growth in female-headed families with children, while growth in employment overall and in jobs such as construction tends to slow the growth in female-headed families with children. The relationship of women's job growth to female-headed families with children changed from the 1980s to the 1990s, suggesting the importance of considering gains in employment for women under different economic conditions. From a policy perspective, these findings suggest four contributions.

First, continued economic restructuring that creates unemployment or poor-quality jobs for men is likely to further undermine family stability, while growth in full-time jobs (which are more likely to offer better wages and benefits) seems to contribute to traditional family formation and stability. Increases in part-time work had different effects for men and women. Increases in part-time work for men were associated with faster growth in female-headed families with children, while increases in the percentage of women working part-time were associated with slower growth in these families. Counties with increases in part-time employment may be experiencing a restructuring of work to include more nonstandard work relationships (McLaughlin and Coleman-Jensen 2008). An increase in part-time work would generally be considered a decline in job quality and would be associated with reduced incomes and availability of benefits. Part-time jobs may provide preferred employment for married or cohabiting women when they have children and their partners are employed, increasing family stability.

Second, given the persistence of gender segregation of jobs and differential effects by gender, it is important to consider men's and women's employment separately. This is essential as localities consider economic development through job attraction, retention and expansion of existing industries, or local entrepreneurship initiatives, and as states craft economic development initiatives. Unfortunately, forces of globalization and declines in worker power in the United States related to economic restructuring and growth in nonstandard work and poor-quality jobs (McLaughlin and Coleman-Jensen 2008) leave communities feeling as though they have little control over the local economy.

Third, the county-level analysis indicates the counties and states that have the highest prevalence of female-headed families also had the fastest growth in those families. These counties and states can use this information to consider improving and expanding services and programs for families with children, thus improving the quality of life of all families; however, the focus must be on those most at risk of poverty and/or family instability. Counties and states with a smaller share of female-headed families with children, or where poverty among these families is low, may provide insight into successful strategies and conditions that support all families.

Finally, the extraordinarily high poverty among female-headed families with children in nonmetro areas is well documented (Snyder, McLaughlin, and Findeis 2006), as are the barriers to improving well-being that these families face (Mills and Hazarika 2003). These barriers include limited availability of good jobs for women, rental housing, child care, and public transportation (Evans and English 2002; Mills and Hazarika 2003; Ward and Turner 2007). If women are leaving abusive relationships, these barriers may be even greater due to limited or no availability of domestic violence counseling or safe houses (Feyen 2001; Websdale 1998). Policies, to this point, seem to have little influence on improving the circumstances of female-headed families with children.

Federal policies often are not intended to reduce inequality across localities, and typically they do not provide flexibility to account for differences in local conditions. Places with the fewest resources of their own often have the largest barriers to improving the well-being of families. The devolution of responsibility for many policies from the federal to local levels and the continued local responsibility for provision of many services that support families suggest that the places with the fewest resources continue to have the most limited ability to meet often greater local needs.

U.S. policy makers at all levels need to recognize that female-headed families with children make up one-fifth of families with children and that these families are an integral and growing part of modern U.S. society in nonmetro and metro areas. Regardless of how national, state, or local decision makers perceive female-headed families with children, attention must turn to improving the well-being of these and all families. The future of U.S. society hinges on strong families with children, whether headed by married couples, cohabiting partners, single women, or single men. Every policy, but especially those related to economic restructuring and employment quality, education, taxation, welfare, and health insurance, should be evaluated with improving the well-being of all families and children in mind.

Table 5.1 Percentage of families with children that are headed by women, 1980, 1990, and 2000

	1980	1990	2000
Nonmetro	12.1	16.1	19.3
Metro	17.5	19.5	21.3

NOTE: 1980 definition of metro, U.S. Census of Population Summary Files. Data are weighted to reflect the population distribution of families with children.

Table 5.2 Weighted least squares regression models of change in percentage of female-headed families with children, 1980 to 1990 and 1990 to 2000

Variable description (all are difference measures unless indicated otherwise)	Total counties (n = 3,061)		Nonmetro counties (n = 2,353)		Metro counties (n = 708)	
	1980 to 1990	1990 to 2000	1980 to 1990	1990 to 2000	1980 to 1990	1990 to 2000
Intercept	7.933***	3.855***b	5.180***	4.524***	8.891*	1.875
Metro in 1980	0.031	-0.039	—	—	—	—
Economic restructuring measures						
Difference in total employed	-0.267***	-0.087***b	-0.166***	-0.046*	-0.304***	-0.100***b
Gain in women's employment	6.574***	3.447*	2.761***c	-0.434	13.957***	3.212 b
Gain in poor jobs	-0.938	0.149	-0.013c	1.280	-3.840*	-0.422
Gain in total manufacturing	-0.233	-0.086	-0.120	0.129	-1.124	-0.785
Gain in professional services	-6.365***	-1.209b	-2.854***c	-0.792b	-11.992***	-1.323b
Gain in FIRE	0.185	-0.247	-0.129	-0.198	1.331	0.143
Gain in construction	0.003	-0.021	0.009	-0.017	0.005	-0.162
Gain in public administration	-0.077	0.341	-0.308	0.229 b	0.526	1.005
Gain in wholesale trade	-0.028	-0.004	0.003	-0.018	0.183	0.427
Total gain in poor jobs	0.614	1.913**	1.065*	0.727	0.493	4.132*
Total gain in total manufacturing	-0.214	-1.858***b	0.148	-0.586c	0.434	-2.764***b
Total gain in professional services	-2.110***	-5.213***b	-0.722c	-0.737c	-3.638***	-5.094***
Total gain in FIRE	-0.030	0.413	-0.271	0.266	0.395	0.402
Total gain in construction	-1.656***	-1.499***	-0.787***c	-1.328***	-2.124***	-0.868
Total gain in public administration	-0.105	0.124	-0.041	0.137	-0.349	-0.138
Total gain in wholesale trade	-0.079	0.031	-0.179	-0.007	0.017	0.671
Percent women employed part-time	-0.041**	-0.036*	-0.032*	-0.069***c	0.009	0.039
Percent men employed part-time	0.039**	0.108***b	0.054***	0.097***b	0.024	0.080*
Difference in median income for women working full-time, full-year in 1989 dollars ($000)	-0.359***	0.095***b	-0.063c	0.129***b	-0.425***	0.059b

Table 5.2 (continued)

Variable description (all are difference measures unless indicated otherwise)	Total counties (n = 3,061)		Nonmetro counties (n = 2,353)		Metro counties (n = 708)	
	1980 to 1990	1990 to 2000	1980 to 1990	1990 to 2000	1980 to 1990	1990 to 2000
Family traditionalism						
South	-0.404***	0.993***[b]	-0.230	0.633***[b]	-0.537**	1.012***[b]
Percent Catholic[a]	-0.028***	0.019***[b]	-0.012[c]	0.005	-0.031***	0.020**[b]
Percent fundamental Protestant[a]	-0.028	-0.007	-0.018	-0.007	-0.035	0.010
Percent Mormon[a]	0.069	0.116**	0.004	0.008[c]	0.114	0.257***
Percent rural	-0.009	0.004	0.008	0.009*	-0.005	0.010
Marital incentives and opportunities						
Percent high school dropout	-0.126***	-0.043*[b]	0.016[c]	0.038[c]	-0.188***	-0.117**
Percent college graduates	-0.205***	-0.214***	-0.118***	-0.106**[c]	-0.146**	-0.221***
Difference in sex ratio (15 to 59 males to females)	-7.358***	-4.682***[b]	-6.467***	-3.057***[b,c]	-9.572***	-6.835***
Difference in welfare benefits[a]	0.004***	0.007***	0.007***	0.004*	0.006**	0.009***
Demographic control variables						
Percent black base year	0.044***	-0.015***[b]	0.091***[c]	0.014**[b,c]	0.025***	-0.026***[b]
Percent black	0.262***	0.306***[b]	0.351***	0.215***[b,c]	0.302***	0.332***
Percent Hispanic	-0.192***	-0.065***[b]	-0.094**	-0.117***[c]	-0.104**	-0.029
Log population	-0.224	-1.341***[b]	-1.021*	-1.520**	-0.263	-1.914**
Models are weighted by number of families with children in a county divided by mean number of families with children across all counties						
Adjusted R²	0.619	0.500	0.390	0.182	0.726	0.645

NOTE: Most data are from the 1980, 1990 and 2000 Summary Files of the U.S. Census of Population and Housing.

[a] The religious adherents data are from the Churches and Church Membership in the U.S. data, 1980, 1990, and Religious Congregations and Membership Study, 2000, from Association of Religion Data Archives. The AFDC/TANF data are from the House Ways and Means Committee Report, SECTION 7—TEMPORARY ASSISTANCE FOR NEEDY FAMILIES, table 7–13.

[b] Coefficients are different over time within residence type (total, nonmetro, metro), p ≤ .05.

[c] Nonmetro and metro coefficients are statistically different in the same decade, p ≤ .05.

Notes

1. The gain in women's employment from 1980 to 1990 is calculated as [(1990 women's employment / 1980 women's employment) divided by (1990 total employment / 1980 total employment)]. A value of one or greater indicates an increase in the share of employment held by women.

PATTERNS OF FAMILY FORMATION AND DISSOLUTION IN RURAL AMERICA AND IMPLICATIONS FOR WELL-BEING

ANASTASIA SNYDER

The link between social and economic change at the macro level and the evolution of rural families has long been recognized by rural scholars (Smith and Coward 1981; Wilkinson 1984). Rural family research in this area has highlighted the association between a declining rural economy and a shift away from traditional family structure, which in turn promotes worse economic outcomes for families and children (Fuguitt, Brown, and Beale 1989; Lichter and McLaughlin 1995; MacTavish and Salamon 2003b; McLaughlin, Gardner, and Lichter 1999). The results are rural family structure and formation patterns that are similar to those in urban areas. Residential differences in two-parent and single-parent family structure once were large but are narrowing (Snyder and McLaughlin 2004), and contemporary family behaviors, such as cohabitation and nonmarital childbearing, are now significant features of rural family life (D. Albrecht and C. Albrecht 2004; Snyder, Brown, and Condo 2004).

Despite the shift away from traditional family structure among rural populations, important differences persist concerning marriage. Rural women remain more likely to marry as both a first-union type and a first-birth context, are more likely to marry after a nonmarital conception, and marry approximately one year earlier than nonrural women (D. Albrecht and C. Albrecht 2004; Snyder et al. 2004). This distinct marriage pattern among rural women is especially interesting because it is occurring at a time when prominent family scholars are noting a society-wide decline in the importance of marriage in adult lives (Amato et al. 2007; Cherlin 2004), and when the economic context in nonmetropolitan (nonmetro) areas is contributing to the destabilization of families (McLaughlin, Gardner, and Lichter 1999). Rural women's affinity for marriage could reveal persistent and distinct family values, an adaptive response to rural economic contexts, or a combination of the two.

This chapter focuses on rural women's divorce and remarriage patterns as a lens to better understand rural families in the context of changing social norms and economic realities. Prior studies have already examined rural women's first-marriage formation experiences; here I build on that work by first studying the proportion of rural women's lives spent in the married state. Then I turn my attention to divorce and remarriage outcomes as a way to better understand the role of marriage in rural women's lives.

Recent Family Changes

Historically, rural and nonmetro families engaged in more traditional behaviors, including earlier marriage and childbearing and larger family sizes, and had a larger percentage of two-parent families (D. Brown 1981; Fuguitt, Brown, and Beale 1989; Heaton, Lichter, and Amoeteng 1989; Myers and Hastings 1995). Over time, rural families have experienced a trend away from more traditional family structure and toward female-headed families, which is viewed as evidence of a shift toward more mainstream family structure in nonmetro areas (Snyder and McLaughlin 2004).

In recent years, however, several studies of more contemporary family forms (nonmarital cohabitation and childbearing) find that despite these changes, rural women maintain a preference for marriage, and that this difference distinguishes rural women from others (D. Albrecht and C. Albrecht 2004; Snyder 2006; Snyder et al. 2004a). That this preference for marriage is occurring at a time when other evidence suggests a societal-wide decline in the importance of marriage in adult lives (as evidenced by delays in age at first marriage, a separation of marriage from childbearing, high divorce rates, and alternatives to marriage, such as cohabitation) makes this finding all the more significant (Amato et al. 2007; Cherlin 2004). A more complete story of rural women's marital behavior, and possible explanations for differences, can only be understood by expanding studies beyond a focus on first-marriage timing to other marriage-related behaviors.

When considering divorce, for example, very little is known about differences between rural and urban populations. Overall, approximately 40 percent of all first marriages will end in divorce within fifteen years (Bramlett and Mosher 2002), and while nonmetro women are less likely to ever divorce (Myers and Hastings 1995), overall rural and urban differences in divorce patterns are unknown. In addition, examining remarriage after a divorce can shed some light on marriage preferences. High divorce rates have contributed to a rise in remarriage rates (Cherlin 1992), although in the past twenty years the odds of remarriage after a first divorce have declined in the United States (Bramlett and Mosher 2002), but again residential differences are unknown. To my knowledge no studies have examined divorce and remarriage patterns among nonmetro populations in recent years. This study adds to that knowledge, with the goal of understanding more about the uniqueness of rural women's marital behaviors.

Family Structure and Economic Conditions

The economic conditions in many rural and nonmetro areas present considerable challenges to the individuals and families who live there. At the contextual level, prevailing economic conditions—including lower wages, economic restructuring, and job loss—are associated with changing family structure and have contributed to the rise in female-headed families (Albrecht 1998; Lichter and McLaughlin 1995; McLaughlin, Gardner, and Lichter 1999). At the family level, economic stress resulting from a changing rural economy contributes to marital instability among rural families (Conger and Elder 1994b). These studies suggest that economic conditions in rural America destabilize families and have contributed to the shift away from a two-parent family structure to female-headed and other family types that contain children.

At the same time, however, the economic conditions faced by rural and non-metro female-headed families are even worse. Poverty among all rural female-headed families is high compared to other family types (Snyder and McLaughlin 2006), and rural working women and mothers face poverty-level wages, and barriers to employment such as a lack of child care (Blau 2001; Gordon and Chase-Lansdale 2001; Lichter and Jensen 2002; McLaughlin and Perman 1991; Rural Sociological Society Task Force 1993; Tickamyer and Bokemeier 1988), that should deter single parenthood. Thus, the rural economic context threatens traditional family stability, but also makes female headship even more difficult to sustain without strategies that rely on other forms of economic support.

Indeed, half of all nonmetro female-headed families receive at least one form of public assistance (Snyder and McLaughlin 2006), and one-fourth live in alternative arrangements that increase their household income and reduce poverty (Snyder, McLaughlin, and Findeis 2006). Thus, in this context marriage provides something of an economic safety net for families with children. Two adults have greater potential than one to work more hours and increase household income. Compared to female-headed and cohabiting households with children in nonmetro areas, married-couple families with children have higher household income, reduced poverty, and less receipt of all forms of public assistance (Snyder and McLaughlin 2006).

In sum, prior studies suggest that the rural economic context makes family life difficult, although it is not clear whether these conditions should promote family instability or encourage marriage. By examining divorce and remarriage patterns, we can investigate both possibilities.

Data and Methods

Data from the 2002 cycle of the National Survey of Family Growth (NSFG) are used to examine divorce and remarriage patterns among metropolitan (metro) and nonmetro women. The NSFG is collected by the National Center for Health Statistics and is a national probability sample of 7,463 women age fifteen to forty-five in 2002. It was designed primarily to examine fertility-related health of American women, but it also contains extensive retrospective information about union formation and dissolution behavior. These retrospective data are used to examine metro-nonmetro differences in (1) the amount of women's lives spent in the married state, (2) the timing of first divorce, and (3) the timing of remarriage after a first divorce. All analyses in this study are weighted, making them representative of U.S. women age fifteen to forty-five in 2002.[1]

Measures

Relevant individual and family background variables are used to examine divorce and remarriage among metro and nonmetro women. Although the 2002 NSFG has extensive and detailed measures of the timing of all union formation and dissolution experiences of women, it does not include good measures of economic context or individual values and attitudes. Instead, these are measured indirectly through individual and family background character-istics, which are closely tied to family behavior (Casper and Bianchi 2002).

OUTCOME VARIABLES

Three outcomes are examined in this study. The first is a measure that describes the percent of *months spent in the married state.* The second is a dichotomous measure of exiting a marriage via *divorce,* among women who have ever married. The third is a dichotomous measure of *remarriage* among women who have ever experienced a first divorce.

INDEPENDENT VARIABLES

Geographic residence is the main independent variable of interest. The geographic residence measure is based on the U.S. Census classification of counties as metro or nonmetro in 2002. Metro residence is further delineated into suburban metro and central city metro residence. In addition, individual characteristics, family behaviors, and family background characteristics are included in the multivariate models.[2]

Findings

DESCRIPTIVE RESULTS

Table 6.1 describes the marital status of women age twenty to forty-five in 2002. Overall, slightly more than half of the women in the sample were married, almost 15 percent were divorced or separated, and 31 percent were never married. Slightly over two-thirds (69 percent) had ever been married. A slightly higher percentage of nonmetro women had ever been married in 2002 (74 percent), which is explained by a higher percentage married (58 percent) and divorced or separated (16 percent). A similar percentage of suburban women had ever been married in 2002, although a slightly higher percentage were currently married and a slightly smaller share were currently divorced or separated. A much smaller share of central city women had ever been married (60 percent) or were currently married (45 percent).

Table 6.2 provides the percentage of months women in nonmetro, central city, and suburban areas spent single, married, and cohabiting. Overall, women spent 49 percent of their months married. Comparing across residence areas reveals that nonmetro women spend a significantly larger percentage of their months married compared to other women—59 percent compared to 51 percent for central city women and 39 percent for suburban women. When the months spent cohabiting are added to those spent married, table 6.2 shows that even though nonmetro women spend a smaller percentage of their months in unmarried cohabiting relationships (11 percent compared to 16 percent for central city women and 11 percent for suburban women), they still spend a significantly smaller share of their months single and unattached. Only 30 percent of nonmetro women's months are spent single, compared to 46 percent of central city women and 38 percent of suburban women. Nonmetro women spend a larger portion of their lives married, and in any type of union, and a smaller percentage single and unattached.

Figure 6.1 presents life table estimates of the cumulative proportion exiting first marriage to divorce within fifteen years of the date of first marriage. As shown, the timing of first divorce does not differ by residence area during the first five to six years following a first marriage. By year seven a higher proportion of women from central city metro areas, and a lower proportion of women from suburban and nonmetro areas, have divorced, although these differences are neither large nor practically significant. Residential differences are large and noticeable, however, when examining entrance into a second marriage in figure 6.2. Here we see clear evidence that rural women make quicker transitions to a second marriage. Starting at two years after the dissolution of a first marriage, a larger cumulative proportion of nonmetro women have remarried for every year observed up to fifteen years. Central city women have the lowest cumulative proportion remarrying for every year observed. In sum, the findings in tables 6.1 and 6.2 and figures 6.1 and 6.2 provide descriptive evidence of nonmetro women's propensity toward marriage. A larger percentage of nonmetro women were ever married in 2002, they spent a larger percentage of their lives married, and a larger cumulative proportion remarried in every year following a first divorce.

Next, table 6.3 presents multivariate discrete-time event history models examining the odds of a first divorce, and a first remarriage, with the goal of determining differences by central city, suburban, and nonmetro women. The "Divorce" column of table 6.3 examines the odds of divorce from a first marriage. Parameter estimates and odds ratios are reported. Women in central city and suburban areas have higher odds of divorcing, controlling for individual characteristics, family behaviors, and family background characteristics. Central city and suburban women are 20–30 percent more likely to divorce compared to nonmetro women.

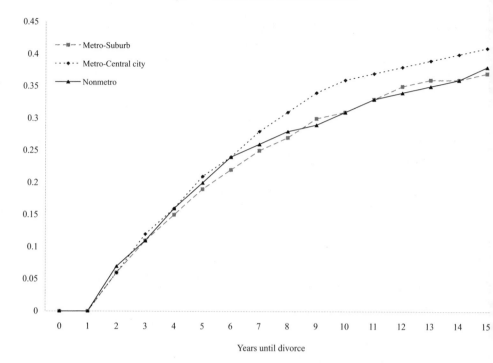

FIG. 6.1   Life table estimates of the cumulative proportion of women exiting first marriage to divorce, by residence

Other variables in the model are also strongly associated with odds of divorce, in the expected direction. Notably, a woman's higher human capital, measured by high school education and full-time employment, increases the odds of divorce, as do some family behaviors. Each year a first marriage is delayed reduces the odds of divorce by approximately 15 percent; a nonmarital birth increases the odds of divorce by 40 percent; and cohabiting prior to marriage nearly quadruples the odds of divorce. Having a college-educated mother increases the odds of divorce, while having a college-educated father slightly lowers the odds of divorce.

The "Remarriage" column in table 6.3 examines the odds of remarriage following the dissolution of a first marriage, and again parameter estimates and odds ratios are reported. Nonmetro women are also distinct in this outcome—suburban and central city women have significantly lower odds of remarriage, ranging from about 20–30 percent lower compared to nonmetro women, controlling for the same characteristics in the model predicting divorce. Again, some interesting control variables are associated with the odds of remarriage, notably family behaviors. Having a first nonmarital birth does not promote marriage—we already saw how this family experience increased

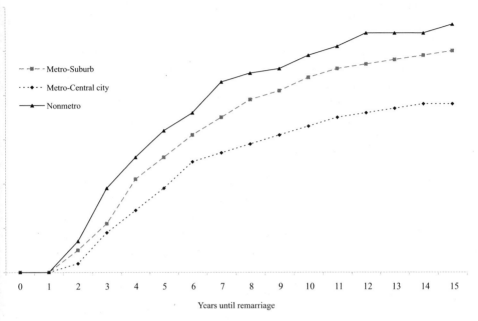

— -■- - Metro-Suburb

· · · ◆ · · Metro-Central city

—▲— Nonmetro

Years until remarriage

FIG. 6.2   Life table estimates of the cumulative proportion of women entering second marriage, by residence

the odds of divorce, and here it decreases the odds of remarriage by approximately 22 percent. Finally, where fathers' higher socioeconomic status raises the odds of remarriage, mothers' socioeconomic status is not associated with odds of remarriage.

These models provide evidence of nonmetro women's affinity for marriage, as evidenced by their lower odds of divorce and propensity for remarriage. These findings, in combination with the descriptive results presented earlier, suggest that marriage remains an important family context for nonmetro women, and more so than for women in suburban or central city areas.

Conclusions

Despite a worsening socioeconomic context in rural America that should destabilize families, nonmetro women retain a preference for marriage. The results from this study provide evidence for more traditional family behavior among nonmetro women in several domains related to marriage. Compared to suburban metro and central city metro women, nonmetro women spend a significantly larger percentage of their lives in the married state, have lower odds of divorce from a first marriage, remarry more quickly following the end of a first marriage, and have higher odds of remarriage.

These findings are intriguing and build on prior studies demonstrating nonmetro women's affinity for marriage. Unfortunately, data limitations in the 2002 NSFG only allow us to control for individual characteristics, family behaviors, and family background characteristics. Even though these are thought to be indirect measures of context and values (Casper and Bianchi 2002), these results cannot determine the relative importance of social norms or economic context. These findings can, however, be placed in the context of other related studies to help us understand their significance.

One explanation for the unique marriage behavior among nonmetro women could be the availability of "marriageable men" in nonmetro areas. Prior studies, however, suggest that this is unlikely, given the declining economic attractiveness of men in general (Oppenheimer 1997; W. Wilson 1996), and nonmetro men in particular (Jensen et al. 1999). Transitions to marriage are generally lower in areas with smaller proportions of economically attractive men (Lichter, Kephart, et al. 1992; W. Wilson 1996), which makes these findings even more unexpected. The economic context of nonmetro areas would suggest a decline in the prevalence of marriage, which is contrary to the results of this study.

Social explanations for family behaviors posit that nonmetro individuals continue to hold more traditional family values, and that these values would be translated into more traditional family behaviors more often if the economic conditions in nonmetro areas did not disrupt the fulfillment of these values (Struthers and Bokemeier 2000). This is a possible explanation for the steady rise in the proportion of rural female-headed households in recent decades. It is also possible that the unique marital behavior observed among nonmetro women stems in part from a challenging economic context. The notion of "enforceable trust" comes from studies that seek to understand, given the current social and economic context in the United States, not why marriage has declined in recent decades, but rather why such a high percentage of the population (90 percent) will still ever marry (Cherlin 2004). The idea is that marriage provides a safety net for families in economically challenging situations, and by entering marriage the couple is making a public statement about future expectations of emotional and economic support not made by entering other union types, such as cohabitation. Given the economic challenges women face as single parents in rural areas, their preference for marriage may be one strategy that provides greater economic stability for themselves and their children, and also allows for the fulfillment of persistent traditional values noted in prior studies of rural populations (Struthers and Bokemeier 2000a).

This study also provides some evidence that policies aimed at improving the macroeconomic context in rural America could also help promote marriage. Rural populations clearly favor marriage, which suggests that the "deinstitutionalization" of marriage in recent decades (Cherlin 2004) has not occurred in rural America to the extent that it has elsewhere. Thus, improving the rural economic context has potentially widespread implications for promoting the economic and social well-being of rural families and children.

Table 6.1 Marital status of women age twenty to forty-five in 2002

	All	Nonmetro	Central city	Suburban
Percent distribution	100.0	17.7	33.3	49.0
Marital status in 2002				
Married	54.4	57.5	44.8	60.0
Divorced/separated	13.9	16.3	14.1	13.0
Widowed	0.5	0.6	0.7	0.4
Never married	31.2	25.6	40.4	26.6
Ever married	68.9	74.4	59.6	73.4

NOTE: n = 6,493 women age twenty to forty-five in 2002, weighted frequencies.
SOURCE: 2002 National Survey of Family Growth (NSFG).

Table 6.2 Percent months spent single, married, and cohabiting

	All	Nonmetro	Central city	Suburban
Single	39.1	30.2	46.0	37.9
Married	48.6	59.2	38.9	50.9
Cohabiting	12.3	10.6	15.1	11.2

NOTE: Mean age for sample is 34.2 overall, 34.6 central city, 33.7 suburban, 34.1 nonmetro. Sample restricted to those twenty and older, includes 957,567 person-month, weighted frequencies.
SOURCE: 2002 National Survey of Family Growth (NSFG).

Table 6.3 Discrete-time logistic regression analyses predicting divorce and remarriage: Parameter estimates and odds ratios

Independent variables	Divorce		Remarriage	
	β	$e^{β}$	β	$e^{β}$
Intercept	−1.57	—	−4.00	—
Time—years in sample	0.12	1.12	0.21	1.24
Residence (nonmetro omitted)				
Suburban	0.17	1.18	−0.19	0.83
Central city	0.25	1.29	−0.33	0.72
Race (non-Hispanic white omitted)				
Non-Hispanic black	0.25	1.29	−0.82	0.44
Hispanic	0.03*	1.03	−0.37	0.69
Other racial/ethnic group	0.28	1.32	−0.75	0.47
Age at interview (over 35 omitted)				
25 and younger	−0.12*	0.89	0.81	2.24
26–35	0.15	1.16	0.71	2.03
Foreign born	−0.07	0.93	0.21	1.24
Age at first marriage	−0.17	0.84	−0.05	0.95
Ever cohabited	1.35	3.87	0.20	1.22
First birth nonmarital	0.35	1.42	−0.25	0.78
High school education	0.21	1.24	0.33	1.39
Full-time work	1.34	3.81	1.13	3.11
Mother's employment in childhood (full-time omitted)				
Part-time	−0.17	0.84	−0.04	0.96*
Did not work	−0.10	0.91	0.07	1.07*
Mother college educated	0.17	1.18	0.01	1.00*
Father college educated	−0.06	0.94	0.32	1.38
Intact family during childhood	−0.12	0.88	−0.23	0.79
-2LL, (df)	9671.57, (17)		4508.74, (17)	
Pseudo R²	0.252		0.268	
N	81,945		33,819	

* Indicated not statistically significant at p ≤ .05 level.
SOURCE: 2002 National Survey of Family Growth (NSFG).

Notes

1. Three data files are constructed for this study, and all are restricted to women age twenty and older in 2002. The first is a person-month file that includes all respondents and is used to examine the percentage of women's months spent married (n = 957,567 person-months). The second file is organized in person-years and is used to examine exits from a first marriage to divorce. This file is restricted to women who ever experienced a first marriage (n = 81,945 person-years). The third is also organized in person years, is restricted to women who ever experienced a first marital dissolution (divorce or widowhood), and is used to examine entrance into remarriage (n = 33,819 person-years).

2. In the 2002 NSFG residence is measured at interview date, and since these analyses rely on retrospective reports of divorce and remarriage this structure presents a problem. The 1995 NSFG included a variable that researchers used to measure how long the respondent lived in the county of interview date, which allowed for numerous prior studies using those data to examine residential differences in the family behavior of interest at the time the behavior occurred (Brown and Lichter 2004; Brown and Snyder 2006; Lichter and Graefe 2001; Snyder, Brown, and Condo, 2004; Snyder 2006). The 2002 NSFG dropped this variable, so that it is only possible to measure residence in 2002, which is the measure used in this study. Despite the intuitive drawbacks of this residence measure, there is ample evidence from prior studies using the 1995 NSFG that the measure of residence described above will provide results that would be very similar to those based on a subsample for which residence at divorce or remarriage is certain. Two studies in particular (Brown and Snyder 2006; Snyder, Brown, and Condo 2004) conducted extensive sample selection analyses on several subsamples of the 1995 NSFG based on length of residence in nonmetro areas, and found that the analyses revealed similar union formation results. Two other studies (Albrecht and Albrecht 2004; Snyder 2006) conducted nearly identical analyses, with different measures of residence timing, and yielded the same conclusions regarding marital status outcomes following a nonmarital conception.

JOB CHARACTERISTICS AND
ECONOMIC SURVIVAL STRATEGIES

The Effect of Economic Restructuring and Marital Status in a Rural County

MARGARET K. NELSON

Over a decade ago, my colleague Joan Smith[1] and I set out to explore how families in a rural county in Vermont pieced together their daily survival strategies. We had in mind an image of something that we called "patching it together"—a notion about how the members of these households could use all the varied resources of the rural locale to sustain themselves. And, in an uncharacteristic fit of nostalgia, we assumed that one of Joan's neighbors—a man who used his tractor to plow her driveway in the winter and to cut the hay on her fields in the summer—could serve as a template for the creative ways in which rural folk joined together participation in the regular labor force, informal economic activities, self-provisioning, and practices like bartering with neighbors to create a life that, if not rich in economic resources, was rich in its links to the land and the community.

And so we set off to find more such families. What we found was entirely different from what we had predicted. We found that the varied survival strategy enjoyed by Joan's neighbor was a "privilege" or "benefit" available not to those who were marginal to the formal economy but, conversely and surprisingly, preserved for those who were most firmly linked to the waged labor force and, indeed, to those linked to the labor force through good employment. What we also found was that as economic restructuring made its way through the area in Vermont we call Coolidge County,[2] it was replacing good jobs with bad ones and thus systematically undermining the capacity of families to get by through an elaborate and multifaceted survival strategy, thereby weakening their ability to ensure the well-being of household members.

To explore these findings, I describe Coolidge County and its particular form of economic restructuring. I then turn to two sets of comparative data. I first compare the survival strategies of married-couple households among what we call "good job" and "bad job" households and demonstrate how both sets of strategies emerge from, and depend on, the household's link to the waged labor force. In the next section I compare the survival strategies of single-mother households to those in married-couple households.

Economic Restructuring in Coolidge County

Driving the back roads of Coolidge County, Vermont, one may get the impression that this is an area that escaped the second half of the twentieth century. This statistically rural county still boasts family farms, sparsely settled woodlands, and quaint villages with white steeples and town greens. Broad vistas suggest a land left behind, and indeed, it is partly this image that is marketed to tourists who visit the county as well as to urban dwellers who find the "made in Vermont" seal an attractive incentive for buying a product. But this image conceals the reality of how Coolidge County residents earn a living, a reality which is more in keeping with the rest of the country than a first impression might suggest.

This has not been the case until quite recently. In 1960 the economy of Coolidge County could not have looked more different from that of an urban industrial center or, indeed, from that of the United States taken as a whole. Three measures of this difference are especially relevant to the argument of this chapter. First, in 1960 over a quarter of the population found employment in the traditional rural sectors of farming, forestry, and fishing, while less than a fifth held jobs in manufacturing.[3] By way of contrast, in urban areas nationally over a quarter of the population was engaged in manufacturing, while only 7 percent were in farming, forestry, and fishing. Second, although in 1960 Coolidge County women were almost as likely as those in urban areas to enter the labor force (presumably to help support the family farm),[4] Coolidge County *men* not only had low labor force participation rates (73 percent), but also demonstrated a relatively strong aversion to wage and salary work (with less than 61 percent so employed); in comparison, almost 79 percent of men in urban areas were in the labor force, and 78 percent of these men held down a waged or salaried job. Third, Coolidge County families were large and likely to include both parents, especially in comparison with those in urban areas, where smaller families and more single-parent families prevailed.

By the end of the twentieth century, these—as well as other—differences had disappeared and even reversed direction. Agricultural employment had dropped to less than a tenth of the labor force, and the level of manufacturing was almost precisely the same as it was for the nation as a whole. The labor force participation rates of *both* men and women in Coolidge County exceeded those of men and women elsewhere, and the proportions of labor force participants who were wage and salary workers were quite similar to those elsewhere. In addition, the proportion of female-headed households (5 percent of those with children) was approaching, even if it had not yet met, the proportion in the nation as a whole (7 percent of those with children).

Between 1960 and 2000, then, Coolidge County appeared to be joining the modern age. However, what appears to be convergence is actually the result of two very different and overlapping waves of change (see table 7.1).

During the first period (roughly 1960 to 1980), Coolidge County actually moved in the *opposite* direction from the rest of the country in at least one important respect: just as urban areas were beginning to deindustrialize, Coolidge County was experiencing a rapid period of both a decline in agricultural activity (from 26 percent in 1960 to 12 percent in 1980) and an intensive period of industrialization that was materializing by 1960 and that escalated for the next two decades. Between 1960 and 1980, the proportion of the labor force employed in manufacturing increased from under 20 to over 22 percent. This period was a good one for the residents of Coolidge County, and it was especially good for male labor force participants, who saw their incomes rise both relative to men in other areas and relative to women in the county. But the promises of industrialization were short-lived.

During the second period of change (roughly 1980 to the present), three significant shifts in the economy occurred. First, after two decades of growth, the proportion of the labor force in manufacturing dropped to 17 percent (below the 1960 level) in 1990 and then down to 14 percent in 2000; in the next five years it dropped further still, to 9 percent in 2005, which was well below the level in the United States as a whole. During the more recent past, then, some firms that had been in Coolidge County for a long time or had located there during the "boom" years moved on to find an even cheaper labor force (Duncan 1992; Gorham 1992); other firms started to downsize and rely on outsourcing (Falk and Lyson 1991; Falk, Talley, and Rankin 1993). Indeed, even as recently as 2006 one of the last remaining large manufacturing firms announced that it too was closing its doors and laying off its workforce of 182, and a second firm closed temporarily awaiting purchase by a new owner.

Second, while the proportion of the labor force in manufacturing was declining, a number of new, locally owned firms started up, and they brought with them a change in the *character* of manufacturing employment. The average size of manufacturing firms dropped precipitously, from sixty-three employees in 1980 to twenty-eight employees in 1993, where it remained until 2004 (U.S. Department of Commerce selected years). This change is significant because smaller firms are less likely than larger ones to offer health insurance, vacations, paid personal leaves, and decent wages (Lobao and Schulman 1991; Stolzenberg 1978; Weissman and Epstein 1994). Third, the service sector—notorious for part-time work and low wages—continued its steady growth: by 1990 more than 37 percent of all labor force participants found employment there; by 2000 this number had risen to 46 percent. And while concentration in the service sector was a consistent feature of women's employment as early as 1960, in the years that followed the proportion of men in the service sector increased substantially. Finally, we might note that although it does not represent a shift in direction, during the 1980s women's employment continued to grow; by 1990 women made up a full 46 percent of the total labor force, and by 2000 they made up 47 percent.

In short, Coolidge County, like other rural areas, was experiencing a change in the distribution of workers across various sectors of the economy, a transformation of the character of employment held by those workers, and alterations in the nature of the workforce itself.

Research in Coolidge County: Methods and Definitions

To investigate the meanings of these changes for families, I explore three sets of data. For the analysis of married-couple families, Joan Smith and I collected data (between 1991 and 1992) in two ways: we conducted a random survey of the population (n = 358) over the telephone, from which a subset of 158 households was drawn that met the criteria for inclusion in the study (see below);[5] we also conducted in-depth, face-to-face interviews with a snowball sample of 117 individuals representing 81 different working-class households.[6] For the analysis of single-mother families, I conducted interviews (between 1995 and 2000) with approximately 70 single mothers.[7]

In this chapter, I use the terms "household" and "family" interchangeably and in the manner in which they are used in conventional speech. However, I am not generalizing about all families. Given that this research was conducted in Vermont, it will come as no surprise that the members of the families studied are white. Second, because Joan Smith and I were interested in what happened to those in the *best* position to cope with a restructured labor market, for the initial survey we included only two-parent families, families in which at least one person had a job in the formal, waged labor force, and families in which both adults were eligible for employment (that is, neither adult had a disability and neither was retired). Two-thirds of those families had at least one child living at home; every single-mother family interviewed in the subsequent study had at least one child under the age of eighteen living with her at least part of the time.

Like the definition of a household, the definition of a survival strategy is quite straightforward. It has an empirical or grounded meaning: it refers to a specific set of economic activities developed to ensure daily life. More specifically, we focus on four distinct practices: *the dual earner strategy,* that is, whether (or not) a married-couple family sends both adults out to work; *moonlighting,* whether one or more of those workers hold down more than one job; *self-provisioning,* the extent to which the family takes care of its own needs with its own labor with respect to such activities as finding firewood or changing the oil in the car;[8] and *interhousehold exchanges,* the extent to which the family relies on others for help in the activities of daily living.

There is one more definition central to this analysis: a measure of the quality of the jobs held by household members. Although designed to capture shifts in employment practices within the county in which this research was conducted, the classification of households relies on a static, dichotomous measure that considers the household's *current* location in the restructured economy. The sample is divided into two groups inelegantly called *good job* and *bad job* households. The notions of good jobs and bad jobs are part of common parlance these days. To operationalize these concepts, we rely on two component features of employment: first, whether the job is full-time and year-round, and second, whether the workplace is bureaucratized, offers benefits like health insurance and vacation pay, and is stable in its employment patterns.

Married-Couple Households in Coolidge County

HOUSEHOLD STRATEGIES AND THE QUALITY OF EMPLOYMENT

Most people are *willing* to work hard, and most people do, in fact, work very hard—whether they live in good or bad job households. However, the good job and bad job families put together the components of a survival strategy in different ways, and bad job families face a unique set of problems when it comes to using their time and energy effectively.

Good job households almost invariably rely on a dual-earner strategy (87 percent) (see table 7.2). In 35 percent of the good job families, at least one earner engages in moonlighting, which, in these families, usually means owning an on-the-side business. For example, a man in a good job household works a regular, full-time job during the day and then comes home and does car repair for pay in his backyard in the evening; a woman in a good job household works at her regular job during the day and then, after dinner, spends time at her dressmaking business.

In addition to having intensive income-producing activities, the members of good job households also engage in both substantial and routine self-provisioning. Almost half of all good job households (in the snowball sample) either constructed their own homes or made extensive renovations on an existing one. We also asked people which of five more common activities, such as growing their own vegetables or changing the oil in the car, they had done during the previous year. A quarter of those in good job families said they had done four or more.

Finally, about half of all good job households make casual exchanges with other households on a regular basis (I bring you tomatoes from my garden; you bring me freshly baked brownies), and many good job households also engage in practices of barter and the negotiation of reduced rates for goods and services (I fix your car and, in exchange, you bring a cord of firewood). In sum, good job households are often busy places with a complex, multifaceted survival strategy.

Because bad job households have lower incomes than do good job households, it might be expected that their members would make special efforts to increase the range of economic activities. And, in fact, these efforts *are* often made. However, bad job households face impediments to accomplishing this expansion of their survival strategy. Most significantly, they are less likely than are good job families to have two earners: three times as many bad job households (33 percent versus 13 percent) rely only on a single earner—and that earner has only a bad job. Second, although the same percentage of bad job and good job households include an individual who moonlights, in bad job families that moonlighting takes on a different form than it does in good job households. Members of good job households moonlight through entrepreneurial activity such as having an on-the-side business of craft work or lawn mowing; members of bad job households simply take on second jobs. A man in a good job family repairs cars in his backyard during his hours away from his main place of work, while a man in a bad job household moonlights at the local Mobil station; a woman in a good job family designs and knits sweaters for sale to her friends and colleagues, while a woman in a bad job family receives wages for sewing for someone else. The two kinds of families also self-provision at different rates and in different ways. As common sense would predict, bad job households do more *routine* self-provisioning—they grow their own vegetables; they chop and split wood to burn in the fireplace; they probably hunt and raise meat; they change the oil in the car themselves; and they plow their own driveways. Yet—and this is significant—bad job households do none of the more substantial projects. In good job households, self-provisioning means building your own house and then, if you have the time, also changing the oil in the car. In bad job households, self-provisioning is just changing the oil. This is not to imply that the activities of bad job families are unimportant, but to suggest that these more routine activities reap smaller savings and that, ultimately, they sustain rather than *improve* peoples' lives. Finally, like the members of good job households, those in bad job families make casual exchanges with members of *other* families. Surprisingly, however, whereas among good job families these exchanges have an inverse relationship to income—those with lower incomes are more likely to rely on help from family and friends—among bad job households the reverse is true.

In short, there is considerable evidence that bad job families cannot make up for the absence of a second worker by intensifying their other economic practices. Instead, among bad job households both routine moonlighting and self-provisioning depend heavily on the presence of (or the conditions that support) the second worker. And whereas among good job households nonmonetary exchanges with other households are intricately associated with other economic activities, among bad job households the practices of interdependence compete with self-provisioning.

There is reason to believe the explanation for these differences inheres in the nature of good and bad work rather than in the characteristics of the individuals located in those two kinds of households.[9] Quite briefly, as will be recalled, good jobs were defined as those that, in addition to being full-time, offered benefits, stability, and discretionary time. These factors are critically important in enabling a family—and especially one with young children—to keep both adults at work. For example, among good job families the ability of family members to take time off from work to respond to inevitable family crises (e.g., a sick child; a pressing appointment) shaped their capacity to maintain employment. As one woman said, "One day when my daughter was sick I came home from work early. Of course I have vacation time. I usually keep a week to two weeks of vacation for a day here if I want to take it or half a day there. My youngest child is supposed to be going in for surgery, so I have kept extra time for that." Among bad job families the absence of these factors impeded their ability to respond to family needs. A man in a bad job household commented, "I just got a written warning a couple of weeks ago because my daughter was up all night and I was up all night with her and I couldn't go to work the next day, and I got a written warning for missing too much time at work."

In addition, by virtue of having at least one member attached to work that pays good wages and carries benefits, good job households can accumulate the resources (e.g., a second car) that help another household member maintain employment, and can keep a second worker in the labor force even when that worker's earnings do not exceed the expenses of employment. Among bad job families, unless the second worker's earnings *do* surpass those expenses, they must be forgone. An alternative practice, that of staggering work schedules so as to avoid the costs of child care altogether, is more common among bad work households. But this practice has its own costs and might contribute to the instability of the household survival strategy (Presser 1999, 2000).

Indeed, bad job families have rapidly fluctuating fortunes based on what is going on in that bad job itself and in the family as a whole. Bad job households were not only more likely than good job households to have had a family member who was laid off from work during the previous year (24 percent versus 11 percent), but only bad job households had experienced *two* such layoffs. One woman in a bad job household described job changes that occurred with dizzying speed, and a constant change in the family deployment pattern:

> I did a paper route. . . . I got up at 2 in the morning and I was done by 5:30 depending on the day. That was seven days a week. . . . I did day care, I forgot about that. I had three children in my home. . . . I did that from September until June. When [my husband] lost his job there was just my babysitting income and . . . from September to November we were both employed. . . . From November until March my babysitting was the only income. In March I started the route, so in March I was doing the paper route and day care. . . . When school got out I quit day care and just did the paper route. . . . He's been back to work about three weeks . . . and that's [a] temporary [job]. . . . But because he's working and leaves at 4 in the morning, I can't do my paper route.

Bad job households with only one worker have enormous incentives for that one worker to moonlight. Yet, it turns out, they face double jeopardy. A household that has trouble supporting two workers also has trouble supporting moonlighting. Consider the Desrosiers. They have young children and badly need the income from more than one job. But they have only one car and have no relatives in the area to help keep down the costs of child care. Therefore, Janet cannot hold down a job. From time to time, Ron moonlights. When he does, Janet is left alone from early morning until late at night. She has no way to shop or to get the children to the doctor. In this household, the tensions that accumulate quickly erode the benefits of Ron's moonlighting.

Substantial projects like building one's own home also depend on resources—such as predictable time and secure pensions—and thus are out of reach of most bad job families. When money is tight, even routine self-provisioning practices may depend on the perks attached to a specific job—if you work for a logger you get free wood and you can borrow a chain saw. But these perks disappear when the job does: this might explain why bad job families do *more* self-provisioning when they have the two-earner strategy than when they only have one—more work means more perks.

Interhousehold assistance and exchange may substitute for the lack of opportunities to self-provision, but, surprisingly, the creation of reliable networks is a privilege of households that do not face urgent financial needs: bad job households with higher incomes are more likely to develop social exchange relationships than are those with lower incomes. In fact, some people in bad job households—and especially those in the most precarious economic position—try to avoid obligations of reciprocity. One member of a bad job family explained it this way: "Brothers and sisters, they can take care of theirselves, and we have to take care of ourself and they have to take care of theirselves—unless you got a rich family and everybody helps each other somehow. But [then in a rich family] the money always comes back to the guy who gives it to you. In a poor family it don't."

Rather than making up for the cost of poor employment by intensifying the various tactics that make up a household survival strategy, bad job families are able only to do exactly the opposite. The much-discussed downgrading of the character of jobs themselves has a hidden, yet significant, underside.

INSIDE THE HOUSEHOLD STRATEGY

I now want to say a word about what these different survival strategies mean for the men, women, and children located within these two sets of households.

Good Job Families

At first glance, in good job households gendered relationships appear to rest on a traditional base—that of male superiority in the labor force. In approximately half of these families husbands have better work (as measured by our quality of employment standard to distinguish between good and bad jobs) than their wives.

Yet, when we look more closely, we see that the simple fact of women's employment outside the home undercuts many "conventional" supports for gender. Most good job households rely on a dual-earner strategy, and in three-quarters of families both husbands and wives work full-time. Moreover, in over half of good job households husbands and wives have approximately equal hourly earnings. Thus, the economic support for male superiority has been eroded. Among good job households this erosion has occurred *not* because men's work has changed, but because women have begun to develop their *own* stable, full-time work histories.

As the normal underpinnings of gendered relationships disappear, men in good jobs appear to struggle to find ways to replace them. The full range of survival tactics plays a role. In these households men are almost twice as likely as women to moonlight through entrepreneurial side-work. And although these activities are a function of opportunity, skill, and necessity, there is strong reason to believe that they also function to restore eroded gender props in good job households: husbands are more than twice as likely to work two jobs when their wives have employment that is equal to theirs in quality than they are when their employment situation is better than that of their wives. Launching a second income-producing activity, then, might be a way to bolster a man's threatened primacy as an earner within the household.

In good job households, self-provisioning is relevant to the recreation of a gender hierarchy as well. In general, men take leadership in home construction and large-scale remodeling. Moreover, the men we spoke with appreciate the occasions on which they work with other men and thereby build up their networks of solidarity. They also enjoy buying equipment that, although necessary, has particular symbolic importance: a pickup truck; a John Deere tractor; a chain saw. There are also important differences in how men and women make exchanges with those in other households. Men more often than women engage in barter, where the exchange of goods and services requires careful assessment of value and clear terms about repayment. In contrast, although women also exchange services—they take care of elderly relatives; they babysit for each other's children—these practices do not require a calculation of worth, and they leave the terms of repayment indefinite. Thus, a different valuation is placed on the work of men and women: men's work is equated with market values even when it doesn't really function as such but is really part of a social economy; women's work is "naturalized," and its market value is slighted.

Simply said, good job households are successful places. Children are the heirs to this good fortune. In this respect, employment benefits are especially important: parents who receive benefits such as paid sick leave and/or paid vacation leave are more likely to stay home with sick children (Heymann 2000) than those who do not receive those benefits. The children thus have the comfort of a familiar figure when they are not feeling well and recover faster from illness (Institute for Women's Policy Research 2007). Stability matters as well: when employment is predictable, it is possible to make consistent arrangements for child care and to cover the costs of that care. This stability is vital for the well-being of children (Macmillan, McMorris, and Kruttschnitt 2004).

Bad Job Households

The situation—for both adults and children—is quite different in bad job households. Some bad work households look like the "traditional" nuclear family of old: men are in the labor force, women remain at home. But appearances are deceiving. Neither the terms of men's employment nor the terms of women's domesticity are the same as they were in the past. Both men and, especially, women in these households move in and out of the labor force, and in and out of jobs. Sometimes these decisions are shaped by simple opportunity. More often they are determined by gender—but there is little in the objective reality to give license to these decisions, since women in these households can often earn as much as their husbands.

Two pieces of evidence suggest that women in bad job households make special accommodations toward preserving their husband's status as the primary wage earner: they are almost twice as likely as women in good job households to hold down part-time work (45 percent versus 23 percent), and they are more likely to confine their employment possibilities to those close to home. Indeed, given that by definition men in bad job households have degraded employment, whatever advantage they retain relative to their wives appears to be a function of their wives' further disadvantage in the labor force. And, in many of these households, trading substitutes for entrepreneurial moonlighting; it is an activity that gives men the illusion of control over scarce resources, but it also—from time to time—becomes extraordinarily disruptive in the lives of individuals in bad job households. Walter Seward, for example, accepted with equanimity that he was better off not getting attached to his belongings:

> WALTER: Just before last Christmas, through November, I was working like a dog, ten hours a day, six days a week. I was making all kinds of money, great money. Things were great. I went out and bought my

mother a VCR for Christmas. It cost a couple hundred bucks. We also bought a Camcorder that year. We were stupid. We should have saved more and spent less.

INTERVIEWER: I saw a snowmobile for sale out there.

WALTER: That's mine. Yeah, I bought that too. That was three thousand dollars.

INTERVIEWER: Why are you selling it?

WALTER: I could use the money more than I can the fun right now. I figure, I'm the type of guy that luxuries mean nothing to me. I can always sell a luxury today and, when things get better tomorrow, I'll buy another one. I'm not attached to anything.

Further discussion with the Sewards indicated that what Walter thought a good deal, his wife, Debbie, viewed as a waste of scarce resources:

WALTER: One time there was a good deal on a boat, I wanted the boat. It was five hundred dollars. . . . That was three boats ago. I bought and sold, bought and sold boats.

INTERVIEWER: Do you make money with all this buying and selling?

DEBBIE: No! No you do not, don't you say you do.

WALTER: Some I do, and some I don't.

DEBBIE: No, never, ever.

WALTER: When you buy something for a thousand dollars and you use it for two years and you sell it for a thousand dollars, I consider that making money. You've used it for nothing.

DEBBIE: When you buy something you never ever get what you put into that, I don't care if you bought it for a thousand. You always put money into it. It's fifteen hundred dollars you've spent, and when you sell it for a thousand dollars you just lost five hundred dollars.

Thus, in bad job households domestic life is complicated by change, by disruptions of employment, by not knowing how much income is coming in, and by the rapid circulation of consumer goods. As men assert control over limited resources, the rate of change intensifies. This instability makes it difficult to anticipate the needs of children, to provide consistent arrangements for their care, and to meet ongoing needs. When we asked the Sewards who usually cooked meals, Walter answered, "Let's put it this way. I'm going to be totally honest with you. About once a week we really have a sit-down meal, the rest of the time it's get what you want out and make it yourself." When we followed up by asking the twelve-year-old child who usually fed him, he answered, simply, "Myself." The pattern whereby young children "assume extensive adult roles and responsibilities within their family networks"—what Burton (2007) refers to as "adultification"—occurs among families facing economic disadvantage. Research demonstrates as well that such events as adult unemployment and family disruption have negative effects on children's development (Fomby and Cherlin 2007; Harland et al. 2002; Strom 2003).

The Case of Single Mothers

In the first part of this chapter I showed that Coolidge County underwent economic restructuring following the 1980s and described the multiple activities made possible by having a good job (a second earner, occasional moonlighting, self-provisioning, and interhousehold exchanges). I also described the scenario that can be viewed as the poverty of bad jobs. That is, I demonstrated that these families are unable to make up for the cost of poor employment by sending more than one person out to earn wages and are disadvantaged when it comes to moonlighting and self-provisioning. Finally, I suggested that these differences had consequences for household security and predictability.

Although I have focused on the intact household up to this point, these findings have implications for female-headed households, which have rapidly increased as a proportion of all families with children in Coolidge County. Below I discuss four issues related to the analysis above.

First, the evidence suggests not only that family disruption is more likely among households that (like the bad job families we interviewed) are already facing some distress (Coontz and Folbre 2002), but that should this disruption occur, women in good job families, although disadvantaged relative to their husbands, are quite privileged relative to married women in bad job families. The survival strategy of good work households *assumes* women's participation in the labor force and ensures it even when a given job does not make a monetary profit. Hence, women in good work households build stable work histories and develop the arrangements necessary for work outside the home when they have young children (e.g., relationships with babysitters, purchase of an automobile). Indeed this was the case among the women I interviewed. One woman who had built up her own career while a member of an "intact" family with two good jobs, reported that she experienced no employment disruption when her marriage ended: while she now had to function on a little less than half the income she had as part of a couple (and thus had to make a new set of economic decisions), she owned a car and had child care arrangements, which provided the infrastructure for her employment; she also had established good enough relationships with her employer that he was willing to be sensitive to her new difficulties and accommodating to a somewhat greater number of absences from work.

By way of contrast, women in bad job households may have to leave the labor force if the costs of employment outweigh its benefits or when their husband finds employment that meshes uncomfortably with theirs. In fact, as wives, they are the group most likely to become bad workers—and not just workers with bad jobs. As a result, should they end up on their own, they will be positioned poorly to be self-supporting. Again, this was precisely the case among the women I interviewed. One woman who had been employed periodically when she was living with her husband found that her checkered work career was held against her when she was divorced and desperately in need of full-time employment.

Second, single mothers with young children face great difficulties when they seek to support their families on their earnings. Given women's lower wages in the labor force, these earnings are likely to be less than those in households (whether good job or bad job households) that rely on the income of a single *male* worker. At the same time, many of the expenses of employment remain constant; in addition a single parent will have the new expense of child care, which is not an issue in a married-couple family with a single earner. Indeed, among married-couple families, relying on a strategy of shift work (although a strategy with its own problems) can ensure that both parents are employed without incurring child care expenses (Mills et al. 2001).[10]

The Manpower Demonstration Research Corporation's (MDRC) final report of Vermont's Welfare Restructuring Project (which analyzed in 2002 the outcome of single parents that year who were applying for or receiving cash assistance in Vermont between 1994 and 1996) indicates that only 73 percent of those single mothers owned a car, 23 percent reported that they did not take a job or had to quit a job because of difficulties with transportation, and 30 percent reported that they did not take a job or quit a job because of difficulties with child care arrangements (Scrivener et al. 2002).

Third, those who have recently entered the labor force—whether they chose to do so or because they are compelled to as a result of welfare-to-work policies—may be doing so in the context of increasing numbers of bad jobs. Indeed, among the single mothers interviewed, a slightly higher proportion held bad jobs than was the case among the individuals in our earlier study of families in the area (63 percent of single mothers, in contrast to 56 percent of the individuals in two-parent families). But, again, we need not rely on this study alone. The MDRC evaluation of the welfare restructuring project (Scrivener et al. 2002) reports that among those who were employed at the time of the final study, 66 percent were in jobs that did not provide health insurance, 70 percent were in jobs that did not provide paid sick leave, and 56 percent were in jobs that did not provide paid vacations or holidays.[11] One woman I interviewed explained how her child's frequent illness—in the absence of benefits that made accommodations possible—had disrupted her efforts to maintain steady employment: "I didn't [work steadily] when [my daughter] was really young. It was always every six months I would have to get a new job, because I would miss work too much because of her asthma, because of court [re. child support], or she was running a high fever and day care wouldn't take her. So that was a very big struggle for me."

Furthermore, 63 percent of the single mothers in the MDRC report worked jobs that had regular daytime schedules; the remainder worked evenings or nights, on split or rotating shifts, or on an irregular schedule. Under these terms of employment, single mothers with young children would have difficulty working consistently and building up stable work histories: taking time off to care for a sick child would mean, at the very least, the loss of a day's pay; more likely, taking that time off would result in a reprimand and, possibly, the risk of job loss. (Among those in married couples in which both members have bad jobs, the cost of these events can be shared.) Recent studies demonstrate that when single mothers cannot afford to take time off from work, they often recruit their adolescent daughters to care for younger siblings; these daughters then experience diminished school attendance and school performance, thus jeopardizing their own futures (Dodson and Dickert 2004; Gennetian et al. 2002).

Moreover, the MDRC report suggests that 41 percent of the single mothers who had previously been or continued to be welfare-reliant found employment in jobs that paid hourly wages of $7.50 or more, while the remainder were working for less; during these years the Vermont legislature estimated that at a minimum a single mother of one child in a rural area would need to earn $13.64 an hour (Kavet et al. 1999).

And finally, if the reported wages of good job families greatly underestimate the basis on which these families actually make do on a daily basis, and if even bad job households are able—through extraordinary effort—to muster some resources for daily survival that reduce the pressure on the wage (e.g., growing some vegetables, changing the oil in the car), the situation is quite different for single parents. Moonlighting is almost a total impossibility: among the single mothers in the interview sample who were employed full-time, only 9 percent held down more than a single job. By way of contrast, almost a full two-fifths of the married-couple households included at least one moonlighter among its members. Self-provisioning—the strategy for substituting one's own labor for the purchase of necessary goods and services—is also more difficult. Not only does self-provisioning use up scarce resources of both time and money, but much of it depends on other resources such as owning a house or tools: only a third of the women said they had vegetable gardens (in comparison with almost three-quarters of the married couples); only a few said they had made extensive renovations on their homes; none of them had changed the oil in the car themselves (see table 7.3). Although few *women* in married-couple families engage in the full range of these self-provisioning activities, in households with young children, men's participation greatly depends on the presence of an adult who can ensure that the children are not underfoot. Single mothers have neither that "other" adult nor the necessary time and energy. While single-parent families do—from necessity and, sometimes, choice—make arrangements with the members of other families to relieve the burdens of child care, to help with transportation, and to cover for each other during emergencies, these arrangements work best when they operate on the basis of fairly balanced reciprocity (Nelson 2000). Hence, interhousehold assistance can become another stressful obligation, which, in a single-parent household, falls on one set of shoulders alone rather than being shared between two adults. Even housework becomes more difficult when there is no second adult available to watch the children. As one woman said when asked about how she managed to complete her housework, "It's just really impossible to get anything done. Like because you do the dishes, and [my toddler's] just destroying another room. That's why there's two parents, I'm sure. It's just very hard alone."

Government statistics suggest the raw depth of the feminization of poverty in Vermont, as in the country as a whole. According to the 2000 census, 24 percent of families with a female householder and no husband present were poor (in comparison with 6 percent of all families). Among these families, a whopping 31 percent of those with a related child under eighteen years of age and 49 percent of those with a related child under five years of age were living below the poverty level. Studies using measures of a livable wage rather than poverty levels alone suggest that the breadth of poverty is far greater than these statistics suggest: for example, the *Vermont Job Gap Study* also estimated that a full 61 percent of single-parent families with one child and 83 percent of single-parent families with two children earn less than a livable wage (Peace and Justice Center 1999). However, the analysis above, which looked at the wealth of resources that married-couple families (even if they only have bad jobs) can bring to bear on their daily living standards, suggests that the poverty of single-parent families may be even more profound than that indicated even by this more "realistic" measure.

Conclusion

In the summer of 2002, Ames Inc. announced that it was closing its 327 discount department stores in fourteen states and the District of Columbia (Herbst 2002). Although the store in Coolidge County had been among the more profitable stores, it too was closing. Unable to keep up with the national retail giants such as Walmart, Kmart, and Target, Ames was going out of business.

The story of the Ames Department Store in Centerville in the heart of Coolidge County provides an interesting illustration of the recent story of economic restructuring in that region. When the first Ames Department Store opened in a small shopping mall in Coolidge County almost thirty years ago, it competed with a thriving downtown. As one local observer wrote, "When I moved to [Centerville] in 1980, there were five stores downtown—all now gone—that sold reasonably priced clothing, general merchandise, and sundries" (*Rutland Herald* 2002).

In Centerville, as elsewhere, these downtown stores found themselves unable to compete with the range and price of goods available in Ames, a relatively small discount store by current standards. One by one the downtown stores folded, giving way to specialty shops carrying high-priced clothing and trinkets. Indeed, this is what the planners promoted: "Development experts advised downtown merchants to develop niche markets for specialty goods for which shoppers would pay a higher price [since] for everyday needs, shoppers were going to the discount stores" (*Rutland Herald* 2002). This tenuous balance, of a "niche" downtown and a discount mall, served the needs of Coolidge County residents well—at least until competition drove Ames out of business. While an Ames closing made barely a ripple in places already served by its competitors, Coolidge Country, like many other rural locations, boasted no such "big-box" stores. Hence, when Ames closed its doors Coolidge County residents were left to face trips of an hour or so to buy underwear and socks; they could find hand-crafted pottery much closer to home.

Like Ames, modern industry was smart to look to Coolidge County some thirty or forty years ago. Not only did the county have an untapped pool of men who had not yet been drawn into the formal labor force (and substantial numbers of men who remained outside the *waged* labor force), but wages were low (in 1960 median earnings for men were but 64 percent of those in the United States as a whole) and relatively few workers were members of unions. Coolidge County also had relatively large, stable families and women "willing" to work outside the home (at wages that were but half of those offered to men). Moreover, as a nostalgic image of the rural past suggests—and the high proportion of the working age population outside waged employment confirms this supposition—Coolidge County workers could assume that a considerable portion of their needs would be met not only by the family itself (through home-based production of essential goods and services), but by purchasing the products of informal labor. They could thus be "expected" to continue to live on lower wages than those required in more urban areas.

However, by coming to Coolidge County, modern industry played a significant role in transforming the conditions that had made the county attractive. As more workers (both men and women) entered the waged labor force, they not only expected better wages, but they became less capable of self-provisioning than had previously been the case. When these new industries downsized and, in some cases, left altogether (as was the case with Ames), they did so not in response to local developments, but in response to broader (and in some cases global) forces that impinged upon and shaped the dynamics within this particular region. They left in their wake more bad jobs that lacked the flexible benefits and predictable employment that had been the hallmark of employment in the burgeoning manufacturing workplace.

The disappearance of good employment has different effects on different groups of people. Those who have managed to keep a household member in good employment can—with enormous effort and enormous initiative—rely on a diversified survival strategy. Though wages stand at the center of this survival strategy, the strategy is supplemented by (even as it supports) self-provisioning, entrepreneurial moonlighting, and interhousehold exchanges. These good job households can also afford to drive an hour or so to the nearest Walmart to stock up on discount household supplies, or they can, in a pinch, make do with what is at hand locally (and is more expensive). Those households characterized by employment that carries fewer benefits and lower wages might well display the same energy and initiative; however, all that energy and initiative goes into more modest forms of self-provisioning, long hours working a second job, and worry about the return rate on exchanges with friends and family members. They thus live in a world transformed less by their own choices, and more by forces over which they have little control.

In one interview, a single mother spoke eloquently about how her husband became defeated as he lost one job after another and about how this defeat eventually turned into anger and threatened violence. Now on her own with a young child, the woman struggles to make ends meet through waged work that pays considerably less than a livable wage and offers little flexibility to meet inevitable contingencies. Though she resides in a rural area, as an apartment dweller living on a small income she has no means to partake of the benefits it offers for self-provisioning or even to enjoy the beauty of the outdoors. In fact, rurality is more of an impediment than an advantage: she has always had to travel long distances by car to get her child to day care and herself to work; she now will have to travel even longer distances to save money on diapers and baby clothes.

If the absence of a "big-box" store in Coolidge County suggests a land left behind, we should understand well that at the beginning of the twenty-first century, to be "left behind" does not mean being immune from the forces of modernization; it means, as with both industry and discount stores, being affected by those forces, and then passed over. Vermont's rural image may still sell products, but the shirtsleeves of its residents get rolled up to do work that bears little resemblance to their forefathers either in the nature of those activities or in the terms of conditions under which they are enacted.

Reversing these activities and conditions will require political struggle at several levels. Livable wage campaigns are clearly important. But these data suggest that wages alone are not enough. Workers—and especially those in families with young children—need paid time off and other benefits as well as sufficient wages if they are to sustain themselves through employment. As these findings have shown, in the absence of workplace benefits and job flexibility, it takes both effort and luck to keep one or more family members in the labor force. Families that cannot keep two workers in the labor force cannot substitute their own labor for the goods and services necessary for daily survival; indeed, access to those goods and services also rests on waged employment. Moreover, low-income families will continue to need state support; this is especially the case for single mothers who need protection from the assumption that a single wage can support a family. Ensuring these basic supports for working families will take a willingness to see the government—at its various levels—as having responsibility for the well-being of all its citizens.

Table 7.1 Industry in Coolidge County and the United States, 1960–2005

Industry	Coolidge County						United States					
	1960	1970	1980	1990	2000	2005	1960	1970	1980	1990	2000	2005
Agriculture, forestry, and fisheries	25.5%	14.4%	11.5%	9.1%	6.9%	5.6%	6.7%	3.7%	3.0%	2.7%	1.9%	1.7%
Manufacturing	19.6%	20.5%	22.2%	17.0%	14.3%	9.3%	27.1%	26.0%	22.4%	17.7%	14.9%	11.9%
Service	15.6%	31.8%	33.2%	37.3%	46.1%	39.7%	14.5%	24.7%	28.7%	32.7%	42.0%	43.8%

SOURCE: Census, selected years.

Table 7.2   Survival strategy of married-couple families*

	All households (n = 158)	Type of household	
		Good job households (n = 86)	Bad job households (n = 72)
Percent with two earners	78%	87%	67%
Percent with at least one moonlighter	39%	35%	43%
Percent with high rates of self-provisioning (4 or more)*	30%	23%	39%
Percent with high rates of informal assistance from others (one or more)	49%	50%	47%

* Nelson and Smith (1999).

Table 7.3   Routine self-provisioning in Coolidge County

	Married-couple households*			
	All married-couple households (n = 156)	Married-couple households without children (n = 67)	Married-couple households with children (n=89)	Single-mother households (n=40)
Percent who change oil	83%	81%	83%	0%
Percent who cut own wood	46%	42%	50%	2%
Percent who grow meat	22%	16%	26%	2%
Percent who garden	72%	68%	75%	30%
Percent who plow	62%	53%	68%	[not asked]
Percent with high rates of self-provisioning (4 or more activities)	34%	30%	38%	0%

* Nelson and Smith (1999).

Notes

1. My colleague Joan Smith died in September 2004. In this chapter, I use "we" to designate work that she and I did together. I use "I" when reporting on work I did on my own.

2. To protect the confidentiality of respondents, we have changed the names of individuals as well as the name of the county in which the research was conducted.

3. Unless otherwise indicated, data are taken from the U.S. Census, selected years.

4. For a discussion of female labor force participation rates in rural areas, see Swanson and Butler (1988) and Lichter (1989).

5. The profile of the households in which these respondents live resembles closely that obtained in the 1990 census with respect to age, education, household income, and occupations.

6. For more information about the sample, see Nelson and Smith (1999).

7. For more detail on this study, see Nelson (2005).

8. Routine self-provisioning is defined to include those activities that "help to guarantee the daily life of the household" (Nelson and Smith 1999, 10), and it was measured in the random survey by asking whether anyone in the household had raised an animal for food, grown vegetables in a garden, changed the oil in the car, cut and gathered their own firewood for heating purposes, or plowed the driveway during the past year. (A similar question was asked of the single mothers, with the exception of plowing, which clearly applied only to those who owned their own homes.) Substantial self-provisioning is defined as those activities that "help to improve the family's living conditions" (10), and it was measured by asking respondents whether they engaged in home construction and major home renovation projects.

9. The two sets of households differed surprisingly little in the characteristics of their members as measured by education and age and in their composition as measured by the presence of children (Nelson and Smith 1999).

10. In 1993 it was found, for example, in the state as a whole that the labor force participation rate of these single mothers was almost exactly what it is for married women, and yet their unemployment rate was three times as high (Livingston and McCrate 1993).

11. These statistics were recalculated from the Manpower Demonstration Research Corporation final report on the Welfare Restructuring Project in Vermont (Scrivener et al. 2002). For issues concerning employment, the MDRC includes in its tables both individuals who were not employed and individuals who were employed at the time of the final study. To analyze the terms of employment, I recalculate those statistics on the basis only of those who were employed.

ECONOMIC HARDSHIP, PARENTING, AND FAMILY
STABILITY IN A COHORT OF RURAL ADOLESCENTS

KATHERINE JEWSBURY CONGER

The white crosses on the courthouse lawn are long gone, but the effects of the agricultural economic crisis in the 1980s still ripple across the landscape of the rural Midwest. Many families who had envisioned their lives on the farm have moved to towns nearby, farm-related businesses have restructured or disappeared from small towns, small towns dependent on agriculture for their existence have become bedroom communities for people driving to larger economic centers for work, and fewer farmers work larger and larger farms to make ends meet. And often, families still working the land also work other jobs to sustain their no longer "idyllic" lifestyle. There is ample evidence that the economic downturn in the 1980s took a toll on towns and communities throughout the Midwest, but many families survived this rural restructuring through their determination not to give up on past dreams or on the notion that future generations of families would be tied to the land.

How have adolescents and their families who lived through these tumultuous times fared? Have they stayed put—linked to the land through deep roots of family history and commitment—or have fathers and mothers sent their children to look elsewhere for less hazardous, more financially rewarding work? Have marriages broken apart or survived the stress and strain of economic hardship? And finally, how have young adults fared after coming of age during the economic turmoil of the 1980s? This chapter examines the processes through which rural economic problems affected the health, well-being, and long-term socioeconomic opportunities of a cohort of adolescents living in the upper Midwest during the Agricultural Depression of the 1980s. In it, I consider the theoretical model developed to explain the connection between economic conditions, family functioning, and developmental change in parents and their children: the Family Stress Model (FSM; R. Conger and K. Conger 2002). This model identifies a set of family dynamics proposed to influence change in individual well-being for rural families dealing with economic hardship. The chapter concludes with a discussion of the implications of these findings for rural families, communities, and policy makers.

Starting with the economic downturn in the midwestern economy in the 1980s, and continuing through today's news of declining wages, home fore-closures, and the increasing debt of American families, researchers and policy makers alike have struggled to explain the linkages between macroeconomic change and the health and well-being of individuals and families. Research increasingly suggests that dynamics within families are the key to understanding this association. Indeed, the economic changes of the past two decades in the United States (e.g., economic recessions, globalization of business, and evidence of increasing income inequality) have enhanced ongoing interest in how economic resources, employment, and social position affect families and the development of children (R. Conger and K. Conger 2002; Duncan and Brooks-Gunn 1997; Hoff, Laursen, and Tardif 2002; Lichter and Eggebeen 1994). Recent research and reviews of the literature provide significant evidence that economic hardship and disadvantage impair the functioning of parents (e.g., Conger and Dogan 2007; McLoyd 1990) and undermine the physical, intellectual, social, and emotional health of children and adolescents (e.g., Bolger et al. 1995; Bradley and Corwyn 2002, 2003; R. Conger, K. Conger, and Martin 2010; McLoyd 1998).

Numerous studies suggest a link between various dimensions of socio-economic status (SES) and physical health, social-emotional well-being, and cognitive functioning for both children and adults (e.g., Berkman and Kawachi 2000; Bradley and Corwyn 2002; McLeod and Shanahan 1996). Regarding the development of children and adolescents, recent findings demonstrate a clear connection between poverty and mental health (e.g., Ackerman, Brown, and Izard 2004; Dearing, McCartney, and Taylor 2001; McLeod and Shanahan 1996), SES and cognitive development (e.g., Ackerman, Brown, and Izard; Dearing, McCartney, and Taylor 2001; Hoff 2003; Hughes et al. 2005; Mezzacappa 2004), and social class position and physical well-being (e.g. Evans and English 2002; McLoyd 1998; Mistry et al. 2002). So how do SES and economic problems influence the health and well-being of children and adults?

One theoretical approach, the Family Stress Model, illustrates the possible concepts and related processes through which SES and economic problems affect parents and children. This conceptual framework is intuitively appealing as it is consistent with people's views about the influence of family economic circumstances. For example, parents and grandparents who lived through the Great Depression of the 1930s, one of the most significant economic calamities in the history of the United States, share personal stories about serious deprivations they experienced during that time, some of which continue to influence their lives today. More extreme responses to the financial collapse were found in the newspapers of the day, which reported on businessmen taking their lives in response to the stock market crash in 1929. Similar reports occurred during the 1980s, when farmers and bankers in the rural Midwest committed suicide at an increased rate during the economic crisis in agriculture (Conger and Elder 1994b). The FSM is consistent with these extreme consequences of economic problems in that it emphasizes the adverse emotional effects of economic hardship.

Stories abound in the rural Midwest of families losing farms, jobs, or businesses in the wake of the agricultural crisis of the 1980s. Children gave up dreams of farming, of college, or of taking over the family business; many couples divorced, unable to withstand the stresses and strains of corrosive financial concerns; and the usually "carefree" time of adolescence was oftentimes overshadowed by concerns about family, friends, schools, and communities (Davidson 1990; Lasley et al. 1995).

Just as important are the stories of families who weathered the crisis without suffering significant disruption: couples who survived economic upheaval without divorcing, families that drew together rather than splitting apart, and children who did well in school. The resilient nature of these individuals and families provides important information about individual characteristics and social processes that were protective and able to promote well-being during these stressful times. Looking back, it seems as if few lives in the rural Midwest were left untouched by the social and economic upheaval associated with the agricultural crisis. Although the suicides of farmers and stockbrokers and the fields of broken dreams represent extreme responses to the influence of economic circumstances on children and families, they provide characterizations of the salient processes that provide the foundation of the model that guides our research.

Responding to Economic Stress: The Family Stress Model

The FSM developed from a social psychological approach, and is consistent with a social causation perspective, which argues that the social and economic circumstances in people's lives directly influence their emotions, beliefs, and behaviors (Conger and Donnellan 2007). The FSM proposes that financial difficulties have an adverse effect on parents' emotions, behaviors, and relationships, which, in turn, affect their parenting abilities or strategies (R. Conger and K. Conger 2002).

The FSM builds on a tradition of research dating back to the Great Depression years of the 1930s. A series of studies at that time provided evidence that severe hardship could undermine family functioning and socialization practices in a fashion that negatively affected the lives of both parents and children (e.g., Angell 1936; Cavan and Ranck 1938; Komarovsky 1940). Elder's research extended this earlier work in a series of reports demonstrating the response of Depression-era parents to economic loss (Elder 1974; Elder and Caspi 1988). These themes have been carried forward in contemporary investigations that both support and modify many of the conclusions reached in these earlier studies (e.g., Leventhal and Brooks-Gunn 2003; McLoyd 1998). Mayer (1997) calls the conceptual ideas emanating from this line of research the "good parent theory," which proposes that poverty or low income has a negative effect on parents' psychological well-being. These psychological disruptions, in turn, are expected to reduce effective parenting practices.

Consistent with this line of research, Conger and Conger and their colleagues developed the conceptual framework, the FSM, which described their efforts to understand how financial problems influenced the lives of Iowa families who experienced the economic turbulence of the 1980s (K. Conger, Rueter, and R. Conger 2000; R. Conger and K. Conger 2002; Conger and Elder 1994b). As shown in figure 8.1, the FSM proposes that conditions of economic hardship lead to economic pressure in the family. Markers of hardship include low income, high debts relative to assets, and negative financial events such as job loss, increasing economic demands, or declining material resources. These hardship conditions are expected to affect family functioning and individual adjustment primarily through the economic pressures they generate. The FSM proposes that economic pressures include (1) unmet material needs involving necessities such as adequate food and clothing, (2) the inability to pay bills or make ends meet, and (3) having to cut back on even necessary expenses (e.g., health insurance and medical care). The model illustrates how experiencing these kinds of pressures gives psychological meaning to living with economic

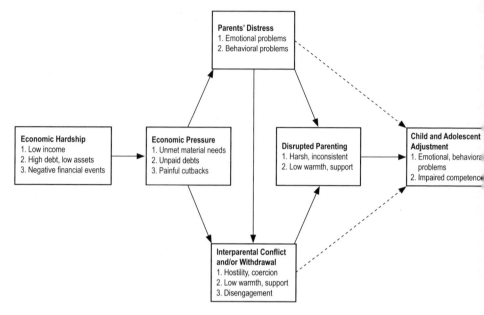

FIG. 8.1   The Family Stress Model linking economic hardship to adolescent adjustment through parents and family social processes

hardship (K. Conger, R. Conger, and Elder 1994; R. Conger and K. Conger 2002; R. Conger, K. Conger, et al. 1992, 1993; Conger and Elder 1994a; Conger, Wallace, et al. 2002).

The FSM proposed that economic pressure has its effect on family life and individual development through its effect on the social, emotional, and psychological well-being of the adults in the family. For example, the model predicts that when economic pressure is high, parents and other adult family members (e.g., members of the extended family) living with children are at increased risk for becoming emotionally distressed, as indicated by feelings of depression, anxiety, anger, and isolation. These markers of emotional problems are broadly defined and also may be related to other problems, such as alcohol and drug use or antisocial behavior, as suggested by earlier research (e.g., R. Conger 1995; Duncan and Brooks-Gunn 1997; McLoyd 1998). In addition, the model proposes that emotional distress creates problems and affects the dynamics of family relationships, including increased conflict and reduced warmth and support in the relations between adults and increased harsh and inconsistent parenting practices (K. Conger, Rueter, and R. Conger 2000; K. Conger, R. Conger, and Scaramella 1997). Research indicates that the prediction of conflict and withdrawal holds not only for biological parents but also for stepparents, cohabiting unmarried romantic partners, and other caregiver relationships such as grand-mothers and mothers raising a child together (Conger, Wallace, et al. 2002). The FSM also proposes that, in addition to parents' emotional distress, marital or interparental conflict and relationship problems will be directly related to disruptions in positive parenting.

The final path in the model shown in figure 8.1 depicts the connection between disrupted family relationships and child and adolescent adjustment. More specifically, the primary hypothesis is that disrupted parenting will mediate or explain the influence of parental distress and interparental conflicts on child development (e.g., Conger et al. 2000). According to the model, then, when families experience economic hardship, children are at risk for decreases in positive adjustment (e.g., cognitive ability, social competence, school success, and attachment to parents) as well as increases in internalizing (e.g., symptoms of depression and anxiety) and externalizing (e.g., aggressive and antisocial behavior) problems. However, the model proposes that the economic effects on children will only be indirect through their effect on the lives of parents and other family members. For single-parent families, the model may omit caregiver conflicts with one another or substitute conflicts with an ex-spouse or current romantic partner, as economic problems are expected to affect these relationships as well (Conger, Wallace, et al. 2002).

In addition to the mediating pathways depicted in figure 8.1, other factors, such as social and psychological resources, may condition or moderate the strength of the associations among variables, thus promoting resilience or exacerbating vulnerability to the effects of economic stress. For example, a high level of support from an older sibling may lessen the effect of hostile, negative parenting on child adjustment (e.g., K. Conger, R. Conger, and Elder 1994a). Thus the hypothesized associations in figure 8.1 provide the basic theoretical and conceptual underpinnings for the program of research reviewed here (R. Conger and K. Conger 2002; Conger, Wallace, et al. 2002; Conger, Lorenz, and Wickrama 2004).

Studying Families Across Time: The Iowa Youth and Families Project

The basic parameters of the model shown in figure 8.1 were first proposed and evaluated in the Iowa Youth and Families Project (IYFP), a study of 451 rural Iowa families. The initial panel study was conducted from 1989 to 1992; the 451 focal children were in the seventh grade when they were first interviewed with a near-age sibling and their parents. Initial findings were reported separately for the 205 boys (R. Conger, K. Conger, et al. 1992) and 220 girls (R. Conger, K. Conger, et al. 1993) who participated in the IYFP during seventh grade and who had complete data for the required analyses. These two-parent families were selected for study because they lived in areas heavily dependent on agriculture and were likely to have experienced the economic and social upheavals caused by the economic downturn of the 1980s. Given the ethnic structure of rural Iowa at that time, all of these families were of European origin.

The IYFP included assessments of all dimensions of the FSM as illustrated in figure 8.1. Each family member (mother, father, seventh grader, and a near-age sibling) reported on his or her personal characteristics, family interactions, relationships with one another, economic and demographic circumstances, and activities and relationships with extended family and friends during two visits to the family each year. Child and adolescent outcomes included negative adjustment (e.g., problem behaviors and emotional distress) and positive adjustment (e.g., school achievement and mastery). In addition to the information gathered from the family members, four structured family interactions were videotaped as part of the second visit to the family. These videotapes were rated by trained observers using the Iowa Family Interaction Rating Scales (Melby and Conger 2001). All of the measures were designed to develop a picture of how families of various economic backgrounds and circumstances were influenced by, and adapted to, changes in the local, regional, and state economy. For a complete description of the study, see Conger and Elder (1994b).

In 1991, a sample of 110 single mother–headed households was added to the study; participants included the mother, a focal child matched in age (a ninth grader) to the focal children in the IYFP, and a near-age sibling. For details regarding this study, see Simons and Associates (1996). These two samples were combined into the study now known as the Family Transitions Project (FTP), and data collection continues to the present day. Continuation of the study has allowed us to assess the long-term effects of coming of age during a time of economic upheaval and social change. Details and initial findings from the FTP are reviewed in R. Conger and K. Conger (2002). The next section of this chapter examines empirical findings related to the hypothesized pathways proposed in the FSM.

Empirical Evidence Related to the Family Stress Model

A review of the findings begins with an assessment of the primary pathway of influence, namely how stressful economic conditions are expected to affect parents' emotional distress through their sense of economic pressure. Our confidence in this pathway, and other aspects of the hypothesized stress process, has been strengthened now that basic results of the FSM have been replicated with more diverse family groups in the United States and abroad (e.g., African American families—see Conger, Wallace, et al. 2002; Scaramella et al. 2008; Czech families—see Hraba, Lorenz, and Pechacova 2000; Finnish families—see Solantaus, Leinonen, and Punamäki 2004; and Latino families—see Parke et al. 2005). Results from these studies as well as those from the Iowa study summarized here illustrate how stress processes operate within families to influence the lives of children and adolescents.

Economic Hardship, Economic Pressure, and Parent Distress

This first section brings to life the notion that conditions of economic hardship, such as losing a job, having unstable income, and being laid off, have their effect on parents' psychological distress through the daily economic pressures associated with these negative financial circumstances. Based on previous research traditions related to economic strain, poverty, and unemployment (e.g., Duncan and Brooks-Gunn 1997; Elder 1974; Liem and Liem 1990), we first assessed parents with a set of measures that would adequately reflect conditions of economic hardship. The measures included: (1) per capita income, which provided a sense of the current economic state of the family; (2) unstable work of the parents; (3) the ratio of debts to family assets such as that used by rural sociologists (e.g., Murdock and Leistritz 1988); and (4) income loss due to changing economic circumstances. Results from the IYFP indicate that these hardship conditions led to economic pressures. That is, in response to diminished economic conditions, families experienced economic pressures such as having to cut back their spending for clothing, housing, leisure activities, and health insurance. Furthermore, parents reported that they frequently had difficulty paying their bills at the end of the month, never seemed to have any money left over, and could not afford many basic necessities of life (e.g., R. Conger, K. Conger, et al. 1992, 1993). And for these Iowa families, these experiences of economic pressure were significantly related to psychological distress for both husbands and wives. In fact, once we took reports of economic pressure into account, hardship conditions themselves had only an indirect effect on emotional distress. Support for this part of the stress process also has been reported in studies of African American and Latino families as well as in families in

Finland and the Czech Republic (see Conger, Wallace, et al. 2002; Hraba, Lorenz, and Pechacova 2000; Parke et al. 2005; Solantaus, Leinonen, and Punamäki 2004, respectively).

Especially striking, parents suffering the greatest economic hardship often reported taking extreme steps to cut expenses, such as canceling health insurance, buying used instead of new, bartering for items, as well as reducing or eliminating donations to their church and other charitable organizations, which is a very public manifestation of economic difficulties. Oftentimes, families living on farms reported having loans and mortgages that involved their aging parents or other family members, thus making it impossible to walk away from a farm that was losing money and rapidly losing value as land prices sank throughout the region (Conger et al. 2000). Thus, assessing the economic pressure brought about by these very real experiences helps us understand how economic conditions are linked to emotional distress and disrupted family relations.

The following illustrates how economic conditions and economic pressure combine to produce emotional distress. A poignant form of distress was observed in some of the videotapes of women who, prior to the farm crisis, were stay-at-home moms who then were thrust into work outside the home to generate income for the family. As might be expected in rural areas of the Midwest, these women did not have a variety of occupational choices and thus went to work for low wages at places like the local restaurant, the local convenience store, or a nearby factory, or commuted to a larger town nearby to help make ends meet. This was not a career move but a decision born of economic necessity, and often "her" paycheck went directly to meet expenses for the farm, the family business, or new shoes for the kids, leaving nothing left over for her own use or enjoyment. Although the money itself was badly needed, wives forced into this situation may have viewed this unwanted work as a violation of their expectations for a breadwinner-homemaker lifestyle. That is, women choosing to raise families in rural settings may have done so in part because of their desire for a relatively traditional family lifestyle. Disappointments related to changes in family life may have been hard for some women to overcome even while acknowledging that their families had little control over these macroeconomic events that swept through rural America (Davidson 1990; Lobao and Lasley 1995). Adding to this distress was the fact that many times the people who had to deny loans or start foreclosure proceedings were the same people whom they sat next to in church or at their kids' softball games; a heart-wrenching circumstance for all concerned.

Economic Pressure, Parent Distress, and Marital Relationships

The next step in the stress process examines how economic pressure and emotional distress can combine to disrupt marital relationships. This step in the process builds on research on the effects of unemployment in the auto industry, which found that adults had increased emotional and physical health complaints, marriages fell apart, and reports of child and spouse abuse increased dramatically (e.g., Kessler, Turner, and House 1988; Perucci and Targ 1988). We hypothesized that couples who reported economic pressure as a result of the massive downturn in the rural economy would experience similar problems (Conger and Elder 1994b).

Just as a thunderstorm rolls across the prairie, we found that the effects of economic pressure reverberated through the lives and relationships of these Iowa couples. First, our results indicated that economic pressure increased emotional distress, such as depression, anxiety, and hostility, for both wives and husbands. This increased emotional distress contributed to either withdrawal in social interactions or increased marital conflict, leading in some cases to separation or divorce even in these long-standing marriages (see Conger et al. 1994). Our research suggests that it is the dynamics of the romantic relationship that predict why some couples are fairly resilient to economic stressors and other life events while others are not. Specifically, patterns of social support and communication during problem-solving interactions were key elements in understanding relationship dynamics in couples. For example, Conger, Rueter, and Elder (1999) found a significant interaction effect between level of observed social support and economic pressure in predicting husbands' and wives' emotional distress (i.e., depression, anxiety, and hostility). Husbands and wives who pulled together and demonstrated high levels of social support (1 SD above the mean) toward each other reported less emotional distress (even after controlling for all exogenous variables). Couples who had low levels of support had higher levels of distress in response to economic pressure.

Consistent with the FSM, results show that economic pressure also contributed directly to marital conflict, and spousal support alone did not explain how some couples avoided increased conflict while others showed increased hostility and withdrawal. Figure 8.2 illustrates the significant interaction obtained by regressing Time 3 marital distress (such as thoughts of ending the marriage) on Time 2 marital conflict for couples with ineffective compared to effective problem solving (R. Conger, Rueter, and Elder 1999). The interaction between problem solving and marital conflict was significant ($\beta = -.16$, $p < .05$)

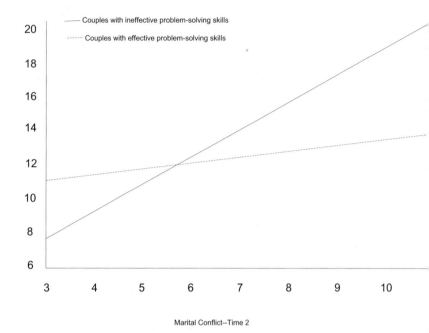

FIG. 8.2   Predicting the association between marital conflict and marital distress as a function of effective problem solving compared to ineffective problem solving (SOURCE: adapted from Rueter, Conger, and Elder 1999)

with all Time 1 predictors, such as economic pressure, emotional distress, and marital conflict, in the equation. Results indicated that couples who were able to solve problems in an effective, constructive, and practical manner diminished the negative effect of marital conflict on marital distress when compared to couples with ineffective problem-solving skills. These findings suggest that effective couple problem solving may act as a protective influence for couples faced with economic adversity (R. Conger and K. Conger 2002). Furthermore, understanding the patterns of marital interaction in response to economic stress helps identify potential points for intervention with families experiencing economic hardship or other negative life events.

In addition to relationship dynamics, previous research suggests that individual characteristics or personal resources may reduce the level of adversity or even suppress the full negative effect of stressors such as economic adversity (Lin and Ensel 1989; Thoits 2006). In this case, the personal resources of parents might reduce the negative influence of economic stress and negative life events. Specifically, we proposed that people with a high sense of mastery or control would be more resilient to negative events and circumstances (Lewis,

Ross, and Mirowsky 1999; Mirowsky and Ross 1998; Pearlin et al. 1981). Results supported this hypothesis. The personal resource of mastery protected parents in two ways; a high sense of mastery decreased the likelihood of experiencing depressive symptoms in response to economic pressure and predicted lower economic pressure over time, even after controlling for income and education (R. Conger and K. Conger 2002). We suggest that persons with a higher sense of mastery or personal control may be more likely to take active steps to reduce expenses and manage resources, thereby reducing economic pressure for the family. Thus, research evidence supports the basic propositions of the first part of the FSM, namely that economic pressure will intensify emotional distress and that both distress and pressure may disrupt marital relationships. The findings also demonstrate, however, that important personal (i.e., mastery) and social (i.e., effective couple problem solving) resources promote resilience to the negative effects of the economic stress process.

Linking Economic Pressure to Parenting and Adolescent Adjustment

The evidence to date also supports one of the central hypotheses of the FSM, namely, that disruptions in parenting behaviors appear to play a key role in transmitting the effects of stressful economic conditions to the development of children (e.g., R. Conger, K. Conger, et al. 1992, 1993; Conger, Wallace, et al. 2002). For example, findings from the study demonstrate that economic pressure serves as a predictor of poor parenting behaviors that put adolescents at risk for problematic adjustment (Conger et al. 1994; Conger et al. 1999).

One area where we observed the effect of economic stress on parenting was related to the stress and strain of having inadequate income to afford life's basic needs or to make ends meet; these difficulties increased the hostility and coercion between parents, which, in turn, often diminished the warmth and support toward children (see K. Conger, R. Conger, and Scaramella 1997; R. Conger, K. Conger, et al. 1992, 1993; Conger, Wallace, et al. 2002). Just as emotional distress interfered with good marital relationships, so too did it interfere with "good" parenting, such as mothers' and fathers' abilities to maintain consistent expectations, effectively monitor their children's activities and school-work, and be available when difficulties arose. Figure 8.3 summarizes results from two studies that tested the full FSM: Study 1 used data from the IYFP, and Study 2 used data from African American parents and children participating in the Family and Community Health Study (FACHS). We found similar patterns of results across the two studies, which indicate that emotional distress in

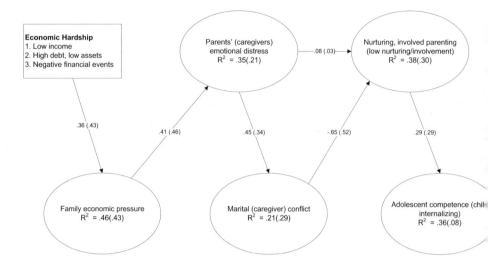

FIG. 8.3   Adolescent competence influenced by family economic hardship via its effect on family social processes and parental adjustment

response to economic pressure had a corrosive effect on both marital (or parent-caregiver) relationships and parent-child relationships (e.g., R. Conger, K. Conger, et al. 1993; Conger, Wallace, et al. 2002), and these relationships, in turn, had a negative effect on child adjustment. Consistent across both studies, results indicate that the effects of economic hardship on children were indirect through their influence on the important adults in their lives. This consistency is perhaps all the more remarkable given that the IYFP results are based on low- to middle-income white families in the upper Midwest and the FACHS results are based on low- to middle-income urban black families in the Midwest and low-income rural black families in the Southeast.

In addition to the tests of the full model, additional analyses indicated that economic pressure predicted interpersonal aggression of adolescents and their siblings indirectly through parental hostility (R. Conger and K. Conger 1996; Williams, Conger, and Blozis 2007). Furthermore, children living with a depressed parent were at higher risk for depression themselves (Reeb and Conger 2009). We propose that how adolescents respond to their parents' emotional distress and hostile, inconsistent parenting can have long-term effects (K. Conger, R. Conger, and Scaramella 1997). For example, decisions made in adolescence could have unforeseen effects on the life course as bad decisions, such as dropping out of school or an unplanned pregnancy, could limit their choices later on in life (e.g., Lewis, Ross, and Mirowsky 1999). This interpretation is consistent with previous research findings that chronic poverty in early life puts young adolescents at risk for poor academic achievement, for developing an array of problem behaviors, and for experiencing decreased opportunities to improve their life chances (Duncan and Brooks-Gunn 1997; Duncan and Magnuson 2003).

However, the picture was not all bleak, as many families demonstrated resilience to the negative effects of economic hardship by maintaining open lines of marital and family communication and by providing warm, supportive parenting. It was this nurturing, involved parenting, which was also low on hostility and cynicism, that buffered or mediated the effect of economic hardship on these Iowa adolescents and predicted more positive outcomes. For example, adolescents who observed their parents solving problems in their marriage, and who experienced constructive problem solving with siblings and with parents, were more likely to experience an increase in their sense of mastery over the years of adolescence (K. Conger, Williams, et al. 2009). Just as a high level of mastery acted as a protective personal resource for parents, we expect that the development of mastery during the teens and early twenties will help explain which adolescents are more likely to be in a position to take advantage of social and educational opportunities. So the findings suggest that while economic pressure and emotional distress oftentimes have a corrosive influence on marital and parent-child relationships, some parents are able to pull together in the face of these stressors. And when they are able to do so, these adults can markedly reduce the adverse consequences of economic problems for their marriages as well as for their children's health and well-being.

Just as support from parents buffered the effects of economic adversity for their children, we found evidence that siblings can serve as a source of support for one another during difficult times. Older siblings in the IYFP who demonstrated warmth and support toward their younger siblings, even under conditions of economic hardship, significantly reduced the negative effect of moms' and dads' harsh, coercive parenting (K. Conger, R. Conger, and Elder 1994; K. Conger, R. Conger, and Scaramella 1997; K. Conger, Shebloski, et al. 2008), and predicted more positive adjustment for these adolescents. Thus, during times of economic and social distress, older siblings may be able to provide that "arena of comfort" that has been identified as important to positive mental health and well-being during adolescence (Call and Mortimer 2001). Taken together, then, the personal resources and the nature of interactions within the family system help explain how some families were able to withstand many of the negative effects of economic hardship and others were not.

Although the influence of economic hardship on children was primarily indirect through its effects on their parents, these adolescents too felt the lack of money as parents had to cut back expenditures for new sneakers or uniforms for basketball, football, or other sports for which schools expect parents to pay their child's expenses. During interviews, these rural adolescents reported taking on jobs after school and on weekends to participate in school activities. In many of these small towns, local schools are *the* social hub of the community, as everyone either has a child participating in sports, music, the debate team, or Future Farmers of America, or knows someone who does. Many parents, particularly mothers who were forced to go to work in low-wage and unfulfilling jobs, were now no longer available to their children after school or on weekends. Fathers also had reduced time with children as they commuted longer distances to find work or took jobs, such as long-haul trucking, that took them away from home for days at a time. Parents in these situations also were less able to volunteer at their child's school, their church, or the local senior center, thus affecting not only their own family but many other lives as the economic effects rippled throughout these small communities (Davidson 1990; Lasley et al. 1995; Lobao and Lasley 1995). Simply put, economically hard-hit families who were forced to withdraw from these activities often lost important sources of support at the same time their need for support increased, creating a double dose of stress that reverberated throughout these rural families and communities (Lasley et al. 1995; Lorenz et al. 1993; Rosenblatt 1990).

Future Research: Studying the Next Generation

The next steps in the Iowa study include an examination of these adolescents as they move through the tasks of early adulthood, such as obtaining additional education, having children, getting married, becoming employed, and establishing themselves as independent adults. How successful they are in negotiating the challenges of early adulthood may depend in part on their experiences in their families during the critical adolescent years. The findings presented in this chapter, as well as those from other studies (e.g., Duncan and Brooks-Gunn 1997; Kokko and Pulkkinen 2000; Lewis, Ross, and Mirowsky 1999; Parke et al. 2005; Scaramella et al. 2008), support this notion. For example, those adolescents who lived in families who felt the full brunt of the economic crisis may have fewer educational and employment opportunities, which in turn can start them on a path of less satisfying work, lower wages, and fewer options for romantic partners (K. Conger, Martin, et al. 2011; Lichter, McLaughlin, and Ribar 2002). Unexpected behavioral outcomes such as early pregnancy and poor choices in romantic partners also may disrupt carefully laid plans (e.g., Lewis, Ross, and Mirowsky 1999).

In contrast, those adolescents who grew up in families who survived the economic challenges of the 1980s with their parents' marriage intact may be in a better position to take advantage of educational, social, and employment opportunities that present themselves in early adulthood. In addition, there may be a cumulative advantage, as these youth acquire more education and place themselves in a position to take advantage of better employment and life opportunities (K. Conger, Martin, et al. 2011). These positive experiences, in turn, may help them establish more satisfying relationships with romantic partners, family members, and friends (Bryant and Conger 2002; Conger, Bryant, and Brennom 2004), thus realizing their dreams made during adolescence.

Implications for Social Policy and Prevention

Results from this study highlight how economic conditions at the local, state, and federal levels can spill over into family life and affect both family functioning and the health and well-being of family members. Policy makers should keep these findings in mind when developing social policy designed to alleviate the negative consequences of economic restructuring in rural America. In particular, these results suggest that it is not only adults who suffer the ill effects of economic hardship; economic pressure in families can create risk for adolescents. Families in rural areas may face unique challenges that compromise their ability to adapt and respond to changing economic conditions. First, geographic isolation may limit access to programs designed to offer assistance to families such as financial management or training for new jobs. Second, many rural communities may have limited support services for youth and families; often there are fewer professionals to deliver services to a widely dispersed population. For example, limited access to health care and lack of public transportation may make it difficult to obtain quality health care services, thus compromising the health of family members (HHS Rural Task Force 2002; Lichter and Jensen 2002; Ricketts 1999). Resources for mental health services in rural areas are often even more limited, thus compounding the negative fallout from the emotional distress experienced by family members. In a recent study by Ontai and colleagues (2008), low-income rural mothers reported that family health concerns negatively affected their confidence as a parent. Single mothers, in particular, reported difficulty in juggling work and family demands to obtain health care when one of their children was ill or had a chronic health condition.

Conger (1997) noted that one challenge in meeting the needs of distressed families in rural America is that parents may avoid using available services due to the stigma attached, particularly with respect to mental health. Rural youth and families may be more receptive to educational programs, mental health services, and prevention programs that are offered through respected local institutions such as churches, schools, cooperative extension, or community health clinics.

Conclusions

Taken together, these findings suggest that the FSM provides a reasonable heuristic model for improving our understanding of how economic conditions influence family members, social interactions, and the adjustment of children and adolescents. We are grateful for the many family members who have been willing to talk to us and participate in this study for twenty years. I think they, too, realize the importance of social scientists and policy makers having a well-informed understanding of the effects of economic hardship on individuals and families. The voices of family members telling us how they survived difficult times help keep the focus on actual events and real people. And this reminds us that decisions made in city councils, state legislatures, and the U.S. Congress are not just anonymous pieces of legislation, but have very real effects on the lives of individuals and families across the country. By understanding the effect of economic hardship on marriages, parents, their children, and their communities in both the short and long term, we lay the foundation for developing multifaceted constructive policies and programs that support healthy, well-functioning families in the twenty-first century.

SECTION 3

LOW-WAGE EMPLOYMENT

PARENTS' WORK TIME IN RURAL AMERICA

The Growth of Irregular Schedules

ELAINE MCCRATE

Making a living in rural America typically involves multiple endeavors, combining low-wage employment in services, trade, or manufacturing with self-employment, both formal and informal (Nelson and Smith 1999; Tickamyer and Wood 2003; refer also to Nelson, chapter 7 in this volume). This economic structure entails coordination of complex and shifting spatial and temporal demands, to ensure that earners are in the right place at the right time.

The constant needs of young children for care are superimposed on the requirements of rural work. Parents need to be able to make *plans* for child care within their painstakingly constructed schedules, and they need to be able to "drop everything" when plans fail because of illness, snow days, mud days, and no-show babysitters. Self-employed and many informal-sector working parents can often (not always) plan ahead, and often they can also drop what they are doing, at least for a short while, without losing their livelihoods. Also, most manufacturing and clerical workers traditionally could count on fairly predictable schedules around which to plan the care of children (as well as time for work in the informal sector), although these workers have generally not enjoyed flexible schedules that let them respond to unforeseen contingencies (McCrate 2003, 2005; Presser 2003).

The last thing most families need is scheduling instability imposed by external authorities, where parents can neither make plans nor respond to last-minute emergencies. In the complex mosaic of rural workers' days, this is even more problematic. The long-term shift in rural areas out of self-employment and into wage labor has meant that employers have gradually gained authority over significant parts of rural parents' time. It has also meant more time spent in a car (Tigges and Fuguitt 2003). Manufacturing, a stronghold of rural employment in the past several decades, has typically featured stable (if rigid) work schedules. However, in recent years, rural work has shifted to sectors that already have more variable schedules (transportation and some services), and virtually all industries, rural and urban, have been moving in that direction. When employers demand strict observance of work schedules, even when these schedules change frequently and at short notice, family care plans and effective responses to unanticipated family needs both become much more difficult. Latchkey child care arrangements, stress, and unstable sleep schedules may follow. While this is equally true in urban and rural areas, the sheer number of income-generating activities that rural families must juggle, along with child care, means that externally imposed erratic schedules are more likely to generate domino effects and vicious circles: if a checkout clerk has to work unexpectedly on Saturday afternoon, then she can't plan ahead to do cleaning or child care for other families during that time (informal sector), and her own child care arrangements are disrupted, so she must disrupt someone else's plans to see that someone is watching her own children. And because of growing rural female labor force participation, as well as rural population decline in some areas, the family and community backups for parents with schedule breakdowns are arguably thinner today than before.[1]

This chapter documents the growth of variable starting and stopping times at work for rural residents, especially for those workers who have little control over the timing of work. It documents the disproportionate concentration of this problem among some rural parents, especially lone parents, and blacks and Hispanics. I discuss some of the reasons for variable scheduling and present some policy proposals.

The Data

Unless otherwise noted, this analysis is based on the May Current Population Survey. In various years, the Bureau of Labor Statistics has administered the Work Schedule Supplement along with its regular May survey. The May CPS includes a variable on metropolitan (metro) vs. nonmetropolitan (nonmetro) residence, where nonmetro is defined as areas with fewer than one hundred thousand people. For convenience, I will use "rural" and "nonmetro" interchangeably; I will do so also for "urban" and "metro," acknowledging that these pairs are hardly alike in many salient respects. (Among other things, the one hundred thousand cutoff blurs the distinction between rural and exurban.) I examine the work schedules of all civilian workers age eighteen to sixty-five with complete data over the years 1997–2004.[2]

Total Weekly Hours of Work

Using data from the May 2004 Current Population Survey, table 9.1 shows the percentages of metro and nonmetro workers who usually work part-time, full-time, and overtime, and those with hours so variable that they are not classified as any of these. Rural residents are 43 percent more likely to have variable total weekly hours than metro residents (12 percent vs. 8 percent, in table 9.1).[3] This kind of schedule is especially common among rural men.[4] Either women are more reluctant to work variable schedules, probably because of family responsibilities, or employers are more reluctant to fill these kinds of jobs with women. However, fathers need to plan family time, too. Variable hours may be a barrier to men trying to be more involved with their families.

Variable hours, however, are not necessarily a sign of trouble for families. Nonmetro areas still have more self-employed people, who usually enjoy greater scheduling flexibility than employees. This chapter will unpack the variability in hours to see how much is involuntary, and for whom it is involuntary—and therefore discover whose children potentially are at risk.

Variability of Starting and Stopping Times

In most industries that use variable scheduling, there is also considerable variation in days worked. In rural economies, with their heavy reliance on resource-based industries such as farming and outdoor recreation, there is substantial seasonal variation in working time as well. My estimates therefore fall considerably short of describing total variability in schedules.[5]

The Work Schedule Supplement of the Current Population Survey provides measures of both control over hours and variability of hours. One question asks, "Do you have flexible work hours *that allow you* to vary or make changes in the time you begin and end work?" (emphasis mine). Respondents may answer yes or no. Other questions ask what time of day the respondent begins work on her main job most days, and at what time she ends work. Respondents may give specific times, or they may answer, "It varies." This option has been available for respondents since 1997.

I cross-tabulated these variables from the May 2004 Work Schedule Supplement and used the results to create the 2 × 2 classification scheme of table 9.2. This table gives examples of the schedule type in each cell.

Figure 9.1 gives the actual weighted percentages on schedule type for all civilian workers in the supplemental interview sample, age eighteen to sixty-five, for rural and urban workers. For this sample, 11 percent of nonmetro workers said they do not have flexible schedules at their main job that allow them to vary their starting and stopping times, but that their starting and stopping times do vary (category D). For D-workers, the implication is that someone else is changing their hours, and indeed D-workers include a lot of workers on split and rotating shifts. This structure also includes many workers who

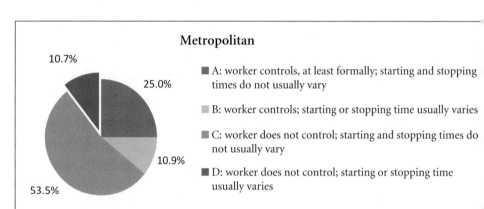

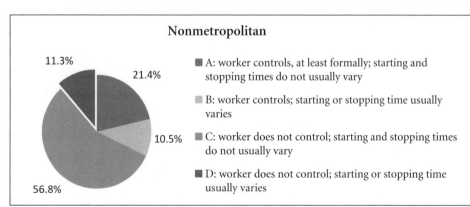

FIG. 9.1   The distribution of schedule types by metropolitan and nonmetropolitan residence, 2004

say they work regular daytime or evening schedules (mostly daytime). These workers appear to be indicating that while their starting and stopping times regularly fall within a daytime (or evening or night) interval, they change enough within that interval to be described as variable.[6] These workers neither enjoy predictability nor have flexibility that they can control.

Most nonmetro workers (57 percent) are in the more conventional group that lacks control over its hours and has fixed starting and stopping times (category C). This situation is typical of the schedules of many manufacturing and clerical workers. These schedules are rigid, but they are predictable.

Many nonmetro workers (21 percent) say that they have flexible work hours that allow them to change their schedules, but in fact give usually fixed starting and stopping times (category A). These workers may be choosing to maintain regular schedules to accommodate the routine needs of families, or there could be a gap between formal control over their schedules and the reality of their workplaces (for example, many lawyers and doctors; MacDermid and Tang 2009). Finally, only 11 percent of rural workers control their hours, and usually in fact vary them (category B).

The schedules of metro and nonmetro workers differ in some important respects. Rural workers are more likely than urban workers to have rigid work hours—that is, schedules that are fixed and that they do not control (category C, 57 percent vs. 54 percent). Thus, rural workers have less ability to respond to unanticipated family needs. While the proportions of rural and urban workers with variable starting and stopping times that they control (category B) and with times that they do not control (category D) are about the same, the overall percentages mask important differences among demographic groups, particularly among household types.

Table 9.3 illustrates this variation, showing the distribution of schedule types among single parents, married parents, and nonparents for whites, African Americans, and Hispanics, in metro and nonmetro areas. Overall, rural parents are more likely to have D-schedules (without control over variable work times); 10 percent of rural parents have such schedules, compared with 9 percent for urban parents. Rural parents are also more likely to have C-schedules (without control over rigid work times): 57 percent vs. 54 percent. This finding implies that rural parents are less likely to have the kind of schedule whereby they do have control over their starting and stopping times (A + B): this proportion is 37 percent for urban parents, and only 33 percent for rural parents.

Single parents, most of whom are women and would be expected to have the greatest need for control over their own schedules, typically have higher frequencies of D-schedules than married parents. The problem is most common in rural areas. Rural single parents are also more likely to have rigid schedules (C) than their married counterparts, and in addition rural single parents are also more likely to have C-schedules than their urban counterparts. Rural single parents are less likely than urban single parents to have schedules that they do control (A + B, i.e., those who can vary the times that they begin and end work).

This pattern is especially striking for blacks and Hispanics. In particular, 20 percent of black rural single parents and 19 percent of Hispanic rural single parents have D-schedules. Furthermore, 66 percent and 67 percent of rural black and Hispanic single parents, respectively, have rigid schedules (C), and fewer of them have schedules that they control (A + B, not shown).

Married parents in rural areas do not fare well, either. For all racial/ethnic groups, they are more likely to have schedules that they do not control (C + D) than married parents in urban areas.

The Role of Economic Restructuring

How much of the variability in work schedules is relatively long-standing, and how much is plausibly attributable to recent economic restructuring? Figure 9.2 shows changes in the four different schedule types since 1997 in metro and nonmetro areas. Variable starting and stopping times have increased, both of the type that workers themselves control and of the type that they do not control. The latter, however, has increased more rapidly. And while the aggregate trends are similar in metro and nonmetro areas, we have seen that erratic schedules strike harder in certain kinds of rural families (female-headed, black, and Hispanic). Furthermore, the impact is likely to be greater in nonmetro areas, where families more often sustain themselves by piecing together several different methods for generating income, in both the formal and informal sectors.

Rural workers' schedules have changed dramatically across all private sector industries. Table 9.4 shows the growth rates of schedule types within industries, and also of broad industry shares of employment for urban and rural areas from 1997 to 2001. By 2004, the Bureau of Labor Statistics had implemented a new, noncomparable industrial classification system; these results are shown in table 9.5. D-schedules among rural residents exploded between 1997 and 2001, except in the field of public administration. By 2004, this type of schedule was especially common in one rural growth industry, leisure and hospitality, as well as in mining, trade, and transportation.

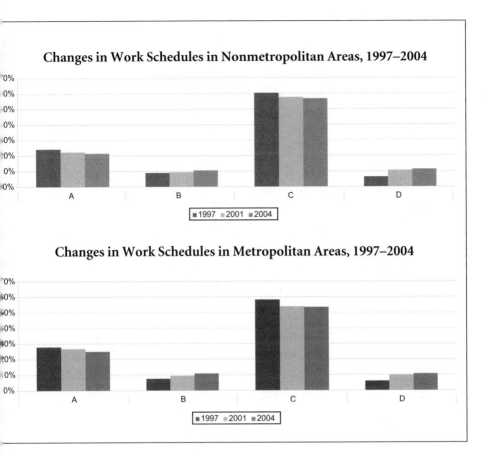

FIG. 9.2   Changes in work schedules by area

C-schedules, rigid but usually regular, decreased gradually for rural workers in all industries except agriculture. Manufacturing, a traditional stronghold of the C-schedule, markedly decreased its overall share of rural employment, contributing to the decline of this schedule type.

While B-schedules (variable starting and stopping times controlled by the worker) increased in most industries for urban residents, they had a more mixed pattern among rural residents, declining conspicuously in transportation, communication, and utilities. The share of A-schedules (regular, and at least nominally controlled by the worker) also decreased for most industries employing rural workers.

Discussion

The forces behind the decline of the C-schedule and the rise of the D-schedule are widespread, traversing nearly all industries. Five trends underlie the growth of erratic hours in rural as well as urban areas. First is the extraordinary increase in women's hours of employment over the past several decades. Women used to be predictable consumers because they were available for shopping and the use of services during regular working hours (remember home milk delivery?). Therefore, the schedules of workers who served them could be predictable. Now women are drawn in many different directions, and in addition to work, they need time to shop and to take children to school,[7] activities, doctor's appointments, and so on. Consequently, the workers who serve them must adjust their own hours to take care of the things they need to do.

Second is the growth of service industries and the decline of manufacturing. Unlike the outputs of manufacturing, the outputs of service industries (and interactions with retail customers) cannot be inventoried. In their study of scheduling practices in several industries, Moss, Salzman, and Tilly (2005) found a number of trends, such as restaurant outsourcing of food preparation to remote manufacturers, that tended to reduce the number of erratic schedules in food service and increase the number of stable (and possibly rigid) schedules in food manufacturing (a common rural industry). But they also found that retail employers are backing off from expanded hours and instead using call centers to achieve 24/7 coverage. The outsourcing of sales work from stores to call centers has increased the proportion of workers on part-time or unpredictable schedules at remote sites. With the increase in women's labor force participation, workers must field more calls during early morning hours, evenings, and weekends. Furthermore, since retail calls tend to spike at discrete times (for example, when the television ad blares, "Call now! Operators are standing by"), workers must be available at times that, from their perspective, are unpredictable and arbitrary.

In some industries, such as retail and food service, D-schedules are part of an aggressive strategy to cut costs and maximize revenue by matching employees' hours to customers' hours, on something like a "just-in-time" basis. At Walmart, the nation's largest employer, increasing the proportion of part-time workers has also gone hand-in-hand with increasing the number of workers on D-schedules[8] (Greenhouse and Barbaro 2006). Also, to the extent that manufacturing and retail firms practice just-in-time inventory control, one other result may be that truck drivers are on the road at less predictable hours. Deregulation in trucking has also contributed to this, as required rest intervals have been reduced in length.

Although services and trade are among the most D-schedule-intensive industries, the practice of erratic scheduling has been growing in all sectors. A third reason for the increased incidence of variable starting and stopping times addresses the growth of this practice across industries. Just-in-time inventory control swept manufacturing in the latter decades of the twentieth century, and because of the low-tech nature of much rural manufacturing work (Barkley 1995), attempts to eliminate slack in production schedules may be among the primary mechanisms by which manufacturers attempt to make their rural establishments competitive. Furthermore, just-in-time principles have begun to permeate areas previously considered beyond their reach, such as financial services, cleaning rooms in hotels, and shipping packages (Lambert 2008).

In turn, workers who do not know when they will be at work probably do not know when they will go shopping and require the services of cashiers and clerks, generating a vicious circle of uncertainty. When an employer suddenly requires a parent to stay longer at work, reducing at-home meal preparation time, the family might go to McDonald's, and McDonald's suddenly needs more labor. Ironically, the achievement of flexibility for some workers—either through explicit personnel practices or through informal actions such as absenteeism—can impose unpredictability on others. Many nurses' schedules are unpredictable because they have to cover the absenteeism of other nurses, who may be off addressing their own family problems. With the growth of female labor force participation and hours worked, workers who would have in the past "dropped everything" to respond to family emergencies themselves now must impose their own scheduling uncertainty on others—for example, the sister-in-law who reluctantly agrees to watch a worker's children at a moment's notice. As the rural population declines in some areas and some rural counties empty out, there is a less dense network of personal support for child care problems. Only in rare cases are there market solutions for these problems.

Fifth, employers are imposing irregular schedules in large part because they can. Employers are taking advantage of workers' declining bargaining power as mass layoffs and worker displacement force many of the unemployed to take jobs with less desirable working conditions (Uchitelle 2006). Federal policies have also reduced worker bargaining power: attention to the enforcement of the overtime provisions of the Fair Labor Standards Act has been less than scrupulous in recent years. Employers' enhanced bargaining power in turn has been exacerbated by welfare reform, which requires many recipients to accept virtually any job offer regardless of working conditions.

What Can We Do About Erratic Work Schedules?

Because D-schedules make it difficult to plan family life, they are likely to be harmful to children. They are especially concentrated in some of the most vulnerable families: those of rural single parents of color. So what can we do about D-schedules? I start this discussion with several principles. First, we need coordinated social intervention to address the problem, because children are public goods. We all benefit when they have positive outcomes, regardless of how much or how little we have contributed to their upbringing (Folbre 1994). Therefore, markets will predictably fail to provide for the care of children, because of the "free rider" problem. Most of us would like children to be provided for, but we would like someone else to pay the bill. As a result, social intervention is necessary in markets that often fail spectacularly to accommodate children's needs.

Second, we don't want to give firms incentives to discriminate against parents. For example, a requirement of company-provided child care for all employees who need it would likely induce firms to hire fewer parents (Heymann 2000).

Third, we need to accept some slack in the system—that is, not all work schedules can be arranged on just-in-time principles without imposing unacceptable costs on parents and on other workers as well. Stores and service providers will have to be a bit "overstaffed" at times, or child care providers will need to maintain excess capacity to absorb the children of workers who get called in to work at the last minute. Someone has to bear the cost of slack; the only question is who. I am remaining agnostic for the time being as to whether we ought to strongly discourage irregular-hour work through disincentives for employers, or whether we ought to accommodate it through backup arrangements for parents. Deciding between these alternatives requires, among other things, more understanding of the preferences of working parents. Therefore, my proposals are of both varieties.

My last principle is that worker bargaining power must increase. Workers who lack a collective voice, and who fear the loss of the jobs they have, cannot negotiate good schedules with their employers. This is a level of policy that we often forget and that often seems daunting or out of reach, but that usually trumps anything else that might be accomplished.

I now offer a variety of proposals that satisfy these criteria: recognizing children as public goods; not creating incentives to discriminate against parents; accepting some slack; and enhancing worker bargaining power. Some of these proposals will require more organizing effort than others. Some are inexpensive and some are more costly. Some are long-standing ideas among scholars and advocates for workers and families, which have been thoroughly researched for effects; others are new and need some preliminary investigation of likely consequences.

1. We need more collective activities for children. Children should have more time in preschool and more supervised activities during the summer and after school. Rural self-sufficiency, at least in child care, is rapidly becoming obsolete as more mothers move into the labor force. The considerable number of states that have already passed school finance reform measures in response to court challenges under their state constitutions will be in a better position to redistribute resources to rural areas to support extended school activities.

2. There should be more licensed drop-off child care, much like France's *haltes-garderies* (Bergmann 1996). At these centers, parents can simply drop off children without advance notice.[9] In low-density rural areas, it might be necessary to maintain some reserve capacity in existing child care arrangements, rather than starting new centers. Social service agencies should compensate care providers for maintaining an overstaffed facility.

3. Welfare recipients must be able to refuse jobs with hours so irregular that they cannot plan for child care while they are at work. At the same time, the clock on welfare eligibility should be stopped at least until a recipient gets an offer that meets minimum criteria in terms of hours and scheduling predictability.

4. Social workers should work with employers, not just with service providers, to try to stabilize schedules, by advocating that their clients who are parents of young children be switched to more regular jobs.

5. To give all parents more flexibility in their work schedules to respond to unforeseen contingencies, we should mandate paid sick leave and vacation time for all employees. The United States is alone among advanced industrialized countries in not doing this (Appelbaum 2001).

6. When possible, firms should consolidate operations that have peaks in client service needs at different times to create more stable hours. This will probably require cross-training (Lambert 2009). It may also require breaking traditional divisions of labor by gender, class, and race, if, for example, maids in hotels are to get more stable hours by also taking on some basic maintenance work or front-desk work. Hotels have increased cross-training in their food and beverage services so that workers can fill

in for absentees, resulting in higher work intensity (Bernhardt, Dresser, and Hatton 2003); in principle, cross-training should be possible to stabilize work schedules.

7. If employers need irregular hours to respond to variations in demand, then employers should pay more, not less. D-workers' average hourly earnings are much lower than the wages of other workers (McCrate forthcoming). We could consider amending the Fair Labor Standards Act to require compensating differentials for irregular working hours (including irregular part-time hours), much as we now do for overtime, but the administrative burden could be prohibitive. Rather, a workplace-based enforcement mechanism is more likely to be successful. In this country, that would be a union. Unions have been losing what little power they have in some of the industries that have been most aggressive in pursuing unpredictable hours. For example, Walmart has moved into the grocery business, undermining the bargaining strength of the United Food and Commercial Workers in many areas. Labor law reform is necessary to make it easier for workers who would like to bargain collectively with their employers to do so. Unions could bargain with employers to reduce the proportion of D-jobs, either by increasing the wage (a disincentive for the proliferation of D-jobs) or through direct controls over schedules. Some unions have been able to negotiate effective language affecting the proportion of jobs that become D-jobs. (See, for example, Bernhardt, Dresser, and Hatton 2003. Also, nurses' unions often address this problem in their contracts.)

8. Public job-generating strategies, such as tax relief for employers, should target the growth of "good" jobs—jobs with livable incomes and family-friendly schedules—especially in depressed rural and inner-city areas. Such strategies should involve public reporting of progress, as well as clawback provisions when industries fail to meet targets for good job growth.

9. Last but not least, fiscal and monetary authorities should increase the bargaining power of all workers through careful expansionary fiscal and monetary policy. They should maintain the dollar at a relatively low exchange rate so that there is less temptation to move "low-road," low-tech rural manufacturing (Barkley 1995; McGranahan 2003) to Asia or Latin America, and hence less temptation in these industries to pursue a just-in-time competitive strategy to keep the jobs here. Parents who do not fear unemployment are in a better position to leave or turn down jobs that harm their families, and hence to negotiate for better jobs.

Conclusion

The American economy is transitioning from a state of predominantly rigid but predictable schedules (manufacturing and clerical work) to a regime with greater reliance on just-in-time principles. This kind of restructuring is happening across industries, although services, trade, and transportation have led the way. Parents, especially rural single parents of color who have particularly acute needs for scheduling stability, end up with much of the burden, unable to plan effectively for family time or child care.

Businesses may increasingly reach the conclusion that the costs of erratic scheduling exceed the benefits, because it seems to increase quit rates (Moss, Salzman, and Tilly 2005). But the growth of services, which cannot be inventoried, suggests that D-schedules are likely to remain a standard part of life for a large segment of the working population for the near future. As long as that is the case, policy makers must take steps to protect families and children.[10]

Table 9.1 Distribution of total usual weekly hours of work for metro and nonmetro residents, 2004

	Variable hours	Part-time (1–34 hours)	Full-time (35–40 hours)	Overtime (more than 40 hours)
Metro	8.2%	14.0%	54.8%	22.9%
Men	8.9	7.6	54.2	29.3
Women	7.4	21.4	55.6	15.7
Nonmetro	11.8%	14.1%	52.3%	21.8%
Men	14.2	6.9	50.2	28.7
Women	9.0	22.5	54.8	13.8

NOTE: n = 56,350.
SOURCE: May 2004 Current Population Survey.

Table 9.2 Control over the variability of starting and stopping times

	Starting and stopping times the same most days	Starting or stopping time varies
Flexible schedule that allows employees to vary starting and stopping times	A: manager has ability to adjust hours but usually maintains a regular schedule	B: self-employed small business owner goes fishing on sunny days, or professional worker sets own schedule
Employees cannot vary starting and stopping times	C: clerical or manufacturing worker has fixed hours Monday through Friday	D: employer provides a different schedule each week to waitress or retail clerk

NOTE: n = 56,350.
SOURCE: May 2004 Current Population Survey.

Table 9.3 Percentage of workers with C and D schedules, by metro/nonmetro residence, race, ethnicity, and family status

	Metro		Nonmetro	
	C: worker does not control; starting and stopping times do not usually vary	D: worker does not control; starting or stopping time usually varies	C: worker does not control; starting and stopping times do not usually vary	D: worker does not control; starting or stopping time usually varies
All parents	53.7	9.2	56.8	10.3
Unmarried	57.1	9.7	59.4	13.1
Married	52.9	9.1	56.3	9.8
All nonparents	53.4	11.6	56.7	12.0
All white parents*	52.2	8.8	56.4	10.0
Unmarried	54.8	9.1	58.4	11.9
Married	51.7	8.8	56.1	9.7
White, not parents*	52.3	11.2	55.7	11.5
All black parents*	61.6	11.96	64.5	14.0
Unmarried	63.5	11.8	65.6	20.0
Married	60.5	12.0	63.8	10.2
Black, not parents*	60.3	14.0	67.1	15.5
All Hispanic parents	63.2	10.9	64.9	14.4
Unmarried	60.8	11.4	66.7	18.8
Married	63.8	10.8	64.7	13.8
Hispanic, not parents	63.6	12.0	63.9	14.6

NOTE: n = 56,350.
* Does not include persons of mixed race.
SOURCE: May 2004 Current Population Survey.

Table 9.4 Rate of change of schedule types within industries, by metro vs. nonmetro area, 1997–2001

	A: worker controls at least formally; starting and stopping times do not usually vary	B: worker controls; starting or stopping time usually varies	C: worker does not control: starting and stopping times do not usually vary	D: worker does not control; starting or stopping time usually varies
Metro				
Agriculture, forestry, and fishing	−28.7	−1.9	−0.2	126.0
Mining	−1.0	3.8	−11.5	61.5
Construction	−15.8	12.6	−2.3	83.3
Manufacturing	−2.3	32.3	−5.1	106.7
Transportation, communication, and utilities	2.7	33.3	−10.0	37.8
Wholesale trade	6.7	−1.2	−6.9	45.0
Retail trade	−13.4	23.1	−9.0	44.7
Finance, insurance, and real estate	8.4	24.1	−13.1	6.9
Services	−3.9	28.8	−7.5	63.5
Public administration	−1.3	54.5	−7.6	7.5
Nonmetro				
Agriculture, forestry, and fishing	−21.7	16.8	5.4	89.5
Mining	−27.1	35.6	−19.6	207.9
Construction	−2.1	−4.0	−5.3	55.7
Manufacturing	−7.9	59.1	−5.1	88.6
Transportation, communication, and utilities	4.9	−15.2	−13.6	110.2
Wholesale trade	−2.7	30.8	−11.1	107.8
Retail trade	−14.9	3.8	−5.1	51.3
Finance, insurance, and real estate	−5.4	−4.0	−2.2	132.0
Services	−5.7	2.3	−2.9	58.8
Public administration	4.0	−4.7	−0.6	−4.4

NOTE: n = 48,416 for 1997, and 46,670 for 2001.
SOURCE: May 2004 Current Population Survey.

Table 9.5 Proportion of workers with C and D schedules within industry, by metro vs. nonmetro area, 2004

	Metro			Nonmetro		
	C: worker does not control; starting and stopping times do not usually vary	D: worker does not control; starting or stopping time usually varies	Overall industry share of urban employment	C: worker does not control; starting and stopping times do not usually vary	D: worker does not control; starting or stopping time usually varies	Overall industry share of rural employment
Agriculture, forestry, fishing, and hunting	41.1	15.5	0.7	31.1	9.2	5.0
Mining	45.9	23.8	0.2	56.7	21.6	1.0
Construction	53.0	10.7	7.4	47.9	10.5	8.5
Manufacturing	62.2	7.2	11.5	74.6	8.8	16.6
Wholesale and retail trade	47.4	15.6	14.8	51.9	15.4	14.2
Transportation and utilities	53.9	17.8	5.0	49.3	21.2	4.9
Information	49.6	9.4	2.8	56.4	9.3	1.4
Financial activities	48.6	5.2	7.7	53.9	5.0	4.4
Professional and business services	44.1	7.0	11.2	45.7	7.1	5.3
Education and health services	64.9	8.4	21.4	69.7	8.2	21.5
Leisure and hospitality	45.5	20.2	8.3	41.0	21.3	7.5
Other services	41.9	9.6	4.9	32.6	10.9	4.9
Public administration	61.3	8.1	4.3	65.5	9.5	4.9
Total			100.0			100.0

NOTE: n = 56,350.
SOURCE: May 2004 Current Population Survey.

Notes

1. Population decline has been most problematic in the prairie states. In many other rural areas, especially those with natural amenities, there has been population increase (Johnson 2003)—but class differences between newcomers and old-timers may militate against the development of informal backup systems for parents.

2. Unlike my previous paper on work schedule variability (McCrate forthcoming), these data include self-employed workers, because of their greater presence in urban areas.

3. Rural residents are also less likely than city dwellers to report working thirty-five hours or more (about 74 percent of the rural sample usually worked full-time or overtime hours, vs. 78 percent for the urban sample). Rural part-time workers are somewhat more likely than their urban counterparts to be satisfied with working less than thirty-five hours, perhaps in part because this most likely undercounts (and accommodates) their substantial activity in the informal sector. Data on preferences for work hours are not shown, but are available from the author.

4. The gender differences are further explored in my other paper (McCrate forthcoming).

5. Among involuntary part-timers, 2.5 percent of rural residents give the seasonal nature of their job as the reason for part-time work, vs. 0.6 percent of urban dwellers (data available from the author). Seasonal variation certainly presents serious challenges to rural working low-income parents trying to organize child care—it is comparable to the problems of all working parents trying to arrange child care during school vacations. But because much of the change can be anticipated weeks or months in advance, parents have greater scheduling elasticity than they do on irregular day-to-day schedules.

6. For an extensive discussion of potential problems with the data, see McCrate (forthcoming). It is worth noting that the growth of D-jobs is not captured in BLS's traditional shift work variable. Most of the increase in D-jobs among nonmetro workers (as for the entire American labor force) has come from people who say that they work regular daytime hours between 6 a.m. and 6 p.m. While D-jobs include a lot of jobs with rotating and split shifts, such shifts have declined at least since 1997. Similarly, the percentage of people who say that they work irregular hours or "some other shift" has fallen. In my previous paper, I conclude that the apparent anomaly of variable starting and stopping times within "regular" shifts cannot be attributed primarily to measurement errors, and that it most likely reflects the real experiences of a growing number of workers.

7. Many rural children attend consolidated schools drawing students from a widely spread population. Rural parents often take their children to school rather than submitting them to bus rides that can take more than an hour in each direction (Howell 2001).

8. Some Walmart employees also charge that increasing demands for irregular schedules is a strategy to force workers with relatively long tenure and high wages out of their jobs by making their jobs less manageable with their personal lives (Greenhouse and Barbaro 2006).

9. Although most of the spaces are reserved for children on unscheduled, occasional visits, some children come part-time on a regular schedule. It is not a big stretch to imagine centers where children could come on persistently irregular schedules.

10. Thanks to Shanna Ratner, Kristin Smith, Doug Hoffer, and Susan Lambert for sharing helpful work, comments, and suggestions.

LOW-WAGE EMPLOYMENT AMONG MINORITY WOMEN IN NONMETROPOLITAN AREAS

A Decomposition Analysis

MARLENE LEE

Because they cannot save, low-wage earners and their families are more vulnerable to economic and health crises. Women's low-wage employment may also be the source of additional problems as market costs for the work many women do at home, such as child care, are often more than women with low wages can afford to pay. In the nonmetropolitan (nonmetro) United States, race and ethnicity are significant factors in women's low-wage employment. The consequences of minority women's low-wage employment are even more important in light of debates over work, marriage promotion, and education provisions of the 1996 welfare reform and its recent reauthorization.

Background

While there were significant economic declines for rural communities during the 1980s and 1990s, new employment opportunities also opened up for women in this period. As rural economic sectors that traditionally employed men (e.g., mining, farming, and manufacturing) contracted, service sectors expanded, creating opportunities for women at the same time that households needed additional wage earners to make ends meet (Falk and Lobao 2004). In addition, because of changing gender norms, women began entering fields traditionally monopolized by men, but these sectors were in decline.

In an earlier study, Lobao and Meyer (1995) examined the effect of restructuring on rural women's farm employment and found that during the 1980s farm crisis, women were more likely than men to seek off-farm employment to supplement family income. Women were also more likely to occupy jobs brought about by restructuring. About one-third were in traditional women's rural professional jobs, such as teaching and nursing, and nearly one-half occupied lower-wage jobs in the more recently expanding service sector. Many women were also self-employed and engaged in informal sector activities such as babysitting, house cleaning, and providing business services.

In a qualitative study of rural women in northern Michigan, Ames, Brosi, and Damiano-Teixeira (2006) investigated the experiences of wage-earning women in the context of economic restructuring. Women expressed concerns over low wages, the lack of jobs with benefits, and the lack of adequate employment for their husbands. Family-owned businesses, some agricultural, provided employment for many women but often only as a supplement to other jobs, as these activities did not pay enough to meet a family's financial needs.

Rural women's employment has also been heavily affected by welfare-to-work legislation. After conducting a descriptive analysis of March CPS data from 1989 to 1999, Lichter and Jensen (2001) found that rural single mothers increased their earnings and that they reduced reliance on public assistance more so than single mothers in metropolitan (metro) areas. Despite the positive effects of welfare reform, nonmetro mothers remain less likely than metro mothers to escape poverty (Lichter and Jensen 2001; Snyder and McLaughlin 2004). For example, 35 percent of working rural single mothers were poor, compared with 29 percent in metro areas (Lichter and Jensen 2001). Part of this disparity is explained by the lower availability of full-time, year-round employment in rural areas, as well as lower levels of remuneration.

Research has demonstrated the existence of geographical disadvantages in wages and place of residence (Gibbs and Cromartie 2001; Logan and Alba 1993). Some regions of the country have systematically lower wages that are not accounted for by the distribution of industries and occupations. Marriage markets have a spatial dimension. Place limits available marriage partners and shapes the economic success of these partners. Opportunities for welfare recipients to pursue higher levels of education and job training in some states also depend on where resources are deployed (Lee, Harvey, and Neustrom 2002). Individuals in more sparsely populated regions of a state may not have access to job training, vocational colleges, or universities near their residence.

Porterfield (2001) did a study of factors that trigger moves out of economic vulnerability for female-headed rural families. Using 1996 SIPP data and logistic regression, she estimated a maximum likelihood model with time-dependent covariates. The dependent variable, a move out of economic vulnerability, was defined as earning 150 percent above the poverty line. Factors positively associated with more stability were having fewer children, marriage, shared family housing, working longer hours, and, most significantly, working full-time. She also found that high levels of education did not affect stability, although having a GED had a positive effect. This may reflect the predominance of low-wage/low-skill jobs in these areas. In fact, wages were so low among rural single mothers that more than one in four of those who worked full-time still experienced economic vulnerability.

Braun and colleagues (2002) investigated the economic well-being of rural mothers, taking into consideration both restructuring and welfare reform. These researchers used both qualitative and quantitative methods in their study of eighty-three low-income women residing in Kentucky, Louisiana, and Maryland. They found that many families fell short of self-sufficiency, even those who supplemented their incomes with public assistance. Among this sample, employment opportunities were concentrated in low-wage sectors, and unemployment was common, with only 42 percent of women being employed, and 31 percent seeking employment. Eighty-one percent of mothers were living below poverty level. Many mothers reported wanting better jobs, but stressed that finding employment that paid a livable wage was extremely difficult.

Existing research and empirical findings suggest that the potential for education, marriage, and job characteristics to affect earnings outcomes differs by race and ethnicity and that geographic context must be taken into consideration. Although considerable attention has been given to low-wage employment, including gender differences, very little attention has been given to whether the relative effect of the sources of low-wage disadvantage is different across population groups. Are some factors more predictive of low-wage earnings among nonmetro Hispanic women than among Hispanic women residing in metro areas? Does education yield the same gains in reducing the probability of low-wage employment for metro and nonmetro residents, regardless of race or ethnicity? Furthermore, given the differences in opportunities available to minorities and women in nonmetro communities, which factors are most important in these settings?

This chapter looks at the relative importance of individual and job characteristics for minority women's low-wage employment. The author does this by applying techniques for analyzing wage gaps to analysis of differences in the rate of low-wage employment among nonmetro women. The results show that for all women, regardless of race or ethnicity, the effect of individual and job characteristics explains at least 30 percent of the metro and nonmetro difference in the rate of low-wage employment. However, differences in returns to endowments and work activity account for most of the higher rate of low-wage employment among nonmetro minority women.

Analytic Strategy and Data

The decomposition of observed racial or gender difference in wages has a long history in scholarly literature (see summaries in F. Jones 1983; Rodgers 2006). The underlying regression technique divides the wage gap into the proportion of the gap attributable to observed differences in characteristics of the two groups (i.e., women compared with men or blacks compared with whites) and the proportion attributable to discrimination and unmeasured factors.

This chapter uses techniques that allow for similar analysis of racial and ethnic differences in the probability of low-wage employment. Blinder (1973) and Oaxaca (1973) developed an extension of the wage gap decomposition that may be applied to binary outcomes such as whether an individual is employed in a low-wage job or not. Their method has been applied to linear probability models, which do not force probabilities to be bounded between 0 and 100. The current analysis relies on decomposition of probabilities estimated from nonlinear logit regression models (Fairlie 2005; Gomulka and Stern 1990; Herzog and Schlottmann 1995). Using the coefficient estimates from logit regressions and sensitivity tests as described by Fairlie (2005) overcomes the problem of limits and indexing associated with the Blinder-Oaxaca approach. These techniques are implemented using the fairlie macro in Stata 9.1.

Probit regressions are used to estimate selection (the inverse mills ratio) into employment for each race and ethnic group. Logit regressions are used to estimate the probabilities of being in low-wage employment and not being in low-wage employment for two groups, controlling for selection into employment. The logit regression coefficients used in the decompositions are means of estimates from matched samples of one thousand from the relevant groups, such as nonmetro non-Hispanic black and metro non-Hispanic black. Because the order in which covariates are entered into the logit regression will affect the results, the order of variables is randomly changed with each of the estimations. Decomposition results are sensitive to which sample's coefficients are used. Sensitivity analyses were conducted to assess how decomposition results are affected by using different sets of coefficients.

The effects of characteristics on differences in the probability of low-wage employment are derived from the regression coefficients estimates (shown in tables 10.2a, 10.2b, 10.2c) by substituting the mean characteristics of one group for the other. This technique answers questions such as what the probability of low-wage employment among nonmetro blacks would be if this group had the same characteristics as metro blacks.

The fairlie decomposition macro in Stata estimates an endowment effect based on statistically significant and insignificant regression coefficients. In the decomposition results (table 10.3), both the overall estimates for all characteristics from the fairlie procedure and estimates for each significant set of variables are provided. One limitation of this implementation in Stata is that the data are unweighted data. This limitation is not a serious concern in the estimation of regression coefficients, as most of the factors on which the weights would be based are included in the regression; however, the unweighted group means used in the decomposition may be biased. That the low-wage employment rates are nearly identical whether we use a weighted or unweighted mean suggests that the chances of bias are very small. Further, the one-to-one matching and one hundred simulations also reduce the likelihood of biased results.

Data for the analyses are drawn from the 2005 American Community Survey. For 2005, the ACS Public Use Microdata Sample (PUMS) was drawn from all counties across the nation. The 2005 PUMS is based on the household population and excludes the institutionalized population. The smallest geographic unit identified in the PUMS is the 5 percent Public Use Microdata Area (PUMA). The PUMAs were created for the Census 2000 5 percent PUMS data files. Each one contains a minimum of one hundred thousand people. For this analysis, each PUMA has been designated as nonmetro or metro based on the percentage of the PUMA population that resided in a metro statistical area at the time of the Census in 2000. PUMAs with less than 50 percent of individuals in metro areas were treated as nonmetro.

The sample used was restricted to women age twenty-five to sixty-four who were not enrolled in school and were employed in a paid civilian wage or salaried position. Earlier descriptive work on female low-wage earners has shown that women age eighteen to twenty-four represent nearly a third of all low-paid wage and salaried women (Kim 2000). However, because this chapter assesses the extent to which differences in education and marriage contribute to racial and ethnic gaps in low-wage employment rates, this age group was excluded from the analysis. These young workers, although not enrolled in school, may yet continue their education. And for women, marriage often takes place after the completion of their education. As in other analyses of employment, this chapter excludes older workers because the transition to retirement affects patterns found in the population age fifty-five and older. However, since the late 1990s, the labor force participation of older men has been increasing after falling in the 1970s and 1980s, possibly reflecting expectations for longer, healthier lives and uncertainties regarding both public and private pensions. Labor force participation for older women has been on the rise for an even longer period. Low-wage workers in particular may retire at older ages because they are more likely not to benefit from private pension plans and to receive lower social security payments.

Following past studies (Gibbs and Cromartie 2001), the author classified women as being in low-wage employment based on a woman's hourly wage (in 2004 dollars) in the job held in the twelve months prior to the survey. An hourly wage less than $9.28 is considered to be below a living wage because even if a woman worked full-time, year-round she would earn less than the weighted average poverty threshold for a family of four in 2004 ($19,307).

How Do Characteristics of Female Workers Differ Across Metropolitan and Nonmetropolitan Areas?

Previous research has identified a number of factors associated with low-wage work among women (Boraas and Rodgers 2003; Kim 2000). There is a larger share of younger workers among low-paid women workers. Lower education levels limit women's earnings, with a higher proportion of low-wage workers having less than a high school education and a much lower proportion having a college degree or higher. Low-wage female workers are also disproportionately single mothers. A much lower share of low-wage female earners have full-time jobs. Related to the prevalence of part-time work among women is the industry-occupation mix, including occupational segregation. Both men and women tend to earn less in female-dominated professions. The variety of factors associated with low-wage employment among minority workers is complicated by geographic patterns of discounted wages (Gibbs and Cromartie 2001).

Minority women employed in rural areas have many of the characteristics associated with low-wage female workers in the United States overall. Employed women in nonmetro areas are less educated than employed women in metro areas (table 10.1a). A higher proportion of working women in metro areas have a college degree when compared to working women in nonmetro areas. Among non-Hispanic blacks and Hispanics, a larger percent of metro women than nonmetro women have four-year college degrees (24 compared with 13 and 17 compared with 10, respectively). Among minority women, nonmetro workers are also more likely than metro workers to have a disability. Among non-Hispanic whites and blacks, there are higher proportions of foreign-born and non-citizen workers among women in metro areas, but the proportions are still relatively low. The percentages of Hispanic female workers who are foreign-born or noncitizens are 37 and 26 percent, respectively, in nonmetro areas and 52 and 32 percent in metro areas. Nonmetro female workers are more concentrated in the South and Midwest (42 and 34 percent) than their nonmetro counterparts, with most nonmetro black female workers in the South and more than 70 percent of both metro and nonmetro female Hispanic workers concentrated in the South and West. Nonmetro blacks and Hispanics are more concentrated in service occupations than metro blacks and Hispanics. Among minority female workers, nonmetro Hispanics are the least likely to work year-round.

Differences between low-paid nonmetro women and other nonmetro female workers in the ACS are similar to those observed in past research (tables 10.1b and 10.1c). Low-wage nonmetro women are less educated than other nonmetro female workers, with a higher percentage of low-wage workers having no high school degree (16 compared with 5) and fewer having a college degree (8 compared with 29). These nonmetro workers are more likely than are other employed women to be service workers (34 compared with 12). They are also much more likely to work in retail (19 compared with 9). Lower shares of low-wage female earners have full-time or year-round jobs. More rural women employed in low-wage jobs report having disabilities, limiting their ability to work (13 compared with 8).

The concentration of non-Hispanic blacks and Hispanics among low-paid women is nearly twice that among workers earning higher wages (7 compared with 3 and 11 compared with 6, respectively). Characteristics of non-Hispanic white women residing in nonmetro areas largely reflect patterns of the total described above. For black (Hispanic) nonmetro female earners, the characteristics of low-wage workers also show some marked differences relative to other black (Hispanic) female workers.

Do Characteristics Explain Metropolitan/Nonmetropolitan Differences in Low-Wage Employment Rates?

REGRESSION MODELS

Non-Hispanic White

For employed white women residing in either metro or nonmetro areas, all individual and job characteristics in the regression model are significantly associated with the odds of low-wage employment. However, the effects of age, education, region of residence, and some job characteristics are not the same in nonmetro and metro areas (table 10.2a). Metro workers age fifty-five and older have lower odds (negative coefficient) of holding a low-wage job than those workers age thirty-five to forty-four. Nonmetro workers in the oldest age group are more likely than the thirty-five- to forty-four-year-olds to be in low-wage jobs. Regardless of metro or nonmetro residence, more educated whites are less likely to be in low-wage jobs, but the buffering effect of a four-year college degree is stronger in nonmetro areas. On the other hand, having a full-time, year-round job does not decrease the odds of low-wage employment for white women in nonmetro areas as much as it does for white women in metro areas. For white women in metro areas, living in the Midwest increases the odds of low-wage employment more than it does for nonmetro white women.

Non-Hispanic Black

Employed black women's odds of low-wage employment, like those of whites, are associated with individual and job characteristics (table 10.2b). However, except for foreign-born status and residence in the southern region of the United States, the effects of these characteristics do not differ significantly for metro and nonmetro blacks. Smaller sample sizes and larger variances for nonmetro blacks in these analyses make it more difficult to detect differences between those residing in metro and nonmetro areas.

Younger employed black women, age twenty-five to thirty-four, have higher odds of low-wage employment than older black women, even than those age fifty-five and older. Lower levels of education, having a disability, being a noncitizen, and residence in the southern or western United States all increase the odds of low-wage employment. Those employed as service workers, in retail, part-time, and for only part of the year have higher odds of low-wage employment. Foreign-born blacks have lower odds of low-wage employment than the native-born do, as do foreign-born whites. Foreign-born black women in nonmetro areas have significantly lower odds of low-wage employment than foreign-born black women in metro areas. For black women in both metro and nonmetro locations, the odds of low-wage employment increase with residence in the southern region of the United States. However, southern residence increases the odds of low-wage employment significantly more for black women residing in nonmetro areas than for black women in metro areas.

Hispanics

Although the effects of individual and job characteristics on the low-wage employment of Hispanic women are similar to those for non-Hispanic black and white women in many ways, there are some striking differences (table 10.2c).

Both the youngest and oldest employed Hispanic women have higher odds of low-wage employment than Hispanic women in prime working ages (thirty-five to fifty-four). As it does for whites, for Hispanics a four-year college degree lowers the odds of low-wage employment in nonmetro areas more than it does in metro areas. Not being a U.S. citizen is associated with higher rates of low-wage employment for all groups except nonmetro blacks, but the effect is strongest among metro Hispanics. Also, the effect of job characteristics on low-wage employment among Hispanic women, as among white women, differs significantly across metro and nonmetro areas. In metro areas, employment as a service worker increases the odds of low-wage employment less than it does in nonmetro areas. On the other hand, full-time, year-round employment decreases the odds of low-wage employment significantly more in metro areas than it does in nonmetro areas.

DECOMPOSITION RESULTS

For all women—whites, blacks, or Hispanics—the effect of individual and job characteristics explains at least 30 percent of the metro and nonmetro difference in the rate of low-wage employment (table 10.3). Regardless of race and ethnicity, relative to other variables, education and job characteristics account for most of the difference explained. For blacks and Hispanics, region of residence also accounts for a substantial amount (10 percent or more) of the nonmetro and metro difference in low-wage employment. These results suggest that for blacks, whites, and Hispanics less than half the difference in low-wage employment rates is explained by differences in the characteristics of the metro and nonmetro population. Differences in the parameter estimates account for most of the metro/nonmetro difference in low-wage employment. Thus, differences in average returns to individual endowments such as education and in average returns to hours worked mostly explain why low-wage employment rates are so much higher in nonmetro areas than in metro areas, particularly among blacks and Hispanics.

Differences in population characteristics do, however, account for the majority of large racial and ethnic differences in nonmetro women's low-wage employment rates—18 percentage points difference between blacks and whites and 20 percentage points difference between Hispanics and whites. For both black and Hispanic women in nonmetro areas, differences in education level and job characteristics explain a substantial proportion of the gap between nonmetro white low-wage employment rates and their own low-wage employment rates (table 10.4).

Education explains the greatest proportion of Hispanic-white differences among employed women in nonmetro areas (table 10.4). Eight points (0.4 × 20) of the 20-percentage-point difference between white and Hispanic women may be attributed to higher levels of education among white women. An additional 3.5 (0.173 × 20) of these percentage points stem from greater concentration of nonmetro whites in full-time, year-round jobs. Hispanic-white differences in age, disability, and region of residence account for about another 2 percentage points.

Region of residence and education contribute equally to black-white differences in women's low-wage employment rates in nonmetro areas (table 10.4). Nearly four points (0.215 × 18) of the 18-percentage-point difference stem from higher education levels among whites. About another 4 percentage points (0.192 × 18) are due to the concentration of nonmetro blacks in the South. Black-white differences in disability and full-time and year-round employment together account for 3 points of the 18-percentage-point difference.

Summary and Conclusion

Women in low-wage employment make up a substantial proportion of all women age twenty-five to sixty-four employed in the civilian labor force, 32 percent of working women in nonmetro areas, and 21 percent of working women in metro areas. Regardless of metro or nonmetro residence, employed non-Hispanic white women are less likely to hold low-wage jobs than employed Hispanic or non-Hispanic black women. The difference in white and nonwhite low-wage employment rates is particularly pronounced in nonmetro areas, where nearly 50 percent of employed working-age Hispanics and non-Hispanic black women are employed in low-wage jobs, compared with about 30 percent of non-Hispanic whites.

Within race and ethnic groups, differences between metro and nonmetro women in education levels and rates of employment in full-time and year-round jobs account for around one-third of the higher rates of low-wage employment in nonmetro areas. However, structural differences in returns to individual and job characteristics account for most of the gap between metro and nonmetro low-wage employment rates within race and ethnic groups. In contrast, most of the racial and ethnic differences in low-wage employment rates in nonmetro areas may be accounted for by differences in population characteristics. For nonmetro blacks, living in the South contributes significantly to higher rates of low-wage employment than whites. For Hispanics, lower education levels are of particular concern.

These results suggest that to narrow the gap between metro and nonmetro women with respect to earning a living wage, geographic disparities in education and job quality need to be addressed. Improving education among nonmetro women would also reduce racial and ethnic inequalities if non-Hispanic black and Hispanic educational attainment were to be increased. Improvements in education and job quality, however, will not close the low-wage employment gap between metro and nonmetro women. To do this, returns to individual endowments and for similar work need to be equalized across metro and nonmetro areas. According to Gibbs and Cromartie (2001), low-wage counties have a lower wage scale across all industries, which is consistent with the finding here that structural metro-nonmetro differences in returns to education and full-time-year-round employment account for much of the higher rates of low-wage employment among nonmetro women.

The lower return to education and full-time, year-round work for women in nonmetro areas means that some steps to assist low-income women will not work equally well in metro and nonmetro areas. For example, the TANF reauthorization act recognizes that average wages of those leaving welfare for work are still too low to ensure family well-being. Major programmatic areas to which TANF resources are directed—more hours of work and employment in higher-paying industries or occupations—all theoretically can assist welfare beneficiaries, predominantly women and disproportionately minorities. However, metro/nonmetro disparities in returns to education and job characteristics may mean that these programmatic activities provide less assistance for women employed in nonmetro areas.

Table 10.1a Characteristics of total sample by race, ethnicity, and place of residence

	All nonmetro	All metro	Non-Hispanic white nonmetro	Non-Hispanic white metro	Non-Hispanic black nonmetro	Non-Hispanic black metro	Hispanic nonmetro	Hispanic metro
Low-wage employment	33%	21%	30%	17%	48%	25%	50%	37%
Age								
25 to 34	25%	27%	24%	24%	28%	29%	36%	37%
35 to 44	29%	29%	28%	28%	32%	31%	33%	32%
45 to 54	29%	28%	30%	30%	28%	27%	22%	22%
55 or older	17%	16%	18%	18%	12%	13%	10%	9%
Education								
Less than high school	9%	8%	7%	4%	15%	10%	33%	28%
High school	35%	26%	35%	25%	42%	30%	30%	28%
Some college	34%	33%	35%	33%	31%	37%	26%	27%
College	22%	33%	23%	38%	13%	24%	10%	17%
Family/marital status								
Own child(ren) under 18 present	58%	60%	59%	63%	55%	57%	46%	50%
Married	66%	58%	69%	63%	39%	37%	61%	56%
Single, previously married	22%	23%	21%	21%	27%	28%	23%	23%
Never married	12%	20%	10%	16%	34%	35%	16%	21%
Health								
Disability	9%	8%	9%	7%	11%	9%	10%	7%
Nativity/citizenship								
Foreign-born	3%	12%	1%	5%	1%	11%	37%	52%
Noncitizen	2%	7%	1%	2%	1%	5%	26%	32%

(continues)

Table 10.1a *(continued)*

	All nonmetro	All metro	Non-Hispanic white nonmetro	Non-Hispanic white metro	Non-Hispanic black nonmetro	Non-Hispanic black metro	Hispanic nonmetro	Hispanic metro
Region								
Midwest	34%	22%	38%	25%	3%	20%	17%	8%
South	42%	36%	37%	32%	94%	53%	46%	33%
West	11%	21%	11%	20%	1%	9%	34%	41%
Northeast	12%	21%	13%	22%	1%	19%	4%	17%
Job characteristics								
Service workers	19%	15%	17%	12%	31%	22%	34%	28%
Retail trade industry	12%	10%	12%	11%	10%	9%	11%	10%
Full-time	77%	78%	76%	77%	80%	84%	77%	80%
Year-round	62%	64%	62%	64%	62%	65%	58%	62%

SOURCE: 2005 American Community Survey (ACS).

Table 10.1b Characteristics of low-wage sample by race, ethnicity, and place of residence

	All nonmetro	All metro	Non-Hispanic white nonmetro	Non-Hispanic white metro	Non-Hispanic black nonmetro	Non-Hispanic black metro	Hispanic nonmetro	Hispanic metro
Low-wage employment	100%	100%	100%	100%	100%	100%	100%	100%
Age								
25 to 34	30%	33%	28%	28%	32%	37%	39%	39%
35 to 44	29%	29%	28%	29%	32%	28%	32%	32%
45 to 54	26%	24%	27%	27%	25%	24%	19%	20%
55 or older	16%	14%	17%	17%	11%	11%	10%	9%
Education								
Less than high school	16%	21%	13%	11%	20%	19%	45%	46%
High school	45%	37%	46%	39%	48%	42%	33%	30%
Some college	31%	29%	32%	34%	28%	32%	19%	18%
College degree	8%	13%	9%	17%	4%	7%	3%	7%
Family/marital status								
Own child(ren) under 18 present	57%	55%	58%	59%	53%	54%	46%	47%
Married	60%	53%	64%	60%	35%	30%	59%	55%
Single, previously married	25%	24%	25%	24%	27%	27%	24%	23%
Never married	15%	23%	11%	16%	38%	43%	17%	22%
Health								
Disability	13%	12%	13%	13%	12%	13%	11%	9%
Nativity/citizenship								
Foreign-born	4%	21%	1%	5%	0%	11%	44%	67%
Noncitizen	3%	15%	1%	3%	0%	6%	34%	49%

(continues)

Table 10.1b (*continued*)

	All nonmetro	All metro	Non-Hispanic white nonmetro	Non-Hispanic white metro	Non-Hispanic black nonmetro	Non-Hispanic black metro	Hispanic nonmetro	Hispanic metro
Region								
Midwest	32%	21%	38%	26%	3%	20%	13%	8%
South	48%	42%	40%	38%	96%	60%	54%	38%
West	11%	21%	10%	17%	1%	6%	31%	41%
Northeast	9%	16%	11%	19%	1%	14%	2%	13%
Job characteristics								
Service workers	34%	34%	32%	29%	43%	40%	46%	43%
Retail trade industry	19%	17%	20%	20%	13%	14%	12%	12%
Full-time	67%	65%	65%	58%	76%	73%	72%	75%
Year-round	54%	51%	53%	48%	60%	55%	55%	56%

SOURCE: 2005 American Community Survey (ACS).

Table 10.1c Characteristics of sample not in low-wage employment by race, ethnicity, and place of residence

	All nonmetro	All metro	Non-Hispanic white nonmetro	Non-Hispanic white metro	Non-Hispanic black nonmetro	Non-Hispanic black metro	Hispanic nonmetro	Hispanic metro
Low-wage employment	0%	0%	0%	0%	0%	0%	0%	0%
Age								
25 to 34	23%	25%	22%	24%	25%	27%	33%	35%
35 to 44	29%	29%	29%	28%	33%	32%	34%	33%
45 to 54	31%	29%	31%	31%	30%	28%	25%	23%
55 or older	17%	16%	18%	18%	12%	13%	9%	9%
Education								
Less high school	5%	5%	4%	3%	10%	7%	21%	17%
High school	30%	23%	30%	22%	35%	26%	28%	26%
Some college	36%	33%	36%	33%	34%	38%	34%	33%
College degree	29%	39%	30%	43%	21%	29%	17%	23%
Family/marital status								
Own child(ren) under 18 present	59%	61%	60%	64%	57%	58%	46%	52%
Married	69%	59%	71%	63%	44%	39%	63%	56%
Single, previously married	21%	22%	20%	21%	27%	28%	22%	23%
Never married	11%	19%	9%	16%	29%	33%	14%	21%

Table 10.1c *(continued)*

	All nonmetro	All metro	Non-Hispanic white nonmetro	Non-Hispanic white metro	Non-Hispanic black nonmetro	Non-Hispanic black metro	Hispanic nonmetro	Hispanic metro
Health								
Disability	8%	6%	7%	6%	10%	8%	10%	6%
Nativity/citizenship								
Foreign-born	2%	10%	1%	5%	2%	12%	29%	43%
Noncitizen	1%	4%	1%	2%	1%	5%	17%	21%
Region								
Midwest	36%	22%	38%	25%	4%	19%	20%	9%
South	40%	34%	36%	31%	93%	51%	37%	31%
West	12%	22%	12%	21%	1%	9%	37%	42%
Northeast	13%	22%	14%	23%	2%	20%	5%	19%
Job characteristics								
Service workers	12%	10%	11%	8%	19%	16%	20%	18%
Retail trade industry	9%	9%	9%	9%	7%	7%	9%	9%
Full-time	81%	82%	81%	81%	85%	87%	83%	83%
Year-round	66%	67%	66%	67%	65%	68%	60%	65%

SOURCE: 2005 American Community Survey (ACS).

Table 10.2a Logit model of low-wage employment among non-Hispanic white women, age twenty-five to sixty-four and employed in the civilian labor force

Independent variables	Metro			Nonmetro		
	Coefficient	Standard error		Coefficient	Standard error	
Age						
25 to 34	0.18	0.02	***	0.20	0.023	***
45 to 54	−0.10	0.01	***	−0.13	0.021	***
55 or older	−0.08	0.02	***	0.07	0.035	***
(35 to 44)						
Education						
No high school diploma	0.53	0.02	***	0.65	0.040	***
Some college / no 4-year						
degree	−0.52	0.01	***	−0.52	0.021	***
Bachelor's degree or						
higher	−1.34	0.02	***	−1.50	0.029	***
(High school diploma /						
no college)						
Health						
Disability	0.59	0.03	***	0.67	0.058	***
Nativity/citizenship						
Foreign born	−0.06	0.04		−0.18	0.129	
Not citizen	0.40	0.05	***	0.36	0.174	**
Region						
Midwest	0.27	0.02	***	0.11	0.025	***
South	0.46	0.01	***	0.38	0.026	***
West	0.04	0.02	**	0.11	0.033	***
(Northeast)						
Job characteristics						
Service worker	1.12	0.01	***	1.06	0.020	***
(not service worker)						
Retail trade	0.89	0.01	***	0.95	0.022	***
(not retail trade)						
Employed full-time	−0.85	0.01	***	−0.60	0.018	***
(part-time)						
Employed year-round	−0.62	0.01	***	−0.43	0.017	***
(part-year)						
Lambda	−0.42	0.05	***	−0.76	0.106	***
Intercept	−0.63	0.02	***	−0.18	0.039	***
Pseudo R^2	0.161			0.1409		
Sample size	310,406			93,190		
Percent in low-wage jobs	16			29		

*** $p < 0.01$; ** $p < 0.05$; * $p < .10$
SOURCE: 2005 American Community Survey (ACS).

Table 10.2b Logit model of low-wage employment among non-Hispanic black women, age twenty-five to sixty-four and employed in the civilian labor force

	Metro			Nonmetro		
Independent variables	Coefficient	Standard error		Coefficient	Standard error	
Age						
25 to 34	0.45	0.030	***	0.45	0.076	***
45 to 54	−0.05	0.032		−0.07	0.074	
55 or older	−0.07	0.055		0.19	0.143	
(35 to 44)						
Education						
No high school diploma	0.48	0.049	***	0.45	0.130	***
Some college / no 4-year degree	−0.59	0.032	***	−0.58	0.079	***
Bachelor's degree or higher	−1.69	0.048	***	−1.80	0.125	***
(High school diploma / no college)						
Health						
Disability	0.60	0.106	***	0.81	0.302	***
Nativity/citizenship						
Foreign born	−0.35	0.056	***	−1.24	0.458	***
Not citizen	0.52	0.076	***	0.67	0.638	
Region						
Midwest	0.44	0.042	***	0.36	0.324	
South	0.58	0.035	***	0.89	0.284	***
West	0.12	0.053	***	1.16	0.453	**
(Northeast)						
Job characteristics						
Service worker	0.92	0.027	***	1.02	0.063	***
(not service worker)						
Retail trade	0.76	0.038	***	0.83	0.095	***
(not retail trade)						
Employed full-time	−0.56	0.029	***	−0.19	0.070	***
(part-time)						
Employed year-round	−0.40	0.024	***	−0.12	0.057	**
(part-year)						
Lambda	−0.65	0.190	***	−1.00	0.448	**
Intercept	−0.77	0.059	***	−0.74	0.307	**
Pseudo R²	0.152			0.1237		
Sample size	49,366			6,506		
Percent in low-wage jobs	24			47		

*** p < 0.01; ** p < 0.05; * p < .10
SOURCE: 2005 American Community Survey (ACS).

Table 10.2c Logit model of low-wage employment among Hispanic women, age twenty-five to sixty-four and employed in the civilian labor force

Independent variables	Metro			Nonmetro		
	Coefficient	Standard error		Coefficient	Standard error	
Age						
25 to 34	0.24	0.027	***	0.26	0.093	***
45 to 54	−0.07	0.030	**	−0.12	0.096	
55 or older	0.09	0.047	**	0.42	0.163	***
(35 to 44)						
Education						
No high school diploma	0.64	0.033	***	0.47	0.122	***
Some college / no 4-year						
degree	−0.62	0.032	***	−0.66	0.101	***
Bachelor's degree or						
higher	−1.27	0.041	***	−1.69	0.157	***
(High school diploma /						
no college)						
Health						
Disability	0.53	0.057	***	0.42	0.206	**
Nativity/citizenship						
Foreign born	0.18	0.029	***	−0.07	0.118	
Not citizen	0.88	0.037	***	0.69	0.149	***
Region						
Midwest	0.18	0.050	***	0.04	0.211	
South	0.54	0.035	***	0.84	0.199	***
West	0.11	0.034	***	0.21	0.201	
(Northeast)						
Job characteristics						
Service worker	0.80	0.025	***	0.90	0.083	***
(not service worker)						
Retail trade	0.54	0.034	***	0.65	0.118	***
(not retail trade)						
Employed full-time	−0.23	0.027	***	−0.21	0.088	**
(part-time)						
Employed year-round	−0.29	0.022	***	−0.15	0.074	**
(part-year)						
Lambda	−0.60	0.103	***	−0.94	0.439	**
Intercept	−0.90	0.054	***	−0.36	0.237	
Pseudo R^2	0.1669			0.1465		
Sample size	47,335			3,877		
Percent in low-wage jobs	35			49		

*** $p < 0.01$; ** $p < 0.05$; * $p < .10$
SOURCE: 2005 American Community Survey (ACS).

Table 10.3 Percent of metro/nonmetro differences in female low-wage employment rates explained by characteristic

	Using metro coefficients			Using nonmetro coefficients		
	Non-Hispanic white	Non-Hispanic black	Hispanic	Non-Hispanic white	Non-Hispanic black	Hispanic
Nonmetro/metro percentage point difference in rate	13	23	14	13	23	14
Percent of difference explained by:						
Age	−1.0	−2.1	−1.2	−1.0	1.4	NS
Education	11.8	15.1	15.8	22.1	22.5	21.8
Disability	0.8	0.6	2.6	1.4	1.6	2.2
Nativity/citizenship	−0.4	0.3	−8.9	0.1	7.5	1.9
Job characteristics	18.2	12.1	11.7	18.7	10.1	12.3
Region	4.6	9.6	10.6	1.2	15.3	13.0
Lambda—selection into employment	−0.6	3.6	−0.9	−1.3	−7.2	−2.0
All characteristics	33.4	39.2	29.7	41.1	51.2	49.1

NOTE: Author's estimates based on analysis of the 2005 American Community Survey. Decomposition estimates use means from one-to-one matched samples of 1000 and mean coefficient estimates from 100 unweighted regressions with random ordering of variables. SOURCE: 2005 American Community Survey (ACS). NS = not significantly different from zero.

Table 10.4 Percent of nonmetro racial or ethnic differences in female low-wage employment rates explained by characteristic

	Black	Hispanic
Percentage point difference in group and non-Hispanic white rates	10.0	20.0
Percent of difference explained by:		
Age	NS	2.5
Education	21.5	40.1
Disability	2.3	1.4
Nativity/citizenship	NS	NS
Job characteristics	14.3	17.3
Region	19.2	4.8
Lambda—selection into employment	−2.0	−9.1
All variables	55.0	57.0

NOTE: Author's estimates from the 2005 American Community Survey. Decomposition estimates use one-to-one matched samples of 1000 and mean coefficient estimates from 100 unweighted regressions with random ordering of variables. Coefficients from non-Hispanic white regression used for decomposition. When black coefficients or non-Hispanic coefficients are used respectively, the percent of the difference explained increases to 73 percent for blacks and 75 percent for Hispanics. NS = not significantly different from zero. SOURCE: 2005 American Community Survey (ACS).

REGIONAL VARIATION OF WOMEN IN
LOW-WAGE WORK ACROSS RURAL COMMUNITIES

CYNTHIA D. ANDERSON AND CHIH-YUAN WENG

The processes of economic restructuring and devolution are seriously chal-lenging the quality of life in rural communities across the United States. The economies of many rural communities have undergone structural change due to globalization, presenting both opportunities and threats to their economic well-being and quality of life. On the one hand, the expansion of global markets provides opportunities for the growth of local businesses. On the other hand, globalization may mean the loss of local jobs due to outsourcing or business relocation and the suppression of local wages due to global competition in labor markets. More and more rural residents must engage in multiple jobs, often without benefits that came with the old economy. The effects of globalization processes have been very uneven across rural communities in the United States. Some rural communities have been able to effectively respond to these changes and elevate their quality of life by developing industries that provide high-skill jobs and increase the incomes of local workers. In contrast, other nonmetropol-itan (nonmetro) communities have been less fortunate and have experienced sharp increases in low-wage employment (Anderson, Schulman, and Wood 2001; Falk, Schulman, and Tickamyer 2003; Lobao, Hooks, and Tickamyer 2007).

At the same time, devolution of responsibility for the delivery of public goods and services has elevated the accountability of governments in rural communi-ties (Dewees, Lobao, and Swanson 2003; Lobao and Hooks 2003). States play a larger role in designing and implementing welfare policy and in finding ways to decrease the number of welfare recipients. Welfare legislature enacted in the late 1990s led to state-defined welfare-to-work policies that included time-limited/work-first programs; the implication was that employment would enable families to escape from poverty (Morgen et al. 2006). While national and state-level studies find increased employment among low-income poor, they also note significant economic hardship and insecurity (see, for example, Kilty and Segal 2006). Indeed, poverty is surprisingly common among working adults in the United States. Conservative estimates suggest that in 2004 about 7.8 million people, or about 6 percent of those in the labor force, were working poor (Bureau of Labor Statistics 2006, 1); more liberal estimates claim over 57 million people as working poor (Newman and Chen 2007). Regardless of the estimate, the problem is magnified in rural areas, where 67 percent of poor families worked at least one job (Gibbs and Parker 2001). These data suggest that a substantial number of jobs in rural America pay low wages, offer few benefits, or consist of part-time or contingent employment.

The processes of economic restructuring and devolution affect communities differently. To better understand the uneven distribution of low-wage workers, researchers must address questions of how and why socially valued resources are differentially allocated across the country. In this chapter, we review labor market and demographic factors that influence the numbers of low-wage workers. We examine the nonmetro low-wage working rates by key demographic characteristics for 1997 and 2007 using data from the Current Population Survey (CPS). We further break down data for 2007 across four regions of the United States: the Northeast, the Midwest, the South, and the West. We contend that the low-wage working population is influenced by the attributes of geographical regions as well as demographic characteristics; the processes of economic restructuring and devolution affected low-wage workers differently across regions. Our chapter concludes with policy recommendations for improving the lives of U.S. workers.

Factors Affecting the Low-Wage Workforce

DECLINE IN MANUFACTURING INDUSTRY

Economic restructuring has a variety of outcomes for regions across the United States. For the most part, the decline in manufacturing has resulted in the loss of well-paying, often unionized jobs with benefits. The globalization movement has led to deindustrialization in some nonmetro communities as manufacturing work continues to be shifted offshore (see, for example, Lobao, Brown, and Moore 2003). However, reflecting the broader, nonmetro growth trend, a substantial number of nonmetro communities have successfully retained and/or attracted new industry as manufacturing work continues to be decentralized from older industrial cities and globalization promotes foreign investment in manufacturing capacity in the United States. For example, the beef-processing industry has expanded in nonmetro areas of the Midwest region (Kandel 2006). Further, the recent movement to develop alternative fuels has resulted in the rapid construction of ethanol bio-refineries in nonmetro communities within the region (Barrett 2007; USDA Economic Research Service 2007a).

RISE IN SERVICE INDUSTRY

Also reflecting broader macroeconomic trends, significant numbers of nonmetro workers within the region are now employed in service sector industries. It is important to emphasize that the service sector includes a substantial number of jobs paying high salaries (e.g., doctors, business consultants, lawyers). However, the vast majority are lower-level, service-provision jobs that pay low wages and are contingent (e.g., retail sales clerks, bank tellers). Jobs in nonmetro service sector industries tend to pay lower wages than jobs in nonmetro manufacturing industries (Gibbs, Kusmin, and Cromartie 2005). Thus, a strong dependence on service sector industries for employment would likely contribute to increasing the size of a rural community's low-wage working population.

INDIVIDUAL FACTORS

The characteristics of workers in a local labor market are also important in influencing the size of the low-wage working population. Acquiring education (i.e., developing human capital) has long been touted as a means of upward mobility and avoiding poverty (Becker 1964; Blau and Duncan 1967). Regions with a highly educated workforce would be more likely to exhibit fewer low-wage workers. Further, particular segments of the labor force (e.g., women, minorities, young adults, and elderly workers) have been found to be more susceptible to accepting low-wage employment and becoming working poor (e.g., Jensen, McLaughlin, and Slack 2003; Rank 2004; Bureau of Labor Statistics 2004).

DEMOGRAPHIC FACTORS

Finally, the demographic characteristics of a community, such as the prevalence of specific household types, have been found to be linked to the size of the low-wage working population. For example, in 1990 single-parent family households headed by employed females were found to be five times more likely to be working poor when compared to married-couple family households with the head and/or spouse employed (Goe and Rhea 2000).

REGIONAL FACTORS

Historically, regions of the United States have been characterized by unique labor markets centered on industry. For example, manufacturing dominated the midwestern "Rust Belt," agriculture (cotton and tobacco) prevailed in the South, and mining provided the backbone for the Appalachian region. The rate of pay for occupations associated with these industries influenced the quality of life for people in these regions. Hence, low-wage worker rates can be expected to vary by region as the role of dominant industries within labor markets changes over time and place.

In this chapter, we examine four distinct regions of the United States: Northeast, Midwest, South, and West.[1] It is important to note that each of the four regions encompasses a diversity of communities, ranging from large metropolitan (metro) areas with millions in population to nonmetro areas with small cities (now called micropolitan areas) to remote rural areas with very small populations. States vary significantly in the concentration of low-wage workers in these types of areas. States within the same region often show markedly different patterns across cities, suburbs, and rural areas in the prevalence of working poverty. Nonetheless, as a broad indicator of labor market composition, attention to regional patterns of low-wage work is important.

The major industrial shift in the nonmetro United States in the past thirty years has been from agriculture to low-tech support services. Metro areas have shifted out of manufacturing to product services (McGranahan 2003). This difference is particularly strong in the South (Falk and Lyson 1988). The rural South, with development policies based largely on attracting low-wage/low-skill manufacturing industry, sustained its competitiveness in the global market longer than other regions because of state-supported policies (e.g., antiunion) and its large supply of low-skilled workers (Anderson, Schulman, and Wood 2001). Research by Berube and Tiffany (2004) on EITC filers (EITC is a refundable federal income tax credit available to families who work but generally earn less than 200 percent of the poverty level) suggests that families in the rural South are more likely to earn low incomes than those in any other part of the nation. These families are disproportionately African American, single mothers, and lack their own transportation (Beale and Cromartie 2004).

Low-wage work in the South and West is more rural in character than low-wage work elsewhere. Counties in the West, unlike other areas of the country, tend to be large, sparsely populated, and separated by great distances (Kirschner, Berry, and Glasgow 2006). Counties in the western region also contain the largest concentration of Native Americans and Hispanic immigrants. Kirschner (2005) documents the diversity of industry in the West, including extractives and agriculture, as well as personal services that revolve around retirement communities and tourism; she finds that a rapidly increasing and largely Hispanic immigrant population serves as low-skilled labor in these industries.

Research found that low-wage working families in the West represent one in six rural tax filers, a higher share than in that region's large cities, suburbs, or small metro areas. The places with the highest rates of EITC receipt in the West are rural areas in and around American Indian reservations, locations along the Mexican border in Arizona and California, and California's Central Valley, home to large Hispanic immigrant populations (Berube and Tiffany 2004). Many counties with large Hispanic populations are characterized by limited English proficiency, lower education, and low earnings (Beale and Cromartie 2004).

Native American high-poverty counties are characterized by very limited male employment, more children living in poverty, and deeper poverty (Beale and Cromartie 2004). One in five Native Americans in high-poverty counties earns an income below 75 percent of the poverty line. These counties report some of the lowest male employment rates for full-time, year-round work, even compared with other high-poverty counties.

The Midwest and the Northeast are characterized by high levels of working poverty in large central cities, and lower levels in their suburbs, small metros, and rural areas. The working poor in the Midwest, like the poor, are disproportionately white, older, and more likely to be found in two-parent families when compared to the nation as a whole (Harrison and Watrus 2005). Poverty rates in the rural Midwest in 2000 were lower than average, in part because of a relatively stable farm-based economy in some areas (Harrison and Watrus 2005). We expect trends on low-wage work to follow similar patterns.

In the Northeast, where manufacturing, farming, fishing, and mining once characterized local labor markets, high-tech industries including computers and communication, as well as education, provide workers with higher than average wages. As such, poverty rates in the Northeast are lower than other regions of the United States.

Data Analysis and Findings

Within the context of a market economy, the concept of "low-wage work" is based on the level of income that is socially defined as adequate for the sustenance of families or other social units. Economic stability is often understood in terms of poverty status, but poverty status is a poor indicator of a family's ability to meet its basic needs. Families must be able to accumulate the necessary resources to finance their housing, food, transportation, child care, health care, and other necessities. This need typically requires earnings two to three times the federal poverty level (Churilla 2006). Academics, community organizers, and citizens often reference the concept of "living wage" as an appropriate estimate for sustainable living. The living wage varies by region and family size, but approximates the median household income as the standard, or the amount that divides households into two equal groups, one having incomes above that amount and the other having incomes below that amount. The median household income in 2006 was $48,200 (DeNavas-Walt, Proctor, and Smith 2007).

We define individuals who work for inadequate wages as "low-wage workers." Our measure uses the CPS definition of "working" that refers to all currently employed individuals. More specifically, our definition of working includes employed members of the civilian labor force age fifteen and over who did any work during the week of the survey. We classify an individual as "low-wage" if they have earnings below 200 percent of the official U.S. poverty threshold for a single person (poverty thresholds provided by U.S. Census Bureau, http://www .census.gov/hhes/www/poverty/threshld.html). For perspective, a family of four was considered to be "low-wage" in 2007 if their family income was below $41,300; a family of three was low-wage if their income was less than $34,340; and a family of two was low-wage if their income was less than $27,380. Workers who earned below these levels were considered "low-wage" workers. This definition captures the large number of economically vulnerable workers, those in unstable low-wage jobs with few or no benefits, limited opportunities for mobility, and perhaps just one crisis away from poverty. Based on this definition, 27.2 million low-wage workers, representing 18 percent of the U.S. workforce, were considered "low-wage" in 2006. Almost five million (4.9) low-wage workers lived in rural areas; low-wage workers made up one-fifth (21 percent) of all rural workers.

Data on low-wage worker rates in rural areas, as seen in table 11.1, show that members of certain groups experience elevated risks of being working poor. In both 1997 and 2007, racial and ethnic minorities, women, female-headed households, female-headed households with children, those in the rural West and rural South, and rural workers with less education all had a greater than average chance of being members of the low-wage workforce.

Table 11.1 also illustrates the decrease in rates of low-wage work from 1997 to 2007 for all groups, in the United States as a whole and in rural areas specifically. The percentage of low-wage workers in the United States decreased from 19 percent in 1997 to 18 percent in 2007. The decrease for low-wage workers in rural areas was more substantial, from 26 percent in 1997 to 21 percent in 2007. For all cases, the female rate of low-wage workers is higher than the male rate and the rural female rate is higher than the overall female rate.

When looking at race, we first have to understand how the Current Population Survey measures the variable. For the 1997 data, the population is divided into five groups on the basis of race: White; Black; American Indian / Aleut Eskimo; Asian and Pacific Islander; and Other races (includes any other race except the four mentioned). The CPS revised its race categories in 2003, allowing respondents to report more than one race. As such, the 2007 data includes six race groups: White; Black or African American; American Indian or Alaskan Native; Asian, Native Hawaiian, or Other Pacific Islander; and Other race. The last category includes any other race except the five mentioned. Because of these changes, our 1997 and 2007 data on race are not directly comparable; caution should be used when interpreting changes in the racial composition of the United States over time.

Nonetheless, we see that rural working poor rates are higher than overall rates for each racial category. African Americans and American Indians / Aleut Eskimos have the highest rates at each point in time. Rates for all groups decreased from 1997 to 2007, with the exception of a nonsignificant increase for American Indians / Aleut Eskimos. In 2007, we are able to look at low-wage worker rates by Hispanic origin. Overall, the low-wage worker rate for Hispanics is 36 percent. The rate is significantly higher in rural areas, at 44 percent.

In terms of age, the sixteen-to-twenty-four-year-old group of workers has the highest rate followed by the twenty-five- to thirty-four-year-olds. Notable is the smaller gap for rural workers when compared with national workers as a whole. For all groups, the rate has decreased from 1997 to 2007. In the thirty-five-to-forty-four and forty-five-to-fifty-four age groups, the decrease in overall rates of working poor is not significant; in the rural areas, the decrease for these groups is a bit larger (3 percent).

Rates of working poor are highest for workers with less than a high school education. While the overall rate for these workers increased, the rate for rural low-wage workers decreased from 40 percent in 1997 to 35 percent in 2007. Similarly, the rate for rural low-wage workers with only a high school degree decreased 2 percent, while the change for overall low-wage rate was insignificant. Important is the fact that rural workers with less than high school education had lower than overall rates in 2007.

Workers who are married with an absent spouse and workers who are separated have the highest rates of low-wage work. Again, rural areas have higher rates than the United States as a whole, and rates decreased over time. Consistent with the literature, female-headed households with children have the highest rates of low-wage work, with rural areas significantly higher than the overall U.S. rate.

Of specific interest for this study is how rates of low-wage work vary by geographic region of the country. As seen in table 11.1, the overall rate of low-wage work did not change significantly for any particular region. The rate for rural low-wage workers, however, decreased for each region. Most notable was the decreased percentage of low-wage rural workers in the West from 29 percent in 1997 to 21 percent in 2006.

RATES OF LOW-WAGE WORK BY REGION

To further explore differences in rural low-wage worker rates by region, we turn to table 11.2. Table 11.2 is limited to rural low-wage workers in 2007 and offers a breakdown of demographic characteristics by region of the country. With only one exception, the South has the highest rate of low-wage work for all indicators. The exception is education, master's degree and above, where the Midwest boasts the highest rate of rural low-wage work.

In 2007 for all rural regions, the female low-wage worker rate is higher than the male low-wage worker rate, ranging from a high of 27 percent in the South to a low of 19 percent in the Northeast. In the South, the rate for American Indians / Aleut Eskimos is the highest (43 percent), followed by Black (38 percent) and multiple racial identities (29.2 percent). In the Northeast, however, the low-wage worker rate for American Indians / Aleut Eskimos is very low (3 percent); the rate for Blacks is the highest in the Northeast (30 percent). In the Midwest,

Blacks have the highest rate of low-wage work (38 percent). In the West, American Indians / Aleut Eskimos have the highest rate (38 percent). In terms of Hispanic origin, the rate is highest in the South and lowest in the Northeast.

When looking at age, we see that the overall rural rate is highest for sixteen- to twenty-four-year-olds. This varies by region, however. In the Northeast, the rate is highest for twenty-five- to thirty-four-year-olds. Workers age sixty-five and over have a 13 percent rate overall, varying from a low of 10.6 percent in the Midwest to 16 percent in the South. Education level by region is consistent with overall rates for education level; it is highest for workers without a high school education. This rate ranges from a low of 25 percent in the Northeast to a high of 40 percent in the South.

The overall rates for those married with spouse absent and separated are 39 percent and 40 percent, respectively. In the Northeast and the South, the rate is higher for married with spouse absent, while in the Midwest and West the rate is higher for separated. For all regions, rates are lowest for married couples, ranging from 11 percent in the Northeast to 17 percent in the South. In terms of family type, the rates are highest for female-headed households with children, ranging from 51 percent in the Northeast to 64 percent in the South.

RATES OF LOW-WAGE WORK BY OCCUPATION

To further understand the variation in rural low-wage worker rates by region, we examine data on occupations. Certain occupational groups have higher than average rates of low-wage workers. As shown in table 11.3, rural low-wage rates in the United States are highest for food preparation (40 percent), health care support (38 percent), building and grounds cleaning and maintenance (38 percent), and farming, fishing, and forestry (35 percent). The only occupation in the Northeast with a greater than 30 percent rate is building and grounds cleaning and maintenance (38 percent). In the Midwest, both food preparation (35 percent) and building and grounds cleaning and maintenance (34 percent) are high. In the West, food preparation (44 percent), building and grounds cleaning and maintenance (42 percent), health care support (38 percent), and farming, fishing, and forestry (31 percent) are high. The South has the largest number of occupations with higher than 30 percent rates: health care support (50 percent), food preparation (47 percent), farming, fishing, and forestry (44 percent), building and grounds cleaning and maintenance (40 percent), construction and extraction (32 percent), and production (30 percent).

Table 11.3 also includes the mean hourly wage for all occupations, with a range from $9.35 (food preparation) to $46.22 (management). The mean wage for the most low-wage occupations is less than $12.31. To put this in perspective, a worker earning $12.31 per hour, working full-time (40 hours/week) year-round (52 weeks/year), would earn $25,605 annually. These earnings are significantly less than the living wage estimates discussed earlier.

Table 11.3 suggests that workers employed in certain occupations, such as health care support, food preparation, cleaning, farming, and personal care, have a greater than expected chance of earning low wages. The average wages for these occupations are above minimum, but create a position of economic vulnerability for the worker. What factors contribute to the preponderance of such occupations? And why are the rates by occupation slightly, but significantly, different across the four regions of the United States?

Regional differences in rates of low-wage work by occupation illustrated in table 11.3 point to the importance of industry and the unique labor markets that characterize each region. Economic restructuring, characterized by deindustrialization, globalization, and automation, has created new labor markets. For example, agriculture is no longer a principal source of income in most rural areas (Johnson 2006; Hamilton et al. 2008). The new labor markets, characterized by technology and service, are bifurcated. These two-tiered markets, known as primary and secondary sectors, create very different environments for work. On one hand, "good" technology and service jobs provide stable employment, opportunities for mobility, tenure, and decent earnings. The jobs generally require not only college education, but also social capital (individual contacts and networks) and access to expanding labor markets (living or being able to move to areas where jobs are located). Examples of these occupations include management, business and financial operations, computers, architects and engineers, legal, and health care practitioners and technicians. As seen in table 11.3, all of these occupational groups have low-wage work rates less than 11 percent.

The opposite is found in secondary sector occupations, or "bad" jobs. It is here where low-wage workers are disproportionately found—health care support, food preparation, building and grounds cleaning, personal care, and farming, fishing, and forestry. These jobs—also related to technology and service industries—are typically unstable, carry few (if any) benefits, and offer limited or no mobility. The jobs require few skills; they offer workers even fewer skills. Yet they are essential to the "success" of the industry and workers in the primary sector occupations.

We call these low-wage secondary sector occupations "job ghettos" because they are nearly impossible to escape. This is especially true in rural areas, where problems such as transportation, social services, child care, and access to good jobs are exacerbated.

Conclusion and Policy Implications

The rates of low-wage workers are not randomly distributed throughout the U.S. population. Scholars of spatial inequality see this as an "uneven process" (Lobao, Hooks, and Tickamyer 2007). Overall, rates of low-wage workers have declined in the past decade. Rates in rural areas tend to be higher than overall rates. Rural rates vary by region, with the South typically having the highest rates and the Northeast the lowest. Low-wage work is associated with particular characteristics that place individuals and families at a disadvantage, including women, female-headed households, blacks, Native Americans / Aleut Eskimo, those with Hispanic origins, those who are separated or have an absent spouse, workers with high school or lower education, and workers between the ages of sixteen and thirty-four. Rates of low-wage work are higher for certain occupations, including food preparation, health care support, building and grounds cleaning, personal care, and farming, fishing, and forestry. Workers in these occupations may be trapped in "job ghettos," unable to access education or labor market opportunities needed to transition out of low-wage labor markets. These workers and their families are economically vulnerable as they balance a fine line between being a "low-wage worker" and "poor." Individuals in low-wage jobs may easily "slip" or move into poverty because of stressful life events, such as job loss, cut in pay and/or hours, or the breakup of family.

While raising the minimum wage may help the poorest of low-wage workers, it will most likely not have an effect on those earning ten to twelve dollars per hour. Increasing the earnings of these workers means access to "good" primary sector jobs. Access, in turn, may require increased education, skills, transportation, child care, and geographic mobility.

Overall, our data point to a decrease in working poor rates for the United States as a whole and for rural areas more specifically. Caution should be used, however, when interpreting the data as they reflect only two points in time. Our next step is to add additional years (e.g., 2001 and 2004) to see if the decrease is part of a trend. Furthermore, research is needed to understand what has happened to the declining numbers of low-wage workers. Have they improved their status and escaped the job ghettos? Have they dropped into poverty? Or perhaps, as some suggest, have they become "discouraged," so that they simply no longer appear in the data?

Another possible explanation is that the characteristics of low-wage workers in rural areas appear to be converging with those in urban areas, in keeping with other forms of rural-urban convergence identified in the conclusion of this volume. While spatial inequality creates unevenness across regions, these boundaries are not always clearly delineated. Rural and nonrural become less meaningful as society globalizes. Dominant industries—service and technology—depend less on geographical land mass and more on infrastructure and communication. Following this logic, we can expect to see the usefulness of region (e.g., Northeast, South, West, Midwest) as a broad indicator of quality of life giving way to more local units of analysis (e.g., county, city, and even neighborhood). Through the process of devolution, this has already happened. Many federal decisions are now made by states, municipalities are more accountable for local social service funding, and faith-based groups are increasingly providing relief to needy populations. The extent to which such groups can significantly change the long-term quality of life for the working poor in rural areas remains to be seen.

Table 11.1 Rates of low-wage work for the United States and nonmetro areas, 1997 and 2007

	Percent U.S. low-wage workers, 1997	Percent rural low-wage workers, 1997	Percent U.S. low-wage workers, 2007	Percent rural low-wage workers, 2007
Total	19.4	26.1	17.8	21.3
Sex				
Male	18.0	23.9	16.7	19.3
Female	21.0	28.5	19.2	23.6
Race				
White-only	17.8	24.0	16.5	19.6
Black-only	30.7	48.4	27.0	37.5
American Indian / Aleut Eskimo	33.1	43.0	34.1	38.6
Asian / Hawaiian / Pacific Islander	19.3	23.7	15.8	18.8
Multiple racial identities	n/a	n/a	21.2	24.8
Hispanic origin				
Yes	n/a	n/a	35.8	44.3
No	n/a	n/a	14.9	20.0
Age				
16–24	28.6	34.5	29.0	32.6
25–34	23.6	33.1	22.9	29.6
35–44	18.5	25.9	18.2	22.7
45–54	12.1	17.4	11.9	14.8
55–64	13.2	18.0	9.7	11.4
65 and over	14.6	17.9	10.7	13.4
Education				
Below high school or without high school diploma	36.7	40.3	37.3	34.6
High school graduate	22.7	26.9	22.6	24.4
Bachelor and below (above high school)	14.1	20.8	12.7	16.4
Professional degree, master and above	4.8	5.7	4.0	5.0
Marital status				
Married—spouse present	13.4	19.6	11.3	14.1
Married—spouse absent	38.2	38.2	35.0	39.2
Widowed	26.5	35.7	21.3	25.9
Divorced	26.9	37.7	22.5	31.0
Separated	35.2	47.0	34.1	39.6
Never married	25.8	34.2	26.1	31.4
Family kind				
Husband-wife family	13.2	19.2	11.2	13.7
Husband-wife family with children under 18	18.3	26.1	16.5	20.3
Other female head	35.0	48.5	32.7	43.6
Other female head with children under 18	48.7	61.1	48.5	58.4
Region				
Northeast	14.6	17.8	14.7	16.7
Midwest	14.5	23.8	14.9	18.6
South	19.9	28.7	18.8	25.2
West	21.2	29.3	18.7	20.6

SOURCE: 1997, 2007 CPS.

Table 11.2 Rural U.S. rates of low-wage work by region, 2007

	U.S.	Northeast	Midwest	South	West
Rural low-wage worker rate	21.3	16.7	18.6	28.7	20.6
Sex					
Male	19.3	15.0	16.5	23.5	18.2
Female	23.6	18.6	21.2	27.1	23.5
Race					
White-only	19.6	16.6	18.2	22.1	20.0
Black-only	37.5	30.3	37.7	37.9	21.4
American Indian / Aleut Eskimo	38.6	3.1	29.5	43.4	38.1
Asian / Hawaiian / Pacific Islander	18.8	20.8	26.5	21.1	15.5
Multiple racial identities	24.8	8.1	28.8	29.2	20.1
Hispanic origin					
Yes	44.3	29.6	41.4	49.0	39.9
No	20.0	16.4	18.0	23.5	17.7
Age					
16–24	32.6	22.5	30.5	38.2	30.6
25–34	29.6	28.4	25.8	33.7	28.3
35–44	22.7	16.2	19.1	27.8	22.8
45–54	14.8	11.1	13.1	17.3	15.9
55–64	11.4	8.9	8.5	14.8	10.8
65 and over	13.4	14.2	10.6	16.4	11.1
Education					
Below high school or without high school diploma	34.6	25.2	28.9	40.3	32.5
High school graduate	24.4	22.7	20.5	28.0	26.2
Bachelor and below (above high school)	16.4	11.2	15.7	18.7	16.3
Professional degree, master and above	5.0	3.9	6.1	4.8	4.5
Marital status					
Married—spouse present	14.1	10.7	12.2	16.8	14.4
Married—spouse absent	39.2	35.9	32.0	49.5	17.5
Widowed	25.9	22.9	21.1	31.5	20.9
Divorced	31.0	24.9	30.5	34.3	26.9
Separated	39.6	31.3	41.0	41.3	38.1
Never married	31.4	24.3	27.6	37.6	30.2
Family kind					
Husband-wife family	13.7	10.3	11.6	16.6	14.0
Husband-wife family with children under 18	20.3	15.6	17.1	24.4	21.7
Other female head	43.6	36.0	42.9	47.2	39.1
Other female head with children under 18	58.4	50.9	56.7	63.6	47.4

SOURCE: 2007 CPS.

Table 11.3   Rates of low-wage work by occupation in regions of the rural United
States, 2007

	U.S.	Northeast	Midwest	South	West	Mean hourly wage
Management occupations	11.0	10.1	10.4	12.2	10.6	46.22
Business and financial operations occupations	10.0	4.2	10.9	10.6	11.7	30.01
Computer and mathematical science occupations	7.0	1.0	7.8	10.9	2.7	34.71
Architecture and engineering occupations	7.3	0.3	11.1	1.7	23.1	33.11
Life, physical, and social service occupations	9.0	0.7	2.3	15.7	13.1	29.82
Community and social service occupations	16.2	15.2	14.6	17.1	18.1	19.49
Legal occupations	6.7	1.2	14.9	6.1	0.0	42.53
Education, training, and library occupations	12.3	9.3	9.2	14.3	17.9	22.41
Arts, design, entertainment, sports, and media occupations	19.4	10.4	17.5	24.9	26.5	23.27
Health care practitioner and technical occupations	10.2	5.8	8.2	14.7	5.8	31.26
Health care support occupations	38.3	23.7	29.1	49.7	38.0	12.31
Protective service occupations	11.4	1.4	9.9	13.9	10.8	18.63
Food preparation and serving–related occupations	40.0	28.5	34.5	47.0	44.2	9.35
Building and grounds cleaning and maintenance occupations	38.1	38.2	34.1	40.2	41.8	11.33
Personal care and service occupations	29.5	29.0	29.5	29.2	31.1	11.53
Sales and related occupations	24.8	17.9	23.6	28.7	22.8	16.94
Office and administrative support occupations	18.4	14.4	17.3	21.1	16.6	15.00
Farming, fishing, and forestry occupations	34.6	17.7	27.8	44.4	31.1	10.89
Construction and extraction occupations	25.5	20.8	19.5	32.4	19.4	19.53
Installation, maintenance, and repair occupations	16.6	19.9	14.5	17.1	16.7	19.20
Production occupations	24.1	21.3	18.7	30.4	24.8	15.05
Transportation and material moving occupations	21.7	18.0	20.4	24.7	18.8	14.75

SOURCE: Bureau of Labor Statistics, May 2007 National occupational employment and wage
estimates (http://www.bls.gov/oes/current/oes_nat.htm).

Notes

1. The Northeast includes Connecticut, New Jersey, Maine, New York, Massachusetts, Pennsylvania, New Hampshire, Rhode Island, and Vermont; the Midwest includes Illinois, Iowa, Indiana, Kansas, Michigan, Minnesota, Ohio, Missouri, Wisconsin, Nebraska, North Dakota, and South Dakota; the South includes Alabama, Arkansas, Kentucky, Louisiana, Mississippi, Oklahoma, Tennessee, Texas, Delaware, the District of Columbia, Florida, Georgia, Maryland, North Carolina, South Carolina, Virginia, and West Virginia; and the West includes Arizona, Alaska, Colorado, California, Idaho, Hawaii, Montana, Oregon, Nevada, Washington, Utah, Wyoming, and New Mexico.

SECTION 4

WORK AND FAMILY POLICY

STRENGTHENING RURAL COMMUNITIES
THROUGH INVESTMENT IN YOUTH EDUCATION,
EMPLOYMENT, AND TRAINING

LILIOKANAIO PEASLEE AND ANDREW HAHN

As the other authors in this volume have shown, economic restructuring has had a significant impact on the economic prospects of rural families. In this chapter, we look at how these trends have affected rural youth and contend that successful rural economic renewal rests on strengthening opportunities for young people. To revitalize rural communities, we must better link well-designed youth education, employment, and training programs with rural economic development plans.[1]

Economic restructuring has had particularly negative consequences for young people, who frequently bear the burden of low wages and high unemployment. As a result, job loss and changing work structures have created two distinct but interrelated problems in rural communities. First, many young people continue to leave rural life in search of better economic opportunities in urban areas. Because individuals with more education tend to be those most likely to migrate, this "brain drain" has weakened the skill base of rural areas and made it difficult to attract employers. Second, the problem of out-migration is compounded by the growing number of young people who are disconnected from both school and the labor market. These "idle" youth are particularly prone to engaging in problem behaviors (drug abuse, early childbearing, criminal activity, etc.), making it unlikely that they will be able to successfully transition to adulthood and putting stress on rural communities' already weakened financial resources.

The challenges facing teens and young adults in rural areas are problems for all of us, as the future of rural America is intimately linked to the well-being of the next generation of youth. A flourishing youth sector is a vital customer base, an economic development stimulus, and a check on further declines in the overall rural population. To make rural communities places where people want to work, live, and play, rural policies must have the dual goal of promoting economic self-sufficiency among disconnected rural youth and creating viable employment opportunities to retain educated workers.

While youth employment and training programs are not new, our state and federal policy responses have been anemic, episodic, fragmented, and poorly rooted in evidence-based research about what works. Without systemic, coordinated reform, we will continue to be unsuccessful in tackling these problems on a large scale. This chapter provides a framework with which to approach the difficult but critical task of strengthening rural education, employment, and training through the integration of rural economic and youth development policies. Rather than simply focus on particular programs, our analysis tries to identify an array of policy alternatives so that rural stakeholders can adapt recommendations to local contexts and resources.

A robust strategy for integrating rural economic and youth development would include the following components:

- Economic development strategies that build on communities' strengths and assets
- School- and community-based youth programming driven by positive youth development principles
- Vocational education and school-to-work programs in traditional high schools informed by emerging labor market demands
- Education and job training programs for disadvantaged out-of-school youth who are disconnected from the local labor market
- A larger career focus in postsecondary education and stronger connections between community colleges and local employers
- Local and regional partnerships that coordinate youth education and employment programs with economic and community development goals
- A research agenda that strengthens the knowledge base around effective human capital development for rural youth

The remainder of this chapter is organized around three broad topics: the need for expanding rural youth policies; the components of effective rural youth policies using the preceding framework; and examples of promising approaches that can help inform the design of a new generation of rural youth education, employment, and training initiatives. We identify a number of economic development strategies that look promising for rural areas, including health care, teaching, and recreation. We then discuss what is known about what makes youth education, employment, and training programs effective, and which programs are most likely to make a difference for rural youth self-sufficiency and for rural economic success.

Rural Youth Are in Trouble:
The Case for Expanding Rural Youth Policy

YOUTH IDLENESS

In 2007, there were 6.8 million rural youth age fourteen to twenty-four, making up 18 percent of the youth population nationwide.[2] Rural teens and young adults face many of the same challenges as youth in urban communities—high levels of poverty, low educational attainment, and high unemployment—but because of the spatial isolation of rural areas, many live in places with poor infrastructure and limited community services.[3] Still, despite inevitable bumps along the way, most rural youth are connected to families or other support systems that can help them move from adolescence to adulthood: they will graduate from high school, get jobs, form and maintain healthy relationships, have families, and embrace and give back to their communities. A growing number of young adults, however, confront insurmountable obstacles and will not successfully make this transition.

Although it is not always easy to predict which young people will "make it" and which will not, certain groups are at higher risk for poor outcomes. Youth populations that face especially significant barriers in transitioning to adulthood include teens in and aging out of foster care; homeless youth; those involved in the juvenile justice system; pregnant and parenting teens; youth with physical, emotional, or mental impairments; substance abusers; and high school dropouts (Wald and Martinez 2003). While national estimates are collected for each of these groups, data on youth in rural areas are not widely available for planning purposes. Some states do benefit from rural-focused policy think tanks who generate such statistics, but many do not have adequate sources of independent policy-relevant information.

One particularly salient indicator that young people are in trouble is the percentage of disconnected or "idle" youth. Young people are considered idle if they are not in school, the labor force (employed or unemployed), or the armed forces. It is a multidimensional measure of hardship and therefore has special value for policy making. Snyder and McLaughlin (2008) indicate that idleness among young adults is a severe and chronic problem. In rural areas, 12 percent of youth age eighteen to twenty-four are idle, surpassing the national average of 10 percent. Among racial and ethnic minority youth in rural areas the figures are particularly discouraging: 17 percent of rural blacks, 19 percent of rural Hispanics, and an astounding 23 percent of rural "other" racial-ethnic groups such as Native Americans are idle. For dropouts, the proportions are higher still, with more than 30 percent of rural dropouts just "hanging around." In each case, these figures are worse for rural youth than those in urban areas.[4] This adds up to an alarming number of young people who have little positive connection to social and economic institutions, face reduced earnings prospects, and have a high chance of engaging in risky behavior.

The high rates of idleness among rural youth stem in large part from the poor educational and employment opportunities in rural areas. Despite widespread recognition that education is essential for today's workers, many young people drop out before finishing high school. Failure to complete high school is one of the largest single predictors of youth idleness. Dropouts are three times more likely to be idle than high school graduates, with half of rural non-Hispanic blacks who have dropped out of high school and nearly one-half (49 percent) of young adult dropouts from low-income families idle (Snyder and McLaughlin 2008).

Clearly, youth policy must place a stronger emphasis on dropout prevention and provide young people with chances to connect and reconnect with education and work. However, simply investing in education will not be enough to solve rural economic decline if young people cannot find jobs. Herein is the rural dilemma: investing in human capital will do little to strengthen rural communities if they cannot retain educated workers, and without educated workers, communities can do little to attract employers. If rural economies are to recover, policy initiatives must stem the tide of youth leaving rural areas in search of better opportunities.

Unemployment and Youth Out-Migration

The lack of high-paying jobs—and of employment in general—in rural communities has resulted in an outflow of higher-skilled and more-educated workers, posing significant barriers to rural economic recovery. While the numbers and rates of youth out-migration are lower than they have been in the recent past, they continue to exceed immigration to rural areas. As a result, half of rural counties experienced overall population losses from 2000 to 2005 (USDA Economic Research Service 2007a).[5]

Economic restructuring has reduced the ability of skilled and unskilled youth to find employment in rural areas. While older workers continue to experience skill deficiencies due to the decline in traditional jobs such as agriculture, timber, mining, and textile production, younger workers are more likely impacted by recent shifts in the service sector.[6] The shift from unskilled to skilled jobs has increased spatial mismatch in nonmetropolitan (nonmetro) areas, as many high-skill industries require more extensive communications infrastructure than is available in many rural areas and opt for locations close to suppliers and customers (Gibbs, Kusmin, and Cromartie 2005). Moreover, global competition, the introduction of new technologies that require more advanced skills, and the outsourcing of low-skill, blue-collar employment has reduced the jobs available for younger, less educated rural workers.

Although young adults with more education still tend to be those most likely to migrate, large numbers of adolescents are increasingly leaving rural areas when they finish high school (Irwin et al. 2004). Rural economic development strategies must therefore foster job growth for youth with a variety of skill and education levels if they are to both reduce youth idleness and discourage rural out-migration.

Sector-Based Strategies for Rural Economic Development

Rural communities share many common features, yet the landscape of rural America is incredibly diverse, with varying levels of natural resources, human capital, and educational and technological infrastructure. Policy makers cannot use a one-size-fits-all approach to economic revitalization. As we have seen, the changing demographics of rural America have presented challenges for rural communities, yet they can also provide opportunities for economic growth. We offer some ideas for economic development below, drawing from sectors currently experiencing shortages in qualified workers and from emerging labor markets where rural planners can capitalize on current demographic and economic trends.

MEETING RURAL HEALTH CARE NEEDS

Many rural communities have limited access to health services; in others, facilities are unable to fill vacancies due to a lack of qualified health workers. This problem is likely to increase in coming years as baby boomers age and retirees continue to move into rural communities. While rural health care facilities have a difficult time finding and retaining workers, studies have shown that rural residents are more likely than nonnatives to stay in their jobs. Investment in local workers, therefore, is an important strategy for maintaining a rural workforce (Helseth 2007).

School-to-work programs, employment programs for disconnected youth, and postsecondary training in community colleges can take advantage of health care shortages by forming partnerships with local health care employers and preparing young people for careers in the health care industry. Moreover, since the health care field encompasses occupations requiring varying degrees of education and training, from nursing assistants to lab technicians to doctors, health sector expansion is an excellent strategy for addressing the employment needs of high-achieving students and of more marginalized youth.

STRENGTHENING RURAL SCHOOLS

Similar workforce shortages are occurring in primary and secondary schools. Teacher vacancies are skyrocketing across the United States, and rural schools are having a particularly difficult time attracting qualified teachers. The most critical need is for teachers trained in math, science, technology, and special education. Barriers to attracting teachers to rural areas include professional isolation, low salaries, and poor resources (National Education Association 2007). However, some states are having success in encouraging new teachers to return to rural areas in exchange for help with training and certification (Collins 1999). Schools can also do more to attract rural students to the profession through early career exposure.

The importance of vibrant rural schools cannot be underscored enough. Given limited social institutions, schools often act as anchors for rural communities—they hold town meetings and elections, host social functions, and offer recreational opportunities. Moreover, in many rural areas, school districts serve as the largest employer. Addressing the rural teaching shortage not only begins to fill rural employment gaps but is critical to helping rural areas maintain a sense of community identity and in ensuring the next generation of well-educated citizens.

DEVELOPING RECREATION AND TOURISM

While young people have been leaving rural communities, retirees and families have been moving into those areas that are rich in natural resources and provide recreational opportunities. Strategic planning between economic development and youth programs can take advantage of this influx to expand job opportunities. Increases in seasonal and part-time work that accompany recreational development can act as an entry into employment for youth who are also attending education or training programs. While many are low-wage service jobs—restaurants, retail stores, and the like—the total earnings per resident are substantially higher (two thousand dollars more per worker) in recreation counties than in other rural counties.[7] At the same time, however, recreational development tends to raise housing costs and attract more-educated migrant workers (Reeder and Brown 2005). Such a strategy, therefore, must also be accompanied by planning for affordable housing and by well-connected school-to-work and training programs that funnel local workers into new jobs.

By no means do these suggestions provide a comprehensive picture of emerging development strategies, nor will they be well suited to all locations. For instance, other industries in which rural regions are finding a niche include green technology, biotechnology, biomedical research, specialty value-added food production, and financial services. What is most important is that rural development strategies reflect regional assets and realistic economic demands and are linked to local employment and training programs. Planners must act in concert with business and the human service community to forecast employment trends, human service needs, and local growth projections.[8]

Designing Rural Youth Employment and Training Programs That Work

If rural economic development strategies are to be successful, we must have comprehensive youth policies that connect young people to schools, jobs, and their communities. Below we discuss four social settings in which human capital development for young people occurs: youth development in after-school programs and community-based agencies; vocational education and school-to-work programs in traditional high schools; education and job training for disadvantaged out-of-school youth; and postsecondary education and training.[9]

IMPROVING YOUTH DEVELOPMENT IN AFTERSCHOOL AND
COMMUNITY-BASED PROGRAMMING

Effective youth employment and training programs must, at their heart, facilitate healthy youth development. Although rural youth face a number of challenges, policy must respond to the emerging literature on positive and healthy youth development that focuses on youth assets and strengths and not just their deficits. Policies, in other words, must provide young people with opportunities to master cognitive, social, emotional, moral, physical, civic, and vocational competencies (Catalano et al. 2004). Thinking about youth capacities can lead to new ways of conceptualizing rural policies and programs.

Heightened awareness of the importance of learning during nonschool hours has greatly expanded youth development programming through new foundation initiatives, organizations promoting afterschool programming, state policies, and even federal initiatives such as 21st Century Schools. Unfortunately, however, rural areas have not enjoyed the same attention to youth development as urban places, and continue to have programs that are underfunded and unevenly located.

Youth development programs can take a variety of forms; they can be offered by schools, community-based organizations, university extension programs, or recreation departments. Since many rural youth have significant transportation challenges, it often makes sense to locate programs in schools and to keep them open in the afternoons, evenings, and weekends (although budgetary pressures can make this difficult). While not all youth development programs are explicitly focused on employment and training, supporting positive youth development addresses the underlying barriers to education and employment and can help youth develop the competencies they need to succeed in school, the labor market, and beyond.[10]

Quality youth programs (though mostly in urban settings) have been linked to a variety of positive developmental outcomes for disadvantaged youth, including enhanced academic performance, decreased substance abuse and teen pregnancy, and higher high school graduation and college enrollment rates.[11] Although specific programs have demonstrated effectiveness through external impact evaluations, successful prevention and intervention lie not in any particular program but in key elements of program design. The evidence-based principles discussed below can be infused into many existing rural youth programs.[12]

Rural youth who are at risk of undesirable life outcomes face multiple barriers to success; many struggle with addiction, have mental or behavioral health problems, are teen parents, or come from families facing considerable economic stress. No program can meet all of the needs of young people without strong connections to social service agencies and other community resources. Yet access to services presents a problem in rural areas, as county, state, and regional offices may be located far from those in need of support. The centrality of schools to rural life and the absence of stigma that is often associated with social welfare programs can make schools prime locations for service coordination.[13]

Effective youth development programs not only address problem behaviors but also seek to develop positive competencies like leadership, social activism, good citizenship, and empathy. Programs should include a variety of activities to reach these goals, such as mentoring, counseling, life-skills training, tutoring and academic support, and community service (Catalano et al. 2004). They must be age and developmentally appropriate, and planners need to pay particular attention to staff and volunteer training, since relationships with adults can make or break a youth development program.

While these strategies and program ideas can be incorporated into a variety of local rural youth programs, there may be benefits to expanding proven programs that have demonstrated effectiveness through external program evaluation. For example, the National 4-H Program is one of the largest and most well-known youth programs in rural areas and provides a good example of the principles outlined above.[14] The organization engages nearly three million rural, farm, and small-town youth, age five to nineteen, in community programs. 4-H emphasizes the use of hands-on, experiential learning in projects that include citizenship, environmental education, technology, the expressive arts, and animal, plant, and consumer science to prepare young people for work and citizenship. The program's ties to the land-grant university system allow it to play a role in advancing research, and it prides itself on the use of youth development principles such as youth-centric programming, youth leadership, and peer learning. Its three-pronged approach of education, prevention, and youth development has been shown to reduce risky behaviors and increase the number of positive characteristics exhibited by participating youth, including a significant proportion from low-income, less educated families (Astroth and Haynes 2002; Kress n.d.).

REFORMING CAREER AND WORKFORCE PREPARATION IN RURAL HIGH SCHOOLS

In addition to the more general prevention and intervention strategies of youth development programs, policies aimed at connecting young people to careers must start with reform of the vocational training in rural secondary schools. Vocational education (also called technical education, school-to-work, or school-to-career education) has traditionally been offered as a distinct track from the college preparatory curriculum. Economic restructuring, however, has made this bifurcated vocational model inadequate for today's youth. All young people—whether they are going on to college or entering the world of work—increasingly need a similar skill base to succeed in the global economy, where employability is contingent on a combination of basic academic knowledge and a range of soft skills, such as working in diverse groups, innovation, empathy, and communication (Act 2006; U.S. Department of Labor 1991). Yet despite these changes, many vocational education and training programs continue to emphasize job-specific skills (which are more easily acquired and more easily outmoded than general skills) and are failing to provide students with the means to adapt to the demands of a changing labor market (National Research Council 1998).

Better integrating vocational and academic learning and encouraging strong connections between schools and employers can (a) make school-based learning more relevant to employment and (b) provide youth with work-based learning experiences tied to what they learn in school.[15] School-to-work programs may include internships and apprenticeships, cooperative education, job shadowing, mentoring, training through school-sponsored enterprises, or Tech Prep programs. Internships, work cooperatives, and apprenticeships have been particularly successful in boosting the employment and earnings of disadvantaged youth (Neumark 2004). Such programs can help make school more meaningful for students who may otherwise drop out and can also encourage college-going students to stay in their communities once they graduate.[16]

While increasing the number of work-based learning opportunities is important, program administrators need to pay close attention to the *quality* of student placements. Early work experience can provide valuable opportunities for adolescent development, yet the jobs held by most young people are disconnected from classroom learning, provide little room for advancement or opportunities to acquire and exercise leadership skills, and offer few meaningful interactions with adult supervisors (National Research Council 1998).

One strategy demonstrating success with reducing dropout rates and increasing postsecondary employment and earnings is the integration of academic and occupational courses into learning communities with a particular career focus. Examples of these "career academies" include health, business and finance, arts and communications, computers, engineering, law, and government. Well-designed programs create links with employers, local colleges, and the community to provide students with exposure to careers and work-based learning opportunities. With their small learning communities and strong work focus, career academies are particularly effective for young men and those most at risk of dropping out of school.[17]

Since limited employment opportunities in rural areas may make it difficult for school-to-work programs to provide students with internships and work-based experiences, rural schools must often find creative ways of linking learning to life. Two such strategies include place-based learning and entrepreneurship education. The former emphasizes linkages with higher education or other local institutions to create community-based learning opportunities; the latter teaches students how to create microenterprises—businesses needing little start-up capital and with few employees—as a way to acquire and apply business, academic, and life skills (James 1996).

While the experiential aspects of both strategies can enhance learning, rural areas may present barriers to using entrepreneurship as a method for experiential learning *if* the expectation is that students will create and launch businesses of their own. The characteristics of rural life that so often lead to rural unemployment—low local demand, poor transportation, and limited technological infrastructure—are likely magnified for young adults with limited experience.[18] Instead, rural students may be more successful in undertaking projects at the classroom, school, or community level that combine place-based learning and innovative business creation to revitalize distressed communities. In rural northern Maine, for example, Lubec High School has formed a partnership with regional colleges to create a community-based aquaculture program. Students raise fish, maintain a hydroponic greenhouse, farm mussels, sell bait, and are engaged in a drift study with local fishermen. While the program has not been subject to structured evaluation, case study data suggest that the program has been effective in realizing its goals of increasing school attendance, decreasing dropout rates, and enhancing students' educational and career aspirations (Hynes 2003).

EXPANDING "SECOND CHANCE" PROGRAMS FOR OUT-OF-SCHOOL YOUTH

While restructuring vocational education with updated school-to-work policies can improve high school completion rates and enhance students' job-readiness skills, school-based programs cannot capture the growing number of idle youth who have already dropped out of school. Rural youth policies must do a better job addressing the developmental and human capital needs of a wide range of young adults. In particular, such programs must invest more effort in reaching older youth and high-risk teens (those who are not in school, who are engaged in high-risk behaviors, or who are court-involved) by expanding opportunities for them to reconnect with education and training. "Second chance" programs can take many forms: alternative high schools for students unable to succeed in traditional settings, offender reentry programs, highly structured residential centers, and less intensive education and training programs often run under the auspices of community-based organizations.

While there are a growing number of positive national evaluations of second chance programs, few have shown significant long-term gains in the education *and* employment of participants, both of which are critical to addressing the needs of idle youth. Therefore, although we try to emphasize principles rather than programs in designing rural youth policy, when it comes to second chance programs we encourage rural communities to expand access to the handful of national programs that have proven effective for disconnected and hard-to-serve youth: Job Corps, Youth Service and Conservation Corps (Youth Corps), and YouthBuild USA.[19] Each combines positive youth development principles with focused education and job training.

Job Corps is a residential education and training program for young people age sixteen through twenty-four that is administered and funded by the U.S. Department of Labor. The program's effectiveness lies in its intensity and comprehensive mix of services. In addition to academic services, job training, and work experience, members receive parenting education; computer and social skills training; health care; counseling and other social supports; and engage in community service activities. Participants receive a stipend while enrolled and transitional support for up to twelve months after they graduate (U.S. Department of Labor 2007; Public/Private Ventures 2002).

Like Job Corps, Youth Corps is designed to increase the educational attainment and labor market success of disadvantaged youth, but the program's ties to the Corporation for National Service translate into a much stronger emphasis on community service and civic engagement. Job skills and personal development occur as members work together to meet community needs through environmental, education, and human service projects. Members receive a stipend, educational benefits, and scholarships (Public/Private Ventures 2002).

Finally, YouthBuild—a program targeting disconnected youth through an integrated approach to youth and community development—points to the power of engaging youth in community problem solving, one of the key elements in positive youth development. The YouthBuild idea was born in East Harlem in 1978 when a high school teacher asked her students how they would improve their community if they had adult support. Their answer was to rebuild houses, take empty buildings back from drug dealers, and eliminate crime. Together they launched the first YouthBuild program, which has now blossomed into a nationally renowned model.[20] Young people enrolled in the program work to achieve their GED or high school diploma and receive job training, leadership, and community service opportunities as they construct affordable housing for homeless and low-income residents (YouthBuild USA n.d.).

Both Job Corps and Youth Corps have been studied through rigorous impact evaluations. Job Corps has shown the most impressive overall effects on education, employment, and earnings for high-risk youth—impacts that have been sustained for thirty months postenrollment—and has demonstrated effectiveness in increasing the employment and earning prospects of young offenders (Public/Private Ventures 2002; Task Force 2000). Findings from national Youth Corps evaluations show positive effects on employment and earnings at fifteen months postenrollment, particularly for African Americans, who made up 50 percent of the sample (Public/Private Ventures 2002). Although assessment of YouthBuild has been limited by a lack of follow-up data and program-wide evaluation, several studies do show positive effects, including high job placement rates and reduced recidivism among youthful offenders (U.S. GAO 2004; Ivry and Doolittle 2003; Leslie 2007).

While program effectiveness for rural youth is not reported in the research findings, each of these programs seems compatible with rural youth employment and training strategies. Youth Corps may be particularly well suited for rural areas, which often lack existing employment opportunities. Programs can be tailored to respond to local economic circumstances, as training typically includes service projects in rural areas such as forests, parks, and rangelands. For example, the Coconino Rural Environment Corps works in partnership with Arizona's land management agencies and organizations. Youth learn about and are trained in a variety of conservation fields, including fuels reduction and forest restoration; trail construction and maintenance; resource monitoring; and survey projects (Coconino Rural Environment Corps 2007).

LINKING POSTSECONDARY EDUCATION AND
TRAINING WITH LOCAL EMPLOYERS

Higher education has a fundamental role to play in rural economic renewal by expanding youth access to postsecondary education and training (thereby increasing their employability). Community colleges play a particularly important role in workforce development. As Secretary of Labor Elaine Chao pointed out in 2006, "Two-thirds of the estimated 18 million new jobs created in the next 10 years will be in occupations that require some advanced education. This can be a 4-year college degree, a 2-year degree from a community college or specialized training like an apprentice program. But completing some form of higher education is critical to building a solid, sustainable career path" (Chao 2006). Unfortunately, even though rural youth are more likely to graduate from high school than are urban peers, they are often disconnected from postsecondary opportunities and therefore less likely to go to college (Rural Families Data Center 2004; Tilly et al. 2004). Increasing educational attainment is an important part of rural economic development: while the returns from education are greater in urban areas, studies show that rural areas with more college-educated adults have higher income and employment levels than regions with lower education levels (Gibbs 2005).

While many community colleges already provide effective GED and other remedial education programs, school-based and out-of-school education and training programs can creatively link with postsecondary institutions to increase pathways to college. The relative accessibility and affordability of community colleges make them prime candidates for disadvantaged rural youth to realize higher education. Community colleges, which typically have open enrollment policies, are also well suited for collaboration with other education and training programs. Many remote areas do not have access to campuses, but the growing trend of distance learning holds promise for rural course expansion.

One important challenge in community college participation is attrition due to economic pressures. While investment in federal programs such as Pell Grants and asset-building policies like Individual Homestead Accounts can help more rural families pay for postsecondary education and training, expanding college access (and completion) for poor rural youth will also necessitate creative solutions from other sectors. The Lumina Foundation, for example, recently launched two programs—DreamKeepers and the Angel Fund—in a number of community colleges and rural tribal colleges and universities to address student attrition. The influence of these initiatives, which provide students with emergency bill paying, scholarships for tuition, support services, and workforce-related skill development, is currently being evaluated by MDRC (Ajose et al. 2007).

Despite the potential for community colleges to play a strong role in rural employment and training, rural campuses are often constrained by their small size. Small and medium-sized rural community colleges offer fewer workforce development programs than do urban, suburban, and large rural campuses. A lack of on-campus child care and limited distance education programs are often cited as barriers to community college enrollment in rural areas. Because they operate without the economies of scale of larger institutions, to enhance resources and decrease student costs it may be necessary to increase state and federal funding to small rural community colleges (Hardy and Katsinas 2007). Combining postsecondary resources with other program funding streams can also create more comprehensive human capital initiatives (Gruber 2000).

Lastly, partnerships with community colleges, land-grant universities, and other postsecondary schools can greatly enhance other types of youth education and training programs and rural development strategies. Most land-grant universities already offer a number of opportunities in rural areas through university extension programs, including 4-H, noncredit and professional development courses, and community and economic development work. These institutions can play a key role in developing program guidelines and in training teachers, program staff, mentors, and employers. Moreover, offering training and technical assistance to local businesses may be more successful in attracting employers to rural areas than traditional strategies such as tax breaks (Whitener and Parker 2007).

CREATING EMPLOYMENT AND TRAINING PARTNERSHIPS
THROUGH A YOUTH POLICY LENS

Rural youth policy—especially addressing employment and training—has been hampered by policy fragmentation and unclear policy responsibilities. Historically, it has been difficult to discern who is responsible for idle and out-of-school rural youth. While states and localities have long played a dominant role in K-12 education, they have not taken the same lead when it comes to programs for dropouts or for high school graduates who are skill deficient. Meanwhile, the federal government response has been weak and extremely disjointed.[21] While there is some movement at the federal level to better streamline resources for youth, local and regional partnerships cannot wait for Washington to act; they must take the lead in moving the rural agenda forward. Fortunately, communities do not need to reinvent the wheel. In many places, collaboration can build off existing structures and take advantage of established funding streams.

The 1998 Workforce Investment Act (WIA) mandates coordination between entities receiving federal job training funds and has directed local workforce investment boards to establish youth councils to help plan and coordinate youth employment services. Although it is not exclusively focused on young people, 30 percent of program dollars must be spent on programs for out-of-school youth (Beaulieu 2000). Many workforce boards and youth councils—particularly in rural areas—are regional in scope and can be a valuable tool for bringing together a wide array of state and local actors. The U.S. Department of Labor has encouraged them to expand their capacity in developing more comprehensive youth systems beyond the mandated inclusion of housing authorities, juvenile justice providers, and parents of WIA-eligible youth (Beaulieu 2000). Constructing rural partnerships that connect youth advocates with economic development can expand the range of actors with a stake in creating effective youth education and training programs, better align youth workforce training with local labor market demands, avoid program duplication, and create more streamlined resources.

Youth councils or similar bodies should plan new policies and reform older ones through a needs assessment that starts with the four youth policy sectors presented in this chapter (youth development, vocational education, second chance programs, and postsecondary education and training). An assessment should consider the following:

- What is being done in each of these areas in your community or region?
- How does money flow through these sectors?
- Which youth populations are served, and how extensive is the scale of enrollment?
- What do we know about their effectiveness, equity, and performance?
- What outcomes are sought, and how do these translate into contracting with local youth service providers?
- What are the levers of change to make sure rural youth are getting their fair share of resources?
- Is there specific rural youth–focused legislation that guides the sector's work?
- Are there close and useful ties with knowledge producers and advocacy organizations in the region?
- How well are these youth programs related to local employment considerations?

In designing such systems, rural policy makers should take advantage of the wealth of knowledge held by rural policy organizations and government research services and the funding opportunities offered by foundations with a rural focus.[22] Partnering with such institutions is important not only in developing well-designed policies but also in measuring their success. As we explain below, strengthening the youth policy research base is paramount to the success of youth education, employment, and training programs.

STRENGTHENING THE YOUTH POLICY RESEARCH BASE

The limited research base with which to guide policy making has been one of the most important hurdles to significant investment in rural youth employment and training programs over the past two decades. The first generation of evaluations of government-sponsored employment and training demonstration projects funded by the Department of Labor under the 1977 Youth Employment and Demonstration Projects Act was largely disappointing. While some of the projects did show promise in dealing with youth unemployment, most evaluations showed few positive results, failed to highlight innovative and effective practices from which others could learn, and ignored the fact that programs often operated with inadequate funding (Hahn and Lerman 1985; Pines 2000). Ultimately, inconclusive findings concerning program impacts led policy makers to conclude that little worked to improve the lives of disconnected youth (Edelman, Holzer, and Offner 2006; Partee n.d.).

In this chapter, however, we have pointed to a number of promising practices that, given more recent studies, are likely to enhance education and learning for at-risk rural youth. Still, if measured by the quality and rigor of program evaluations, the research findings on youth programming continue to be mixed. Although there have been a number of national evaluations of youth education, employment, and training, few have had an explicitly rural focus. For example, the New York City–based MDRC has contributed enormously to the field by studying disadvantaged youth programs through random assignment methods, but their research is an exception rather than the norm, and rural youth are rarely included in their studies. Moreover, many program evaluations suffer from an underenrollment of young people who would most benefit from the program (typically youth most at risk), inconsistent participation by those enrolled, and high rates of attrition (Ivry and Doolittle 2003).

A youth policy agenda must strengthen the research base around effective youth education and training programs. Given the potential challenges in implementing these strategies in rural communities, it is imperative that rural youth be included in well-designed evaluations to address rural differences. Policies rooted in proven practices are particularly important today as programs compete for scarce resources and well-designed, evidence-based research drives funding priorities. The ability to demonstrate the effectiveness of investments in rural youth education and training is vital to securing program funding and further expanding related social policies.

Policy Recommendations for Investing in
Rural Human Capital Development

A multifaceted approach to rural human capital development must include multiple settings and provide numerous opportunities for young people to connect with education, employment, and training in their communities. While there is no question that better studies of rural youth policies and programs are needed, we strongly believe that a relevant policy agenda for rural youth—and for rural America—need not and cannot afford to await the development of a definitive base of research studies. As outlined in the beginning of this chapter, policy makers must begin investing in rural communities and should take the following actions in developing plans for rural economic revitalization:

- *Build on communities' strengths and assets in economic development strategies.* Rural America is extremely diverse; unique economic contexts, varying levels of public infrastructure, and differing levels of capacity for solving local problems mean that the challenges faced by rural communities cannot be solved with a one-size-fits-all approach. While research and funding for youth programs need to occur at the national, state, and local levels, policy making must also enhance the problem-solving capacity of rural communities so that strategies can be better tailored to the needs of rural youth.
- *Expand school and community-based youth development programs.* Expand the movement of afterschool programming in rural communities. Help schools stay open longer and support transportation to connect youth to positive youth development programming. Support community-based organizations to have more rural coverage and encourage school-CBO partnerships.
- *Reform vocational education and school-to-work programs in secondary schools.* Rural youth policy must be linked first and foremost to education policy. The career and workforce training needs of students and employers can be enhanced by strengthening school-to-work programs in traditional high schools. Support legislation to facilitate linkages between schools, employers, and postsecondary institutions.
- *Focus on education and job training programs for disadvantaged out-of-school youth disconnected from the local labor market.* Education, employment, and training programs tend to have the largest effect on youth who enter programs with the poorest chances for success in school and

the labor market, but resources are particularly limited for older youth and young adults. Increase rural access to proven programs like Job Corps, Youth Corps, and YouthBuild. Programs can extend their impact by targeting outreach to higher-risk populations, including high school dropouts, youthful offenders, and chronically unemployed youth.

- *Encourage a larger career focus in postsecondary education and stronger connections between community colleges and local employers.* Expanding access to postsecondary education and training in rural communities is essential to increasing the ability of young people to find well-paying jobs and keeping them from leaving rural areas. Moreover, a well-educated workforce and industry-specific training programs can attract employers to rural areas. Encourage linkages between community colleges, land-grant universities, and local employers to design area-specific education and training programs.

- *Create local and regional partnerships to coordinate youth education and employment programs with economic and community development goals.* Youth employment and training programs have been limited by policy fragmentation. Regional partnerships must better align youth and economic development policies. To facilitate multisector collaboration, persuade Congress to expand funding for grants that specifically target distressed rural areas.

- *Strengthen the knowledge base around effective rural practices.* The ability to demonstrate the effectiveness of investments in rural youth education, employment, and training is paramount to securing program funding. While there is increasing evidence around effective programs for disadvantaged youth, we need to develop a more robust knowledge base about what works in rural communities. Demonstration projects must include rural places, evaluations should oversample rural and disengaged youth, and national evaluations that include rural places need to specify rural outcomes in their findings and discussions.

Conclusion

Successful rural economic revitalization will not be an easy task. It involves reconnecting idle rural youth, strengthening the tenuous connections of at-risk youth, and improving the economic base of rural areas so that young people are able to stay in their communities. Because we believe that youth are essential to the future of rural recovery, we have focused here on programs and policies to enhance the economic and life prospects of young people through the expansion of rural education, employment, and training programs.

Still, while youth are a critical component of healthy communities, better youth programs are only part of the answer. Comprehensive rural policy must also do more to enhance adult education and training, address the needs of rural families, strengthen early childhood and elementary education, and expand prevention programs. We can no longer afford to ignore rural communities or continue to approach policy in a weak, haphazard manner. This investment is crucial to reviving rural communities, preserving the competitiveness of the American economy, and ensuring the next generation of productive, engaged citizens.

Appendix: Elements of Effective Youth Programming

The following outline distills lessons learned from a number of metaevaluations of programs targeting high-risk, out-of-school or out-of-work youth and geared toward enhancing youth development, academic achievement, dropout prevention, school-to-work transitions, or youth employment. Few of the programs reviewed incorporate every strategy—and none focus explicitly on rural youth—but all share common principles about what makes youth programming successful (see Brand et al. 2000; Pines 2000; Jurich and Estes 2000; Public/Private Ventures 2002; Ivry and Doolittle 2003; Hammond et al. 2007; Partee n.d.).

Program Design
- Use evidence-based strategies and program designs
- Target multiple risk and protective factors
- Promote high standards for participants and staff
- Provide academic support and enhance basic skills
- Expose youth to a broad array of education and career opportunities
- Prioritize job placement
- Provide participants with financial incentives (paid work and internships)
- Provide experiential learning that is tied to employment opportunities and work-based learning that reinforces education and training components
- Create opportunities for youth to exercise leadership and civic engagement
- Reinforce positive social norms
- Make a long-term commitment to youth that extends past program enrollment

Appropriate Learning Environments
- Emphasize personal attention (e.g., small learning communities)
- Use a variety of strategies and activities to enhance competencies
- Offer age-appropriate programming

Personal Relationships
- Establish connections with caring adults through staff, mentors, councilors, and employers both from within the program and from other sources

Coordination and Collaboration
- Link school-based or second chance programs and postsecondary education and training
- Maintain relationships with employers to provide youth with positive work experiences
- Create partnerships with intermediary/brokering institutions to provide staff, volunteer, and employer training
- Link with external service providers to address basic needs and barriers to employment (child care, housing, food, medical care, legal support, etc.)

Planning and Implementation
- Implement programs as they were designed
- Include youth and frontline youth workers in program planning
- Provide strong staff and executive leadership and ongoing training
- Build in program evaluation that is tied to program goals
- Target outreach to enroll hard-to-reach youth

Notes

1. Research on rural areas uses a number of different definitions of "rural." The federal government alone has more than a dozen different methods for measuring rurality. Our population estimates come from Census Bureau figures, but we use other statistics from a number of different sources. Throughout this chapter we use "rural" and "nonmetro" interchangeably. For more detailed information on rural measurement methods, see Coburn et al. (2007). There are also a number of different definitions of the youth population. For example, the United Nations and the World Bank classify youth as those age fifteen to twenty-four. Other measures include individuals as young as ten years old or stop at age twenty-one. Since this essay is concerned with education and employment programs beginning at the high school level and with addressing the large number of idle rural youth, we have included young people age fourteen to twenty-four in our estimates.

2. Calculations are from the July 2007 Current Population Survey.

3. Rural poverty rates are higher than urban rates in every region except the Northeast, and nearly one-fourth of the rural population is considered persistently poor (Strong et al. 2005). Dropout rates vary significantly across the United States, from a low of 5 percent of teens age sixteen to nineteen in rural areas of North Dakota to a high of 17 percent in rural parts of Florida (Annie E. Casey Foundation 2004). Youth consistently experience unemployment rates nearly three times the rates reported in general employment statistics (for 2006 nonmetro unemployment rates were slightly higher than in metro areas, at 4.9 percent and 4.6 percent, respectively; Economic Research Service 2007b).

4. The only exceptions to urban-rural comparisons where urban youth fare somewhat worse on idleness than rural youth are among dropouts who are female, Hispanic, or from families above the poverty line (Snyder and McLaughlin 2008).

5. Mining and farming counties in the Great Plains, Corn Belt, and Appalachia and in a number of Southern manufacturing counties had the greatest population loss over the period.

6. Contrary to persistent views of rural America, only 6.5 percent of the rural labor force is engaged in farming (and just 1.78 percent of rural residents earn a primary living from farm income). Another 12.4 percent are employed in manufacturing, while 66 percent of rural employment is in the service sector (see Johnson 2006; Davis and Marema n.d.; and Gibbs et al. 2005).

7. Reeder and Brown utilize Johnson and Beale's (2002) typology of nonmetropolitan recreation counties in their calculations. The measure identifies recreation counties based on levels of employment and income in tourism-related industries, the presence of seasonal housing, geographic location, natural amenities, and form of recreation.

8. Regional planning may be particularly important in innovation-based industries since most rural areas are at a competitive disadvantage in attracting businesses and capital investment. For more on rural industry clusters, see R. Atkinson (2004) and Porter (2004).

9. We borrow this typology from Edelman, Holzer, and Offner (2006). In our review of effective programs, we did not rely exclusively on experimental and quasiexperimental research findings but turned to them when available. A number of case studies and process evaluations of rural employment and training programs exist. While their conclusions may not be as robust as evaluations with more rigorous research designs, such research can provide practitioners with rich examples of what is being done in the field.

10. Prevention programs play an important role in employment and training initiatives. This includes not only dropout prevention but also a focus on substance abuse: when the Indianapolis Private Industry Council sought to enroll dropouts in a life sciences curriculum offering training and jobs in the drug industry, many youth could not pass the mandatory urine- and drug-testing screening.

11. See, for example, Hahn, Leavitt, and Aaron's (1994) evaluation of the Quantum Opportunities Program; Tierney, Grossman, and Resch's (1995) evaluation of Big Brothers / Big Sisters' mentoring program; and Philliber, Kaye, and Herrling's (2001) evaluation of the Children's Aid Society's Carrera Adolescent Pregnancy Prevention Program.

12. A summary of the factors associated with effective youth education and training programs is included in an appendix at the end of this chapter.

13. The full-service school model provides a good example of strong school–social service collaboration. For an overview see Dryfoos and McGuire (2002). While schools are well suited for service coordination, it is important for services to follow youth when they leave school, whether they drop out, graduate, move, or become incarcerated. The high mobility of families with children makes program continuity particularly important for rural youth.

14. While 4-H is the largest youth program in rural areas, nationwide 55 percent of youth served by 4-H programs are from cities and suburbs (National 4-H Headquarters 2006). For more information on programs and locations see http://www.4-h.org/.

15. The 1994 School-to-Work Opportunities Act (STWOA) provided funds for schools to link with employers and postsecondary education and training institutions and represented one of the most comprehensive policies concerning workforce development. The Act funded an array of activities designed to strengthen school-to-work transitions. An important principle of the legislation was that unlike many other employment and training programs, STWOA grants were designed to integrate academic and vocational education for all students, not just particular populations considered at risk. However, the STWOA was not reauthorized after its initial five years.

16. Huang et al.'s (1997) longitudinal study of the High School and Beyond program found that schools that placed a strong emphasis on academic programs graduated students who were more likely to migrate from rural areas, while schools that focused on vocational training were more likely to graduate students who remained in their communities. The findings were similar for college-going and non-college-going youth.

17. For a summary of the evidence around career academies, see Ivry and Doolittle (2003), Kemple and Scott-Clayton (2004), and Public/Private Ventures (2002).

18. A number of national organizations exist dedicated to youth entrepreneurship education; Rural Entrepreneurship Through Action Learning (REAL) specifically targets rural youth. Although the field of entrepreneurship has expanded enormously in recent years, program evaluations remain mixed, and rural data are largely absent from these studies.

19. Another program is the National Guard's ChalleNGe program, a two-year federally funded program that like Job Corps has many rural program sites. ChalleNGe includes a six-month residential component and then mentoring and services to promote education and training. It is only now being researched and so is not discussed further here.

20. YouthBuild is funded by both public and private sources. In 2006, Congress transferred authority of competitive federal grants for YouthBuild programs from the Department of Housing and Urban Development to the Department of Labor. The transfer was designed to better align YouthBuild with other workforce education and training programs as well as to enhance program evaluation (U.S. GAO 2004).

21. For example, the 2002 White House Task Force for Disadvantaged Youth identified over three hundred active programs (administered by twelve agencies) that targeted vulnerable young people. The task force concluded that "the complexity of the problems faced by disadvantaged youth is matched only by the complexity of the traditional federal response to those problems. Both are confusing, complicated, and costly" (2003). The 2006 Tom Osborne Federal Youth Coordination Act was designed to better coordinate disparate youth policies and funding sources across government. Unfortunately, funding for the Act's implementation through a Federal Youth Development Council was not included in the 2007 or 2008 budgets. The Coordinating Council on Juvenile Justice and Delinquency Prevention coordinates a number of federal prevention programs, but their focus is on youth already involved in the juvenile justice system.

22. There are dozens of local and regional organizations that focus on rural policy. Some national organizations with a rural focus include the Carsey Institute, the Rural Youth Network, the USDA Rural Information Center, the USDA Cooperative State Research, Education, and Extension Service, W. K. Kellogg Foundation's Rural People, Rural Policy Initiative, and the Annie E. Casey Foundation's Rural Family Economic Success Initiative.

CHILD CARE IN RURAL AMERICA

NICOLE D. FORRY AND SUSAN K. WALKER

Changes in employment practices and rural family life over the last fifty years have increased the need for dependable, affordable child care. Largely, a shift in job availability and public policies have sent women who traditionally cared for their children at home into the workforce. The rural economy was traditionally based on manufacturing, natural resource extraction, and agriculture, and the jobs were held mostly by men. But with the reduction in these industries, and the growing economic importance of tourism, service work now predominates (Johnson 2006; Kelly 2007). Service jobs are frequently held by women, are paid hourly, offer few benefits, and may demand work during nontraditional hours. In addition, since the welfare reform legislation of 1996, parents are required to work to receive assistance. Consequently, the rural labor force has seen an influx of low-income mothers whose families are dependent on their incomes, heightening the need for services that support women's employment. Child care, especially for single or low-income mothers, is one such service (Bainbridge, Meyers, and Waldfogel 2003; Blau and Tekin 2003). But limited access to child care, or child care that is too costly or inconvenient in terms of location and hours, is a barrier to employment (U.S. GAO 2004; Ghazvini et al. 1999; Hobbs and Chang 1996; Hofferth and Collins 2000; Kimmel 1998; Reschke and Walker 2006; Walker and Reschke, 2004).

Decades of research on children's early learning potential and later academic achievement also highlight the value of child care as a setting that influences child development. Compared to low-quality child care, high-quality child care has been associated with positive short- and long-term outcomes, including better language and premathematics skills, later academic achievement, improved social skill development, higher future earnings, and less involvement in the criminal justice system (Burchinal et al. 1996, 2000; Garces, Duncan, and Curie 2002; Kaplan 1998; Lombardi 2003; NICHD Early Child Care Research Network 2005; Posner and Vandell 1994). These effects are particularly pronounced among low-income children (Votruba-Drzal, Coley, and Chase-Lansdale 2004). Analyses revealing that rural children are behind in preacademic skills compared to nonrural children (Grace et al. 2006) have prompted a more careful examination of the quality of early care and education settings for rural children, and of potential barriers to availability of and access to high-quality child care, particularly in rural settings.

This chapter further investigates child care in rural America as both an employment support for low-income families and an educational support for children. The first section presents information on the use of various child care arrangements in rural settings as well as considerations and barriers in the selection of child care providers among those families. Empirical differences between rural and nonrural populations are highlighted to elucidate the specific influence of context (rurality) over other factor differentials among families (e.g., income, child age). The second section examines supports related to child care for rural families, from federal public policies that help families pay for care to local programs that support quality. The chapter concludes with recommendations for policies and programs that enhance rural parents' child care choices and opportunities for rural children's growth and development.

Use of Child Care in Rural Areas

Census data on the child care utilization patterns of young children with employed mothers reveal both similarities and differences across rural and urban areas. Analyses of 2001 Survey of Income and Program Participation (SIPP) data exploring all child care arrangements used for children from birth to five years of age show relative care to be used most often, followed by organized care (e.g., center-based and school-based arrangements), parental care, and informal nonrelative care regardless of rural/urban dwelling (Smith 2006). Though this same pattern holds when considering the primary care arrangements of rural children, the greatest proportion of urban children birth to age five use an organized care arrangement for their primary arrangement (Smith 2006). The Early Childhood Longitudinal Study—Kindergarten Class of 1998–99 (ECLS-K) baseline data also reveal underrepresentation of rural children in center-based care arrangements, other than Head Start, the year prior to entering kindergarten (Grace et al. 2006). Representation in Head Start during this year, however, is higher among rural than nonrural children (Grace et al. 2006).

A higher proportion of rural children than urban children in kindergarten through eighth grade use parental care after school (Kleiner, Nolin, and Chapman 2004). Among school-aged children who are in nonparental care, fewer rural children are in a center/school-based afterschool arrangement. Additionally, rural children age six to eleven are more likely to stay home alone (U.S. Department of Health and Human Services 2005).

Factors That Influence Child Care Selection

Universal factors exist that might influence rural and urban parents' use of specific types of care; some of these factors are related to family income and thecost of care, and others are related to geography. For example, most families across all economic levels prefer relative or informal providers for their infants and toddlers. As children enter the preschool years (age three to five), parents generally switch to formal care arrangements (Huston et al 2002; Mulligan et al. 2005). This difference by child age is in part due to a shift in parents' priorities for their child's care. For example, parents of infants and young toddlers tend to be most concerned with safety and nurturance of their child; whereas parents of preschoolers tend to focus on learning and social opportunities that will prepare their child for school. Because of the limited availability, location of, and access to formal providers in rural areas (Brooks et al. 2002; DeMarco 2008; Fuller et al. 2002; Smith 2006), low-income families in general, and rural families in particular, are less likely to use formal child care providers than higher-income families or urban families (Colker and Dewees 2000; Ehrle, Adams, and Tout 2001; Walker and Reschke, 2004). Adding to these practical dimensions, many families with strong kith-and-kin ties feel that care provided by family, friends, and neighbors offers both a degree of trust and an expectation of service not found in formal care (Reschke and Walker 2006). A closer examination of the dimensions of cost, availability, and quality will further elucidate factors influencing rural families' childcare choices and needs for support.

COST

Among employed mothers with a child under age six, rural employed mothers pay less for child care than urban parents in terms of average monthly expenses (Smith and Gozjolko 2010). In relative terms, however, rural low-income families pay more for care than their urban counterparts. Using 2005 SIPP data, Smith and Gozjolko (2010) found rural families with an employed mother and child under age six to spend an average of 9 percent of their household income on child care, compared to 8 percent among their urban counterparts. This disparity is more pronounced among families in which the mother has less than a high school education and among families receiving a child care subsidy.

The cost of child care relative to family income is high regardless of location (Davis and Weber 2001; Smith 2006; Swenson 2007). In a national study by Schulman (2000), child care costs in rural areas were estimated to be three thousand to six thousand dollars annually for the care of preschool-aged children and over forty-five hundred dollars annually for the care of an infant. Some studies have shown the relative cost of child care to be even higher among some low-income rural families. For example, Walker and Reschke (2004) found low-income rural single-parent families with an infant or toddler spent an average of 37 percent of their income on regulated infant care.

AVAILABILITY

The availability of child care varies depending on the age of the child, the hours, and location of care. It is well documented that infant/toddler care and care for school-aged children is inadequate in many rural and nonrural communities (Rural Policy Research Institute 1999; Hofferth 1999). The lack of infant care may be due to higher regulatory standards for child-to-caregiver ratios or the greater demands and costs of providing such care. Other limiting factors for parents attempting to access high-quality, regulated care involve the hours and location of needed care. Many parents, especially parents in the service industry, work during nontraditional hours or have inconsistent hours. The availability of formal, regulated child care providers before 7 a.m. and after 6 p.m. is limited (Hofferth 1996). Parents also need a convenient location for child care (e.g., close to work or home or en route between work and home) to maintain their ability to arrive at work on time.

As Colker and Dewees (2000) note, due to the geographic spread of rural areas and the smaller number of formal providers in rural areas, finding a conveniently located provider can be problematic. Regulated child care centers are less likely to be found in low-income and rural communities (Rural Policy Research Institute 1999; Hofferth et al. 1991). In Gordon and Chase-Lansdale's (2001) analysis of 1990 Current Population Survey data, they found the potential unmet need for center care to be greater for poor nonmetropolitan (nonmetro) areas than other subgroups. This likely results from the lack of large capital investments in child care due to limited financial resources and geographic dispersion within low-income and rural communities (Cochi Ficano 2006; Gordon and Chase-Lansdale 2001). Public data about the number of regulated child care slots available to children in rural counties provide further proof of the dearth of providers. For example, a report on children in Arkansas and Oklahoma (Annie E. Casey Foundation 2004) reported that there were three children competing for every child care space available in both of those two states. In some rural areas, programs such as Head Start, a free preschool program for impoverished three- to four-year-olds, is the only formal care available (Colker and Dewees 2000).

Infant/toddler care and school-aged child care are particularly limited in rural areas as sparsely distributed populations diminish the demand for child care providers and therefore result in fewer regulated providers (Rural Policy Research Institute 1999; Beach 1997; Colker and Dewees 2000; Shoffner 1986; Smith 2006). Walker and Reschke (2004) note that in addition to long distances between regulated providers, issues of quality can contribute to the limited child care in rural areas. In an anecdote cited in this study, in one rural county in Maryland parents reported that one of the two infant care centers in the county closed due to charges of infant abuse, thus leaving only one regulated infant provider for a thirty-mile radius.

Transporting children to providers is another barrier to accessing available care in rural areas. Many rural areas do not have public transportation, and those that do often have inefficient routes that run on restricted schedules (Fisher and Weber 2002). Due to the wide geographic spread of rural areas, the lack of public transportation poses greater challenges to rural parents than urban parents in accessing child care.

QUALITY

Studies suggest that the quality of care in rural areas may be lower than in other areas due to the lower wages earned by rural child care providers and a less educated and trained workforce (A. Atkinson 1994; Beach 1997). Rural areas also face unique challenges to maintaining strict licensing standards compared to metropolitan (metro) areas (Colker and Dewees 2000). The Cost, Quality, and Child Outcomes Study Team (1995) determined that rural states have fewer state licensing employees and longer distances to travel, making it more difficult to enforce standards and to maintain specialized training for child care professionals.

Partly due to the high relative cost of care and the limited availability of regulated care, particularly during nontraditional hours, many low-income rural families turn to family, friends, and neighbors to provide child care. Though this choice may be an economic or practical necessity or a preference by the family, many informal providers are not required to receive training in child development and early education and are not regulated by states (Porter and Kearns 2006). Thus, the safety and quality of these arrangements are largely unknown. Additionally, family, friend, and neighbor care (i.e., informal) arrangements tend to be less reliable than formal care and more fraught with interpersonal issues and emotional costs that can leave working parents in a bind (Reschke et al. 2006).

In summary, low-income families in rural areas face significant constraints in finding, accessing, and paying for high-quality child care. Regulated environments are often limited in number and proximity, particularly for infants, toddlers, and school-aged children. Public transportation is nonexistent in many rural areas, and the cost for regulated programs is relatively high. As a result, many rural low-income families turn to the source of care most available, cost-effective, and possibly preferred though perhaps less safe, less effective in promoting children's early learning, and potentially demanding on personal relationships: other family members, friends, and neighbors.

Policies/Programs Designed to Support Rural Families' Use of Quality Child Care and Facilitate Parental Employment

Many federal and state programs are in place to facilitate parental employment via child care provision and to aid families in obtaining high-quality child care. These programs ease the financial burden of care to families, increase the quality of existing child care programs, and increase the availability of high quality programs. Each of these major public initiatives will be reviewed below, with specific application to the rural context. Following this, exemplary programs designed to supplement mainstream federal/state programs will be highlighted.

Alleviating the Cost of Child Care

CHILD CARE SUBSIDIES AND COST/CHOICE OF CARE

The Child Care and Development Fund (CCDF) provides child care subsidies to low-income families. It is a federally funded, state-administered program with two primary goals: to support parental employment and the availability of high-quality child care (Blau 2001). Because CCDF is a block grant provided to states, states have a great deal of flexibility in implementing this program.

State policies that affect parents' choice or ability to use CCDF child care subsidies include income eligibility and application procedures, subsidy waiting lists, family copays, and provider reimbursement rates. Given that states have latitude in policy administration, examining the practices of states that possess areas with significant rural populations can reveal areas that aid or that challenge their low-income residents. A review of the 2008–9 state plans for CCDF subsidies reveals that eleven of the twelve *least* generous states in terms of income eligibility[1] (i.e., those who cap the income eligibility for child care subsidies at or under 50 percent of the state median income) possess areas with significant rural populations, as do five of the six states that require in-person applications, as well as the District of Columbia,[2] a barrier to accessing subsidies for families without access to transportation or time off work to travel to the subsidy office. Families who are eligible and apply for a subsidy are not guaranteed benefits. As of 2008, seventeen states, many of which possess areas with significant rural populations, responded to an inability to meet the demand for subsidies by instituting a wait list or freezing subsidy enrollment.[3] High family copayments may negatively affect rural families' choice to access a child care subsidy. Parents may perceive subsidies as providing a small return for the high burden of applying and recertifying for the subsidy. Finally, reimbursement rates are not accepted by some providers whose price is higher than the CCDF reimbursement rate. In states where market rates are not determined statewide,[4] rural providers are often offered lower reimbursement rates due to the high rates of poverty in rural areas (Davis and Weber 2001). States also offer a lower reimbursement rate to informal (e.g., family, friends, and neighbors) than to formal providers, thereby affecting the overall financial aid available to rural families whose feasible child care options are limited to kith or kin, or who choose such care to keep income within the family system (Uttal 1999).

Studies on child care subsidies among rural and nonrural families reveal variation in how long subsidies are used and subsidy recipients' choice of providers. Davis, Grobe, and Weber (2007) found that families in extremely rural areas (i.e., with no population clusters over ten thousand) received child care subsidies for a shorter period of time than families in micropolitan (rural with population clusters greater than ten thousand but less than fifty thousand) and metro areas (areas with population clusters of over fifty thousand). As this effect remained even when family, community, and policy characteristics were taken into account, the authors hypothesized that the shorter duration of child care subsidy used in rural areas is due to stronger feelings about stigma in these communities (an idea supported by the research of Sherman 2007).

Davis and Weber (2001) found differences in subsidized compared with nonsubsidized parents' choice of care providers. Almost half of the providers with subsidized children in Davis and Weber's rural subsample were unregulated (i.e., informal providers). This pattern is inconsistent with the choices of metro/urban child care subsidy recipients, who tend to use formal providers (Forry 2007; Huston, Chang, and Gennetian 2002; Tekin 2005; Wolfe and Scrivner 2004). Given that informal care providers tend to be less educated in early childhood development and education, child care subsidies utilized in rural communities may be less successful in fostering child development than those in metro/urban communities.

TAX BENEFIT PROGRAMS:

CHILD AND DEPENDENT CARE TAX CREDIT

The federal Child and Dependent Care Tax Credit (CDCTC) is a progressive tax credit designed to reimburse families a proportion of their out-of-pocket child care costs. The CDCTC is a nonrefundable tax credit that covers a portion of one's employment-related child and dependent care expenses for the care of children under thirteen and dependents of any age. The CDCTC has some limitations that affect low-income families universally. First, the benefit received from the CDCTC can be small or nonexistent, depending upon whether and how much the family owes in federal income taxes, the amount the family paid for child care, and whether the child care provider (in the case of informal providers) is willing to provide the parent with his or her social security number and a receipt of payment (Forry and Anderson 2006). No research has been conducted on the utilization rate of the CDCTC among low-income rural families. Cochi Ficano (2006), however, used multivariate methods and found that expansion of formal child care is more sensitive to increases in the CDCTC in rural than urban areas.

In addition to the federal Child and Dependent Care Tax Credit, a number of states offer their own child/dependent care tax provision, which is applied to state income taxes. The provisions of state-level child and dependent care tax benefits differ by state with regard to their structure (i.e., credit vs. deduction), benefit level, refundability, and maximum benefits offered. States usually design their child/dependent care tax benefits as a percentage of the federal CDCTC. As of 2008, twenty-eight states had a state child/dependent care tax provision,[5] many of which possess areas with significant rural populations. Studies have not yet documented a direct effect of the existing federal or state child/dependent care tax provisions on maternal employment.

Few states in the United States have implemented an At-Home Infant Care (AHIC) program. AHIC is a state-implemented program that subsidizes low-income parents to care for their infants (up to age one or two, depending on the state). AHIC programs have been implemented in a few states that possess areas with significant rural populations (e.g., Minnesota, Montana; National Partnership for Women and Families 2005). Given the lack of infant care universally offered in the United States, particularly in rural areas, AHIC is a unique program that allows parents to earn a wage while caring for their own child at home. Legislation to develop a federal AHIC program has been introduced numerous times without success. By their nature, AHIC programs preclude women from working full-time outside the home. It is likely for this reason that legislation to create a federal AHIC program has failed.

Enhancing the Quality of Care

Enhancing the quality of child care has direct effects on both child development outcomes (Clarke-Stewart et al. 2002) and maternal employment (Chaudry 2004). Reschke and Walker's (2006) study of low-income rural mothers documented their hesitancy and periodic unwillingness to work if it meant their child was in an unsafe or low-quality child care arrangement. Programs and policies that set minimum standards for child care quality (i.e., state regulations) or that facilitate the use of high-quality care (i.e., child care subsidies and public pre-kindergarten) may thus enhance maternal employment directly.

State regulation of child care providers fosters higher-quality care by ensuring that health and safety measures are taken and some structural/caregiver characteristics associated with quality are met (i.e., child:staff ratios, caregiver education requirements). Standards for the regulation of child care providers are developed by each state and vary widely across the United States. In a recent publication by the National Association of Child Care Resource and Referral Agencies states that possess areas with significant rural populations comprised the bottom ten states in ratings of both child care center regulation and oversight (NACCRRA 2009).

In rural areas, child care regulation faces multiple challenges. First, the geographic distance between providers makes it difficult for regulators to conduct regular site visits or facilitate accessible training sessions for providers. Second, perhaps because there are fewer child care providers to regulate, rural areas tend to have fewer state licensing employees per capita (Cost, Quality, and Child Outcomes Study Team 1995). This shortage of staff further compounds the struggle of visiting and training providers that are not within close proximity of one another.

CHILD CARE SUBSIDIES AND QUALITY OF CARE

In addition to interceding with the cost of child care among eligible families, the CCDF program mandates that states set aside at least 4 percent of CCDF funds to improve both the availability and quality of child care. Activities financed through these set-aside funds include providing training and education to providers (including some distance learning programs), increasing reimbursement rates, and providing wage supplements, scholarships, and start-up and expansion grants (U.S. DHHS 2009). Set-aside funds aimed at increasing quality of care are used to financially support child care resource and referral agencies that train providers and assist with evaluation activities, efforts at monitoring compliance with licensing and regulatory requirements, and activities that support children's development (U.S. DHHS 2009). States also use CCDF set-aside funds to support the development of quality rating and improvement systems (QRIS). These state-wide systems use quality ratings to market information on child care providers' quality to parents and to set standards of quality for providers. As of 2009, sixteen states, some of which have a significant rural population, had a fully operational QRS, and a number of other states were in the process of developing/piloting systems (Tout et al. 2009).

PUBLICLY PROVIDED CARE AND EDUCATION PROGRAMS

Head Start

Head Start programs are funded through grants provided directly to community-level public agencies, private nonprofit and for-profit organizations, Indian tribes, and school systems (U.S. DHHS 2004). Head Start offers a range of services, including educational intervention; medical, dental, and mental health services; and parent involvement activities (U.S. DHHS 2004).

Head Start programs are available in rural counties and tribal territories across the United States. Though Head Start programs are not available in all rural communities, in many rural communities Head Start represents the only center-based early education and care provider for three- to five-year-olds (Colker and Dewees 2000). Head Start also has the National Migrant and Seasonal Head Start Quality Improvement Center, which provides culturally and linguistically appropriate training and technical assistance to Migrant and Seasonal Head Start programs. Despite the efforts of Head Start to be sensitive and proactive regarding rural issues, parents' commutes to center-based Head Start programs may tend to be long and inconvenient. Perhaps for this reason many rural parents do not use this service (Walker and Reschke 2004).

Universal Pre-kindergarten

A recent movement to better prepare children for school has been the development of universal pre-kindergarten programs (pre-K). Pre-K programs are implemented by states and offer families a half or full day of educational programming for four-year-old children, utilizing licensed teachers and a developmentally appropriate curriculum. States are in various stages of offering universal pre-K to their residents. As of 2008, twelve states, all of which possess areas with significant rural populations, do not have a public pre-kindergarten program.[6]

A study by the U.S. Department of Education (T. Smith et al. 2003) found fewer public elementary schools offered pre-K classes in rural areas (34 percent) compared to urban areas (45 percent). Additionally, pre-kindergarten teachers were less well educated in rural areas than in urban areas (percent with a bachelor's degree or higher was 83 percent and 91 percent, respectively). Finally, pre-kindergarten teachers were less likely to be on the elementary school teacher pay scale in rural areas than in urban areas (T. Smith et al. 2003).

As with all other programs reviewed thus far, rural families face unique struggles in accessing public pre-kindergarten programs due to a dearth of pre-kindergarten classrooms in rural areas, geographical spacing, and transportation issues. A map of pre-kindergarten availability by state shows that many states that possess areas with significant rural populations serve only a small percentage of four-year-old children.[7]

21st Century Learning Centers

The 21st Century Community Learning Centers (21CCLC) initiative through the U.S. Department of Education, originally authorized under Title X, Part I of the Elementary and Secondary Education Act (ESEA), provides funding for schools and community-based agencies to offer elementary and middle school children a safe environment in which they can continue learning after school hours (U.S. Department of Education 2010). Funds are allocated to high-poverty, low-performing schools. A recent report on the 2004–5 21CCLC grantees found 33 percent of grantees to be in rural areas, compared to 43 percent in urban areas and 24 percent in suburban areas (Naftzger et al. 2006).

Exemplary Programs and Recommendations

Though federal and state programs have made efforts to improve the availability, accessibility, and quality of child care, many of these programs are not responsive to the unique needs of rural families, or their existence is unknown to families. Either way, public supports in many rural areas go underutilized. Fortunately, state and local exemplary programs across the United States supplement federal efforts. In this section, a variety of exemplary programs that have been acknowledged in the literature for their success in improving the affordability, availability, and quality of child care in rural areas will be highlighted, and recommendations for future programs will be offered.

Exemplary Programs

AFFORDABILITY OF CARE

Increasing access to child care subsidies is one way rural communities have increased the affordability of child care. Three exemplary collaborations have accomplished this through financial support, building infrastructure, and addressing identified community needs. In Florida, the Child Care Executive Partnership[8] was developed to address the shortage of child care subsidies. Through this partnership a program was developed in which employers could make contributions to the child care subsidy program for their eligible employees. If a contribution was made by the employer, the employee, who was on a wait list for a child care subsidy, was automatically provided a subsidy. The state matched each dollar employers contributed. This effort produced $6 million in contributions from employers, which allowed three thousand families to receive a child care subsidy (Wright 2003).

The Coalition for Valley Families facilitated collaboration among private and public sector human service providers in the Rio Grande Valley of Texas.[9] This coalition developed task forces that engaged in community needs assessments and advocacy efforts leading to the development of a Workforce Development Board that has the authority to adjust child care subsidy reimbursement rates. In addition to taking efforts to make child care more affordable, the Coalition has engaged in training and technical assistance activities to support child care providers in obtaining grants (Wright 2003).

The North Carolina Smart Start Initiative provided funding and technical assistance to county-level public-private partnerships in conjunction with their community's child care needs.[10] These partnerships identify needs in the county and channel Smart Start funds to these needs. Across the state, 42 percent of Smart Start funding goes to child care subsidies. As of 2003, over fifty thousand children had been provided child care subsidies through the Smart Start Initiative. Smart Start efforts also support the professional development of child care providers through scholarships to training programs (Wright 2003).

AVAILABILITY OF CARE

Collaborative efforts to increase the availability of child care have found success by leveraging employer support, offering free or subsidized recruitment and training activities to child care providers and potential providers, and financing facility development and renovations for child care providers. In Huntsville, Arkansas, for example, the Butterball Turkey plant, in collaboration with a local Head Start and regional child care nonprofit agency, financed in large part the building of a child care facility. The facility is available to employees, but also serves as an additional child care site for the community (Wright 2003).

Building child care provider capacity through training and recruitment efforts has also been successful. In Arkansas, a program was developed to recruit child care providers in the town of St. Francis. Potential child care providers were enrolled in a licensing training, then took a six-week small business planning course. The effort provided four new child care providers (U.S.

GAO 2004). In Harlan County, Kentucky, a Child Care Resource and Referral agency partnered with Early Head Start to develop curricula on infant/toddler care. Providers trained in these curricula received certification, which allowed them to increase the number of infants/toddlers in their care and receive higher child care subsidy reimbursement rates (U.S. GAO 2004). Finally, at the state level, child care resource and referral networks offer training and technical assistance to local child care facilities and workers and aid parents in locating care for their children. A statewide, coordinated system of resource and referral agencies allows rural state programs to collaborate and share resources, ensure standardization of service and quality, and maximize available public dollars (Bailey and Warford 1995).

Finally, two initiatives increased the capacity of child care providers in rural areas by financing child care facility construction and renovation. Coastal Enterprises is an initiative in Maine that offers child care providers loans for developing and improving child care facilities throughout the state.[11] As of 2003, a total of $7.4 million was provided to ninety-seven child care providers in Maine as a result of the project (Wright 2003). The Community Investment Collaboration for Kids is a national initiative that partners with federal agencies to fiscally support the construction and renovation of child care facilities. By 2003, at least $3 million was provided to rural child care providers through this program (Wright 2003).

QUALITY OF CARE

Efforts at improving the quality of child care in rural areas are largely focused on training and credentialing providers. Training and preparation for credentialing are implemented by a variety of federal and national, state, and local organizations. The largest early education nonprofit in the United States, the National Association for the Education of Young Children (NAEYC),[12] offers technical assistance and small grants to local areas, including rural communities and tribal regions, to help centers complete steps in the accrediting process. At the state level, child care resource and referral networks offer training and technical assistance to local child care facilities and workers, and a university-based system of training and assistance to providers is offered through the Cooperative Extension Service (CES). The Cooperative Extension Service's use of computer technology has enabled its host universities to provide distance learning over the Internet and through satellite communication. Some state efforts, such as Cornell's Cooperative Extension, offer informational support programs for family, friend, and neighbor child caregivers (CES 2007).

Specific state and regional child care projects have also been developed to enhance the quality of child care in rural areas specifically. In Lee County, Alabama, the Employers' Child Care Alliance has been developed with four goals, one of which is to enhance the quality of child care in the county. Efforts of this project include matching child care centers with employers who provide scholarships to support the training of center staff and assisting centers in obtaining accreditation through training and support (Wright 2007). The Early Childhood Professional Development Project (New York) is a partnership designed to enhance early care and education in rural areas. This partnership has a special focus on child care provider training. Its efforts include recruiting mentors to work with less educated and less experienced providers, providing scholarships and increasing salaries as supports to stay in the field and achieve higher levels of professionalism, and building public awareness for the need to educate and financially support child care workers. An initiative through the Families and Work Institute called Sparking Connections has provided funds to support regional efforts to enhance the quality of informal child care by offering education and training, social support, and supplies and materials in rural areas (Wright 2007).

Recommendations for Future Policies and Programs

The aforementioned local, state, and national programs designed to increase the affordability, accessibility, and quality of child care in rural areas are promising innovations. They remind us of what is possible and point the way toward improvements for rural families. However, several critical dimensions of child care must be addressed. First, federal policies to help address the high cost of child care for low-income families must continue to be financially supported and scrutinized. State CCDF policy levers (e.g., parental copayments, subsidy waiting lists, and provider reimbursement rates) compete for the same funds. Thus, research is needed on the most effective decisions for each policy lever, and block grants allocated to states should reflect the cost of effectively administering this program to families.

Next, all initiatives related to child care must be examined through a family-centered lens. Parents' selection of care reflects consideration of the practical realities of cost, convenience, and availability, and parents' choice in care for the persons most trustworthy and most meaningful to the child must be respected. Therefore, if informal arrangements are preferred or are the most accessible form of care for rural families, efforts to improve quality must address the interests of informal family, friend, and neighbor providers. Training programs for informal providers will likely not take the shape of traditional training for child care professionals. Rather, efforts to increase provider understanding of learning activities, responsive care, and health and safety will need to be sensitive to the interests, locations, and schedules of the family members, friends, and neighbors providing care (Porter and Kearns 2006).

Another consideration regarding the use of informal care should be addressed through subsidy programs. As mentioned, the reimbursement rate for informal providers is lower than that of formal providers in many states. Closing the gap between reimbursement rates would make subsidies more attractive to families who prefer or have no choice but to use informal providers. To improve the quality of informal care, reimbursement rates for informal providers could be graduated based on quality indicators, such as the amount of training received. This tiered reimbursement system could reflect those used with formal providers in some states (see U.S. DHHS 2009). Subsidy programs could also be responsive to the needs of families living in rural areas by extending the period between recertification and employing methods that do not mandate in-person visits.

One recommendation to help families afford child care is to expand the Child and Dependent Care Tax Credit. Expansion of this credit is important for rural families because the CDCTC makes no restrictions on the type of care used and requires no in-person application or recertification visits. The federal CDCTC is currently nonrefundable, meaning it has no benefit for low-income families who do not owe federal taxes (Forry and Anderson 2006). Making this tax credit refundable would correct for this limitation and result in a more progressive tax credit. Additionally, adjusting the credit to automatically adjust for inflation would maintain the value of this credit over time.

Finally, efforts to increase the availability of formal care, including Head Start and pre-K programs, can follow the lead of exemplary programs highlighted above. Providers can be supported to gain certifications and accreditations that enable them to care for infants and toddlers, trained to provide developmentally appropriate care, paid a fair wage, and given financial support to hire additional staff. Additionally, through training and incentive programs, the myriad factors that lead to burnout and turnover can start to be addressed in an attempt to keep quality providers.

Conclusions

Due to the small, geographically dispersed populations and limited resources of rural areas, rural parents face unique barriers that hinder them from selecting high-quality child care at a reasonable price. This dynamic is of particular concern as rural mothers with young children are employed in increasing numbers (Smith 2006), and multiple indicators suggest the quality of rural child care to be lower than that in urban areas (Beach 1997; Colker and Dewees 2000; Cost, Quality, and Child Outcomes Study Team 1995; Galinsky et al. 1994). Solutions to overcome these barriers require innovative policy changes and program development. In creating such policies and programs, policy makers and administrators should focus on the needs, desires, and strengths of the rural community.

Notes

1. These eleven states are Alabama, Florida, Idaho, Indiana, Iowa, Michigan, Minnesota, Missouri, Nebraska, New Hampshire, and Rhode Island (U.S. DHHS 2009).

2. These six states are Colorado, Iowa, Nebraska, New Mexico, Utah, and West Virginia (U.S. DHHS 2009). As a note, the majority of states that offer in-person applications also offer application options via another method (e.g., mail/phone). Also, five significantly rural states offer Internet applications (Kansas, South Dakota, Vermont, Washington, and Texas; U.S. DHHS 2009).

3. These states were Alabama, Arkansas, California, Florida, Georgia, Indiana, Maine, Massachusetts, Minnesota, New Jersey, New York, North Carolina, Pennsylvania, Texas, and Virginia (Schulman and Blank 2008).

4. According to 2008–9 CCDF State Plans, market rates were determined statewide in the District of Columbia, Hawaii, Iowa, Louisiana, Mississippi, New Hampshire, New Jersey, North Dakota, Rhode Island, Vermont, West Virginia, and Wyoming (U.S. DHHS 2009).

5. These states are Arkansas, California, Colorado, Delaware, the District of Columbia, Georgia, Hawaii, Idaho, Iowa, Kansas, Kentucky, Louisiana, Maine, Maryland, Massachusetts, Minnesota, Montana, Nebraska, New Mexico, New York, North Carolina, Ohio, Oklahoma, Oregon, Rhode Island, South Carolina, Vermont, and Virginia (Campbell et al. 2006; Campbell, Matsui, and Brens 2009).

6. These twelve states are Alaska, Hawaii, Idaho, Indiana, Mississippi, Montana, New Hampshire, North Dakota, Rhode Island, South Dakota, Utah, and Wyoming (Barnett et al. 2008)

7. See http://www.preknow.org/resource/mapping/accessmap.cfm.

8. http://www.ccep.bz/.

9. http://www.tvcof.org/programs.cfm?section=Coalition%20for%20Valley%20Families.

10. http://www.smartstart-nc.org/.

11. http://www.ceimaine.org/.

12. http://www.naeyc.org/.

HEALTH INSURANCE IN RURAL AMERICA

DEBORAH ROEMPKE GRAEFE

Census Bureau estimates indicate that 7.5 million—or almost one in six—rural Americans were without health insurance coverage in 2006 (DeNavas-Walt, Proctor, and Smith 2007). And, just as in metro places, the proportion without health insurance in rural places has been on the rise since before the turn of the century—a problem expected to have worsened with the recent economic recession. Overall, rural residents were as likely to be without coverage as metro residents (approximately 16 percent of both groups were uninsured), but the demographic, social, and economic diversity of rural places makes health coverage in some rural locations much less likely than in others.

Rural residents living in counties not adjacent to an urban county are significantly less likely to have health coverage and more likely to remain not insured for longer periods (Ziller et al. 2003). Furthermore, they are 1.5 times more likely to be covered by Medicaid, and coverage gaps are more likely with Medicaid than with private insurance because of limited eligibility periods (M. Smith et al. 1996). They also are less likely to work for employers who offer health benefits. Ziller and colleagues (2003) found that more than two-thirds of unemployed workers in rural counties were employed in small businesses, often with fewer than twenty employees. Working adults in rural counties are also more likely to earn low wages, making the purchase of health insurance coverage difficult even if possible. When adults are uninsured, most experience relatively long gaps without coverage (Kaiser Commission 2007).

This chapter sets the stage for understanding patterns of health coverage among rural populations, with a brief review of national trends in coverage. Patterns of health coverage among rural populations are then examined against counterpart populations in urbanized settings. Three nationally representative cohorts from the Survey of Income and Program Participation provide comparisons for minorities, single-parent families, and poor families—especially vulnerable groups—in metropolitan (metro) and nonmetropolitan (nonmetro) areas.[1] The importance of economic restructuring for health coverage patterns is then examined, with comparisons for rural areas on the basis of declines in manufacturing and growth in service-sector employment, as well as chronic poverty.

The Rise and Fall of Health Coverage Rates

Health insurance coverage is a relatively recent benefit, first widely offered by employers in the 1940s and 1950s. A time of economic and industrial growth, labor union strength, and changes in the federal income tax code made health coverage as an employee benefit a means of increasing compensation to attract employees (Thomasson 2000). As more and more employers offered health insurance and medical technologies advanced, its public health value increased. The federal government eventually began programs to provide health coverage for economically disadvantaged families, creating Medicaid and Medicare in 1964. Within the next fifty years, dramatic health care cost increases and the related disadvantage resulting from a lack of coverage would create a demand for overhaul of the health care system that is front and center of health and public policy debates today.

A steady rise in the number and percentage of Americans without health coverage has been observed over the past twenty years, interrupted only during times of a robust national economy, low unemployment rates, and relatively slow growth in health premiums (Kaiser Commission 2007). Estimates from the Current Population Survey for 1987 through 2005 show an increasing trend in the percentage of the population who lacked health insurance coverage that peaked in 1998, then declined slightly until rising again to just under 1998 levels at 16 percent in 2005 (DeNavas-Walt, Proctor, and Smith 2007). A peak number of 46.6 million persons were without health insurance coverage in 2005. The most recent estimates of persons without coverage are based upon data collected prior to the December 2007 start of the recession, which resulted in dramatic increases in unemployment and further decreased the number with employer-sponsored health insurance.

The stalled economy in 2001, for example, together with an increasing cost of premiums, brought a decline in employer-sponsored coverage and a climb in publicly provided health insurance, although this increase was not sufficient to completely offset the losses in private-sector coverage. Employer-provided coverage further declined after 2004, despite economic improvements bringing increased family incomes. Mainly, this decline occurred because fewer workers were offered health benefits, but most recently even some with higher incomes have gone without health insurance coverage. While most people obtain coverage through their employer, private health insurance coverage has declined recently, from nearly two-thirds in 2000 to under 60 percent in 2007. In 2006, 80 percent of the uninsured were in families with employed heads, and most of these families were headed by at least one full-time worker (Kaiser Commission 2007). When uninsured employees do not have employer-sponsored coverage, most often it is because their employers do not offer the benefit.

An important reason for lower rates of private coverage in rural areas, where many businesses have fewer than one hundred employees, is that small businesses are less likely than larger ones to offer the health coverage benefits. Also particularly salient in rural places is the fact that the employee share of insurance premiums is often not affordable, especially for low-income workers. Nevertheless, many of these employees will not have incomes low enough to qualify for publicly sponsored coverage. Those living in households earning less than twenty-five thousand dollars annually, working-age individuals, the foreign-born, Hispanics and African Americans, and persons living in the South or, to a lesser extent, the West were more likely to be without health coverage in 2006. Provisions in the new health care reform legislation requiring individuals to have health coverage, and strategies to make coverage affordable, including subsidies to persons with low incomes and Medicaid expansions, will be important for rural residents.

Some states have expanded Medicaid eligibility to include low-income parents, but as a factor reducing the numbers of uninsured, growth in public health insurance (including Medicaid and the Children's Health Insurance Program, CHIP) applies primarily to children's coverage. Under federal law, states must provide coverage for poor children (under age nineteen), and CHIP complements Medicaid by covering children who do not qualify for Medicaid. Together these programs provide coverage for one in four American children and more than half of all rural poor children (Ziller et al. 2003). Public-sector programs are a critical source of coverage in rural areas, where over a third (nearly 4 million) of all children rely on Medicaid or CHIP for their access to health care (O'Hare 2007). This compares with around 20 percent of urban children who rely on these public programs—a difference that results mostly because a larger share of rural children are found in low-income families. Still, almost one in five low-income rural children have no health care coverage, and 11 percent of children living in rural areas—1.3 million children—remained uncovered in 2005. Almost 16 percent of uninsured American children live in a rural community.

Health Coverage Variations by Rural or Urban Location

A general metro/nonmetro comparison of health insurance coverage finds little or no difference in the likelihood of having coverage for urban and rural residents. And as in urban places, the types of jobs available, a lack of unionization, and a preponderance of small employers contribute to poorer insurance coverage among rural workers (Collins et al. 2003). Yet these are issues more likely to plague rural than urban areas, and low-income workers, who are more likely to be found in rural places, are less likely to be offered health insurance and to take it if it is offered because they cannot afford the high premiums (Guendelman and Pearl 2001; Monheit and Vistnes 2000). Furthermore, race and residence come together to influence the likelihood of insurance coverage (Duncan, Seccombe, and Amey 1995). Thus, a simple metro/nonmetro comparison masks important differences in accessibility and affordability of health care coverage.

Unfortunately, investigations of rural/urban differences in health coverage have been hampered by the lack of sufficient data. Most national surveys do not provide sufficient numbers of respondents who live in rural places to provide reliable estimates, particularly for the most vulnerable population groups. In some cases, this problem has been overcome by aggregating more than one panel of a survey that repeats over time but uses a new sample each time (e.g., Glover et al. 2004). This solution makes clever use of the available data but does not permit within-person multiyear comparisons over a relatively short time frame. Large data sets that provide samples adequate for analysis of rural respondents are often not longitudinal or cover short time periods and do not include geographic information for linking files with area economic characteristics. Studies able to look beyond a simple metro/nonmetro difference have utilized restricted, as opposed to public-use, files to determine the degree of rurality of respondent county of residence. Perhaps the most informative of these, by the Kaiser Family Foundation, provides evidence of rural/urban differences by comparing rural places surrounded by other rural counties. That study used restricted data from the Medical Expenditure Panel Survey (MEPS) for 1996–99. "Restricted" data are the survey-sponsoring agency's original data files containing geographic identifiers. Researcher use of such data is strictly limited, making the detailed study of rural issues a challenge (Kaiser Commission 2007).

Data for the Current Comparisons

The Survey of Income and Program Participation (SIPP) provides longitudinal data with monthly indicators of individual and family social and economic well-being—including employment and schooling, income and earnings, benefits (e.g., health insurance coverage), and public program participation (e.g., Medicaid and Medicare)—which are useful for examining the health coverage experiences of rural and urban populations over time. Respondents are interviewed every four months regarding their economic, social, and demographic characteristics, including health insurance coverage, in each of the current and past three months. A household-level survey, SIPP information is collected for each person in the household, each of whom is followed for up to four years once he or she enters the sample household. Demographic measures of particular interest that are provided by SIPP are race and ethnicity, family structure, and family poverty level.

Three aspects of health coverage are examined here: (1) the percentage of the population who were ever without coverage during a sixteen-month observation period, (2) the percentage who were without coverage for a total of one to four, five to eight, or more than eight months over the observation period, and (3) the percentage who were covered only by private health insurance, only by Medicaid, only by Medicare, by a combination of Medicaid and Medicare, and by a combination of private and public (either Medicaid or Medicare) health insurance, and who were without coverage for the entire sixteen months. All ages are analyzed together to get an overall picture of health coverage in rural America. Since rural areas have slightly older population structures than urban areas, Medicare should be somewhat more prevalent there.

Several panels of SIPP have been fielded over the years, beginning in the 1980s, and each panel focuses on a different nationally representative sample of around forty thousand households. When weighted, respondents for each panel are representative of the U.S. noninstitutionalized population during the study period. Panels begun in 1996, 2001, and 2004 are used here to demonstrate how health insurance coverage differs for rural populations over sixteen-month periods from 1998 to 1999, 2001 to 2002, and 2004 to 2005.[2] The observation period length was dictated by the availability of only the first five waves of 2004 SIPP Panel data at the time this study was conducted. These waves provide sixteen monthly observations. Thus, all available monthly observations were utilized from the 2004 Panel. For equivalent comparisons across time, approximately equal separations between study periods were maintained by beginning the sixteen-month observation in 1998 for the 1996 Panel (a four-year panel) and in 2001 for the 2001 Panel (a three-year panel). Using longitudinal data permits examination of change over time in coverage status and change in the types of health coverage used. Using data for three different time periods shows trends in these outcomes across different economic periods.

Importantly, SIPP data provide place-of-residence indicators giving (1) the metro versus nonmetro status of the respondent's residential location and (2) the state of residence. An exception is that state subsample sizes in SIPP for Wyoming, North and South Dakota, Vermont, and Maine are too small for individual state-level estimates. As a result, survey participants from Wyoming and North and South Dakota and from Maine and Vermont are aggregated as two state-group categories.[3] The data do not provide information about the characteristics of respondents' geographic locations, but these two geographic indicators for state of residence and metro or nonmetro residence can be used to link year- and state-specific rural/urban sector-specific job growth measures to individual SIPP records (except for respondents in the five aggregated states) to characterize the economic growth in the state's metro and nonmetro areas.

Economic restructuring eliminates better paying jobs with better benefit packages and may result in declines in private health coverage and increases in publicly sponsored coverage. The classic case of economic restructuring involves a decline in manufacturing (although recently in mining, forestry, etc., as well) and an increase in service-sector employment. Thus, for instance, average nonmetro service-sector job growth for a particular state and year is linked with the records of SIPP respondents living in a nonmetro area of that state in that year. The records of respondents living in a metro area of that state are linked with the state's average service-sector job growth in metro areas in that year.

Job growth statistics are from the Regional Economic Information System (REIS) county-level employment files. These contextual data were aggregated up, based on 2003 Beale codes for the rural-to-urban continuum (available from http://www.ers.usda.gov/Data/RuralUrbanContinuumCodes), to create state metro- and nonmetro-area job growth measures.[4] Of particular interest here are places with positive growth in service-sector employment and places with negative growth, or decline, in manufacturing-sector jobs, as these represent basic indicators of economic restructuring.

Patterns in the Lack of Health Coverage

Figure 14.1 graphs the percentage of metro and nonmetro residents who ever went without health insurance coverage over each of the three sixteen-month periods. These estimates are considerably higher than cross-sectional estimates based on decennial census data, but are consistent with estimates for twelve-month periods using Current Population Surveys and MEPS. In the earliest economically robust period of the late 1990s, there was no difference between rural and urban places in the likelihood of having a spell without health coverage. After 2000, however, nonmetro residents were significantly more likely to experience a gap in coverage. Although the percentage going without health coverage dropped in the 2004–5 period compared with the 2001–2 period, in

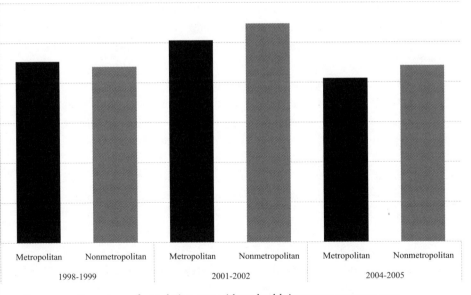

FIG. 14.1   Percentage of population ever without health insurance coverage over sixteen-month observation, by period and metropolitan/nonmetropolitan residence (SOURCE: 1998–99, 2001, 2004–5 Survey of Income and Program Participation [SIPP])

both periods rural residents were 8 percent more likely to be without coverage than urban and suburban residents. At minimum, one in five rural residents experienced a gap in coverage; in the 2001–2 period, almost one in three had at least a month's gap in coverage.

The first two rows of numbers in table 14.1 are for the total metro and nonmetro populations. Reading across each row in the table, we see the percentages of the population (indicated by the stub on the left) who were without coverage for a total of four or fewer months, for five to eight months, for nine to sixteen months, or for any time during the 1998 through 1999 observation period, then corresponding figures for the 2001–2 period and, in the last four columns, for the 2004–5 observation period. Based on these percentages, the overall period increase between the 1990s and 2001–2 resulted from a growth in the percentage of individuals experiencing small amounts of time without coverage. However, most who experienced any gap in coverage were without health insurance for a total of nine months or more, regardless of rural residence. In the later two periods, the rural/urban differences observed in the proportion ever without coverage were made up of individuals who were in this group. This means that the increase in the percentage without coverage for more than eight months resulted in a greater likelihood of lost coverage after 2000.

The 2001–2 period shows higher percentages without coverage for all subgroups as well. Furthermore, each of the subgroups examined was more likely to be without coverage than the general population. More importantly, minorities and persons from poor families were more likely to be without coverage in post-2000 nonmetro than in metro America. The distributions of months without coverage for poor families became quite similar in the 2004–5 period, and the share experiencing time without health insurance was notably high— two in five persons in poor families experienced a gap in coverage. It is likely that job losses in the recent recessionary period have increased both gaps and the length of gaps in health insurance coverage even more.

Probst and colleagues (2004) argue that minorities living in rural places experience a doubly disadvantaged status when it comes to health disparities— disadvantage due to minority status as well as due to rural residence. However, as they note, most studies fail to identify the extent to which rural residence is linked with disparate health insurance and health care experiences. Using National Health Interview Survey data for 1999–2000, they found that rural racial/ethnic minorities under age sixty-five were less likely to have health coverage than others and were less likely to have supplemental insurance if Medicare-eligible. When covered, however, they were more likely than nonminority rural residents to have publicly provided insurance. Thus, understanding health coverage in rural areas also requires a look at the types of coverage rural people have.

Patterns in the Type of Health Coverage

Whereas figure 14.1 shows the percentages of rural and urban populations who ever experienced a gap in health coverage during the sixteen-month observation period, figure 14.2 graphs the shares of the total rural and urban populations who never had coverage and who always had some type of coverage, by coverage types, throughout the sixteen months. Categories of coverage here include private health insurance coverage, Medicaid, Medicare, both Medicaid and Medicare, both private and a type of public coverage, or no coverage. The "no coverage" category is different from having experienced any gap in coverage (discussed above); individuals with "no coverage" were without coverage for the full sixteen months. Although, as discussed above, gaps in coverage were most likely during the 2001–2 period for all groups, going without coverage for the entire sixteen months was least likely for metro residents during this period. For nonmetro residents, however, there was no decline from the earlier period. Furthermore, over the three time periods the percentage of nonmetro residents with no coverage increased more than for metro residents. In the most recent period, rural residents were 24 percent more likely to have had no coverage compared with urban residents.

The nonmetro population was less likely to have had only private health coverage, although, consistent with a declining trend in employer-sponsored coverage in recent years, both rural and urban residents saw a decline in private coverage over the three periods. Public coverage is clearly important, and increasingly so, for coverage access in rural areas. In the 1998–99 period in both metro and nonmetro areas, 7 percent of the population was covered only by Medicaid. For nonmetro residents, this percentage climbed to 11 by 2005–6. Medicare coverage was quite similar by rural/urban status, but combining Medicaid and Medicare—that is, having Medicaid some of the time and Medicare some of the time—was twice as likely in rural areas. This finding is not surprising since rural areas tend to have larger proportions of older American residents than urban areas (DeNavas-Walt, Proctor, and Smith 2007). Notable, however, is that in rural areas the elderly were more likely to have relied upon Medicaid at some time during the sixteen-month period. This finding is indicated by the combined Medicaid and Medicare category.

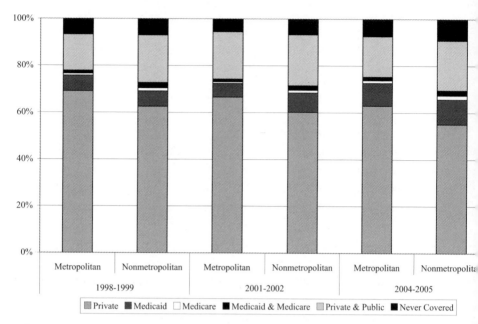

FIG. 14.2   Distribution of types of health insurance coverage: percentage of the population with each coverage type, by period and metropolitan/nonmetropolitan residence (SOURCE: 1998–99, 2001, 2004–5 Survey of Income and Program Participation [SIPP])

More frequent than relying on public coverage alone, however, was a combination of private and public coverage. Adding together the percentages ever using public coverage, we see that reliance on public aid for health insurance has grown, especially in rural areas. In 1998–99, nearly a third (30 percent) of the population used public coverage at some point during the period. In 2004–5, the figure was more than a third (36 percent). While children of poor parents are more likely to be covered by public programs than their parents, this increase (together with the increase in the percentage without coverage) nevertheless points to economic changes in rural places as part of the story about health coverage in rural America.

Health Coverage in Economically Distressed Rural America

The role of the economic health of the geographic area where individuals live is important. Few population-based investigations of rural health insurance coverage can consider the part played by community economic characteristics, as the data for such studies are relatively rare. An exception is a study conducted for 1991 and 1994 to determine why health insurance coverage varies across the nation and across counties in Wisconsin, a state with a unique household survey that collects health coverage information for a sample that represents county residents (Marsteller et al. 1998). This study showed that county-level variations in coverage were explained primarily by county unemployment rates. It also found that the effect of unemployment was greater when the economy was strong, in 1994, than during the 1991 recessionary year. Also in 1994, higher hospital prices and having fewer physicians—and thus less competition and higher physician prices—were linked with reduced rates of coverage. Both factors—employment and prices due to lower supplies of health care resources—are endemic to impoverished rural places.

Figure 14.3, which is based on SIPP data for our sixteen-month observation periods beginning in 1998, 2001, and 2004, mirrors the finding that the effect of area economic health varies according to national economic cycles. This figure shows the percentages of the population without health coverage in nonmetro areas where manufacturing jobs declined and where service jobs

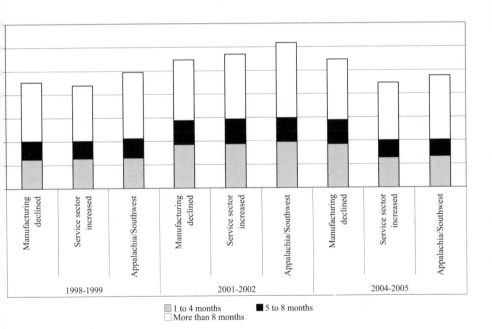

FIG. 14.3   Percentages of population in nonmetropolitan areas with decline in manufacturing or growth in service jobs and in Appalachian/southwestern states who lacked health insurance coverage for one to four, five to eight, and more than eight months, by period (SOURCE: 1998–99, 2001, 2004–5 Survey of Income and Program Participation [SIPP])

increased, as well as where poverty has been a chronic issue and rural minorities are concentrated—Appalachia and southern states along the Gulf of Mexico. These rural areas experienced the same rise in the percentage of uninsured, as is observed in figure 14.1, during the 2001–2 economic downturn period. But in rural areas with growth in service-sector employment and in the chronically depressed nonmetro areas of Appalachia and the South, the increase in time without health coverage was larger, reaching 30 percent in the latter area.

The effect of decline in manufacturing-sector jobs might appear less important than chronic poverty or growth in the service sector because in rural places that experienced such restructuring, the percentage without health coverage is the same as for rural areas overall—about 22 percent—in all three periods. These figures demonstrate marginal differences, but a multivariate regression model can show the importance of a personal or residential characteristic relative to other characteristics in the model. Table 14.2 presents results from logistic regression models estimating (1) the rural/urban difference in the likelihood of having a gap in coverage versus having coverage for the entire observation period, net the effects of personal and area economic restructuring characteristics; and (2) the effects of personal and area restructuring characteristics on the likelihood of having a gap in coverage, net the effects of other personal and area economic restructuring characteristics, for rural and for urban residents. All characteristics are coded as "yes/no" to share the same metric, and the table reports odds ratios for ease in comparing the effects.[5] Model 1 controls for an individual's family poverty and minority status and the area's decline in manufacturing jobs and growth in service jobs. During 1998–99, living in a nonmetro area multiplies the odds of having a coverage gap by 1.1, effectively increasing the risk of lacking coverage 10 percent compared with metro residents. After 2000, the risk is 30 percent higher for rural residents. The disadvantage faced by rural residents has increased considerably since 2000.

The model 2 specification indicates that economic restructuring had little to no effect on the likelihood of a gap without coverage before 2000. Indeed, during this period, an increase in service-sector jobs decreased the odds of a gap in coverage 10 percent for rural residents. This analysis does not differentiate the types of service jobs, some of which involve high communication and technical skills and are likely to come with employee benefits. Possibly, the service jobs that became more plentiful at this time—a period of economic strength and growth nationally—were jobs offering benefits.

After 2000, economic restructuring became a more important force behind gaps in coverage. In the 2001–2 period—a time of economic downturn for the nation as a whole—a decline in manufacturing increased the odds of a coverage gap 40 percent in rural areas. This disadvantage is greater than that observed for urban areas at this time. Also after 2000, service-sector increases were associated with 20 percent greater odds of experiencing a gap in coverage. These findings support the notion that economic restructuring has made it more difficult for rural residents to maintain health coverage.

Still, the most important factors influencing a coverage gap are minority status and family poverty. The model 2 specifications in table 14.2 show that, controlling for poverty and economic restructuring, rural minorities have been more than twice as likely as non-Hispanic whites to experience a coverage gap. During the economic downturn period, they were three times more likely to be without coverage. The most important factor influencing coverage gaps, however, is family poverty, and this factor is more important for rural than for urban residents. In the most recent period, the odds of a coverage gap were almost seven times greater for someone from a family in poverty than for near-poor and non-poor rural family members.

Patterns in the percentages having different types of coverage or no coverage for nonmetro areas with manufacturing-sector declines, shown in figure 14.4, are also similar to patterns for nonmetro areas generally, as is shown in figure 14.2. In each of the three types of nonmetro areas shown in figure 14.4, there is a decline in the percentage of the population that was covered only through private health insurance programs and growth in the percentage without coverage for the entire sixteen months. Where manufacturing declined, the percentage of the population that was covered by a public program at some point during the sixteen months increased between 1998–99 and 2001–2. While private coverage continued its drop in the 2004–5 period, public coverage did not increase further, and the percentage of the population that was uninsured for the entire period increased. In rural places with service-sector growth or chronic poverty, publicly sponsored coverage increased slightly more over time, compensating somewhat for the decline in private coverage. Nevertheless, this figure indicates that the trade-off between public and private coverage has not kept up with the increasing numbers of uninsured in rural America.

Poverty is higher in rural compared with urban and suburban areas generally—15 percent versus 12 percent were below poverty, respectively, in 2006. And minority individuals are more likely to be impoverished than non-Hispanic white Americans—24 percent of African Americans and 21 percent of Hispanics, compared with 8 percent of non-Hispanic white Americans in 2006 (DeNavas-Walt, Proctor, and Smith 2007). Approximately three-quarters of rural African Americans live in Mississippi, Georgia, North and South Carolina, Alabama, Louisiana, and Texas, and about a fourth of rural Hispanics live in Texas (Probst

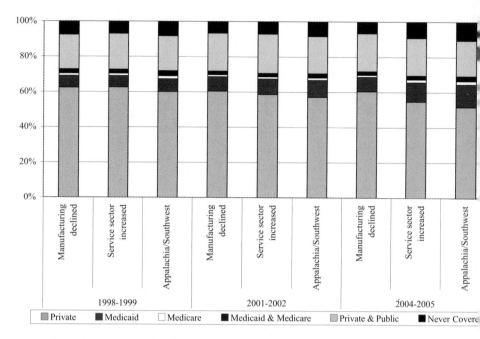

FIG. 14.4   Percentages of population in nonmetropolitan areas with decline in manufacturing or growth in service jobs and in Appalachian/southwestern states with each coverage type, by period (SOURCE: 1998–99, 2001, 2004–5 Survey of Income and Program Participation [SIPP])

et al. 2004), the state distinguished as having the most uninsured (DeNavas-Walt, Proctor, and Smith 2007).

Glover and colleagues (2004) found that rural minority health coverage disparities are tied to regional differences in minority population concentrations in the South and West, which result in disparate economic opportunities for occupational attainment and income. Living in areas surrounded by places with greater African American concentration has been found to increase occupational inequality for African American women and wage inequality for men and women (Beggs, Villemez, and Arnold 1997). This situation, combined with an occupational structure with high proportions of service occupations, makes places like the "black belt" of southern states (Falk, Talley, and Rankin 1993) areas where insurance coverage is less likely, particularly for minorities.

Working-age minorities in rural areas are less likely to have health insurance compared with rural working-age whites; if they are insured, they are more likely to be covered by public programs (Glover et al. 2004). These differences and U.S. regional variations in coverage can be explained by variations in resources including education, income level, employment status, and whether employers offer insurance coverage. Nevertheless, in a recent call for public health and other professionals to address the worldwide connection between poor health and poverty, rural Mississippi was targeted as the place to start (Jack 2007).

Job losses in Mississippi in recent years have led not only to decreases in income, but to losses in health insurance coverage (Roberts 2006). The American Federation of Workers and Congress of Industrial Organizations (2004) reports, for example, that among industries where jobs are declining in Mississippi, more than two-thirds (70 percent) of employed workers have employer-sponsored health insurance; among industries experiencing job growth, just under three-fifths (59 percent) of employed workers have employer-provided coverage. For such reasons, we observe the largest percentage of the uninsured in rural areas of Appalachian and southern Gulf-bordering states.

Policy Solutions and Implications

Arguments favoring health insurance coverage for all are powerful. A healthy population is crucial to sustaining community productivity and maintaining strong families—indeed, for creating a bright future (U.S. DHHS 2000). Many argue that access to good health should be a basic right of all Americans—like clean water to drink and air to breath. Yet a recent survey of Pennsylvania's rural population reveals a lack of affordable health care as the most important unmet health care issue faced by farm workers and rural residents today (Hessert 2008).

Having coverage or not affects decisions about seeking care when experiencing illness (Glied and Little 2003), the level of care received if sought (Baker et al. 2001), as well as health outcomes (Seccombe and Amey 1995). Estimates of the importance of various contributors to premature mortality put inadequate health care at the root of 10 percent of early deaths (Lee and Paxman 1997; McGinnis, Williams-Russo, and Knickman 2002). A more influential factor underlying premature death—behavioral patterns and lifestyle—may also be influenced by attention to preventative health care. Several solutions to increasing the percentage of individuals who maintain health coverage have been discussed among policy makers for some time and continue to be at the forefront of political debates today, but the best solutions for rural residents will be mindful of factors underlying the lack of coverage there.

With expansion of Medicaid and CHIP coverage to cover low-income individuals without children as well as parents, as many as two-thirds of the uninsured population could have health insurance (Ziller et al. 2003). This solution addresses the role of family poverty as well as job loss and inaccessibility to employer-sponsored coverage, but would require increased federal and state funding of these programs. Clearly, that is likely to depend on strong state economies and a federal commitment to health coverage as a basic right. The new health reform law expands Medicaid eligibility to those with incomes 133 percent of poverty and subsidizes coverage for those with incomes between 133 and 400 percent of poverty. Whereas this strategy promises greater access to coverage for individuals living in rural areas, it is important to remember that coverage gaps are more likely for individuals with Medicaid, and government budgetary constraints could critically impair coverage retention in rural areas.

While health care coverage and access to high-quality health care has been debated at the federal level for some time and is at the forefront of the Obama presidential administration agenda, some states have recognized that health care for the uninsured cannot wait. Massachusetts led state action toward universal coverage, providing the nation with its first test of strategies that require all citizens to purchase health insurance, just as they are required to purchase automobile insurance to drive their cars. The plan has been tremendously successful in enrolling the financially disadvantaged, whose premiums are government subsidized, but expected costs to taxpayers in coming years have the legislated insurance's proponents and opponents alike on edge regarding its affordability. Bringing down the costs of care will be an important part of such a plan's success.

Marsteller and colleagues (1998) point out that states can influence coverage rates through health insurance market policies also. They found that states with policies to guarantee coverage by small businesses had lower uninsured rates, but warn that if strategies such as this one are combined with other solutions such as insurance premium rate restrictions, they may counteract each other. Exchange programs such as introduced in the current health care reform proposals, however, are expected to increase the ability of small businesses to provide coverage for their employees. Marsteller and colleagues (1998) also note that increasing the supply of health care facilities and physicians in rural areas can increase competition and reduce the cost of premiums—a solution with a payoff both for businesses that cover their workers and for individuals purchasing coverage. They argue that Medicare and Medicaid, as important sources of patient revenue in rural areas, should be utilized to leverage cooperation among rural health care providers. This may help to facilitate the community health centers advocated by the last Bush administration for every poor county in the country.

The recently proposed Cover All Pennsylvanians (CAP) provides an example of ways to concurrently address both increased access to care and improved affordability of health care. With this plan, affordability is expected to increase through financial incentives to health care providers to expand their availability across more time (for instance, evenings and weekends) and in more places, particularly in underserved rural areas; by including pharmaceuticals and behavioral health issues among health services covered; and by funding health insurance coverage subsidies, for example, through state taxes on tobacco products and assessments against businesses failing to offer health insurance to employees.

Since most uninsured adults are employed, increasing workplace-based coverage has long-reaching potential benefits. Indeed, employer-provided health insurance can pay off in employee productivity (O'Brien 2003). This solution would require either incentives (e.g., tax incentives) or legislative mandates for employers to provide health coverage benefits for all employees. Group insurance options have been proposed that would permit self-employed individuals and small businesses to bargain together as a larger insurance purchasing agent, potentially increasing bargaining power and reducing insurance premiums (Rosenbaum, Borzai, and Smith 2000). Since rural self-employment increases the risk of being uninsured compared with urban self-employment, and since approximately four in five who live in rural counties not adjacent to a metro area and who lack health insurance come from families with at least one full-time worker (Ziller et al. 2003), this solution appears practical.

Rural Americans tend to have lower incomes than urban residents, with a median income in 2006 of just over thirty-eight thousand dollars, compared with more than fifty thousand dollars in metro statistical areas and just under fifty-six thousand dollars in metro areas outside principal cities (DeNavas-Walt, Proctor, and Smith 2007). Likewise, 15 percent of rural residents had below-poverty incomes that year, compared with 12 percent of urban residents. Nearly half of residents in rural counties not adjacent to an urban county have family incomes less than 200 percent of the federal poverty level. The majority of the uninsured in these most rural counties are impoverished according to this standard (Ziller et al. 2003). For these families, subsidies may be needed *before* they can purchase health coverage, rather than as a tax return after the fact.

Of course, tax reforms that would offer a tax deduction for individuals who purchase health insurance on their own could be combined with tax credits for low-income individuals and families so that health insurance premiums would be more affordable to them. Again, the cost of this strategy to the government is not likely to be trivial.

Interestingly, some point out that increasing area attractiveness to industry (e.g., through improved school systems) and industry recruitment efforts by local economic developers may offer the best all-round solution for persistent-poverty areas (Glover et al. 2004). However, job growth has been slower in rural than in urban areas since the late 1990s. For example, rural employment grew by around 1.3 percent annually between 2003 and 2006 compared with 1.9 percent annual growth in urban areas (Kusmin 2007). Furthermore, dual-worker families in the rural areas surrounded by rural counties are at greater risk of lacking health coverage than their counterparts in urban and suburban areas because employer-sponsored coverage is unavailable to them, and only about 33 percent of low-wage workers have access to employer-sponsored coverage regardless of rural or urban residence (Ziller et al. 2003). Personal services and entertainment industry workers are least likely to be offered coverage by their employers, especially in rural areas. As shown in this chapter, the problem is greater when the national economy declines. For this strategy to pay off, all jobs will need to offer affordable coverage as a benefit of employment. The new health reform legislation is expected to promote this solution by creating special health benefit exchanges through which small business can purchase affordable coverage for their employees and by penalizing larger employers who fail to provide self-effective coverage options for their workers.

The most promising, and equitable, path to increasing health coverage for rural residents will be the same as that for providing *all* Americans coverage—it will require the financial cooperation of large and small employers providing coverage, individuals purchasing coverage, and the government subsidizing coverage (Collins, White, and Kriss 2007; Lambrew and Gruber 2006). It will depend as well on expanding health care facilities in rural areas and decreasing health care costs. Whether achieved through health care market strategies or legislated health coverage plans, the continued reliance of rural residents on subsidized care is likely to be a reality reinforced by aging rural populations and the low-wage service-sector employment available in many rural labor markets. Furthermore, as was shown here, shorter periods without coverage contribute substantially to the number of uninsured, indicating a need for affordable alternatives to close the gaps for low- and middle-income families. In sum, the current heavy reliance on publicly sponsored coverage in rural areas means that a private solution alone cannot solve the problem of the uninsured in rural America.

Table 14.1 Percentage of population groups in metro and nonmetro areas without health coverage for one to four, five to eight, nine to sixteen, and any months, by period

		1998–1999 Months without coverage				2001–2002 Months without coverage				2004–2005 Months without coverage			
		1–4	5–8	9–16	Any	1–4	5–8	9–16	Any	1–4	5–8	9–16	Any
Total population	Metro	7	4	12	23	9	5	11	25	6	4	11	21
	Nonmetro	6	4	12	22	9	5	13	27	6	4	12	22
Minority population	Metro	10	7	21	38	14	8	21	43	8	6	17	21
	Nonmetro	9	6	23	38	16	10	23	49	15	9	21	45
Population in single-parent families	Metro	12	8	19	39	17	9	18	44	10	7	15	32
	Nonmetro	10	7	21	38	18	8	18	44	9	5	14	28
Population in poor* families	Metro	13	10	27	50	16	9	42	67	10	7	24	41
	Nonmetro	12	7	28	47	19	9	44	72	10	5	25	40

* Less than 100% Federal Poverty Level.

SOURCE: 1998–1999, 2001–2002, 2004–2005 Survey of Income and Program Participation (SIPP).

Table 14.2 Odds ratios showing significant partial effects of residential and personal characteristics on the likelihood of ever lacking health coverage during each period

		1998–1999		2001–2002		2004–2005	
Model 1	Rural residence	1.1		1.3		1.3	
		Rural	Urban	Rural	Urban	Rural	Urban
Model 2	Decline in						
	manufacturing	No effect	No effect	1.4	1.3	No effect	0.8
	Increase in						
	service jobs	0.9	No effect	1.2	1.3	1.2	0.8
	Minority	2.4	2.5	3.2	3.4	2.1	2.8
	Poor family	3.3	3.2	5.3	5.1	6.7	4.2

NOTE: All odds ratios were derived from partial coefficients in multivariate models. Separate models were estimated for each observation period and in the case of Model 2, separate models were estimated for rural and urban areas. Model 1 included rural residence, decline in manufacturing, increase in service jobs, minority status, and poor family indicators; only the effect of rural residence is shown since effects for the other covariates are for rural and urban areas combined. Model 2 shows the effects for those covariates for rural and for urban areas for each observation period. Effects are statistically significant at the 99 percent confidence level. The interpretation of odds ratios is explained in note 5.
SOURCE: 1998–1999, 2001–2002, 2004–2005 Survey of Income and Program Participation (SIPP).

Notes

1. Although the terms "rural" and "nonmetropolitan" may not mean exactly the same things in the strictest sense, they are used interchangeably throughout this chapter for ease of discussion.

2. The 1996 panel provides 13,935, the 2001 provides 14,962, and the 2004 provides 16,942 respondents (unweighted) living in a nonmetropolitan location for most of the observation period. In each year, these respondents represent approximately 20 percent of the weighted total sample (including both urban and rural respondents).

3. SIPP's public use geographic identifiers do not permit an evaluation of how rural a nonmetropolitan residence is, and SIPP's method of assigning metro/nonmetro status to respondents tends to bias rural/urban comparisons by reducing potential differences. This bias occurs because in states where the nonmetropolitan sample is very small, a randomly selected portion of the metropolitan sample is coded as living in a nonmetropolitan area (Westat 2001). A comparison of the results presented here with published results from other surveys (see Bhandari 2004) indicates that such bias in the figures presented in this chapter, although of little concern, will slightly minimize the rural/urban differences.

4. Before REIS county-level data were merged with SIPP records, counties were coded as either metropolitan or nonmetropolitan based on Beale codes. Counties having a Beale code of below 4 range from urban areas with population of twenty thousand or more to areas that either are completely rural or are small urban areas having a population of twenty-five hundred or less. These areas are considered nonmetropolitan, or rural, in the analysis. Counties with Beale codes above 3 range from the largest metropolitan areas to counties in metro areas with a population less than two hundred fifty thousand. These areas are considered metropolitan, or urban. These county-level records were then aggregated up to the metropolitan and nonmetropolitan levels for each state in each year—1998, 2001, and 2004. These

records were then used to create state average metropolitan and nonmetropolitan measures of job growth, which were merged to SIPP respondent records by state, metro/nonmetro status, and year.

5. Odds ratios here are interpreted as the number of times more likely it is for a person with the characteristic to be without coverage compared with someone with the reference characteristic. An odds ratio of 1 means that persons with the characteristic and persons with the reference characteristic are equally likely to be without health coverage. Odds ratios greater than (less than) 1 indicate that a person with the characteristic is more (less) likely than a person with the reference characteristic to lack health coverage. For example, an odds ratio of 2 for minority status would mean that the odds of being uninsured are twice as high for minority persons as for nonminorities. An odds ratio of 0.2 would mean the odds would be 0.2 times as likely (or 80 percent less likely) to lack coverage.

LIVELIHOOD PRACTICES IN THE SHADOW
OF WELFARE REFORM

ANN R. TICKAMYER AND DEBRA A. HENDERSON

Welfare reform created massive changes in the policies, expectations, and practices of poor persons. The two major components of the new policy are time limits to cash benefits and devolution of authority from federal to state and local jurisdictions. Placing time limits on cash assistance meant that the majority of welfare recipients face pressure to find paid employment, yet studies of urban low-income working and welfare dependent groups, both prior to welfare reform and after, demonstrate that low-wage working women are no better off (or even worse) than those who combine welfare with other income sources as a livelihood strategy. There is little comparable research in poor rural settings where work is scarce and additional obstacles to employment such as lack of transportation and child care are endemic. In theory, devolution permitted greater understanding and responsiveness to local conditions and need, but also raised the possibility of increasing the burden on areas with few resources for managing new responsibilities.

We examine sources of income and livelihood practices for low-income rural recipients of public assistance at both the early stages of welfare reform and after the policies had been in place and were well established. The purpose is to determine the effect of welfare reform on livelihood practices by creating a profile of income sources and other resources for recipients in poor rural communities in Appalachian Ohio at three points in time over a seven-year period. Data collected in 1999, 2001, and 2005 represent times early, midway, and late in implementation of these policies. We focus on two primary comparisons: the differences between those who have fulfilled the expectation of welfare reform and have some form of paid employment and those who do not; and community level differences embodied in county social and economic characteristics and human service agency operations.

Background

By now it is well known that the passage of PRWORA, the Personal Responsibility and Work Opportunity Reconciliation Act of 1996, more commonly known as "welfare reform," effectively implemented the political promise "to end welfare as we know it." It changed the contours of the safety net initiated during the Great Depression and further elaborated in War on Poverty programs that entitled means-qualified recipients to public assistance. Most notably, it marked the end of the primary program of cash assistance, AFDC (Aid to Families with Dependent Children), and substituted more circumscribed TANF (Temporary Assistance to Needy Families), whose purpose was seen as temporary, limited, and geared toward moving recipients into self-sufficiency through formal labor market employment. The legislation gave states great flexibility in designing and implementing their own welfare programs, but a primary parameter was a sixty-month lifetime limit for assistance. Many states, including Ohio, designed programs that placed far lower limits on eligibility, usually restricting it to two or three years maximum. States' policies also differed in their emphasis on goals of reducing welfare rolls or increasing employment among former recipients (Nathan and Gais 2001). A few states (including Ohio) took devolution one step further and gave counties much greater responsibility for program design and implementation. Regardless of strategy differences adopted for reducing welfare use, the avowed purpose of the radical restructuring of the welfare state was to reduce welfare dependency and increase self-sufficiency by moving recipients off cash assistance and into waged labor.

Numerous assumptions about poverty, welfare use, and outcomes of welfare reform were embedded in political discourse leading up to this policy revolution. Foremost among these was the issue of dependency and its sources. Increasingly, the prereform welfare system was redefined as the cause of poverty and dependency, rather than its remedy. There was a widely shared belief among the public and policy elites alike that welfare recipients were unwilling to work and were assisted in their disinclination by an overly generous and permissive welfare system. While the most influential of these attacks came from the Right in a "war on welfare" that reversed the logic of the War on Poverty by inverting the causal link between poverty and welfare (Gilder 1981; Gingrich et al. 1994; Murray 1984), belief in the structural disincentives to work embodied in welfare was also embraced by liberal analysts who argued for the need to restructure programs to make work pay (Bane and Ellwood 1994). Even feminists argued that the old system, embedded in a patriarchal state, created dependency through the devaluation of care work and a two-tiered social welfare–provision system (Abramovitz 1988; Fraser 1990). Thus, there was widespread agreement that the old system was broken and needed to be fixed and great support for changing the incentive structure. Empirical research from before welfare reform provides a more complex picture of welfare recipients' livelihood strategies than is evident from public polemics. Rather than finding that welfare and employment are oppositional or mutually exclusive practices, research on how recipients and low-income workers make ends meet demonstrates a diversity of income-generating activities that often include a mix of formal and informal employment, self-provisioning, and use of government and private transfers, sometimes alternating, sometimes supplementing, sometimes conducted within the rules and regulations of the system in which they operate, more often in violation of the system (Edin and Lein 1997; Fitchen 1981; Harris 1997; Nelson and Smith 1999; Stack 1974).

Prior to welfare reform, Edin and Lein (1997) studied low-income single mothers in four U.S. cities. In support of the idea of a dysfunctional incentive structure, they found that neither work nor welfare alone provides adequate income to meet the needs of single mothers' families, and that all used a wide variety of private and public sources of income to cover basic living expenses. Contrary to popular belief, mothers with formal labor market participation were worse off than women on welfare. Formal employment reduced their access to income from "side jobs" (informal or off the books) or from public and private assistance.

Edin and Lein also argued that social structural context influences survival strategies. Their study was conducted in four urban areas to represent a range of welfare benefits, size, characteristics of both formal and informal economies, and child support programs. Their results varied by place, confirming their view that structural characteristics of place influence survival strategies and the costs and benefits of different practices.

The effect of welfare reform on income-generating and livelihood practices remains a matter of debate. While cash assistance rolls have been drastically reduced—up to 50 percent—there are large gaps in the research on how poor and low-income groups fare. There is little research comparable to the Edin and Lein study. Instead, the numerous studies of "leavers"—those who exit welfare as a result of welfare reform—rarely provide the same detail. While research demonstrates that leavers are better off than those who remain on cash assistance, it is inconclusive about how both groups manage or their ultimate fate (Jones-DeWeever, Peterson, and Song 2003). Many studies show that poverty rates remain high for former recipients (Lichter and Jayakody 2002; Loprest 1999; Moffitt 2002) and that they continue to struggle with a variety of hardships, lack of resources, and support (Hays 2003). Furthermore, despite numerous state-based studies, there is little attention to context or spatial variation in these findings.[1] In the rare cases where community-level factors are examined, it becomes clear that these have an effect (Parisi, McLaughlin, Grice, and Taquino 2006).

There also has been little comparable research conducted among the rural poor, especially in high-poverty locations either before or after welfare reform. Yet there is substantial evidence that conditions of rural poverty differ from the urban inner-city circumstances documented by Edin and Lein (Lichter and Jensen 2002; Snyder, McLaughlin, and Findeis 2006), and a number of studies document that rural women are worse off and face different economic circumstances than their metropolitan (metro) peers (Brown and Lichter 2004; Lichter and Jayakody 2002; Lichter and Jensen 2001; Snyder and McLaughlin 2004; Snyder, McLaughlin, and Findeis 2006). Similarly, while still highly debated, there is broad speculation and accumulating evidence that the contours of welfare reform differ for remote rural areas compared to urban and metro locations. Rural areas lack the jobs, social services, human and social capital, and infrastructure to facilitate the transition off cash assistance and into paid employment required by the new system (Fisher and Weber 2002; Parisi, McLaughlin, Grice, and Taquino 2006; Parisi, McLaughlin, Grice, et al. 2003; Partridge and Rickman 2006; Pickering et al. 2006; Tickamyer et al. 2007; Weber, Duncan, and Whitener 2002). Few studies directly examine variation within rural areas.

We examine changes brought about by welfare reform by examining the ways that residents of poor rural areas made ends meet early in the implementation process for welfare reform, before the end of eligibility for cash assistance, again two years later after the initial period of eligibility had run out in the study area, and then again four years after that. Additionally, we examine sources of income and noncash survival strategies among the rural poor to determine general patterns of livelihood practices in poor rural areas and how they vary by employment status and characteristics of place.

Research Design and Methods

The final version of welfare reform devolved responsibility to the states for design and implementation of specific programs, but required maximum lifetime limits of five years on eligibility and specific goals for removing recipients from welfare rolls and into employment. In Ohio, under a plan called Ohio Works First (OWF), a thirty-six-month lifetime limit was adopted, beginning October 1997, and stringent work requirements were imposed. The primary characteristic of the Ohio plan was further devolution to the counties. County officials and agencies, assisted by an infusion of state and federal funds to permit local program initiatives, assumed major responsibility for specific program design and implementation. Counties vary in the types of measures they have adopted and in their capacity to meet the requirements of reform measures.

The twenty-nine counties of Appalachian Ohio constitute a region of historically high levels of poverty and unemployment that is largely rural, remote, the product of deindustrialization, lacking in investment and capital necessary for economic development, and with relatively little access to state and federal policy makers and circles. Even within this relatively homogeneous region, however, there are large differences in levels of social and human capital, employment opportunities, and local capacity to implement and administer welfare reform programs (Tickamyer et al. 2007). We selected four counties in this region for intensive study that represent similar high levels of poverty and unemployment but have varying degrees of urbanization, isolation, access to human resources, and social and investment capital to draw on for the process of welfare reform. The four counties range from a nonmetropolitan (nonmetro), nonadjacent, completely rural population county to one that is officially part of a small metro area but nevertheless retains its small-town and rural character.[2] Table 15.1 shows county characteristics for these four counties in comparison with the state. The data show that while all four counties perform substantially below the state average, there are also large differences between the counties. The two more urban counties tend to have higher economic indicators (although not uniformly) than the two completely rural counties. The latter also have less human capital and generally are more isolated economically and socially.

The primary data for this chapter come from surveys administered in the waiting rooms of human service agencies in four counties in Appalachian Ohio during the summer of 1999, one and a half years into the beginning of the thirty-six-month eligibility window for Ohio recipients of cash assistance, and again during the summers of 2001 and 2005, well after the end of the eligibility window.[3] Eligible respondents include recipients of welfare benefits, including cash assistance, food stamps, and medical programs. Survey items ranged from basic demographic and household characteristics to detailed information on program use, employment, welfare use, other livelihood strategies, and attitudes about poverty and welfare reform. It should be emphasized that this is a trend study. Respondents are not the same individuals surveyed at three points in time, but rather represent a snapshot of human service clients in the same welfare offices at each point in time. The results permit a comparison of changes in the social and economic characteristics of welfare users early and late in the welfare reform process, but not of the changing fortunes of individual recipients.[4] A total of 1,246 usable surveys resulted—399 from 1999, 401 from 2001, and 446 from 2005.

We examine income sources for survey respondents and how these influence total household income for each of the years in which data were collected. Also, we compare total household income and indicators of hardship for respondents with and without formal labor force employment. Income is measured by responses to the question "If you added together all of the money that you and people living in your home got during the past year (including OWF/TANF), what would the total amount be?" Response categories were five-thousand-dollar intervals ranging from zero to twenty-five thousand dollars and up, recoded to the category midpoint. Information about a very large variety of income sources, both cash and noncash, public and private, formal and informal, was requested as well as basic demographic, household, and family information. Labor force participation is indicated by a positive response to a question about whether the respondent currently works for pay. Indicators of economic hardship ranging from lacking money for food to experiencing homelessness are also examined. County capacity uses degree of rural/remoteness and a variety of other measures of social and human capital, economic development, and employment opportunities to group the four counties into "high" and "low" categories. The two most urbanized counties are classified as high capacity; the two most rural are labeled low capacity (see Tickamyer et al. 2007 for details).

Findings: Survey Data

Table 15.2 provides information about the social and demographic characteristics of survey respondents by year, the changes from years 1999 to 2005, and counties grouped by capacity. Very few differences exist by year. As expected in this rural area, the vast majority are white women having an average age in the mid-thirties and an average of two children. The majority of respondents have children under eighteen at home, and a substantial number live in households with persons who are not members of their nuclear family. This number increased substantially between the first year of the survey and the subsequent two. Educational attainment of respondents has improved across the three surveys, with a large decrease in percentage without a high school diploma and corresponding increases in those who have completed high school (or its equivalent) or who have some type of additional schooling, with the biggest change occurring between 1999 and 2001.

Partitioning the data into high- and low-capacity counties produces few significant changes from the total sample. With minor exceptions, demographic characteristics are essentially the same across the counties. Respondents are somewhat older in low-capacity counties in the two subsequent surveys. Both types of counties have marked decreases in the number of respondents who do not have a high school diploma or its equivalent, but the decline is much larger for high-capacity counties, possibly the result of more aggressive campaigns to improve the educational credentials of welfare recipients.

Table 15.3 partitions the demographic data by whether respondents are currently employed in the formal labor market across the three time periods. A number of differences appear by work status, although the trends are not uniformly linear. Workers are initially younger, older in 2001, and again younger in 2005. Fewer workers are married in the first two surveys, but this reverses in 2005. Workers have more children living in their homes, but fewer live in households with persons not part of their immediate family. Only in the first year does total household size differ significantly between workers and nonworkers. Finally, workers are better educated than nonworkers, and this improves substantially across this time period.

Table 15.4 displays detailed economic characteristics of Appalachian users of human services in the three survey years and by county capacity. There were notable changes in work effort between 1999 and 2001 and again in 2005, rising from almost 28 percent to 36.5 percent and then declining to just over one-third. Other changes include an increase in the percentage who ever have worked for pay and in monthly earnings and household income, although these are not statistically significant. The percentage looking for work declines in 2005, presumably because they are working or have some barrier to employment. Average monthly earnings increase across the years, but not significantly. Especially noteworthy is the low income of respondents, even for impoverished households in a region of persistently high poverty levels, unemployment, and underemployment. In 2005, the average household income is slightly over

$10,000 per year, a low figure considering that households average close to four members and this is just barely over the poverty line for a single individual.

When these data are partitioned by county capacity, there are large differences between the more urbanized locations and the more rural counties in percentage of recipients who are employed in the first two years, with higher employment rates in the high-capacity counties. The difference diminishes in 2005. Similarly, an initial large gap between high- and low-capacity counties in the percentage looking for work is also reduced in the subsequent years. There is very little difference in monthly earnings. An initial large gap between high- and low-capacity counties in household income diminishes and, somewhat surprisingly, reverses by 2005.

Table 15.4 also shows the sources of income for respondents and their households for the previous year. The most obvious change is in cash assistance. There is a marked decrease in the percentage of respondents who receive OWF/TANF, with the biggest decrease taking place between 1999 and 2001. Food stamp use, on the other hand, decreases substantially in 2001 but then rises again to slightly higher than its original level in 2005. It should be noted that large majorities received food stamps in all three years, unlike OWF, which declines from almost 42 percent to slightly more than a quarter of the respondents by 2005. Other significant changes are decreases in the number of persons reporting that someone in their household received social security or a pension and disability and an increase in receipt of unemployment benefits.

When these data are partitioned by county capacity, interesting differences emerge. There are large differences within year by capacity for welfare receipt. Low-capacity counties have higher percentages reporting receiving OWF/TANF and food stamps and a much more dramatic decline in their receipt than higher-capacity counties. Significant differences also emerge in WIC (the Special Supplemental Nutrition Program for Women, Infants, and Children) that were not evident in the unpartitioned data. Generally, low-capacity counties have higher rates of use, except in the middle survey year, where the relationship is reversed. Other differences are found in transfers. There are no significant differences between counties in 1999 and few in 2005, but in 2001 more residents of low-capacity counties report receiving social security, a pension, or disability, and fewer report benefiting from the EITC (Earned Income Tax Credit) or child support.

A substantial percentage of the population uses informal sources of income and ways of making ends meet in both years, with odd jobs for pay (but off the books) and bartering or trading goods and services most often reported. These two activities also have statistically significant changes from the early to later surveys, with a decrease in performing odd jobs and an increase in barter. High-capacity counties have more respondents who report earning money from odd jobs (except in 2005) and trading goods and services.

Generally, there is a small increase in self-provisioning and accessing some form of either public or private food assistance over the years. Use of food pantries increased from 1999 to 2001 and then declined slightly. There is a significant difference between high- and low-capacity counties in food pantry use in 2001, with much greater reported use in the two lower-capacity counties.

If the same economic variables are examined by whether the respondent is currently working, it becomes obvious that households where the respondent is formally employed are somewhat better off. Table 15.5 shows that their income is substantially higher in all years, and they have lower levels of welfare receipt (significantly lower in 2005). Employment decreases food stamp use, even as it increases for everyone in 2005. Workers are also less likely to have someone in the household on a pension or disability, but they are much more likely to receive child support and to take advantage of the EITC. Differences in informal activity are small and generally not significant. However, it is interesting to note that more respondents who are currently employed also report income from odd jobs and from trade and barter, in opposition to previous speculation that formal labor force participation decreases likelihood of informal work. Finally, food pantry use, which is high across the board, declines for working respondents in 2005.

Based on the descriptive analysis for each survey year, we constructed a multivariate model of influences on household income using ordinary least squares regression. Income is regressed on current work status, county capacity, and controlling for individual and household characteristics, including age, marital status, number of children under eighteen in the home, the presence of non–family members in the household, having less than a high school education, and receipt of public assistance including OWF/TANF, food stamps, and WIC, to determine how each factor contributes to household finances. Table 15.6 shows that in all years, employment increases income substantially and significantly, whereas county capacity has little effect after controlling for other variables in the model. Living in a low-capacity county reduces income in the first two survey years and increases income in the third, but the effect is not significant in any year. The explanatory power of the models is modest and declines slightly over the three years. However, it is not out of line with other studies of income prediction.

In 1999, statistically significant positive contributions to household income come from age, being married, having others in the household (in this case, an adult child living at home), as well as formal labor market employment. Negative effects on income are the result of not having a high school diploma and receiving welfare benefits (OWF/TANF or food stamps).

In 2001, the positive contribution of working is almost the same as in the previous year (about eighteen hundred dollars). The effect of being married is smaller, but having an adult child at home has a larger contribution to income and the presence of children under eighteen is now significant. Not having a high school diploma has a bigger effect than in 1999. The effects of both working and receiving welfare benefits are very stable over the first two survey years, with a sizable boost to income from employment and even larger decreases from receiving cash benefits and food stamps.

Differences in both size and direction of effects appear in 2005. Most notably, the size of the unstandardized regression coefficient for working, at almost thirty-two hundred dollars, is much larger than in the previous two surveys. Age, dependent children, and receiving WIC have positive effects on yearly household income; receiving food stamps has a large negative effect. The WIC coefficient is positive, a reversal from 1999, and many times larger than in the previous survey. Getting food stamps has a much larger negative effect, while receiving cash benefits, although still substantial, is smaller in absolute value than in earlier years. Having less than a high school education is no longer significant and has a smaller depressing effect on income.

Finally, we were interested in how these welfare recipients and low-income workers experience their economic circumstances. Table 15.7 examines economic hardships experienced by respondents and their families by year and county capacity. Indicators of hardship include running out of food stamps or money for food during the past year, lacking food for either oneself or one's children, lacking medical insurance for self, spouse, or children, failing to see a doctor when necessary, and experiencing an episode of homelessness. There has been a notable change across the years, with large decreases from 1999 to 2005 after initial increases in 2001 for all but the health insurance variables. When county capacity is controlled, a few differences between high- and low-capacity counties emerge but diminish over time. Perhaps the most interesting outcome, although not statistically significant, is that at each survey year, more persons in high-capacity counties report having experienced at least one hardship.

Table 15.8 partitions the data by whether the respondent is formally employed during each survey year. Differences by work status are small, and none hold up across all three years, with hardship generally declining by 2005. Somewhat surprising, however, is that in a number of cases workers have higher levels of hardship, although the difference is not statistically significant.

Findings: Panel Data

Evidence from the panel study assists in the interpretation of these findings.[5] Respondents report mixed views of the effect of welfare reform on their lives. A common theme among the interviewed women, especially those who were employed or had employed partners, was that there had been real improvements in their lives: "I think it's [welfare reform] workin'. 'Cause a lot of people that had been on it [welfare] are off an' find out that they can do the job, they can go out and get jobs and have somethin' better in life than a check that comes in once a month that won't get them nowhere" (Cindy, married and subsequently divorced, one child). They are especially pleased to be able to provide for their families' needs: "I think my family's better off. I really feel strongly that my family's much better off. I'm able to do things for my kids I wasn't able to do before. Not everything I'd like, but, ya know. I don't go vacationing for two weeks down in Florida. [laughs] But um, when school comes around and they have their list of school supplies, I can actually go buy those school supplies. It's sometimes hard" (Beth, married, one child). Cindy, the woman first quoted, elaborates: "Well, I'm glad I'm not receiving assistance anymore. Because, you know, on the check you got, three hundred dollars a month. You couldn't do anything . . . like I pay for any extra thing Brady does. . . . He's in Boy Scouts. So I pay for like his camping money, stuff he needs for Boy Scouts and stuff like that. And we wouldn't have been able to do it if we's still on assistance. . . . Um, any time they go on a camping trip it's at least ten dollars for the parents."

A number identified benefits to their sense of efficacy and self-esteem. Cindy articulates this view in a way that resonates with many of the women's experience: "I'm smarter than what I thought I was. Especially, ya know, like I said about my, that my dad would always put us down an' everything an' it's, if nothin' else I've proved to myself that I can do it. . . . I'm a lot stronger than what I used to be." Another woman described how "when I was first on assistance, I had no self-confidence, didn't even care if I ever got off assistance. I didn't care. I was just so down. And everybody has their ups and downs, but a lot of times, at the end of the day, I'm just proud of myself that I am, although it's difficult, I have a good job, that I can, you know, come home from work every day. An' put a roof over my kids' head an' there's food on the table an' my kids tend to be, seem to be happy" (Diane, single mother of three children).

Having discretionary income and being able to make decisions on how to spend it was particularly valued. As Mary, a divorced mother of four, states, "Spend it [my money] the way you want to. I don't have to have anybody tell you how to do it." On the other hand, these decisions aren't always easy: "It's really hard though, trying to decide, 'Okay, do we need to buy diapers or pay the electric bill?' I mean, hm, choices, choices . . . poopy babies or freeze to death" (Whitney, single mother of three in long-term cohabiting relationship).

In general, respondents continue to have numerous problems and no illusions about the difficulties they face: "Just because you're working doesn't mean that you're making enough money to live. . . . Because, you know, we all know Walmart hirin' always. But they're only hirin' ya for twenty-five hours at minimum wage. Then you got to have, you know, what do they always, like thirty before they give you any benefits" (Karen, widow in her thirties with two children). Similarly: "You're always behind on something or something's going to bounce or, there's always something not right. You can never get to the point where you can pay your bills plus buy groceries" (Joyce, married, one child). And Beth, a married mother of one child, agrees: "Seems like I have more bills. I feel like I struggle more now." This is not for lack of effort. Beth works two jobs, as she describes: "I'm working. . . . I'm lucky to have one day a week off. An' I'm workin' my one job I work thirteen hours an' the other job I'm workin' eight and a half every day an' it's like, ya know, I am workin' my butt off an' I am working every day and I don't call off, but I'm still struggling."

One particularly graphic example offered by Whitney demonstrates the ongoing problems of the working poor, in this area, always living on the edge: "I needed a part that was like two hundred an' some dollars, an' all the body work was done, but the part I need to, for the car to run. . . . Clay lost his job because we lost the car. The car broke down so he had no way to drive to Columbus every day. So he lost his job. So then we didn't have the money to pay for the part for the car." This story is particularly illustrative of the problems for those who seemingly successfully transition off of welfare. The job in Columbus (the state capital and a major metro area) represented a very long commute (approximately two hours each way) for a tenuous position that could barely pay enough to cover the costs of the trip. Yet finding work often requires this kind of effort, given the lack of employment opportunities in the study counties.

Discussion

The results of this study suggest a number of outcomes of welfare reform for low-income populations. First, the overall demographic profile of the users of human services is remarkably similar across the years. The biggest change is an increase in educational attainment, undoubtedly reflecting efforts by human service agency personnel early in welfare reform to push recipients to complete at least a GED. Second, even though the demographic characteristics of the samples don't change very much, their livelihood practices do. The number of persons in the labor force increase, as does the percentage of respondents who have ever worked for pay. At the same time, receipt of cash benefits decreases. There are large declines in the percentage of the population who receive OWF/TANF, while food stamps first decrease, then increase. There are also declines in other sources of transfer income, including social security and disability, while unemployment compensation increases slightly. Informal income sources decline, but barter increases substantially. Half or more of the sample gets food from self-provisioning or from taking advantage of public and private food sources. Although income increases in dollar value, the difference is not significant across years. Third, there are very few significant differences between the more rural counties characterized as low capacity and the more urbanized, higher-capacity locations. Finally, there are clear differences between labor force participants and nonworking respondents, with different patterns in both demographic and economic characteristics. Working respondents are better off in general, with significantly higher incomes, less frequent use of public and private transfers, and a greater likelihood of benefit from the EITC and child support. Their mix of income sources and livelihood practices differs from that of their nonworking counterparts.

These changes herald a reduction in hardships experienced by these low-income respondents by the time of the last survey. After initial increases in the hardships reported by respondents in the first two years, there is marked decline by 2005. These changes undoubtedly have been compounded by the ups and downs of the national and regional economy. As the data were being collected in 2001, the economic boom that had assisted in placing welfare recipients into jobs at the time of the initial survey had ended and rising unemployment rates were threatening the fragile accommodations many families had made. The economy showed signs of recovery by the third survey in 2005, and in the areas under study a number of rural development initiatives were in place. Nevertheless, hardships reported still remain distressingly high, and work status has no significant effect on hardship reports.

The multivariate analysis confirms that while work remains a strong predictor of household income for respondents across the first two years, local capacity washes out controlling for individual demographic and economic factors. Income predictors, including welfare benefits, are stable in their effects. There are higher levels of work effort later in the welfare reform process, but, with some exceptions, the pattern of influences on income remains very much the same.

It appears that even in persistently poor rural areas, welfare reform has mandated major shifts in the livelihood practices of low-income residents.

Opportunities for income acquisition differ in rural compared to more urbanized areas, but within a region of persistent poverty such as the four counties in this study, differences in county capacity and resources available to implement welfare reform do not show up as differences in recipient characteristics and outcomes. Employment, on the other hand, has more obvious effects. While we are not able to say definitively whether working respondents are better off than nonworking clients, these data are suggestive of support for the often heard claim for the goals of welfare reform that employment does have a beneficial effect. In these data, clients who are more dependent on public assistance sources are substantially worse off in their access to disposable income.

The in-depth interviews with the panel of recipients this period, beginning at the time of the first survey, reinforce this finding. Respondents indicate strong support for the goals of welfare reform, particularly moving from welfare to work. Although those who experienced the transition reported enormous adjustment and financial problems, they also indicated great pride in working and in having control over cash, being able to spend money as they thought best, and serving as positive role models to their children.

Nevertheless, it should be remembered that regardless of income source, the data indicate very low incomes for almost *all* respondents to this survey—well below the poverty line, on average. Workers have higher incomes, but the amounts they are able to earn or piece together still make them among the poorest members of society, and they experience severe and significant hardship, such as running out of food or being unable to see a doctor when necessary. The kind of work available to these individuals, typically at or slightly above minimum wage with limited hours and no benefits, is not likely to lift them out of poverty, making the very real issues of poverty an ongoing problem that has not been adequately addressed by welfare reform. These findings reinforce structural theories of poverty that argue that impoverishment is the result less of individual failings, welfare dependency, or unwillingness to work than of deficiencies in the economic system and safety net that do not provide adequate opportunities or social support (Rank 2004). This situation is all the more pressing for these rural residents.

Policy Implications

Restructuring the welfare state has created new exigencies for poor persons in poor places. The effort to move persons off cash assistance and into the labor market has had some success, with both financial and psychosocial benefits.

Nevertheless, the results of this study indicate the severe limits on income strategies for rural residents and the difficulties they experience in earning a living with limited state assistance. Furthermore, the continued dependence on forms of public and private assistance by low-income workers and the evidence of widespread hardship regardless of employment status suggest that the safety net has "holes" that need to be mended to make the goals of welfare reform more of a reality.

Some forms of intervention are obvious and have been discussed extensively elsewhere. In isolated places with little economic activity, finding jobs, let alone jobs with living wages, for those who are able and capable will remain a challenge that is exacerbated by lack of dependable transportation and child care. Programs to subsidize quality child care, vehicle availability and maintenance, and health care access for *all* family members would go a long way in assisting low-wage workers to prosper and others to enter the labor force with greater chance of success. Similarly, pegging the minimum wage to the cost of living would assist the working poor to stay afloat. While it may not be realistic to expect that all remote rural areas can create jobs adequate to the needs of the poor, programs that tip the balance to make work pay (as was one of the original goals of some proponents of welfare reform) would reinforce the positive outcomes for many low-wage workers. Macro-level policies and rural economic development initiatives to create more jobs are also necessary, but may have only limited success in remote areas. Assisting poor people to become more employable through some combination of improved access to education, child care, health care, and transportation, while also limited, can at least have success at the margins. Finally, a realistic understanding of the limits of employability as a universal outcome and corresponding assistance programs targeted to "hard cases" should be incorporated into more comprehensive welfare provision policies. Unfortunately, reauthorization of PRWORA in 2005 and subsequent implementation rules put more emphasis on ideological goals than pragmatic ones. The new regulations increase work requirements, restrict substitution of education for work hours, and emphasize marriage promotion rather than skill enhancement at the individual level or job creation and mending the safety net in aggregate.

The ongoing evolution of welfare reform makes it all the more necessary to continue to follow the lives of current and former recipients as they struggle to make ends meet in and out of the labor market. Ironically, devolution, a central component of welfare reform, is largely responsible for one of the major difficulties in assessing impacts of welfare reform and evaluating the effectiveness of specific programs and provisions. The huge variation in implementation strategies across place and space makes it virtually impossible to definitively assess outcomes even if the political will exists to conduct the complex (and expensive) comparative studies necessary to evaluate effects of different policies and programs for different populations. To date there has been relatively little interest in providing the resources necessary to conduct these comprehensive studies, resulting in lots of piecemeal research with specific goals and foci for limited geography. They are often dependent on state and local interests and support, but contain no overall strategy for systematic evaluation and comparison. Some of this gap may be filled over time as long-term longitudinal and panel studies such as the Survey of Income and Program Participation (SIPP) and the National Longitudinal Surveys (NLS) accumulate sufficient cases and data to permit systematic comparison. However, these are unlikely to be able to fill all the holes, especially for the kinds of locations without the political clout necessary to make their voices heard. Research on the well-being of rural families as they struggle with the implications of restructuring of both the economy and the welfare state needs to have higher priority than has been the case. This becomes even more pressing when the hardships imposed by structural changes in the economy and the safety net are exacerbated by severe economic decline and loss of employment as experienced during the second half of the first decade of the twenty first century.[6]

Table 15.1 Economic characteristics of Appalachian Ohio study counties

	Washington		Athens		Meigs		Vinton		Ohio	
Beale Code*	3		4		6		9		NA	
Year	1999/00~	2004/05/06^	1999/00~	2004/05/06^	1999/00~	2004/05/06^	1999/00~	2004/05/06^	1999/00~	2004/05/06^
Population	63,251	61,867^	62,223	61,860^	23,072	23,092^	12,806	13,519^	11,353,140	11,478,006^
Median household income ($)	33,426	36,297^	28,965	29,785^	25,223	28,859^	26,697	32,086^	40,956	43,371^
Per capita income ($)°	22,735	26,37°	17,875	21,928	19,763	20,307	17,208	19,453	28,205	31,860
Percent of persons in poverty	12.3	12.2^	19.1	20.2	20.4	18.1^	18.7	16.8^	10.6	11.7^
Unemployment rate (%)	4.6	5.9^w	11.1	6.4^	10.0	9.8^M	9.0	8.1^v	5.0	5.9°
Percent of female-headed households with children under 18 in poverty	44.6	na	47.0	na	55.2	na	50.7	na	34.6	na
Percent with less than high school degree	11.6	na	12.8	na	18.6	na	20.3	na	12.6	na
Percent of population in the labor force	61.6	na	56.9	na	54.6	na	55.7	na	64.8	na

* From http://www.ers.usda.gov/Data/RuralUrbanContinuumCodes.
~ From http://quickfacts.census.gov (Census 2000).
^ From http://quickfacts.census.gov/qfd/states/39000.html.
w http://www.odod.state.oh.us/research/files/S0/Washington.pdf.
^ http://www.odod.state.oh.us/research/files/S0/Athens.pdf.
v http://www.odod.state.oh.us/research/files/S0/Vinton.pdf.
M http://www.odod.state.oh.us/research/files/S0/Meigs.pdf.
° http://www.odod.state.oh.us/cms/uploadedfiles/Research/s100.pdf.

Table 15.2 Demographic characteristics of Appalachian Ohio human service users by year and capacity

	All counties				1999		2001		2005	
	1999 (n = 399)	2001 (n = 401)	2005 (n = 446)	% change	High (n = 200)	Low (n = 199)	High (n = 201)	Low (n = 200)	High (n = 226)	Low (n = 220)
Percent female	85.3	82.0	79.0	−7.4	84.0	86.2	85.7	78.3	80.4	77.5
Percent white	96.2	95.3	94.2	−2.1	97.0	96.6	95.6	95.0	93.8	94.5
Mean age	34.5	35.3	35.4	2.6	34.3	34.6	32.6	37.9	34.7	36.2
Percent currently married	38.9	40.4	36.1	−7.2	36.0	41.9	32.3	49.0	34.5	37.7
Mean birth children	2.4	2.3	2.3	−4.2	2.2	2.5	2.1	2.5	2.3	2.3
Mean children under 18 at home	1.7	1.7	1.6	−5.9	1.6	1.8	1.8	1.7	1.6	1.6
Percent with nonnuclear members of household	29.3	38.4	36.2	23.5	34.8	37.8	43.3	33.5	37.2	35.2
Total household size*	3.7	4.0	3.8	3.8	3.5*	3.9	4.0	4.0	3.8	3.8
Education[A]***										
Percent less than high school	31.1	20.5	20.9	−32.8	33.6	28.5	17.2	23.7	19.0	22.8
Percent high school	50.5	54.5	54.6	8.1	47.9	53.2	51.0	57.4	52.9	56.3
Percent more than high school	18.4	25.0	24.5	33.2	18.5	18.4	31.7	18.9	28.1	20.9

NOTE: Significance of dependent variables indicates significant F tests for all counties across years and significant t tests for differences between high- and low-capacity counties within year.

[A] Education tested with chi-square.

* Difference statistically significant at p < .05.

** Difference statistically significant at p < .01.

*** Difference statistically significant at p < .001.

Table 15.3 Demographic characteristics of Appalachian Ohio human service users by year and current work status

	1999		2001		2005	
	Not working (n = 277)	Working (n = 107)	Not working (n = 251)	Working (n = 144)	Not working (n = 251)	Working (n = 127)
Percent female	86.9	86.9	81.5	84.4	79.4	78.7
Percent white	95.7	97.2	95.6	95.1	93.6	95.3
Mean age	35.1	32.4*	32.4	36.7***	37.4	32.2***
Percent currently married	40.2	37.4+	43.2	36.8**	34.7	37.0
Mean birth children	2.4	2.5	2.3	2.3	2.4	2.8*
Mean children under 18 at home	1.7	2.0*	1.6	2.1***	1.5	1.7+
Percent with nonnuclear members in household	36.7	16.2***	41.0	33.3+	34.5	32.8
Total household size	3.7	3.7	3.8	4.4**	3.7	3.8
Education[A]		**		**		***
Percent less than high school	33.0	23.8	23.0	15.1	23.4	8.9
Percent high school	52.1	47.6	57.4	49.6	53.2	54.0
Percent more than high school	15.0	28.6	19.6	35.3	23.4	37.1

[A] Education tested with chi-square.
+ Difference statistically significant at $p < .1$.
* Difference statistically significant at $p < .05$.
** Difference statistically significant at $p < .01$.
***Difference statistically significant at $p < .001$.

Table 15.4 Economic characteristics of Appalachian Ohio human service users by year and capacity

	All counties				1999		2001		2005	
	1999 (n = 399)	2001 (n = 401)	2005 (n = 446)	% change	High (n = 200)	Low (n = 199)	High (n = 201)	Low (n = 200)	High (n = 226)	Low (n = 220)
Percent currently working for pay**	27.9	36.5	33.6	20.4%	34.5	21.1**	43.0	29.7**	35.2	31.8
Mean hours of work per week	35.3	33.4	34.5	-2.3%	35.4	35.0	33.6	33.2	33.0	36.5+
Percent who have ever worked for pay+	82.1	87.4	87.5	6.6%	85.7	79.3	88.0	87.0	90.4	84.6+
Percent looking for work	49.0	50.2	42.2	-13.9%	56.8	42.5*	52.9	48.0	42.6	41.9
Mean earnings per month	650	705	800	23.0%	650	651	731	669	800	754
Mean annual household income	8,514	9,715	10,266	20.6%	9129	7,858+	10,155	9,219	9,962	10,560
Mean grocery bill per month	282	295	315	11.5%	280	285	330	288	310	320
Income sources for the past year (percent of respondents receiving . . .)										
Welfare										
OWF/TANF***	41.9	30.7	27.1	-35.3%	33.3	51.1***	25.5	36.3*	22.6	31.8*
Food stamps***	81.6	68.0	82.8	1.5%	78.2	85.1+	65.6	70.6	81.7	84.0
WIC	38.1	36.0	31.8	-16.5%	32.3	43.9*	43.8	27.4***	30.6	33.2
Transfers (percent with someone in the household receiving . . .)										
Social security / pension***	30.9	17.7	18.2	-41.1%	31.1	30.8	12.1	24.0**	17.3	19.1
Disability***	27.5	16.9	13.7	-50.2%	23.6	31.5	13.7	20.5+	10.2	17.3*
EITC	23.7	21.3	20.9	-11.8%	25.7	21.7	26.8	15.2**	21.7	20.0
Unemployment*	5.5	10.0	10.3	87.3%	6.8	4.2	8.9	11.1	9.7	10.9
Child support	20.6	19.7	18.2	-11.7%	18.9	22.4	23.2	15.8+	19.0	17.3
Gift	9.6	9.7	15.5	61.5%	10.1	9.1	11.1	8.2	16.8	14.1

Table 15.4 (continued)

	All counties				1999		2001		2005	
	1999 (n = 399)	2001 (n = 401)	2005 (n = 446)	% change	High (n = 200)	Low (n = 199)	High (n = 201)	Low (n = 200)	High (n = 226)	Low (n = 220)
Informal income sources (percent with someone in household receiving . . .)										
Flea market $	7.9	7.2	12.3	55.7%	6.1	9.8	5.8	8.8	12.8	11.8
Odd job $+	17.9	12.7	15.5	−13.4%	21.6	14.0+	14.7	10.5	12.8	18.2+
Selling homegrown or homemade goods	3.4	1.7	0.9	−73.5%	2.7	4.2	1.1	2.3	0.4	1.4
Selling firewood or mushrooms	1.0	0.6	2.2	120.0%	0.7	1.4	0.5	0.6	1.8	2.7
Other	5.2	5.0	2.9	−44.2%	6.1	4.2	5.3	4.7	2.7	3.2
Traded goods/services**	22.4	31.4	34.6	54.5%	26.5	18.2+	34.3	28.2	37.4	31.8
Food (percent who . . .)										
Self-provision	50.6	48.1	51.7	2.2%	48.0	53.3	49.3	47.0	41.9	54.3
Food from public or private sources	59.2	61.6	74.3	25.5%	59.0	59.3	62.2	61.0	73.1	75.5
Food pantry/bank	40.6	45.0	38.9	−4.2%	38.1	43.2	38.1	52.4**	38.4	39.4

NOTE: Significance of dependent variables indicates significant F tests for all counties across years and significant t tests for differences between high- and low-capacity counties within year.

+ Difference statistically significant at p < .1.

* Difference statistically significant at p < .05.

** Difference statistically significant at p < .01.

*** Difference statistically significant at p < .001.

Table 15.5 Economic characteristics of human service users by year and current work status

	1999		2001		2005	
	Not working (n = 277)	Working (n = 107)	Not working (n = 251)	Working (n = 144)	Not working (n = 251)	Working (n = 127)
Mean annual income	7,933	10,025**	8,768	11,349**	9,203	13,340***
Mean grocery bill per month	281	287	277	325*	331	299+
Income sources for the past year (percent of respondents receiving . . .)						
Welfare:						
OWF/TANF***	43.8	38.7	32.2	27.9	30.7	18.9**
Food stamps***	83.6	76.4+	72.2	60.9*	87.2	70.9***
WIC	38.1	38.2	35.1	37.7	31.5	36.4
Transfers (percent with someone in the household receiving . . .)						
Social security / pension***	36.2	17.1**	25.8	5.1***	25.1	6.3***
Disability***	30.0	19.7+	20.8	10.3**	15.1	3.9***
EITC	16.4	43.4***	15.4	31.6***	15.9	37.0***
Unemployment*	4.7	7.9	10.9	8.8	10.4	13.4
Child support	17.4	28.9*	16.3	25.7**	15.9	26.0*
Gift	11.7	3.9*	9.5	10.3	16.3	17.3
Informal income sources (percent with someone in household receiving . . .)						
Flea market $	7.5	9.2	7.7	6.6	11.2	17.3+
Odd job $+	17.4	19.7	11.8	14.7	15.1	16.5
Selling homegrown or homemade goods	3.3	3.9	0.9	2.9	0.4	1.6
Selling firewood or mushrooms	0.5	2.6	0.5	0.7	2.0	1.6
Other	4.7	6.6	6.3	2.2+	2.4	4.7
Traded goods/ services**	21.3	26.8	29.4	35.7	37.8	38.4
Food (percent who . . .)						
Self-provision	53.3	50.9	52.8	45.8	51.9	54.5
Food from public or private sources	59.8	60.7	58.3	63.8	74.3	78.5
Food pantry/bank	40.9	40.4	46.3	42.6	41.5	30.6*

NOTE: Significance of dependent variables indicates significant F tests for all counties across years and significant t tests for differences between working and not working respondents within year.
+ Difference statistically significant at p < .1.
* Difference statistically significant at p < .05.
** Difference statistically significant at p < .01.
***Difference statistically significant at p < .001.

Table 15.6 Regression of household income on social and economic characteristics of human service recipients, 1999, 2001, 2005

Variable	1999			2001			2005		
	B	Std error	Beta	B	Std error	Beta	B	Std Error	Beta
(Constant)	8192	1804		7984	1860		6615	2294	
Low-capacity county	-660	695	-0.05	-657	776	-0.05	988	870	0.05
Working	1807*	749	0.14	1838*	772	0.13	3177***	987	0.17
Age in years	40***	35	0.07	58	37	0.09	67	43	0.09
Married	2959***	773	0.22	1969**	839	0.13	3919	980	0.22
Number under 18 at home	827	267	0.17	510+	280	0.10	702*	351	0.11
Others in household	1527+	813	0.12	2055*	970	0.12	2545***	794	0.17
Less than high school	-1911**	761	-0.13	-3311***	971	-0.18	-1985	1086	-0.09
Received OWF/TANF	-2058*	750	-0.16	-2728**	885	-0.18	-1667+	982	-0.09
Received food stamps	-3823***	961	-0.22	-3516***	853	-0.23	-4974***	1196	-0.21
Received WIC	-313	845	-0.02	282	866	0.02	2182*	1058	0.12
Informal income sources	-107	798	-0.01	-739	864	-0.04	684	876	0.04
R^2, adj R^2	.28, .25***			.25, .22***			.20, .18***		

+ Difference statistically significant at $p < .1$.
* Difference statistically significant at $p < .05$.
** Difference statistically significant at $p < .01$.
*** Difference statistically significant at $p < .001$.

Table 15.7 Economic hardship of human service users by year and county capacity

	All counties				1999		2001	
Percent of respondents who(se):	1999 (n = 399)	2001 (n = 401)	2005 (n = 446)	% change	High (n = 200)	Low (n = 199)	High (n = 201)	Low (n = 200)
Ran out of money for food	78.4	79.9	73.9	−5.7	75.7	81.3	75.6	84.6*
Lacked food for children	26.8	35.2*	9.0	−66.4	21.8	31.8+	31.7	39.2
Lacked food for self	51.8	57.8	30.1	−41.9	50.8	52.9	55.7	60.1
Lacked medical insurance	30.8	20.2**	19.9	−35.4	35.0	26.2+	16.6	24.2+
Spouse lacked insurance	16.6	12.3	8.2	−50.6	13.4	20.0	8.6	16.6*
Children lacked insurance	15.6	7.5***	8.2	−47.4	15.3	15.9***	6.9	8.3
Did not see a doctor when needed	57.4	62.2	18.8	−67.2	58.2	60.7	62.2	62.2
Were homeless	25.4	34.4**	11.7	−53.9	25.8	24.8	34.0	35.0
Experienced more than 1 hardship	85.7	80.1*	82.5	−3.7	88.0	83.4	82.6	77.5

+ Difference statistically significant at p < .1.
* Difference statistically significant at p < .05.
** Difference statistically significant at p < .01.
*** Difference statistically significant at p < .001.

Table 15.8 Economic hardship of human service users by year and county capacity

	1999		2001		2005	
	Not working (n = 277)	Working (n = 107)	Not working (n = 251)	Working (n = 144)	Not working (n = 251)	Working (n = 127)
Ran out of money for food	73.7	80.7	75.4	82.3	76.3	73.2
Lacked food for children	25.8	27.8	32.1	36.8	11.9	6.1+
Lacked food for self	56.2	43.4*	55.9	58.7	33.3	30.7
Lacked medical insurance	44.3	25.0***	24.0	16.7+	18.3	23.1
Spouse lacked insurance	15.9	17.3	9.6	14.3	7.6	11.1
Children lacked insurance	20.5	13.5	6.4	8.4	5.4	11.1+
Did not see a doctor when needed	60.8	58.2	61.8	62.2	17.5	27.6*
Were homeless	25.5	25.8	35.9	31.6	11.4	13.9
Experienced more than 1 hardship	85.9	89.7	79.3	81.9	82.0	84.3

+ Difference statistically significant at p < .1.
* Difference statistically significant at p < .05.
** Difference statistically significant at p < .01.
***Difference statistically significant at p < .001.

Notes

1. As a result of devolution, states vary widely in their policies and programs, making comparability problematic, especially for evaluation and assessing outcomes. Most evaluations are state-based and statewide, with little effort to examine variation within states or between states. While there have been a few comparative studies as well as efforts to compare (or at least compile) results across locations (see, e.g., CLASP 2001), few systematically examine spatial variation or look at contextual effects.

2. For details of county selection and classification, see Tickamyer et al. (2002, 2007). Relative rurality is determined by Beale codes, a rural–urban continuum based on "a classification scheme that distinguishes metropolitan counties by size and nonmetropolitan counties by degree of urbanization and proximity to metro areas." Beale codes vary from 1 to 9, with 1 representing central counties of metro areas with a population of 1 million or more and 9 designating completely rural counties containing no urban areas with a population of twenty-five hundred or more and not adjacent to a metro area. The four counties include one small county that comes under the smallest metro designation (Washington, Beale code = 3); a formerly nonmetropolitan county that by Census reclassification in 2000 is now considered "micropolitan" (Athens = 4); and two nonmetro counties, one under the most rural

designation (Vinton = 9) and one slightly less remote (Meigs = 6) (http://www.ers.usda.gov/Data/RuralUrbanContinuumCodes).

3. Although the state agency publishes monthly county-level statistics on program use, this information is not available by individual, and we did not have access to county records. Therefore, it is not possible to compare our sample with the county population of agency clients. However, county regulations require their clients to physically check in at least once a year, making the waiting room a crossroads where virtually all users of agency services show up. While the ensuing sample is not a probability sample, the procedures used to collect the data make it representative of the clients of the human service agency in each county at that time.

4. Changes in individual circumstances were collected through in-depth interviews with a panel of twelve recipients in each county (forty-eight total) across the years. See Henderson et al. (2002a, 2002b).

5. The forty-eight recipients who agreed to be part of the panel study were recruited either by volunteering at the time of the initial survey or through snowball sampling. They consented to one- to two-hour semistructured interviews, initially for two sessions, but for the majority of the sample, third and, in some cases, fourth interviews were conducted with their eager consent between 1999 and 2004. By the third interview, thirty-four of the women remained available. Panel members were very similar to the survey respondents in demographic characteristics. For details see Henderson et al. (2002a).

6. Support for this research comes from the Joyce Foundation, the National Research Initiative of USDA, Ohio State Legal Services Association and Legal Aid Society of Greater Cincinnati (OSLSA/LASGC), the University of Kentucky Center for Research on Poverty, and Ohio University.

POVERTY, WORK, AND THE LOCAL ENVIRONMENT

TANF and EITC

DOMENICO PARISI, STEVEN MICHAEL GRICE,
GUANGQING CHI, AND JED PRESSGROVE

The importance of work is a topic that regularly emerges in the debate on poverty and public policy, with the major argument being that getting a job is the first step toward becoming self-sufficient, even if the job is not full-time or does not pay well (Pavetti and Acs 2001). Today there are two federal assistance programs that embrace and enforce the work-first orientation: Temporary Assistance for Needy Families (TANF) and Earned Income Tax Credit (EITC). Over the past ten years, both TANF and EITC have contributed to the decline of welfare use and the increase of work, especially among poor single mothers (Lichter and Jensen 2002). As a result, the TANF and EITC programs have enjoyed stronger public support than welfare policies had before the 1996 welfare reform.

Notwithstanding the positive outlook represented by national statistics on the performance of TANF and EITC, many working poor continue to struggle to make ends meet. Among the most vulnerable are those whose local environment provides limited access to economic and social resources. The importance of the local environment and the differential opportunities imposed by it are often dismissed in the discussion of poverty and public policy. In fact, a general criticism of TANF and EITC is that they reflect primarily an urban antipoverty political agenda (Lichter and Jayakody 2002) and thereby fail to recognize that local economic opportunities vary across urban and rural populations (Parisi, McLaughlin, Taquino, et al. 2002). This shortcoming is understandable given that a larger number of the U.S. poor are urban Americans. However, a larger percentage in rural America are poor, 14 percent, compared to 12 percent in urban America (Lichter and Johnson 2007). Most importantly, many rural low-income families live in communities with highly concentrated and persistent poverty, and unlike similar impoverished urban communities, rural communities are spatially isolated from major economic hubs. As a result, many rural low-income families often are confronted with more barriers to work than their urban counterparts (Lichter, Parisi, Grice, et al. 2007a; Lichter, Parisi, Taquino, et al. 2008).

This chapter addresses an often ignored question: what does it mean for TANF and EITC if the conditions for obtaining, retaining, and developing a job in the local environment do not exist? To anticipate the answer, when the conditions to promote work exist in the local environment, the EITC helps maintain attachment to the labor market by rewarding work, especially if it does not pay enough. In contrast, when the conditions to secure and retain a job do not exist in the local environment, TANF becomes a main source of income to maintain and support family well-being. However, such support from TANF is limited to a maximum of five years in one's lifetime.

A simultaneous evaluation of the performances of the EITC and TANF programs provides an ideal strategy to illustrate the links between work, poverty, and the local environment. For example, if a poor single mother on TANF lives in a community that provides economic opportunities—along with social and public support services—to gain, retain, and develop a job, she will be able to become self-sufficient by earning wages, therefore enabling herself to reap the benefits of the tax credit under the EITC program. On the other hand, if a poor single mother on TANF lives in an economically and socially distressed community, she will face serious barriers to work and will therefore be unlikely to enjoy the supplemental income provided by the EITC program. To illustrate the links between work, poverty, and the local environment, we first present a brief description of the differences in the local environment between urban and rural populations. Next, we use data from the Current Population Survey to generate national estimates of EITC participation rates to illustrate how work differentially rewards low-income working families across urban and rural populations. We also analyze the TANF program in Mississippi to show how work does not pay when the local environment is not conducive to a life without welfare.

The Local Environments of Urban and Rural Populations

Today, approximately 84 percent of the U.S. population is classified as urban. Urban Americans are those residing in the 366 U.S. metropolitan (metro) areas, which, according to the Office of Management and Budget (2008), are broadly defined as Core Based Statistical Areas, that is, areas based on a recognized population nucleus and adjacent communities that have a high degree of integration with that nucleus (2008). Metro areas must have at least one urbanized area of fifty thousand or more inhabitants.

Rural Americans are those residing in 2,041 nonmetropolitan (nonmetro) U.S. counties covering 83 percent of the nation's land. These counties fall outside metro areas and have no cities with fifty thousand or more inhabitants. Nonmetro counties are further divided into micropolitan and noncore areas (OMB 2003). Micropolitan areas have at least one urban cluster of ten thousand or more inhabitants but less than fifty thousand and often include more than one county. Any areas that fail to meet these criteria are defined as noncore areas, which are delineated by single-county boundaries (OMB 2003). Of the total U.S. population, 10 percent live in micropolitan areas and 7 percent in noncore areas.

Urban and rural populations are also economically and socially distinct. Unlike urban populations, rural populations live in local environments where labor markets typically offer low-wage, part-time, and temporary jobs mostly available in the service sector (Beaulieu 1999; Beaulieu et al. 2000; Bloomquist et al. 1993; Gorham 1992; Lichter, McLaughlin, and Cornwell 1995). Rural residents also have limited means of transportation to labor markets with "good jobs," or jobs that pay well and are available all year. Low levels of human capital in terms of educational attainment, job experience, and job skills are other barriers faced by rural populations in securing good jobs (Beaulieu 1999; Beaulieu et al. 2000; Haleman et al. 2000; Lichter and Jensen 2002). Continuing out-migration of rural residents with higher levels of education and better job skills has eroded rural America's stock of human capital and therefore its long-term economic viability (Lichter, McLaughlin, and Cornwell 1995). Globalization has contributed substantially to shrinking the pool of good jobs in rural America, as many manufacturers find it more cost-effective to produce abroad. The continuing erosion of economic opportunities and underinvestment in human capital have undermined the ability of rural populations to develop locally based social infrastructures necessary to establish their problem-solving capacities for maintaining, preserving, and promoting community well-being (Flora and Flora 1993; Luloff and Swanson 1995; Wilkinson 2000).

To be sure, there are significant ecological, demographic, economic, and social differences that clearly distinguish rural and urban populations. Rural populations are at a greater disadvantage than their urban counterparts for three important reasons. First, differences between local environments with thriving economies and those with high and persistent poverty are more pronounced in rural populations than in urban populations (Lichter and Johnson 2007; Weber et al. 2005). Second, places with high concentrations and persistence of poverty are also those with the highest percentages of minorities, especially African Americans (Lichter, Parisi, Taquino, et al. 2008). Third, rural populations are more divided across class and racial lines than their urban counterparts (Lichter, Parisi, Grice, et al. 2007a, 2007b). The implication is clear: public policies that fail to recognize rural disadvantages because of an urban bias might hurt rather than help rural America.

The EITC Program and Its Differential Effect on Working Low-Income Families

The EITC is a refundable tax credit available to families with income levels up to 200 percent above the poverty line. It was established in 1975 with the intent of rewarding working families by reducing their tax burdens (Caputo 2006).

Under this program, an eligible family receives a wage supplement when the credit for which it qualifies exceeds the amount of taxes it owes. The EITC is based on three income ranges: phase-in or subsidized stage, maximum credit or flat range, and phase-out (Caputo 2006; Scholz 1994). In tax year 2006, for example, the credit for a family with two dependent children was 40 percent of the first $11,430 earned (phase-in), and if the family's income ranged between $11,430 and $14,810, it received a maximum credit (flat range) of $4,536. The credit phased out if the family's income exceeded $14,810, reaching a credit of zero if the family's income was more than $36,348. This federal program has enjoyed substantial bipartisan support, and its relatively small credit size has been expanded considerably, making the EITC the largest and most effective antipoverty program for working poor families in the United States (Caputo 2006). In 2005, more than $42 billion was credited to eligible claimants, with more than $37 billion being refunded. In the next few years, the EITC is expected to exceed $50 billion.

We use national data from the Current Population Survey March Supplements from 1994 to 2006 to address the differential impact of the EITC on low-income, working single female–headed households. We limit our analysis to this population because it is the most vulnerable group in terms of receiving public support. Specifically, we first examine whether there is a relationship between work and poverty across rural and urban low-income, single female–headed households (including both central city and suburban residents). Second, we examine whether the work-first initiative stemming from the 1996 Welfare Reform Act might have contributed to the increased number of low-income families using the EITC. Third, we examine the extent to which the EITC differentially lifts poor single mothers out of poverty across urban and rural populations. Finally, we examine work, poverty, and the EITC across racial groups within rural populations.

.

National Estimates on Work, Poverty, and the Local Environment

Our data clearly show there is a relationship between work and poverty among poor single-female households, but this relationship holds only when poor single mothers gain full-time jobs. In the United States, the poverty rate among single female–headed households dropped from 44 percent in 1993 to 32 percent in 2005. During the same period, the percentage of working single females with children increased from 58 to 65 percent. On the other hand, the number working part-time remained relatively constant at approximately 15 percent.

Similar trends can be observed in central cities, rural areas, and suburban areas. However, single female–headed households in central cities continue to have slightly higher poverty rates than those in rural areas, and such households in central cities and rural areas continue to have substantially higher poverty rates than those in suburban areas. In central cities, poverty rates dropped, on average, from 53 percent in 1993 to 38 percent in 2005, while in rural areas they dropped from 46 to 36 percent. Suburban areas experienced the lowest drop in poverty rate, from 32 to 26 percent.

As expected, we find more single female–headed households working in suburban areas than in central cities and rural areas. However, central cities experienced the largest increase in the percentage of single mothers working full-time. Between 1993 and 2005, this percentage increased from 47 to 62 percent. In rural areas, it increased from 55 to 61 percent, and in suburban areas, it increased from 60 to 69 percent. Furthermore, more single female–headed households work part-time in rural areas than in central cities and suburban areas.

National Estimates on EITC Participation Rates, Poverty, and the Local Environment

Prior to the 1996 welfare reform legislation, single female–headed households with children in rural America had a lower EITC participation rate than those in central cities and suburban areas. Two years after 1996, the EITC participation rate in rural areas became higher than that in central cities and suburban areas. By 2005, the EITC participation rate for suburban residents had dropped to the lowest level among all areas. A possible explanation is that because jobs in suburban areas tend to be better than those available in central cities and rural areas, the EITC becomes more important for residents in central cities and rural areas.

Our analysis also reveals that EITC lifts more people out of poverty in suburban areas than in central cities and rural areas. This finding can be explained by the fact that jobs in suburban areas provide higher income than those in other areas. Thus, residents in suburban areas are more likely to reap the benefits of the EITC as long as their income is not above the upper level of the phase-in income range. For example, in 2006 a family with two dependent children making an average income of $12,000 received a maximum credit of $4,536. In contrast, a family that made an average of $8,000 received a credit of only $3,200.

Work, Poverty, and Race in Rural America

The relationship among work, poverty, and race is reported in figure 16.1. The figure displays three general trends: (1) number of single mothers working full-time, (2) number of single mothers working part-time, and (3) percent of poor single mothers working full-time. The results show that work indeed pays off, especially when single mothers work full-time.

Our results also confirm that in rural America, blacks remain the most disadvantaged racial group and are most at risk of becoming and remaining poor (Lichter, Parisi, Taquino, et al. 2008). In fact, for many blacks, work does not provide the same payoff that it does for other groups such as whites and Hispanics (see figure 16.1). For example, 62 percent of black single female–headed households with children worked full-time in 2005, but 49 percent remained in poverty. In contrast, 61 percent of white single female–headed households with children worked full-time in 2005, but only 31 percent remained in poverty. For Hispanics, 61 percent worked full-time in 2005, but 38 percent remained in poverty. Clearly, work is not as rewarding for blacks as it is for other groups.

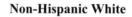

Non-Hispanic White

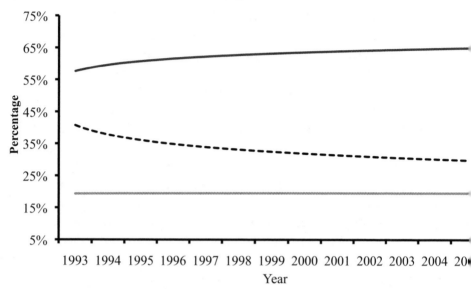

Non-Hispanic Black

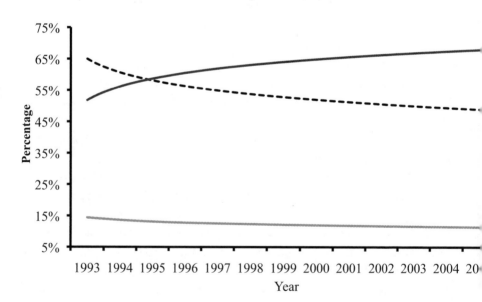

FIG. 16.1   Work, poverty, and race in rural areas (SOURCE: Current Population Survey 2007)

EITC, Poverty, and Race in Rural America

Between 1993 and 2005, Hispanics experienced the fastest growth in the use of the EITC and were also more likely to be lifted out of poverty compared to their white and black counterparts. A plausible explanation for this racial differential may be the migration of Hispanics to rural America. Unlike early Hispanic immigrants who chose to move to urban areas because they could receive social and network support, those who move to rural areas do so for economic reasons. They typically move to small towns with meat-processing plants or areas that offer jobs in oil, timber, furniture, carpentry, textiles, and other nondurable manufacturing (Crowley, Lichter, and Qian 2006). Because these jobs provide relatively good sources of earning, it is no surprise that rural Hispanic immigrants might be more likely to reap the benefits of work when compared to rural black and white residents (see figure 16.2).

TANF and Its Differential Effect on Low-Income Families

The TANF program, created by the Personal Responsibility and Work Opportunity Reconciliation Act (PRWORA) of 1996, replaced the Aid to Families with Dependent Children (AFDC) program. Unlike AFDC, TANF is funded through block grants to states, and low-income families are denied benefits if they do not engage in allowable work activities within two years of receiving assistance. Furthermore, recipients are limited to receiving cash assistance for five years over their lifetime. Individual states, however, have the flexibility to impose stricter time limits.

One explicit goal of the welfare reform legislation was to balance the right of welfare receipt with one's obligation to become a productive working member of society. The act sought to promote job preparation and work so that low-income families could rely on paychecks rather than welfare checks and move onto a path to self-sufficiency. The act also required states to meet work participation rates or face severe financial penalties. With these changes, PRWORA placed responsibility on the individual to gain employment and on the state to facilitate welfare-to-work transitions.

The introduction of time limits on benefits was a major break from past policy. Time limits were seen as the main vehicle to encourage poor single mothers on welfare to engage in forward-looking behavior. The main assumption was that single mothers on welfare would come to the realization that their

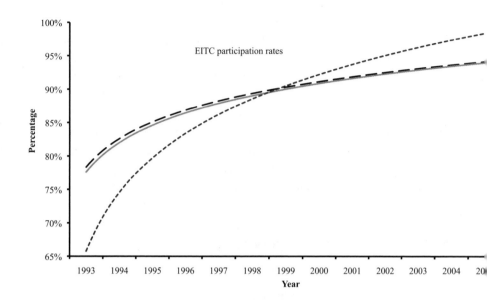

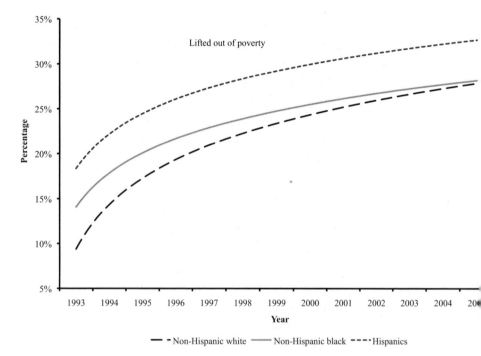

FIG. 16.2   EITC, poverty, and the local environment: single female–headed households with children (SOURCE: Current Population Survey 2007)

current choices have long-term consequences on their well-being and the well-being of their children (Pavetti and Bloom 2001). That is, imposing time limits would force poor single mothers to choose work as a means to provide a future for their families outside the welfare system while "banking" their remaining months of eligibility for rainy days (Moffitt and Pavetti 1999).

Another important change in TANF legislation was the idea of embracing *devolution:* the process by which federal responsibility is transferred to states and local jurisdictions. Within this framework, states can engage in first- and second-order devolution. With first-order devolution, states have greater flexibility to develop their own sets of rules and combine different program parameters to design and implement TANF. With second-order devolution, states build partnerships with local jurisdictions, especially with local civic- and faith-based organizations (Liebschutz 2000; Parisi, Harris, et al. 2005).

Since the passage of the 1996 welfare reform legislation, the nation has experienced the most dramatic decline in welfare caseloads in its history (more than 60 percent), reaching the lowest level of welfare participation since 1960 (Parisi, McLaughlin, Taquino, et al. 2002). This trend has created a public perception that the 1996 welfare reform has been successful in moving poor single mothers into the workforce. National studies show that the share of earnings in the income packaging of poor single mothers increased substantially across urban and rural populations (Lichter and Jensen 2002). These studies also indicate that of those who leave welfare rolls, approximately two-thirds are able to work at some point (Lichter and Crowley 2002), but many are unable to secure permanent jobs or jobs that pay a living wage (Lichter and Jensen 2002). Other studies, however, show that many TANF recipients leave involuntarily. These families leave the welfare rolls because they have exhausted their time limits, are unable to meet work requirements, are forced to bank eligibility, or are removed as a result of diversion strategies aimed at reducing welfare caseloads (Parisi, Harris, et al. 2005). Approximately two million families continue to rely on welfare for reasons such as lack of job opportunities, child care, quality education and training, or public transportation (2008; Parisi, McLaughlin, Grice, and Taquino 2006). This situation means that to have a life without welfare, a poor single mother must be in a local environment where the conditions to obtain, retain, and develop a job exist.

We use data from a study conducted in Mississippi to illustrate how the local environment influences welfare use across different populations when the conditions of the local environment are not conducive to promoting and supporting work (Parisi, Harris, et al. 2005; Parisi, McLaughlin, Grice, and Taquino 2006; Parisi, McLaughlin, Taquino, et al. 2002). This study's research design involved the use of multiple sources of data. First, we used monthly data from the Mississippi Department of Human Services (MDHS) for the period between October 1996 and July 2004. These data were used to generate two measures. The first measure gauged local TANF participation rates, defined as the number of TANF participants in a local area per one thousand people. Essentially, this measure gauged the level of reliance on welfare in a local population. The second measure gauged individual TANF spell duration in months and number of spells.

The second source of data came from a case study designed to understand how the local environment influences reliance on welfare at both the aggregate and individual levels. The case study was conducted in Coahoma County, and data were collected through personal interviews with thirty TANF clients using the life history calendar technique (Harris and Parisi 2007). Coahoma County is one of eighteen counties that define the Mississippi Delta, a region characterized by a history of underdevelopment, high and persistent concentration of poverty, and divisions across class and racial lines. The population in Coahoma County is overwhelmingly black (69 percent). Approximately 40 percent of its population has less than a high school education, and approximately 36 percent lives in poverty. The industry structure in Coahoma County is dominated by low-wage, part-time jobs in the service industry.

The third source of data came from a statewide key informant survey. These data were collected to understand how state policy influences present and future reliance on welfare. The key informants were selected using a snowball sampling procedure. In this study, a key informant was defined as an individual referred by others as being knowledgeable about welfare policy and its implications on poor single mothers. Following this rationale, we were able to select forty key informants after making four hundred contacts throughout the state (Parisi, Harris, et al. 2005).

TANF Patterns and the Local Environment

Since the implementation of TANF, Mississippi has experienced more than an 80 percent drop in welfare caseloads. As a result, there are no longer poor single mothers who draw welfare checks in several counties, especially those in rural settings. However, Delta counties remain the most reliant on welfare use. We find that local populations in the Mississippi Delta have TANF participation rates more than double those outside the Delta—on average, sixty per one thousand population (Parisi, McLaughlin, Taquino, et al. 2002). Our data also reveal that TANF clients in the Delta have longer and more frequent welfare spells than those in any other rural and urban population in the state. During their first TANF spell, poor single mothers in the Delta rely on welfare for approximately ten months. More than 42 percent of TANF clients in the Delta have at least one return spell, and spell duration declines as the number of spells increases. This finding suggests TANF clients in the Delta might start banking their eligibility as they approach the time limits. In contrast, approximately 37 percent of TANF clients in rural and urban populations outside the Delta have return spells, with the first spell being no longer than ten months (see table 16.1).

Understanding Barriers to Work in a Poor Local Environment

When we asked TANF mothers in Coahoma County why they continued to rely on welfare, a consistent theme emerged: "there's no jobs here." Our participants also indicated that they have to wait long periods of time, generally two years, to gain a job. Typically, when they were able to gain jobs, they were temporary and low-wage. This situation creates disaffection with the local labor market and a sense that life cannot go on without welfare. This sense of hopelessness is exacerbated by other barriers to work, such as transportation and child care.

While Coahoma County provides few economic opportunities, neighboring Tunica County offers ample opportunities to gain employment in the casino industry. These jobs include housekeeping, food service, and related service jobs. Although the jobs in the casino industry are seen as good jobs and pay more than ten dollars an hour, few poor single mothers opt to secure such jobs. Our participants indicated that distance was one of the reasons for not considering casino jobs. The casinos are approximately forty-five miles from our participants' residences and could be reached only by bus, given that the mothers did not have their own transportation. The issue with this form of transportation is that it offers limited stops to drop off and pick up children at child care facilities. Furthermore, the bus schedule was such that it took several hours for the mothers to arrive at their work destinations, and most importantly, they had to leave their children unattended because jobs were offered primarily for night shifts. This experience was clearly expressed by two of our participants. One woman recounted some of the troubles she experienced with "going up the road," and recalled how "sometimes you have to leave like two or three hours before you have to be at work [to catch a bus] . . . and then it'd take you about two or three hours to get back sometimes. . . . That's a long time, especially when you have kids to see about." Another woman remarked, "So I just started gettin' me a daytime job so I could be home with my kids at night." Ultimately, the issue was not working night shifts or commuting for several hours. Poor single mothers in Coahoma County were reluctant to secure jobs in the casino industry because they were concerned about the safety of their children while they were away from home.

Understanding Barriers to Work in the Context of State Policy

The difficulties these women face were corroborated by several of our key informants. One of the principal issues raised by the informants was that the TANF policy in Mississippi is not designed to make work pay but rather to reduce the caseload. This view was clearly expressed by one of the key informants, who stated,

> The Welfare Reform Act in Mississippi was very welcomed but not from the standpoint of moving people to self-sufficiency. It was very welcomed because the administration had a strong sense that people had to get off their butts and get to work. . . . So, there was a strong sense that what we needed to do was force these people [food stamp and TANF clients] back to work so that that part of it took on a very punitive stance and it is my understanding Mississippi percentage-wise put more people off the rolls than any other state.

While our key informants acknowledged that the state put some effort into addressing the issue of transportation, such efforts did not reflect the needs of poor single mothers. Specifically, the state failed to recognize that most of the jobs available in the local labor market are second- or third-shift jobs and therefore outside normal working hours. A similar issue was with child care, where the state provided services for child care but ignored the fact that many poor single mothers needed it during night hours. These two views were clearly expressed by our key informants. One indicated, "The easiest jobs to get are the five-to-nine shifts because people want to be home with their families, but the mass transit system stops running. So people can get to work but can't get home." Another indicated that many overlook the problem of transportation in remote rural communities, as "it [Mississippi] is a very rural state. . . . We are talking about people being miles away from each other and the transportation not being there. Transportation is not [in] existence for a lot of people in the counties." Finally, another single mother eloquently raised the issue of transportation and child care: "[Transportation] wasn't provided for taking children to child care before you go to work, or picking children up after you get off work. So, what has happened as the result of the [TANF] program is that a lot of children are in informal care, children who should be getting early childhood education experiences are staying with parents or grandparents or the friend down the street or somebody."

The greatest barrier that many low-income families faced in Mississippi after the implementation of TANF was the failure to build strong relationships and responsibility in the local area. This failure created confusion about the implementation of the policy and often resulted in the mistreatment of people. This unfortunate outcome was explained clearly by one of the key informants, who said, "Every county was interpret[ing] the DHS regulations the way the county wanted to interpret them. . . . There was very subjective interpretations on what should put people off of welfare. That became a major issue because people were declared work ready and their time clock began to tick even though we were uncertain that any of them could actually go to work."

The sentiment was the government had failed to take responsibility, especially for those local populations that did not have the resources to shoulder the responsibility to take care of their own. This view was clearly expressed by one key informant: "We have to be very careful that we don't allow the government to advocate their responsibility to the people they are to serve. . . . What is the government doing? What is the role of government to serve the poor and to take care of the poor in the country? We have to be careful that devolution [transfer of responsibility] doesn't mean that everybody else is responsible for the people except for the federal government and the state."

Of all barriers to work, discrimination and class division were seen as the most critical barriers to overcome. This fact was expressed eloquently by one of our key informants, who stated, "The very people who were financing the campaigns that were saying, 'we need to kick people off welfare,' these were the same people who couldn't, wouldn't hire them. Didn't want to hire welfare mothers." The issue of class division and the importance of giving a voice to the low-income families were also eloquently expressed by another key informant:

> If [welfare reform was] going to be successful [it] had to get out of the plantation system [permanent class division] and . . . address issues [of] collaboration, giving up turf, doing away with racism, building a sound economic program. . . . You will have a plantation system as long as you don't give people a voice in their lives. That was what slavery was. Slavery

was not giving people a voice in their own lives. So, as long a[s] devolution doesn't give people a voice in their own lives, then we perpetuate the plantation system.

Conclusion

TANF and the EITC were designed to encourage and reward work. However, they fail to recognize that equal opportunities for work do not exist uniformly across local environments. Because work opportunities are embedded in the social and economic context of the local environment, the potential benefits of TANF and EITC policy are not equally realized. This differential is often ignored in the ongoing debate on poverty and public policy aimed at promoting and rewarding work.

For TANF, the "work-first" philosophy, which emphasizes steady employment as the primary means of moving out of poverty, results in an uneven policy that exacerbates the disadvantages of single female–headed households faced with barriers to work beyond their personal control. When the conditions to obtain, retain, and develop jobs do not exist, single female–headed households must continue to turn to welfare payments as a major part of their income packaging strategy and derive no benefits from the idea of increasing personal responsibility. In fact, it can be argued that personal responsibility is what prevents many of these women from working, especially when they are faced with the choice of spending considerable time commuting or being with their children. Commuting to work means relying on public transportation and jobs far away from their homes. When public transportation is available, it is often not convenient. Generally, the commute for single mothers can be two hours or more, extending their time away from home and their children. Another barrier is that when any jobs are available, they are often second or third shift, making arrangements for taking care of their children even more difficult.

For EITC, our data show that even when the conditions for work exist, work pays off differentially. In terms of reducing or alleviating poverty, work has a greater influence in central cities than in rural areas. In rural areas, blacks benefit less than any other group, confirming their disadvantaged position in the labor market. This situation threatens to further exacerbate racial and ethnic disparities. In terms of the number of working poor benefiting from EITC participation, rural residents have higher rates of use than their urban counterparts. In terms of EITC lifting people out of poverty, those in suburban areas benefit the most. This inequality confirms the disadvantaged position of residents in economically depressed areas in terms of access to good jobs. Despite these differences in the influence of the EITC on the working poor, the program has contributed to improving the quality of life of the working poor and has helped maintain their attachment to the labor market.

The lesson learned is clear: one-size-fits-all policies do not provide equal opportunities to all. The ongoing debate on poverty and work should shift its attention to differential opportunities within particular local environments. To be sure, the focus should be on developing place if our objective is to lift people out of poverty.

Table 16.1   TANF duration and TANF spells, 1996–2004

	MS	Delta	Nonmetro	Metro
Average in-spell duration				
Spell 1	8.3	9.6	8.1	7.3
Spell 2	6.6	7.5	6.2	6.1
Spell 3	6.2	6.8	5.9	6.0
Spell 4	5.6	6.2	5.1	5.4
Spell 5	5.5	5.8	4.8	5.8
Percent experiencing a spell				
Spell 1	60.6	57.2	62.3	61.3
Spell 2	23.3	24.6	22.9	22.6
Spell 3	9.6	10.3	9.2	9.5
Spell 4	4.1	5.1	3.6	4.0
Spell 5	2.4	2.8	2.0	2.7

SOURCE: Authors' tabulations of data from the Mississippi Department of Human Services.

CONCLUSIONS

ANN R. TICKAMYER AND KRISTIN E. SMITH

Policy to Meet the Needs of Rural America

You go into these small towns in Pennsylvania and, like a lot of small towns in the Midwest, the jobs have been gone now for 25 years and nothing's replaced them. . . . And they fell through the Clinton administration, and the Bush administration, and each successive administration has said that somehow these communities are gonna regenerate and they have not. . . . And it's not surprising then they get bitter, they cling to guns or religion or antipathy to people who aren't like them or anti-immigrant sentiment or anti-trade sentiment as a way to explain their frustrations.
—Barack Obama, 2008

President Barack Obama's often quoted statement about rural America while campaigning drew wide attention and quick condemnation from across the political spectrum and the rural-urban divide. The brief firestorm it created, as well as its subsequent disappearance from public and media attention, highlights several realities about rural America that have yet to be properly addressed.

First, rural areas have been hit hard by waves of economic restructuring that have left their residents hard pressed to earn a living and faced with all the negative ramifications for community and family stability and well-being that accompany economic hardship. Jobs have disappeared, seldom to be replaced with others that sufficiently meet the needs of rural Americans, either individually or collectively. Just as the Great Depression had been preceded by years of rural and agricultural recession long before the stock market crash of 1929 brought the crisis to Wall Street and beyond, many parts of rural America were struggling long before the current economic crisis became widely felt and acknowledged.

Second, these problems rarely are directly addressed by policy makers or politicians, regardless of which side of the political aisle they occupy. There are few policies specifically targeted to rural families and communities. The few explicitly rural policies such as the farm bill are focused on commodity production and trade issues and have little relevance for the majority of rural places and populations (Bokemeier 2008).

Finally, as both the negative stereotypes embodied in the final part of the quote and many of the responses illustrate, there is profound ignorance among opinion leaders and policy makers about the real conditions in rural America. The careless caricature evoked in this statement and the politically motivated responses underscore that the realities of life in rural America are increasingly remote for large segments of the population. This reality is true for policy makers, pundits, and much of the general public.

This volume addresses each of these issues. It focuses on the effects of economic change on rural individuals, families, and communities to provide a better understanding of the economic trends and conditions that influence livelihoods and the viability of life in small towns and rural places. It addresses policy in both its absence and presence to determine how current policies and practices affect rural residents and what types of policies and programs would be of benefit to rural America. And in accomplishing these objectives, it brings these issues clearly into the light, where they can be scrutinized and evaluated and, hopefully, recognized as a topic for study, debate, and action. As the opening quote illustrates, ultimately these are political issues, and an important purpose of this volume is to provide the information to put these on the political agenda.

IMPACTS OF ECONOMIC CHANGE

This volume is not an examination of economic change per se but about the effects of this change on rural families and communities, focusing on the consequences for the men, women, and children who constitute rural populations. Economic restructuring, accelerated by globalization, is part of the ongoing movement of capital and industry to seek cheaper production costs and higher profits. Initially, rural communities benefited when urban industries relocated to rural areas to take advantage of cheap land and labor, especially as the steady decline of agriculture and natural resource industries continued to deplete rural America of its traditional livelihoods. However, successive waves of deindustrialization and offshore relocation, initially from manufacturing but more recently including services, have left many rural communities with few options for earning a living, providing for daily necessities, or engaging future generations. Even where jobs remain or new ones are created, they often lack stability, and they rarely pay the wages and benefits of their urban counterparts (Falk, Schulman, and Tickamyer 2003). While not unique to rural areas, their smaller and less diversified economies provide fewer options when plants close or relocate. Although the changes themselves vary from region to region and place to place, the common thread is that jobs that once provided stable livelihoods and the means for families to survive and prosper are in scarce supply in rural communities. Furthermore, restructuring is not unique to industry but, in the form of welfare reform, also characterizes government programs and the safety net, directly affecting the policy apparatus that responds to economic hardship.

Job scarcity and all the concomitant problems were evident prior to the financial crisis and economic collapse of 2008. Global recession on top of persistent hard times leaves few options for many families in rural America, especially when the safety net has large holes and constraints. Emergency programs such as extended unemployment benefits and retraining programs are potentially helpful but may have limited value for those who had been left behind prior to current events. Thus, food pantries, which were already overburdened, are straining to serve rising numbers of users; similarly, social service organizations are laying off workers at the same time that there are increased demands on their services. The media carry myriad stories of hardship, rarely differentiating between rural and urban places, but there is reason to believe that rural areas are once again particularly hard hit (Morgan, Lambe, and Freyer 2009, 2).

However, rural America is diverse, perhaps increasingly so, as chapters by Lichter and Graefe, Anderson, Lee, and others remind us, both in economic conditions and in all other social and demographic characteristics. Similarly, it is resilient, as many of the authors demonstrate. Opportunities and amenities vary by complex mixes of characteristics of persons and place, described by one of the authors as "complex *spatial* inequality," where multiple intersecting social, economic, political, and geographic factors play out unevenly across space and place, building on Leslie McCall's breakthrough research on "complex inequality" (McCall 2001). This complexity makes it difficult to generalize about all of rural America, especially if analysis moves beyond crude dichotomies and proxies for rural and urban places as represented by the metropolitan-nonmetropolitan (metro-nonmetro) classification. Substantial differences exist between and among rural areas as well as across the rural and urban divide, even as many differences between metro and nonmetro places diminish and converge over time, in part as the outcomes of similar processes of long-term economic restructuring.

Thus, understanding the effects of economic restructuring requires simultaneously recognizing variation across rural places and the points of convergence that make rural America look increasingly like the rest of the nation. In fact, somewhat ironically, many of the differences between metro and nonmetro locations create the conditions that spur social outcomes that represent convergence. For example, the lagging incomes and growing inequality characteristic of rural areas described by Lichter and Graefe most likely are also behind the increase in rural married women with children entering the labor force (Jensen and Jensen, Smith), making these rates more similar to urban areas. The rise of women and decline of men breadwinners documented by Jensen and Jensen and Smith reflect the changing nature of the labor market as traditional industries that provided jobs for rural men disappear to be replaced by service sector jobs more characteristic of women's employment. Similarly, more rural families experience distress and marital dissolution, bringing divorce rates more in line with national figures (McLaughlin and Coleman, Snyder), presumably in part from the economic conditions that make it more difficult to find economic security (McCrate, Nelson). Predictable outcomes of family stress are exacerbated by the lack of other opportunities and family support services (Conger, Forry and Walker), as well as family values that prescribe rigid forms of masculinity and support patriarchal family structures and relations (Sherman).

The authors of these chapters have meticulously described numerous points of convergence and divergence that describe rural fortunes. In many cases, the differences are matters of degree rather than kind, but in combination with each other and the more limited opportunities and amenities generally available in rural places, they have a large impact. The result is that rural areas end up as sites described by what they lack: they lack jobs, investment, infrastructure, transportation, human and social capital, and the institutions and organizations that provide social support for human capital development.

Of course, many of these "lacks" represent larger structural conditions and don't reflect the attractions and the amenities of rural living that keep many of its residents in place and attract others to these areas. The population turnaround experienced by rural areas during the final third of the twentieth century demonstrates the pull of rural areas, especially since the source of rural population increase was and most likely will remain the result of net migration (Johnson and Cromartie 2006). Individuals and families make decisions to forgo urban services and opportunities for rural amenities and lifestyles, incidentally contributing to the convergence in rural and urban sociodemographic characteristics that is found in the research reported here.

Policy Dilemmas

The remedies for many of the problems created or exacerbated by economic restructuring are often obvious and recur in chapter after chapter in this volume—more jobs, better wages, more control over working conditions, affordable health care, child care, transportation, housing, and support for numerous other services and amenities. All seek to expand opportunities that have either diminished or never existed in rural areas. The policy dilemmas come from how and under what circumstances these can be made to happen. Whose responsibility is it to implement them? How can and should they be paid for? These and related questions create difficult issues for citizens and their representatives. Some of these require a national effort; others can be left to state and local jurisdictions. Most will require some level of government assistance and intervention rather than relying on market and volunteer mechanisms, and again, the levels and means by which these occur are the subject of political debate themselves.

This reality flies in the face of the political trends of the past several decades, which have promoted laissez-faire policies, state devolution, volunteer, and market solutions to social problems. Sometimes labeled the neoliberal agenda, these policies have directly affected rural areas' ability to provide services for their residents both in the lack of state assistance for depressed regions and in the forms of public assistance available as described by Tickamyer and Henderson, Parisi and colleagues, and others. The large-scale investments necessary to revitalize many rural places will require collective action and planning efforts at odds with recent government policies. This requirement may change with the change in administration and an associated political philosophy that supports large-scale government action, especially as an emergency remedy for what is widely acknowledged as the deepest economic crisis since the Great Depression. However, even during administrations where state investment and intervention are promoted, rural problems still tend to be ignored or considered peripheral. There have already been reports that rural areas with demonstrable need are disproportionately neglected in allocation of federal stimulus funds by state governments. Thus, it remains to be seen how new political philosophy, policies, and programs will play out in rural areas.

The need for new policy is evident from recent economic developments ranging from the housing and financial crises to unstable fuel prices, with numerous and complex implications for rural areas that often are not market responsive. To take just one example, energy needs demonstrate the many complexities for rural peoples and places. Transportation costs are a persistent problem for rural residents, as pointed out by numerous authors in this volume. This fact was especially obvious during the recent precipitous rise in fuel costs just prior to the recession, which exacerbated the problem and substantially contributed to it, especially for rural residents who often have to travel long distances to jobs and have little access to public transportation. At the same time, it created new incentives for the development of alternative fuel sources such as biofuels, wind power, "clean" coal technology, and oil shale development (ignoring for the moment the environmental and other costs these are sure to incur) and new political will to pursue these alternatives, which, in turn, provide new opportunities for rural economic development and jobs as well as their more direct role in addressing the energy crisis. The point, however, is that rural communities, families, and individuals are likely to be affected directly and indirectly in a multitude of complex ways that would benefit from serious policy analysis and ultimately policy interventions rather than the hope that some sort of market magic will sort through these issues or trickle down from programs designed for urban populations. If the accounts in this volume have any common underlying theme beyond the specific issues they tackle, it is that markets have failed rural America and its families and that deliberative social policy is a desirable corrective.

Historically, rural policy has centered on agriculture policy, food supply, and natural resource management (Brown and Swanson 2003; Browne 2001; Buttel et al. 1993). While many of these have important spillover effects both for rural populations and for the nation as a whole, they have relegated community and family issues to the margins (Bokemeier 2008). Thus, the latest "Farm Bill" (2008 Food, Conservation, and Energy Act, or FCEA), similar to its predecessors, provides support for the largest antipoverty measure in the country—food stamps and nutrition assistance programs. Given rural poverty rates, this is an important source of assistance for rural residents, but since it does not recognize special rural needs, including lower take-up rates, cannot claim to be a rural policy other than in its influence on commodity supply and prices. The FCEA also allocates large amounts of public funds to prop up a very small number of farmers and their families, but certainly not the majority of either farmers (already a tiny proportion of rural residents) or other rural populations. Other policies such as energy policies similarly affect segments of rural peoples and places, but are not targeted in any sort of holistic manner to rural families and their communities.

Yet other obstacles prevent the kind of collective action necessary to create effective rural development policy. The very heterogeneity of rural places geographically, economically, and socially, divisive demographic factors rooted in historic race and ethnic divisions, persistent poverty and lack of capital, and small population numbers diminish political effectiveness and contribute to the inability to create necessary policies and programs. Nevertheless, many of the policies that would benefit rural communities and families are the same as those that are important to every American regardless of location. A minimum wage pegged to cost of living, universal access to health care, and affordable child care are issues that rural America shares with the entire country. The needs are the same; what will vary is the way to implement them.

Policy Needs and Recommendations

With these complications in mind, it should be noted that most of the policies recommended by the authors of this volume fall into several broad categories:

1. Employment needs—stable jobs that pay a living wage with benefits and predictable or controllable schedules. In a society that bases its primary source of entitlement on employment, creating jobs and preparing individuals for jobs is a top priority. However, new and creative ways to make this happen have to be considered. Old methods of local jurisdictions competing to provide concessions and tax subsidies have done little but promote a "race to the bottom" and are increasingly costly and ineffective in an era of increasing global competition. Some opportunities lie in new technologies, especially energy and green technologies, as the perils of global warming and depletion of energy sources become widely accepted and incorporated into policy initiatives. Local amenity development has also provided jobs for rural residents, although these rarely match the compensation levels of those that leave. Nevertheless, a combination of aging populations and conservation efforts makes these potential growth areas.

2. Service/amenity needs—schools, health care, day care, transportation, recreation, social services, and affordable housing. Along with employment, these are the heart of the policies and programs that will make rural communities and families viable and sustainable. It will be necessary to find innovative

ways of funding and delivering these services to make rural areas viable places for raising families and for all generational needs, from human capital development to elder care. Among the possibilities already in practice in selected areas are partnering with urban areas, using new technologies, and providing greater flexibility and funding sources for local initiatives. For example, rural health care needs can be met by a combination of rural triage and routine care provision, along with partnering with urban hospitals and specialty services. However, such an approach requires much more than planning for medical services, but also transportation, training, communications, and so on. Other service needs will require similar policy innovation.

3. Investment needs—infrastructure for new information technologies, broadband Internet access, and public services that will assist in the support of new jobs and enterprises as described in point 1 and service/amenity provision as in point 2. Even in an era when the failure to maintain aging physical capital, let alone new investment, has gained increasing recognition and support for its reversal, the lagging condition of rural America goes largely unnoticed. The decision back in the New Deal to make rural electrification a universal public good is often cited as an important precedent for new infrastructure development such as universal broadband access. Nevertheless, there has been little political will to treat broadband access as a similar public utility, and new effort for this and related issues is necessary. At the same time, old infrastructure needs remain problematic. If anything, for rural places far from the interstate highway system, the needs are even more pressing. A decline in public transportation, including rail lines and buses that serve rural areas, makes them increasingly isolated. Support for rural transportation needs requires attention from policy makers.

Finally, in addition to policies targeted at rural places, policies that directly affect all distressed families, including rural residents, remain an important priority but need to be further targeted for specific populations. Thus, tax credits such as the Earned Income Tax Credit have a major role in assisting rural families, but greater efforts need to be made to make sure that rural families understand and make use of these programs. Rural residents often have lower take-up rates on policies and programs that could assist them, even when they are available.

Research and Data Needs

Good policy requires good data to supply the foundation for informed choices on conditions, needs, and preferences. An ongoing struggle for anyone concerned with rural conditions and realities is the difficulty in finding or creating adequate data about rural people and places. This difficulty begins with Census data and extends to much of the additional information available from both public and private sources. Obtaining small area estimates between decennial censuses for both research and application has always been a problem. With the substitution of the American Community Survey (ACS) for long-form Census data, detailed demographic data for many rural communities are not yet available, and rural analysts who turn to the Census for up-to-date information on rural communities are bound to be frustrated before the full rollout of ACS data. While the ACS will increase information on a variety of topics, the reduction in ACS sample size and the use of multiyear averages for small areas (five years for places smaller than twenty thousand persons) create serious problems for reliable and timely data on rural communities that have yet to be resolved (U.S. GAO 2004).

Census data are not the only problem. Surveys designed to study special issues and topics often do not have sufficient rural respondents to be useful, let alone generalizable to rural populations. Even in very large data-generating projects, rural issues are often overlooked, and it is a struggle to make sure they are incorporated into study design and methodology. For example, the National Children's Survey, a massive new federally sponsored longitudinal initiative to determine factors influencing health and well-being for a nationally representative birth cohort, initially had little interest in distinguishing rural and urban issues and outcomes. This neglect is more widespread than is often obvious. Initial reports that the mortgage foreclosure crisis was less severe in rural America have subsequently been corrected with the information that the original reporting system ignored many rural places.

In addition to data, there are perennial problems with the definition of rural that at least partly rest on data issues. Because of lack of data for small areas, the most commonly used proxy for rural and urban is the metro-nonmetro distinction. This shortcoming was augmented by a micropolitan category in the 2000 Census, but these still represent crude proxies for rural and urban areas. Besides introducing a great deal of noise in the designation of rural and urban places, they totally obfuscate differences within rural areas. Classifications of rural counties constructed by the USDA based on population density and proximity to metro locations or dominant economic activity provide useful ways of classifying rural counties, but these are county based and therefore require county geography to be of use, something that is not often available in national surveys.

These are not solely academic concerns or distinctions. Policy initiatives require having the data to know what the problem is and who will be served.

The recent example described above on housing foreclosure rates is a case in point. It turned out that the primary data source used focused on urban rates, grossly underrepresenting the extent of the problem in rural areas and skewing understanding of the geography and demography of the problem.

Conclusions

The studies in this book demonstrate a commitment to studying rural people and places both in comparison to urban environments and to understand variation within rural settings. Collectively, they illustrate the wide variety of ways that the lives of rural families have changed in response to long-term economic restructuring punctuated by numerous episodes of economic hardship. The purpose is to gain better understanding of how families have been affected by these changes and what can be done to assist them as they adapt to changing circumstances. Economic downturn and recession repeat episodically with all the anxieties and hardships they entail, but even more salient is that when recovery comes, the long-term trend of restructuring remains. Yet rural families and communities have demonstrated time and again their resilience and adaptability, and the accounts in this volume are no different. Gender roles change to accommodate changing economic opportunities. Men and women find new jobs when old ones disappear; they persist and survive even in the face of economic hardship and a safety net not designed to meet their needs. Children continue to grow and develop as their parents struggle to provide for their futures. We argue that there are few mysteries about what specific policies and programs can be of assistance; the general outlines are reasonably well known. The bigger issue is how to make them happen. The first step is to recognize the claims that rural families have on the nation and to find the political will to support their efforts to remain a part of the larger policy agenda.

References

Abramovitz, Mimi. 1988. *Regulating the Lives of Women: Social Welfare Policy from Colonial Times to the Present.* Boston: South End Press.

Ackerman, Brian P., Eleanor D. Brown, and Carroll E. Izard. 2004. "The Relations Between Persistent Poverty and Contextual Risk and Children's Behavior in Elementary School." *Developmental Psychology* 40:367–77.

Act. 2006. "Ready for College and Ready for Work: Same or Different?" http://www.act.org/research/policymakers/reports/workready.html.

Ahearn, Mary C., Janet E. Perry, and Hisham S. El-Osta. 1993. "The Economic Well-Being of Farm Operator Households, 1988–1990." USDA Economic Research Service.

Ajose, Lande, Casey MacGregor, Leo Yan, and Michael Pih. 2007. "Emergency Financial Aid for Community College Students: Implementation and Early Lessons from the Dreamkeepers and Angel Fund Programs." MDRC, New York.

Albrecht, Don E. 1998. "The Industrial Transformation of Farm Communities: Implications for Family Structure and Socioeconomic Conditions." *Rural Sociology* 63:51–64.

Albrecht, Don E., and Carol Mulford Albrecht. 2004. "Metro/Nonmetro Residence, Nonmarital Conception, and Conception Outcomes." *Rural Sociology* 69:430–52.

Albrecht, Don E., Carol Mulford Albrecht, and Stan L. Albrecht. 2000. "Poverty in Nonmetropolitan America: Impacts of Industrial, Employment, and Family Structure Variables." *Rural Sociology* 65 (1): 87–103.

Albrecht, Don E., Carol Albrecht, and Edward Murguia. 2005. "Minority Concentration, Disadvantage, and Inequality in the Nonmetropolitan United States." *Sociological Quarterly* 46:503–23.

Albrecht, Don E., and Stan L. Albrecht. 1997. "Changing Employment Patterns in Nonmetropolitan America: Implications for Family Structure." *Southern Rural Sociology* 12:43–59.

Alexander, Karl L., Doris R. Entwisle, Doris Cadigan, and Aaron Pallas. 1987. "Getting Ready for First Grade: Standards of Deportment in Home and School." *Social Forces* 66 (1): 57–85.

Alexander, Karl L., Doris R. Entwisle, and Maxine S. Thompson. 1987. "School Performance, Status Relations, and the Structure of Sentiment: Bringing the Teacher Back In." *American Sociological Review* 52:665–82.

Amato, Paul R., Alan Booth, David R. Johnson, and Stacey J. Rogers. 2007. *Along Together: How Marriage in America Is Changing.* Cambridge, Mass.: Harvard University Press.

American Federation of Workers and Congress of Industrial Organizations. 2004. "The Mississippi Jobs Crisis."

Ames, B. D., W. A. Brosi, and K. Damiano-Teixeira. 2006. "I'm Just Glad My Three Jobs Could Be During the Day: Women and Work in a Rural Community." *Family Relations* 55:119–31.

Anderson, Cynthia D., Michael D. Schulman, and Phillip J. Wood. 2001. "Globalization and Uncertainty: The Restructuring of Southern Textiles." *Social Problems* 48 (4): 478–98.

Anderson, Elijah. 1990. *Streetwise: Race, Class, and Change in an Urban Community.* Chicago: University of Chicago Press.

Angell, Robert C. 1936. *The Family Encounters the Depression.* New York: Charles Scribner's Sons.

Annie E. Casey Foundation. 2004. *City and Rural KIDS COUNT Data Book.* Baltimore: Annie E. Casey Foundation.

Appelbaum, Eileen. 2001. *Shared Work / Valued Care: New Norms for Organizing Market and Unpaid Care Work.* Washington, D.C.: Economic Policy Institute.

Arthur, John A. 1991. "Socioeconomic Predictors of Crime in Rural Georgia." *Criminal Justice Review* 16:29–41.

Astroth, Kirk A., and George W. Haynes. 2002. "More than Cows and Cooking: Newest Research Shows the Impact of 4-H." *Journal of Extension* 40. http://www.joe.org/joe/2002august/a6.php.

Atkinson, Alice M. 1994. "Rural and Urban Families' Use of Child Care." *Family Relations* 43:16–22.

Atkinson, Robert D. 2004. "Reversing Rural America's Economic Decline: The Case for a National Balanced Growth Strategy." Progressive Policy Institute, Washington, D.C.

Autor, David H., Lawrence F. Katz, and Melissa S. Kearney. 2006. "The Polarization of the U.S. Labor Market." *American Economic Review* 96:189–94.

Bailey, Sandy, and Billie Warford. 1995. "Delivering Servicing in Rural Areas: Using Child Care Resource-and-Referral Networks." *Young Children* 50:86–90.

Bainbridge, Jay, Marcia K. Meyers, and Jane Waldfogel. 2003. "Child Care Policy Reform and the Employment of Single Mothers." *Social Science Quarterly* 84 (4): 771.

Baker, David W., Joseph J. Sudano, Jeffrey M. Albert, Elaine A. Borawski, and Avi Dor. 2001. "Lack of Health Insurance and Decline in Overall Health in Late Middle Age." *New England Journal of Medicine* 345:1106–12.

Bane, Mary Jo. 1986. "Household Composition and Poverty." In *Fighting Poverty: What Works and What Doesn't,* edited by S. Danziger and D. H. Weinberg. Cambridge, Mass.: Harvard University Press.

Bane, Mary Jo, and David Ellwood. 1994. *Welfare Realities: From Rhetoric to Reform.* Cambridge, Mass.: Harvard University Press.

Barker, Kathleen, and Kathleen Christensen. 1998. *Contingent Work: American Employment Relations in Transition.* Ithaca, N.Y.: ILR Press.

Barkley, David L. 1995. "The Economics of Change in Rural America." *American Journal of Agricultural Economics* 77 (5): 1252–57.

Barnett, W. Steven, Dale J. Epstein, Allison H. Friedman, Judi Stevenson Boyd, and Jason T. Hustedt. 2008. "The State of Preschool, 2008." National Institute for Early Education Research, New Brunswick, N.J.

Barrett, Scott. 2007. "Proposal for a New Climate Change Treaty System." *Economists' Voice* 4 (3).

Beach, Betty A. 1997. "Perspectives on Rural Child Care." *ERIC Digest.*

Beale, Calvin, and John Cromartie. 2004. "The Defining Charactersitics of Regional Poverty." *Perspectives on Poverty, Policy, and Place* 2 (3): 3–5.

Beale, Calvin L., and Robert M. Gibbs. 2006. "Severity and Concentration of Persistent High Poverty in Nonmetro Areas." *Amber Waves* 3 (February): 21–27.

Beaulieu, Lionel J. 1999. "Improving Job Opportunities for Low Income People: The Hope of the Workforce Investment Act of 1998." Southern Rural Development Center, Mississippi State University.

———. 2000. "Rural Schools and the Workforce Investment Act." ERIC Clearinghouse on Rural Education and Small Schools. http://www.ericdigests.org/2001-3/rural.htm.

Beaulieu, Lionel J., Frank M. Howell, Domenico Parisi, and Lynn Reinschmeidt. 2000. "Access to Opportunities: Welfare to Work Challenges in a Rural Mississippi County." Southern Rural Development Center, Mississippi State University.

Beaulieu, Lionel J., and David Mulkey, eds. 1995. *Investing in People: The Human Capital Needs of Rural America*. Boulder, Colo.: Westview Press.

Becker, Howard S. 1964. *The Other Side*. New York: Free Press.

Beggs, John J., Wayne J. Villemez, and Ruth Arnold. 1997. "Black Population Concentration and Black-White Inequality: Expanding the Consideration of Place and Space Effects." *Social Forces* 76:65–91.

Bergmann, Barbara. 1996. *Saving Our Children from Poverty: What the United States Can Learn from France*. New York: Russell Sage Foundation.

Berkman, Lisa F., and Ichiro Kawachi. 2000. *Social Epidemiology*. New York: Oxford University Press.

Bernhardt, Annette, Laura Dresser, and Erin Hatton. 2003. "The Coffee Pot Wars: Unions and Firm Restructuring in the Hotel Industry." In *Low-Wage America: How Employers Are Reshaping Opportunity in the Workplace*, edited by Eileen Appelbaum, Annette D. Bernhardt, and Richard J. Murnane. New York: Russell Sage Foundation.

Bernstein, Jared, and Dean Baker. 2003. *The Benefits of Full Employment: When Markets Work for People*. Washington, D.C.: Economic Policy Institute.

Berry, E. Helen, Audrey M. Shillington, Terry Peak, and Melinda M. Hohman. 2000. "Multiethnic Comparison of Risk and Protective Factors for Adolescent Pregnancy." *Child and Adolescent Social Work Journal* 17 (2): 19–37.

Berube, Alan, and Thacher Tiffany. 2004. "The 'State' of Low-Wage Workers: How the EITC Benefits Urban and Rural Communities in the 50 States." Brookings Institution, Washington, D.C.

Bhandari, Shailesh. 2004. "People with Health Insurance: A Comparison of Estimates from Two Surveys." Survey of Income and Program Participation Report No. 243. U.S. Census Bureau, Washington, D.C.

Binkley, Marian. 2000. "'Getting by' in Tough Times: Coping with the Fisheries Crisis." *Women's Studies International Forum* 23 (3): 323–32.

Blank, Rebecca M. 2002. "Evaluating Welfare Reform in the United States." *Journal of Economic Literature* 40 (4): 1105–66.

Blank, Rebecca, and Heidi Shierholz. 2005. "Explaining Gender Differences in Employment and Wage Trends Among Less Skilled Workers." In *Working and Poor: How Economic and Policy Changes Are Affecting Low-Wage Workers*, edited by Rebecca M. Blank, Sheldon H. Danziger, and Robert F. Schoeni, 23–58. New York: Russell Sage Foundation.

Blau, David M. 2001. *The Child Care Problem: An Economic Analysis*. New York: Russell Sage Foundation.

Blau, David, and Erdal Tekin. 2003. "The Determinants and Consequences of Child Care Subsidies for Single Mothers." NBER Working Paper 9665.

Blau, Francine D. 1998. "Trends in the Well-Being of American Women, 1970–1995." *Journal of Economic Literature* 36:112–65.

Blau, Francine D., Marianne A. Ferber, and Ann E. Winkler. 2002. *The Economics of Women, Men, and Work*. Upper Saddle River, N.J.: Prentice-Hall.

Blau, Peter Michael, and Otis Dudley Duncan. 1967. *The American Occupational Structure*. New York: John Wiley and Sons.

Blinder, Alan S. 1973. "Wage Discrimination: Reduced Form and Structural Variables." *Journal of Human Resources* 8:436–55.

Bloomquist, Leonard E., Christina Gringeri, Donald Tomaskovic-Devey, and Cynthia Truelove. 1993. "Work Structures and Rural Poverty." In Rural Sociological Society Task Force on Persistent Rural Poverty.

Bluestone, Barry, and Bennett Harrison. 1982. *The Deindustrialization of America: Plant Closings, Community Abandonment, and the Dismantling of Basic Industry.* New York: Basic Books.

Bokemeier, Janet. 2008. "How the New Farm Bill Affects Families." Paper presented at the Annual Meeting of the Rural Sociological Society, July 28–31, Manchester, N.H.

Bokemeier, Janet L., and Lorraine E. Garkovich. 1991. "Meeting Rural Family Needs." In Flora and Christenson 1991, 114–27.

Bolger, Kerry E., Charlotte J. Patterson, William W. Thompson, and Janis B. Kupersmidt. 1995. "Psychosocial Adjustment Among Children Experiencing Persistent and Intermittent Family Economic Hardship." *Child Development* 66:1107–29.

Boraas, Stephanie, and William M. Rodgers III. 2003. "How Does Gender Play a Role in the Earnings Gap? An Update." *Monthly Labor Review* (March): 9–15.

Bornstein, Marc H., and Robert H. Bradley, eds. 2003. *Socioeconomic Status, Parenting, and Child Development.* Mahwah, N.J.: Lawrence Erlbaum.

Bourgois, Philippe. 1995. *In Search of Respect: Selling Crack in El Barrio.* Cambridge: Cambridge University Press.

Bradley, Robert H., and Robert F. Corwyn. 2002. "Socioeconomic Status and Child Development." *Annual Review of Psychology* 53:371–99.

———. 2003. "Age and Ethnic Variations in Family Process Mediators of SES." In Bornstein and Bradley 2003, 161–88.

Bramlett, Matthew D., and William D. Mosher. 2002. "Cohabitation, Marriage, Divorce, and Remarriage in the United States." *Vital and Health Statistics* 23 (22): 1–93.

Brand, Betsy, Glenda Partee, Barbara Kaufmann, and Joan Wills. 2000. "Looking Forward: School-to-Work Principles and Strategies for Sustainability." American Youth Policy Forum, Center for Workforce Development, and Institute for Educational Leadership, Washington, D.C.

Braun, Bonnie, Frances Lawrence, Patricia Dyk, and Maria Vandergriff-Avery. 2002. "Southern Rural Family Economic Well-Being in the Context of Public Assistance." *Southern Rural Sociology* 18 (1): 259–93.

Brody, Gene H., Velma McBride Murray, Sooyeon Kim, and Anita C. Brown. 2002. "Longitudinal Pathways to Competence and Psychological Adjustment Among African American Children Living in Rural Single-Parent Households." *Child Development* 73:1505–16.

Brooks, Fred, Ed Reisler, Claire Hamilton, and Larry Nackerud. 2002. "Impacts of Child Care Subsidies on Family and Child Well-Being." *Early Childhood Research Quarterly* 17 (4): 498–511.

Brown, Adell, Ralph D. Christy, and Tesfa G. Gebremedhin. 1994. "Structural Changes in U.S. Agriculture: Implications for African American Farmers." *Review of Black Political Economics* 22 (4): 51–72.

Brown, David L. 1981. "A Quarter Century of Trends and Changes in the Demographic Structure of American Families." In Coward and Smith 1981, 9–25.

Brown, David L., Nina Glasgow, László Kulcsár, Benjamin C. Bolender, and Marie-Joy Arguillas. 2008. *Rural Retirement Migration.* Dordrecht: Springer.

Brown, David L., and William A. Kandel. 2006. "Rural America Through a Demographic Lens." In Kandel and Brown 2006, 3–25.

Brown, David L., and Louis E. Swanson. 2003. *Challenges for Rural America in the Twenty-First Century.* University Park: Pennsylvania State University Press.

Brown, David L., and Mildred E. Warner. 1991. "Persistent Low-Income Nonmetropolitan Areas in the United States." *Policy Studies Journal* 19:22–41.

Brown, J. Brian, and Daniel T. Lichter. 2004. "Poverty, Welfare, and the Livelihood Strategies of Nonmetropolitan Single Mothers." *Rural Sociology* 69:382–401.

Brown, Susan L., and Anastasia R. Snyder. 2006. "Residential Differences in Cohabitors' Union Transitions." *Rural Sociology* 71:311–34.

Brown, William P. 2001. *The Failure of National Rural Policy: Institutions and Interests.* Washington, D.C.: Georgetown University Press.

Bryant, Chalandra M., and Rand D. Conger. 2002. "An Intergenerational Model of Romantic Relationship Development." In *Stability and Change in Relationships,* edited by Anita L. Vangelisti, Harry T. Reis, and Mary Anne Fitzpatrick, 57–82. Cambridge: Cambridge University Press.

Budig, Michelle J., and Paula England. 2001. "The Wage Penalty for Motherhood." *American Sociological Review* 66:204–25.

Burchinal, Margaret R., Joanne E. Roberts, Laura A. Nabors, and Donna M. Bryant. 1996. "Quality of Center Child Care and Infant Cognitive and Language Development." *Child Development* 67:606–20.

Burchinal, Margaret R., Joanne E. Roberts, Rhodus Riggins Jr., Susan A. Zeisel, Eloise Neebe, and Donna Bryant. 2000. "Relating Quality of Center-Based Child Care to Early Cognitive and Language Development Longitudinally." *Child Development* 71:339–57.

———. 2009. "Developments in Federal and State Child and Dependent Care Tax Provisions in 2008." National Women's Law Center, Memorandum, April 7. National Women's Law Center, Washington, D.C.

Bureau of Labor Statistics. 2003. "Household Data Series from the Monthly A-Table." http://www.bls.gov/cps/cpsatabs.htm.

———. 2004. "A Profile of the Working Poor, 2002." Report 976, September. U.S. Department of Labor, Washington, D.C. http://www.bls.gov/cps/cpswp2002.pdf.

———. 2009. "The Employment Situation—October 2009." News Release, November 6. USDL-09-1331. U.S. Department of Labor, Washington, D.C. http://www.bls.gov/news.release/archives/empsit_11062009.pdf.

———. 2010. "The Employment Situation—August 2010." News Release, September 3. USDL-10-1212. U.S. Department of Labor, Washington, D.C. http://www.bls.gov/news.release/pdf/empsit.pdf.

Bursik, Robert J., Jr. 1988. "Social Disorganization and Theory of Crime and Delinquency: Problems and Prospects." *Criminology* 26 (4): 519–51.

Burstein, Nancy R. 2007. "Economic Influences on Marriage and Divorce." *Journal of Policy Analysis and Management* 26 (2): 387–429.

Burton, Linda M. 2007. "Childhood Adultification in Economically Disadvantaged Families: A Conceptual Model." *Family Relations* 56 (October 4): 329–45.

Buttel, Frederick H., William P. Browne, Susan Christopherson, Donald Davis, Philip Ehrenshaft, David Freshwater, John Gaventa, and Philip McMichael. 1993. "The State, Rural Policy, and Rural Poverty." In Rural Sociological Society Task Force on Persistent Rural Poverty, *Persistent Poverty in Rural America,* 292–326.

Call, Kathleen T., and Jeylan T. Mortimer. 2001. *Arenas of Comfort in Adolescence: A Study of Adjustment in Context.* Mahwah, N.J.: Lawrence Erlbaum.

Campbell, Nancy Duff, Joan Entmacher, Amy K. Matsui, Cristina Martin Firvida, and Christie Love. 2006. "Making Care Less Taxing: Improving State Child and Dependent Care Tax Provisions." National Women's Law Center, Washington, D.C.

Campbell, Nancy D., Amy K. Matsui, and Arlene Brens. 2009. "Developments in Federal and State Child and Dependent Care Tax Provisions in 2008." National Women's Law Center, Memorandum, April 7. National Women's Law Center, Washington, D.C.

Cancian, Maria, and Deborah Reed. 2000. "Changes in Family Structure: Implications for Poverty and Related Policy." *Focus* 21:21–26.

Caputo, Richard K. 2006. "The Earned Income Tax Credit: A Study of Eligible Participants vs. Non-Participants." *Journal of Sociology and Social Welfare* 33 (1): 9–29.

Carroll, Matthew. 1995. *Community and the Northwestern Logger: Continuities and Changes in the Era of the Spotted Owl.* Boulder, Colo.: Westview Press.

Casper, Lynne M., and Suzanne M. Bianchi. 2002. *Continuity and Change in the American Family.* Thousand Oaks, Calif.: Sage.

Catalano, Richard F., M. Lisa Berglund, Jean A. M. Ryan, Heather S. Lonczak, and J. David Hawkins. 2004. "Positive Youth Development in the United States: Research Findings on Evaluations of Positive Youth Development Programs." *Annals of the American Academy of Political and Social Science* 591:98–124.

Cavan, Ruth S., and Katherine H. Ranck. 1938. *The Family and the Depression: A Study of One Hundred Chicago Families.* Chicago: University of Chicago Press.

Center for Law and Social Policy (CLASP). 2001. "Frequently Asked Questions About Working Welfare Leavers." CLASP, Washington, D.C.

Chao, Elaine L. 2006. Remarks Delivered by U.S. Secretary of Labor Elaine L. Chao, Workforce Innovations 2006 Opening Plenary, Anaheim, California, Tuesday, July 11. http://elainelchao.com/index.php/speeches-2006/workforce-innovations-2006.html.

Chaudry, Ajay. 2004. *Putting Children First: How Low-Wage Working Mothers Manage Child Care.* New York: Russell Sage Foundation.

Cherlin, Andrew. 1992. *Marriage, Divorce, and Remarriage.* Cambridge, Mass.: Harvard University Press.

———. 2004. "The Deinstitutionalization of American Marriage." *Journal of Marriage and Family* 66:848–61.

———. 2009. *The Marriage-Go-Round: The State of Marriage and the Family in America Today.* New York: Alfred A. Knopf.

The Child Care Partnership Project. n.d. "Rural Partnership Profiles." Retrieved July 3, 2007. Available from http://www.nccic.org/ccpartnerships/profiles/rural.html.

Churilla, Allison. 2006. "Low-Income Families in New Hampshire." Carsey Institute Issue Brief No. 3. Carsey Institute, Durham, N.H.

Clarkberg, Martin. 1999. "The Price of Partnering: The Role of Economic Well-Being in Young Adults' First Union Experiences." *Social Forces* 77:945–68.

Clarke-Stewart, K. Alison, Deborah Lowe Vandell, Margaret Burchinal, Marion O'Brien, and Kathleen McCartney. 2002. "Do Regulable Features of Child-Care Homes Affect Children's Development?" *Early Childhood Research Quarterly* 17 (1): 52.

Clogg, Clifford C. 1979. *Measuring Underemployment: Demographic Indicators for the United States.* New York: Academic Press.

Clogg, Clifford C., and Teresa A. Sullivan. 1983. "Demographic Composition of Underemployment Trends, 1969–1980." *Social Indicators Research* 12:117–52.

Coburn, Andrew F., A. Clinton MacKinney, Timothy D. McBride, Keith J. Mueller, Rebecca T. Slifkin, and Mary K. Wakefield. 2007. *Choosing Rural Definitions: Implications for Health Policy.* Rural Policy Research Institute Issue Brief #2 (March). Rural Policy Research Institute, Columbia, Mo.

Cochi Ficano, Carlena K. 2006. "Child Care Market Mechanisms: Does Policy Affect the Quantity of Care?" *Social Service Review* 80 (3): 453–84.

Coconino Rural Environment Corps. 2007. "About CREC." http://www.crecweb.org/about.

Cohany, Sharon R., and Emily Sok. 2007. "Trends in Labor Force Participation of Married Mothers of Infants." *Monthly Labor Review* 130 (2): 9–16.

Cohen, Philip N., and Suzanne M. Bianchi. 1999. "Marriage, Children, and Women's Employment: What Do We Know?" *Monthly Labor Review* 122 (12): 22–31.

Colker, Laura J., and Sarah Dewees. 2000. "Child Care for Welfare Participants in Rural

Areas." Rural Welfare Issue Brief. Administration on Children and Families, U.S. Department of Health and Human Services, Washington, D.C.

Collins, Sara R., Cathy Schoen, Diane Colasanto, and Deirdre A. Downey. 2003. "On the Edge: Low-Wage Workers and Their Health Insurance Coverage." Issue Brief. Commonwealth Fund, New York.

Collins, Sara R., Chapin White, and Jennifer L. Kriss. 2007. "Whither Employer-Based Health Insurance? The Current and Future Role of U.S. Companies in the Provision and Financing of Health Insurance." Issue Brief. Commonwealth Fund, New York.

Collins, Timothy. 1999. "Attracting and Retaining Teachers in Rural Areas." *ERIC Digest.* ERIC Clearinghouse on Rural Education and Small Schools, Charleston, W.V.

Condron, Dennis J., and Vincent J. Roscigno. 2003. "Disparities Within: Unequal Spending and Achievement in an Urban School District." *Sociology of Education* 76:18–36.

Conger, Katherine J., Chalandra M. Bryant, and Jennifer M. Brennom. 2004. "The Changing Nature of Adolescent Sibling Relationships: A Theoretical Framework for Evaluating the Role of Relationship Quality." In Conger, Lorenz, and Wickrama 2004, 319–44. Mahwah, N.J.: Lawrence Erlbaum.

Conger, Katherine J., Rand D. Conger, and Glen H. Elder Jr. 1994. "Sibling Relations During Hard Times." In Conger and Elder 1994a, 235–54.

Conger, Katherine J., Rand D. Conger, and Laura V. Scaramella. 1997. "Psychological Control and Adolescent Adjustment." *Journal of Adolescent Research* 12 (1): 113–38.

Conger, Katherine J., Monica J. Martin, Ben T. Reeb, Wendy M. Little, Jessica L. Craine Barbara Shebloski, and Rand D. Conger. 2011. "Economic Hardship and Its Consequences Across Generations." In *Oxford Handbook of Child Development and Poverty,* edited by Valerie Maholmes and Rosalind B. King. Oxford: Oxford University Press.

Conger, Katherine J., Martha A. Rueter, and Rand D. Conger. 2000. "The Role of Economic Pressure in the Lives of Parents and Their Adolescents: The Family Stress Model." In *Negotiating Adolescence in Times of Social Change,* edited by Lisa J. Crockett and Rainer K. Silbereisen, 201–23. Cambridge: Cambridge University Press.

Conger, Katherine J., Barbara Shebloski, Vivian T. M. Wong, and Wendy M. Little. 2008. "Perceptions of Sibling Support and Adolescent Adjustment." Manuscript in preparation.

Conger, Katherine J., Shannon T. Williams, Wendy M. Little, Katherine E. Masyn, and Barbara Shebloski. 2009. "Development of Adolescent Mastery: The Role of Family Problem Solving." *Journal of Health and Social Behavior* 50 (1): 99–114.

Conger, Rand D. 1995. "Unemployment." In *Encyclopedia of Marriage and the Family,* edited by David Levinson. New York: Macmillan.

———. 1997. "The Special Nature of Rural America." In *Rural Substance Abuse: State of Knowledge and Issues,* edited by Elizabeth B. Robertson, Zili Sloboda, Gayle M. Boyd, Lula Beatty, and Nicholas J. Kozel, 37–52. NIDA Research Monograph 168. National Institute on Drug Abuse, Rockville, Md.

Conger, Rand D., and Katherine J. Conger. 1996. "Sibling Relationships." In *Understanding Differences Between Divorced and Intact Families,* edited by Ronald L. Simons, 104–21. Thousand Oaks, Calif.: Sage.

———. 2002. "Resilience in Midwestern Families: Selected Findings from the First Decade of a Prospective, Longitudinal Study." *Journal of Marriage and Family* 64:361–73.

Conger, Rand D., Katherine J. Conger, Glen H. Elder Jr., Frederick O. Lorenz, Ronald L. Simons, and Leslie B. Whitbeck. 1992. "A Family Process Model of Economic Hardship and Adjustment of Early Adolescent Boys." *Child Development* 63:526–41.

———. 1993. "Family Economic Stress and Adjustment of Early Adolescent Girls." *Developmental Psychology* 29:206–19.

Conger, Rand D., Katherine J. Conger, and Monica J. Martin. 2010. "Socioeconomic Status, Family Processes, and Individual Development." *Journal of Marriage and Family* 72 (3): 685–704.

Conger, Rand D., and Shannon J. Dogan. 2007. "Social Class and Socialization in Families." In *Handbook of Socialization,* edited by Joan E. Grusec and Paul D. Hastings, 433–60. New York: Guilford Press.

Conger, Rand D., and M. Brent Donnellan. 2007. "An Interactionist Perspective on the Socioeconomic Context of Human Development." *Annual Review of Psychology* 58:175–99.

Conger, Rand D., and Glen H. Elder Jr., eds. 1994a. *Families in Troubled Times: Adapting to Change in Rural America.* Hawthorne, N.Y.: Aldine de Gruyter.

———. 1994b. "Families in Troubled Times: The Iowa Youth and Families Project." In Conger and Elder 1994a, 3–20.

Conger, Rand D., Xiaojia Ge, Glen H. Elder Jr., Frederick O. Lorenz, and Ronald L. Simons. 1994. "Economic Stress, Coercive Family Process, and Developmental Problems of Adolescents." *Child Development* 65:541–61.

Conger, Rand D., Frederick O. Lorenz, and K. A. S. Wickrama. 2004. *Continuity and Change in Family Relations: Theory, Methods and Empirical Findings.* Mahwah, N.J.: Lawrence Erlbaum.

Conger, Rand D., Martha A. Rueter, and Glen H. Elder Jr. 1999. "Couple Resilience to Economic Pressure." *Journal of Personality and Social Psychology* 76:54–71.

Conger, Rand D., Lara E. Wallace, Yumei Sun, Ronald L. Simons, Vonnie C. McLoyd, and Gene H. Brody. 2002. "Economic Pressure in African American Families: A Replication and Extension of the Family Stress Model." *Developmental Psychology* 38:179–93.

Connell, R. W. 1995. *Masculinities.* Berkeley: University of California Press.

Coontz, Stephanie, and Nancy Folbre. 2002. "A Discussion Paper from the Council on Contemporary Families." Paper read at Fifth Annual CCF Conference of Marriage, Poverty, and Public Policy, April 26–28.

Cornell Cooperative Extension (CES). n.d. "Children in My Care." Cornell University, Ithaca, N.Y.

Cosby, Arthur G., Tonya T. Neaves, Ronald E. Cossman, Jeralynn S. Cossman, Wesley L. James, Neal Feierabend, David M. Mirvis, Carol A. Jones, and Tracey Farrigan. 2008. "Preliminary Evidence for an Emerging Nonmetropolitan Mortality Penalty in the United States." *American Journal of Public Health* 98:1470–72.

Cossman, Ronald E., Jeralynn S. Cossman, Arthur G. Cosby, and Rebal M. Reavis. 2008. "Reconsidering the Rural–Urban Continuum in Rural Health Research: A Test of Stable Relationships Using Mortality as a Health Measure." *Population Research and Policy Review* 27 (4): 459–76.

Cost, Quality, and Child Outcomes Study Team. 1995. "Cost, Quality, and Child Outcomes in Child Care Centers." Department of Economics, University of Colorado at Denver.

Cotter, David A., JoAnn DeFiore, Joan M. Hermsen, Brenda Marstellar Kowalewski, and Reeve Vanneman. 1996. "Gender Inequality in Nonmetropolitan and Metropolitan Areas." *Rural Sociology* 61:272–88.

Cotter, David A., Joan M. Hermsen, and Reeve Vanneman. 2004. "Gender Inequality at Work." In Farley and Haaga 2004, 107–38.

Cottle, Thomas J. 2001. *Hardest Times: The Trauma of Long-Term Unemployment.* Westport, Conn.: Praeger.

Coward, Raymond T., and William W. Smith Jr., eds. 1981. *The Family in Rural Society.* Boulder, Colo.: Westview Press.

———. 1982. "Families in Rural Society." In *Rural Society in the U.S.: Issues for the 1980s,* edited by Don A. Dillman and Daryl J. Hobbs, 77–84. Boulder, Colo.: Westview Press.

Cronk, Christine, and Paul D. Sarvela. 1997. "Alcohol, Tobacco, and Other Drug Use Among Rural and Urban Youth." *American Journal of Public Health* 87:760–64.

Crowley, Martha, and Daniel T. Lichter. 2009. "Social Disorganization in New Latino Destinations?" *Rural Sociology* 74 (4): 573–604.

Crowley, Martha, Daniel T. Lichter, and Zhenchao Qian. 2006. "Beyond Gateway Cities: Economic Restructuring and Poverty Among Mexican Immigrant Families and Children." *Family Relations* 55:345–60.

Curran, Laura, and Laura S. Abrams. 2000. "Making Men into Dads: Fatherhood, the State, and Welfare Reform." *Gender and Society* 14 (5): 662–78.

Dalton, Graham, John Bryden, Mark Shucksmith, and Ken Thompson. 2003. *European Rural Policy at the Crossroads*. Aberdeen: Arkelton Institute.

Daniel, Jessica H., Robert L. Hampton, and Eli H. Newberger. 1983. "Child Abuse and Accidents in Black Families: A Controlled Comparative Study." *American Journal of Orthopsychiatry* 53:645–53.

Daniels, Steven E., and Joan M. Brehm. 2003. "Fur, Fins, and Feathers: Whose Home Is It Anyway?" In Brown and Swanson 2003, 329–39.

Daniels, Steven E., Corrine L. Gobeli, and Angela J. Findley. 2000. "Reemployment Programs for Dislocated Timber Workers: Lessons from Oregon." *Society and Natural Resources* 13:135–50.

Danks, Cecilia. 2000. "Community Forestry Initiatives for the Creation of Sustainable Rural Livelihoods: A Case from North America." *Unasylva* 51 (3): 53–63.

Davanzo, Julie, and M. Omar Rahman. 1993. "American Families—Trends and Correlates." *Population Index* 59:350–86.

Davidson, Osha Gray. 1990. *Broken Heartland: The Rise of America's Rural Ghetto*. New York: Free Press.

Davis, Dona L. 1993. "When Men Become 'Women': Gender Antagonism and the Changing Sexual Geography of Work in Newfoundland." *Sex Roles* 29:457–75.

———. 2000. "Gendered Cultures of Conflict and Discontent: Living The Crisis in a Newfoundland Community." *Women's Studies International Forum* 23 (3): 343–53.

Davis, Elizabeth E., and Stacie A. Bosley. 2007. "The Impact of the 1990's Economic Boom on Less Educated Workers in Rural America." *Community Development* 38 (1): 59–73.

Davis, Elizabeth E., Deana Grobe, and Roberta B. Weber. 2007. "Participation and Employment Dynamics of Child Care Subsidy Users in Rural and Urban Oregon." Rural Poverty Research Center Working Paper 07-01. Rural Poverty Research Center, Columbia, Mo.

Davis, Elizabeth E., and Roberta B. Weber. 2001. "The Dynamics of Child Care Subsidy Use by Rural Families in Oregon." *American Journal of Agricultural Economics* 83 (5): 1293–1301.

Dearing, Eric, Kathleen McCartney, and Beck A. Taylor. 2001. "Change in Family Income-to-Needs Matters More for Children with Less." *Child Development* 72:1779–93.

DeHaan, Laura, and James Deal. 2001. "Effects of Economic Hardship on Rural Children and Adolescents." In Moore 2001, 42–56.

DeMarco, Allison. 2008. "A Qualitative Look at Child Care Selection Among Welfare-to-Work Participants." *Journal of Children and Poverty* 14:119–38.

DeNavas-Walt, Carmen, Bernadette D. Proctor, and Jessica C. Smith. 2007. "Income, Poverty, and Health Insurance Coverage in the United States." U.S. Census Bureau, Current Population Reports, P60-233.

Department of Social and Rehabilitation Services, Agency of Human Services, State of Vermont. 2000. "Vermont Child Care: A Study of Wages, Credentials, Benefits and Market Rates, July 2000." Prepared by Mills and Pardee, Inc., for Child Care Services Division, Waterbury, Vt.

Dewees, Sarah, Linda Lobao, and Louis E. Swanson. 2003. "Local Economic Development in an Age of Devolution: The Question of Rural Localities." *Rural Sociology* 68 (2): 182–206.

Dodson, Lisa, and Jillian Dickert. 2004. "Girls' Family Labor in Low-Income Households: A Decade of Qualitative Research." *Journal of Marriage and the Family* 66 (May): 318–32.

Donato, Katharine M., Melissa Stainbeck, and Carl L. Bankston. 2005. "The Economic Incorporation of Mexican Immigrants in Southern Louisiana: A Tale of Two Cities." In Zuñíga and Hernández-León 2005, 76–100.

Donnermeyer, Joseph F. 1992. "The Use of Alcohol, Marijuana, and Hard Drugs by Rural Adolescents: A Review of Recent Research." In Edwards 1992, 31–76.

Dryfoos, Joy G., and Sue Maguire. 2002. *Inside Full-Service Schools.* Thousand Oaks, Calif.: Corwin Press.

Duncan, Cynthia M., ed. 1992. *Rural Poverty in America.* New York: Auburn House.

———. 1999. *Worlds Apart: Why Poverty Persists in Rural America.* New Haven: Yale University Press.

Duncan, Greg J., and Jeanne Brooks-Gunn. 1997. "Income Effects Across the Life Span: Integration and Interpretation." In *Consequences of Growing up Poor,* edited by Greg J. Duncan and Jeanne Brooks-Gunn, 596–610. New York: Russell Sage Foundation.

Duncan, Greg J., and Katherine A. Magnuson. 2003. "Off with Hollingshead: Socioeconomic Resources, Parenting, and Child Development." In Bornstein and Bradley 2003, 83–106.

Duncan, R. Paul, Karen Seccombe, and Cheryl Amey. 1995. "Changes in Health Insurance Coverage Within Rural and Urban Environments, 1977–1987." *Journal of Rural Health* 11 (3): 169–76.

Edelman, Peter, Harry J. Holzer, and Paul Offner. 2006. *Reconnecting Disadvantaged Young Men.* Washington, D.C.: Urban Institute Press.

Edin, Kathryn. 2000. "What Do Low-Income Single Mothers Say About Marriage?" *Social Problems* 47:112–33.

Edin, Kathryn, and Laura Lein. 1997. *Making Ends Meet: How Single Mothers Survive Welfare and Low-Wage Work.* New York: Russell Sage Foundation.

Edwards, Ruth A., ed. 1992. *Drug Use in Rural American Communities.* New York: Harrington Park Press.

Eggebeen, David J., and Daniel T. Lichter. 1991. "Race, Family Structure, and Changing Poverty Among American Children." *American Sociological Review* 56:801–17.

Ehrle, Jennifer, Gina Adams, and Kathryn Tout. 2001. "Who's Caring for Our Youngest Children? Child Care Patterns of Infants and Toddlers." Urban Institute Occasional Paper 42. Urban Institute, Washington, D.C.

Elder, Glen H., Jr. 1974. *Children of the Great Depression: Social Change in Life Experience.* Chicago: University of Chicago Press.

———. 1994. "Time, Human Agency, and Social Change: Perspectives on the Life Course." *Social Psychology Quarterly* 57 (1): 4–15.

Elder, Glen H., Jr. and Avshalom Caspi. 1988. "Economic Stress in Lives: Developmental Perspectives." *Journal of Social Issues* 44:25–45.

Elder, Glen H., Jr., Jacquelynne S. Eccles, Monika Ardelt, and Sarah Lord. 1995. "Inner City Parents Under Economic Pressure: Perspectives on the Strategies of Parenting." *Journal of Marriage and the Family* 57:771–84.

Elder, Glen H., Jr., Elizabeth B. Robertson, and Monika Ardelt. 1994. "Familes Under Economic Pressure." In Conger and Elder 1994a, 79–104.

Elder, Glen H., Jr., Elizabeth B. Robertson, and Michael Foster. 1994. "Survival, Loss, and Adaptation: A Perspective on Farm Families." In Conger and Elder 1994a, 105–26.

England, Lynn, and Ralph B. Brown. 2003. "Community and Resource Extraction in Rural America." In Brown and Swanson 2003, 317–28.

Evans, Gary W., and Kimberly English. 2002. "The Environment of Poverty: Multiple Stressor Exposure, Psychophysiological Stress, and Socioemotional Adjustment." *Child Development* 73:1238–48.

Fairlie, Robert W. 2005. "An Extension of the Blinder-Oaxaca Decomposition Technique to Logit and Probit Models." *Journal of Economic and Social Measurement* 30:305–16.

Falk, William, and Linda Lobao. 2003. "Who Benefits from Economic Restructuring? Lessons from the Past, Challenges for the Future." In Brown and Swanson 2003, 152–65.

Falk, William W., and Thomas A. Lyson. 1988. *High Tech, Low Tech, No Tech: Recent Occupational and Industrial Changes in the South.* Albany: State University of New York Press.

———. 1991. "Rural America in the Industrial Policy Debate." In Flora and Christenson 1991, 8–21.

Falk, William W., Michael Schulman, and Ann Tickamyer. 2003. *Communities of Work: Rural Restructuring in Local and Global Contexts.* Athens: Ohio University Press.

Falk, William W., Clarence R. Talley, and Bruce H. Rankin. 1993. "Life in the Forgotten South: The Black Belt." In *Forgotten Places: Uneven Development and the Loss of Opportunity in Rural America,* edited by Thomas A. Lyson and William W. Falk, 53–75. Lawrence: University Press of Kansas.

Farley, Reynolds, and John Haaga, eds. 2004. *The American People: Census 2000.* New York: Russell Sage Foundation.

Fernández-Kelly, M. Patricia, and Richard Schauffler. 2004. "Divided Fates: Immigrant Children in a Restructured Economy." In *Race, Ethnicity, and Gender, Selected Readings,* edited by Joseph F. Healey and Eileen T. O'Brien, 55–75. Thousand Oaks, Calif.: Pine Forge Press.

Feyen, Carol K. 2001. "Isolated Acts: Domestic Violence in a Rural Community." In Moore 2001, 101–27.

Findeis, Jill L., and Leif Jensen. 1998. "Employment Opportunities in Rural Areas: Implications for Poverty in a Changing Policy Environment." *American Journal of Agricultural Economics* 80:1000–1007.

Fisher, Monica G. 2005. "On the Empirical Finding of a Higher Risk of Poverty in Rural Areas: Is Rural Residence Endogenous to Poverty?" *Journal of Agricultural and Resource Economics* 30:185–99.

Fisher, Monica, and Bruce A. Weber. 2002. "The Importance of Place in Welfare Reform: Common Challenges for Central Cities and Remote Rural Areas." Brookings Institution Center on Urban and Metropolitan Policy and Rural Policy Research Institute Research Brief 1. Brookings Institution, Washington, D.C.

Fitchen, Janet. 1981. *Rural Poverty in America: A Case Study.* Boulder, Colo.: Westview Press.

———. 1991. *Endangered Spaces, Endangered Places: Change, Identity, and Survival in Rural America.* Boulder, Colo.: Westview Press.

———. 1991. "Homelessness in Rural Places: Perspectives from Upstate New York." *Urban Anthropology* 20 (2): 177–210.

Flora, Cornelia B., and James A. Christenson, eds. 1991. *Rural Policies for the 1990s.* Boulder, Colo.: Westview Press.

Flora, Cornelia B., and Jan L. Flora. 1993. "Entrepreneurial Social Infrastructure: A Necessary Ingredient." *Annals of the American Academy of Political and Social Science* 529:48–58.

Folbre, Nancy. 1994. *Who Pays for the Kids? Gender and the Structures of Constraint.* New York: Routledge.

Fomby, Paula, and Andrew J. Cherlin. 2007. "Family Instability and Child Well-Being." *American Sociological Review* 72 (April): 181–204.

Forry, Nicole D. 2007. "The Impact of Child Care Subsidies on Child Care Problems, Child Care–Related Work Disruptions, and Mothers' Desire to Switch Care." Ph.D. diss., University of Maryland, College Park.

Forry, Nicole D., and Elaine A. Anderson. 2006. "The Child and Dependent Care Tax Credit: A Policy Analysis." *Marriage and Family Review* 39:159–76.

Fraser, Nancy. 1990. "Struggle over Needs: Outline of a Socialist-Feminist Critical Theory of Late-Capitalist Political Culture." In *Women, the State, and Welfare,* edited by Linda Gordon, 199–225. Madison: University of Wisconsin Press.

Freedman, Audrey. 1985. "The New Look in Wage Policy and Employee Relations." Conference Board Report 865. Conference Board, New York.

Freudenberg, William R. 1986. "The Density of Acquaintenceship: An Overlooked Variable in Community Research." *American Journal of Sociology* 92 (1): 27–63.

Fuguitt, Glen V., David L. Brown, and Calvin L. Beale. 1989. *Rural and Small Town America.* New York: Russell Sage Foundation.

Fuller, Bruce, Sharon L. Kagan, Gretchen L. Caspary, and Christiane A. Gauthier. 2002. "Welfare Reform and Child Care Options for Low-Income Families." *Future of Children* 12 (1): 97–119.

Furstenberg, Frank F., and Mary Elizabeth Hughes. 1997. "The Influence of Neighborhoods on Children's Development: A Theoretical Perspective and a Research Agenda." In *Neighborhood Poverty: Policy Implications in Studying Neighborhoods,* vol. 2, edited by Jeanne Brooks-Gunn, Greg J. Duncan, and J. Lawrence Aber, 23–48. New York: Russell Sage Foundation.

Galinsky, Ellen, Carolee Howes, Susan Kontos, and Marybeth Shinn. 1994. "The Study of Children in Family Care and Relative Care: Highlights of Findings." Families and Work Institute, New York.

Garces, Eliana, Thomas Duncan, and Janet Curie. 2002. "Longer Term Effects of Head Start." *American Economic Review* 92:999–1012.

Garner, Jennifer. 1995. "Worker Displacement: A Decade of Change." *Monthly Labor Review* 118 (4): 45–57.

Gennetian, Lisa A., Danielle A. Crosby, Aletha C. Huston, and Edward D. Lowe. 2002. "How Welfare and Work Policies for Parents Affect Adolescents: A Synthesis of Research." Manpower Demonstration Research Corporation Working Paper. Manpower Demonstration Research Corporation, New York.

Ghazvini, Alisa S., Ann K. Mussi, Ronald L. Mullis, and Jennifer J. Park. 1999. "Child Care Issues Impacting Welfare Reform in the Rural South." Welfare Reform in the Rural South 9. Southern Rural Development Center, Mississippi State University.

Gibbs, Robert. 2001. "Nonmetro Labor Markets in the Era of Welfare Reform." *Rural America* 16 (3): 11–21.

———. 2005. "Education as a Rural Development Strategy." *Amber Waves* (November). http://www.ers.usda.gov/AmberWaves/November05/Features/Education.htm.

Gibbs, Robert, and John B. Cromartie. 2001. "Low-Wage Counties Face Locational Disadvantages." *Rural Conditions and Trends* 11 (2): 18–26.

Gibbs, Robert, Lorin Kusmin, and John Cromartie. 2005. "Low-Skill Employment and the Changing Economy of Rural America." Economic Research Report 10. USDA Economic Research Service, Washington, D.C.

Gibbs, Robert M., and Timothy S. Parker. 2001. "Earnings: Nonmetro Earnings Continue Upward Trend." *Rural America* 16 (2): 38–40.

Gilder, George. 1981. *Wealth and Poverty.* New York: Basic Books.

Gingrich, Newt, et al. 1994. *Contract with America.* New York: Times Books.

Glasmeier, Amy, and Priscilla Salant. 2006. "Low-Skill Workers in Rural America Face Permanent Job Loss." Carsey Institute Policy Brief 2. Carsey Institute, Durham, N.H.

Glauber, Rebecca. 2008. "Race and Gender in Families and at Work: The Fatherhood Wage Premium." *Gender and Society* 22 (1): 8–30.

Glied, Sherry, and Sarah E. Little. 2003. "The Uninsured and the Benefits of Medical Progress." *Health Affairs* 22:210–19.

Glover, Saundra, Charity G. Moore, Janice C. Probst, and Michael E. Samuels. 2004. "Disparities in Access to Care Among Rural Working-Age Adults." *Journal of Rural Health* 20 (3): 193–205.

Goe, W. Richard, and Anisa Rhea. 2000. "The Spatial Shift in the Growth of Poverty Among Families Headed by Employed Females, 1979–89." *Journal of Sociology and Social Welfare* 27 (2): 79–95.

Gold, Rachel, Ichiro Kawachi, Bruce P. Kennedy, John W. Lynch, and Frederick A. Connell. 2001. "Ecological Analysis of Teen Birth Rates: Association with Community Income and Income Inequality." *Maternal and Child Health Journal* 5 (3): 162–67.

Goldin, Claudia. 1990. *Understanding the Gender Gap: An Economic History of American Women.* New York: Oxford University Press.

Goldman, David, and Michael Watts. 1994. "Reconfiguring the Rural or Fording the Divide? Capitalist Restructuring and the Global Agro-food System." *Journal of Peasant Studies* 22 (1): 1–49.

Goldscheider, Frances K., and Linda J. Waite. 1991. *New Families, No Families? The Transformation of the American Home.* Berkeley: University of California Press.

Goldschmidt, W. 1978. *As You Sow: Three Studies in the Social Consequences of Agribusiness.* Monclair: Allanheld, Osmun.

Gomulka, Joanna, and Nicholas Stern. 1990. "The Employment of Married Women in the United Kingdom, 1970–83." *Economica* 57:171–99.

Gordon, Rachel A., and Lindsay Chase-Lansdale. 2001. "Availability of Child Care in the United States: A Description and Analysis of Data Sources." *Demography* 38:299–316.

Gorham, Lucy. 1992. "The Growing Problem of Low Earnings in Rural Areas." In Duncan 1992, 21–40.

Gornick, Janet C., and Marcia K. Meyers. 2003. *Families That Work: Policies for Reconciling Parenthood and Employment.* New York: Russell Sage Foundation.

Gouveia, Lourdes, and Donald D. Stull. 1995. "Dances with Cows: Beefpacking's Impact on Garden City, Kansas, and Lexington, Nebraska." In *Any Way You Cut It: Meat Processing and Small-Town America,* edited by Donald D. Stull, Michael J. Broadway, and David Griffith, 85–108. Lawrence: University Press of Kansas.

Gozdziak, Elzbieta M., and Micah N. Bump. 2004. "Poultry, Apples, and New Immigrants in the Rural Communities of the Shenandoah Valley: An Ethnographic Case Study." *International Migration* 42:149–64.

Grace, Cathy, Elizabeth F. Shores, Martha Zaslow, Bretty Brown, Dena Aufseeser, and Lynn Bell. 2006. "Rural Disparities in Baseline Data of the Early Childhood Longitudinal Study: A Chartbook." National Center for Rural Early Childhood Learning Initiatives, Mississippi State University Early Childhood Institute.

Graefe, Deborah R., and Daniel T. Lichter. 1999. "Life Course Transitions of American Children: Parental Cohabitation, Marriage, and Single Motherhood." *Demography* 36 (2): 205–17.

———. 2002. "Marriage Among Unwed Mothers: White, African American, and Hispanic Experiences Compared." *Perspectives on Sexual and Reproductive Health* 34 (6): 286–93.

Greenhouse, Steven, and Michael Barbaro. 2006. "Wal-Mart to Add Wage Caps and Part-Timers." *New York Times,* October 2.

Griffith, David C. 2005. "Rural Industry and Mexican Immigration and Settlement in North Carolina." In Zuñiga and Hernández-León 2005, 50–75.

Gringeri, Christina. 1994. *Getting by: Women Homeworkers and Rural Economic Development.* Lawrence: University Press of Kansas.

Gruber, Gary. 2000. "Using Educational Resources for Out-of-School Youth." In *The 21st Century Challenge: Moving the Youth Agenda Forward,* edited by Marion Pines, 51–72. Baltimore: Johns Hopkins University.

Guendelman, Sylvia, and Michelle Pearl. 2001. "Access to Care for Children of the Working Poor." *Archives of Pediatric Adolescent Medicine* 155:651–58.

Gunderson, Craig, and James P. Ziliak. 2004. "Poverty and Macroeconomic Performance Across Space, Race, and Family Structure." *Demography* 41:61–86.

Hahn, Andrew, and Robert Lerman. 1985. "What Works in Youth Employment Policy: How to Help Young Workers from Poor Families." National Planning Association, Washington, D.C.

Hahn, Andrew, Tom Leavitt, and Paul Aaron. 1994. "Evaluation of the Quantum Opportunities Program: Did the Program Work?" Heller Graduate School, Brandeis University, Waltham, Mass.

Haleman, Diana L., M. Sargent, J. Zimmerman, and D. Billings. 2000. "The Impact of Welfare Reform on Kentucky's Appalachian Counties." University of Kentucky Appalachian Center, Lexington, Ky.

Hamilton, Brady E., Joyce A. Martin, and Stephanie J. Ventura. 2009. "Births: Preliminary Data for 2007." *National Vital Statistics Reports* 57 (12). Hyattsville, Md.: National Center for Health Statistics.

Hamilton, Lawrence C., Leslie R. Hamilton, Cynthia M. Duncan, and Chris R. Colocousis. 2008. "Place Matters: Challenges and Opportunities in Four Rural Americas." Carsey Institute Reports on Rural America 1 (4). Carsey Institute, Durham, N.H.

Hammond, Cathy, Dan Linton, Jay Smink, and Sam Drew. 2007. "Dropout Risk Factors and Exemplary Programs." National Dropout Prevention Center, Communities in Schools, Inc., Clemson, S.C.

Hamrick, Karen S. 2001. "Displaced Workers: Differences in Nonmetro and Metro Experiences in the Mid-1990s." USDA Economic Research Service.

———. 2005. "Displacement of Textile and Apparel Workers." Paper presented at Globalization and Restructuring in Rural America Conference. USDA Economic Research Service and Farm Foundation, Washington, D.C.

Hardy, David E., and Stephen G. Katsinas. 2007. "Classifying Community Colleges: How Rural Community Colleges Fit." In *Rural Community Colleges: Teaching, Learning, and Leading in the Heartland,* edited by Pamela Lynn Eddy and John P. Murray, 3–17. New Directions for Community Colleges 137. San Francisco: Jossey-Bass.

Harland, P., S. A. Reijneveld, E. Brugman, S. P. Verloove-Vanhorick, and F. C. Verhults. 2002. "Family Factors and Life Events as Risk Factors for Behavioural and Emotional Problems in Children." *European Child and Adolescent Psychiatry* 11 (4): 176–84.

Harris, Deborah A., and Domenico Parisi. 2007. "Adapting Life History Calendars for Qualitative Research on Welfare Transitions." *Field Methods* 19:40–58.

Harris, Katherine. 1997. "Life After Welfare: Women, Work, and Repeat Dependency." *American Sociological Review* 61:407–26.

Harrison, David, and Bob Watrus. 2005. "Responding to the Complex Causes of Poverty in the Northwest." *Perspectives on Poverty, Policy, and Place* 3 (1): 7–10.

Hauser, Philip M. 1974. "The Measurement of Labor Utilization." *Malayan Economic Review* 19:1–17.

Hays, Sharon. 2003. *Flat Broke with Children: Women in the Age of Welfare Reform.* Oxford: Oxford University Press.

Health and Human Services (HHS) Rural Task Force. 2002. "One Department Serving Rural America: HHS Rural Task Force Report to the Secretary." HHS Rural Task Force, Washington, D.C.

Heaton, Timothy B., Daniel T. Lichter, and Acheampong Amoeteng. 1989. "The Timing of Family Formation: Rural-Urban Differences in First Intercourse, Childbirth, and Marriage." *Rural Sociology* 54:1–16.

Heck, Katherine E., John A. Borba, Ramona Carlos, Ken Churches, Susan Donohue, and Arlene Hyde Fuller. 2004. "California's Rural Youth." 4-H Center for Youth Development, Davis, Calif.

Helseth, Candi. 2007. "Recruiting Local People to Fill Health Care Needs." *Rural Monitor* (Summer). http://www.raconline.org/newsletter/web/summer07.php.

Henderson, Debra A., Ann Tickamyer, Julie White, and Barry Tadlock. 2002a. "From Where I Stand: Recipient Views on the Success of Welfare Reform in Rural Appalachia." Paper presented at the Annual Meeting of the Rural Sociological Society in Chicago, August.

————. 2002b. "Rural Appalachia Families in the Wake of Welfare Reform." *Family Focus* 6 (4): 7–9.

Henry, Mark S. 2001. "Impacts of Welfare Reform on Rural Families and Implications for the Reauthorization Debate: Comments." *American Journal of Agricultural Economics* 83 (5): 1310–11.

Henry, Mark S., and Lewis Willis. 2001. "Welfare Reform: Remedy for Persistent Poverty in the Rural South?" *Rural America* 15 (4): 59–67.

Herbst, Masha. 2002. "Ames, One of the Last of the Regional Discounters, to Shut Down." Associated Press State and Local Wire, August 15, Business News.

Hernandez, Donald J., and Evan Charney. 1998. *From Generation to Generation: The Health and Well-Being of Children in Immigrant Families.* Washington, D.C.: National Academy Press.

Herzog, Henry W., and Alan M. Schlottmann. 1995. "Worker Displacement and Job-Search: A Regional Analysis of Structural Impediments to Re-employment." *Journal of Regional Science* 33 (4): 553–77.

Hessert, S. William, Jr. 2008. "Agromedicine Program Continues to Explore Agriculturally Related Health Concerns." *Pennsylvania Rural Health* (Summer): 15.

Heymann, Jody. 2000. *The Widening Gap: Why America's Working Families Are in Jeopardy—and What Can Be Done About It.* New York: Basic Books.

Hobbs, Beverly B., and I. Joyce Chang. 1996. "Identifying and Meeting the School-Age Child Care Needs of Rural Families." *Journal of Family and Consumer Sciences* 88 (4): 13–16.

Hochschild, Arlie, and Anne Machung. 1989. *The Second Shift.* New York: Avon Books.

Hoff, Erika. 2003. "The Specificity of Environmental Influence: Socioeconomic Status Affects Early Vocabulary Development via Maternal Speech." *Child Development* 74:1368–78.

Hoff, Erika, Brett Laursen, and Twila Tardif. 2002. "Socioeconomic Status and Parenting." In *Handbook of Parenting,* vol. 2, *Biology and Ecology of Parenting,* edited by Marc H. Bornstein, 231–52. Mahwah, N.J.: Lawrence Erlbaum.

Hofferth, Sandra L. 1996. "Child Care in the United States Today." *Future of Children* 6 (2): 41–61.

————. 1999. "Child Care, Maternal Employment, and Public Policy." *Annals of the American Academy of Political and Social Science* 563:20–38.

Hofferth, Sandra L., April Brayfield, Sharon Deich, Pamela Holcomb, and Frederic Glaniz. 1991. "National Child Care Survey, 1990." Urban Institute, Washington, D.C.

Hofferth, Sandra L., and Nancy Collins. 2000. "Child Care and Employment Turnover." *Population Research and Policy Review* 19:357–95.

Horne, Michael S., Thomas Samuel Williamson, and Anthony Herman. 2005. *The Contingent Workforce: Business and Legal Strategies.* New York: Law Journal Press.

Howard, John. 1996. "Beleaguered Timber Town Confronts End of an Era." *Reno Gazette-Journal.*

Howell, Craig. 2001. "The Rural School Bus Ride in Five States." Rural School and Community Trust, Washington, D.C.

Hraba, Joseph, Frederick O. Lorenz, and Zdenka Pechacova. 2000. "Czech Families Ten Years After the Velvet Revolution." *Journal of Contemporary Sociology* 29:643–81.

Huang, Gary G., Stanley Weng, Fan Zhang, and Michael P. Cohen. 1997. "Outmigration Among Rural High School Graduates: The Effect of Academic and Vocational Programs." *Educational Evaluation and Policy Analysis* 19:360–72.

Hughes, Claire, Sara R. Jaffee, Francesca Happé, Alan Taylor, Avshalom Caspi, and Terrie E. Moffitt. 2005. "Origins of Individual Differences in Theory of Mind: From Nature to Nurture?" *Child Development* 76:356–70.

Huston, Aletha C., Young E. Chang, and Lisa Gennetian. 2002. "Family and Individual Predictors of Child Care Use by Low-Income Families in Different Policy Contexts." *Early Childhood Research Quarterly* 17 (4): 441–69.

Hynes, Michelle. 2003. "Revitalizing Economics Around Cobscook Bay." In *Engaged Institutions: Impacting the Lives of Vulnerable Youth Through Place-Based Learning*, 9–22. Arlington, Va.: Rural School and Community Trust.

Institute for Women's Policy Research. 2007. "Women and Paid Sick Days: Crucial for Family Well-Being." Technical Report No. B254a. Institute for Women's Policy Research, Washington, D.C.

Irwin, Michael, Troy Blanchard, Charles Tolbert, Alfred Nucci, and Thomas Lyson. 2004. "Why People Stay: The Impact of Community Context of Nonmigration in the USA." *Population* 59:567–91.

Ivry, Robert, and Fred Doolittle. 2003. *Improving the Economic and Life Outcomes of At-Risk Youth*. New York: MDRC.

Jack, Leonard, Jr. 2007. "Thinking Aloud About Poverty and Health in Rural Mississippi." *Preventing Chronic Disease* 4 (3): 1–4.

James, Donna Walker. 1996. "Can Schools Help Build the Entrepreneurial Economy? Lessons from the REAL (Rural Entrepreneurship Through Action Learning) Experience." Forum Brief, American Youth Policy Forum, Washington, D.C.

Jargowsky, Paul. 1997. *Poverty and Place: Ghettos, Barrios, and the American City*. New York: Russell Sage Foundation.

———. 2003. *Stunning Progress, Hidden Problems: The Dramatic Decline of Concentrated Poverty in the 1990s*. Living Cities Series. Washington, D.C.: Brookings Institution.

Jensen, Leif. 2006. "New Immigrant Settlements in Rural America: Problems, Prospects, and Policies." Reports on Rural America 1 (3). Carsey Institute, Durham, N.H.

Jensen, Leif, Jill L. Findeis, Wan-Ling Hsu, and Jason P. Schachter. 1999. "Slipping into and out of Underemployment: Another Disadvantage for Nonmetropolitan Workers?" *Rural Sociology* 64:417–38.

Jensen, Leif, Diane K. McLaughlin, and Tim Slack. 2003. "Rural Poverty: The Persisting Challenge." In Brown and Swanson 2003, 118–31.

Johnson, Kenneth M. 2003. "Unpredictable Directions of Rural Population Growth and Migration." In Brown and Swanson 2003, 19–31.

———. 2006. "Demographic Trends in Rural and Small Town America." Reports on Rural America 1 (1). Carsey Institute, Durham, N.H.

———. 2011. "The Continuing Incidence of Natural Decrease in American Counties." *Rural Sociology* 75 (forthcoming).

Johnson, Kenneth M., and Calvin L. Beale. 1995. "The Rural Rebound Revisited." *American Demographics* 17:46–49, 52–54.

———. 2002. "Nonmetro Recreation Counties: Their Identification and Rapid Growth." *Rural America* 17 (4): 12–19.

Johnson, Kenneth M., and John B. Cromartie. 2006. "The Rural Rebound and Its Aftermath: Changing Dynamics and Regional Contrasts." In Kandel and Brown 2006, 25–49.

Johnson, Kenneth M., and Daniel T. Lichter. 2007. "Demographic Components of Population Change: Immigration and the Growing Hispanic Population in New Rural Destinations." Paper presented at the annual meeting of the Rural Sociological Society, Santa Clara, Calif., August.

———. 2008. "Natural Increase: A New Source of Population Growth in Emerging Hispanic Destinations in the United States." *Population and Development Review* 34 (2): 327–46.

———. 2010. "Growing Diversity Among America's Children: Spatial and Temporal Dimensions." *Population and Development Review* 36:151–75.

Johnson, Kenneth M., Paul R. Voss, Roger B. Hammer, Glenn V. Fuguitt, and Scott McNiven. 2005. "Temporal and Spatial Variation in Age-Specific Net Migration in the United States." *Demography* 42 (4): 791–812.

Jolliffe, Dean. 2004. "Rural Poverty at a Glance." Rural Development Research Report 100. USDA Economic Research Service, Washington, D.C.

Jones, F. L. 1983. "On Decomposing the Wage Gap: A Critical Comment on Blinder's Method." *Journal of Human Resources* 18 (1): 126–30.

Jones, Hezekiah S. 1994. "Federal Agricultural Policies: Do Black Farm Operators Benefit?" *Journal of Black Political Economics* 22 (4): 25–50.

Jones-DeWeever, Avis, Janice Peterson, and Xue Song. 2003. *Before and After Welfare Reform: The Work and Well-Being of Low-Income Single Parent Families.* Washington, D.C.: Institute for Women's Policy Research.

Juhn, Chinhui, Kevin Murphy, and Brooks Pierce. 1993. "Wage Inequality and the Rise in Returns to Skill." *Journal of Political Economy* 101:410–42.

Jurich, Sonia, and Steve Estes. 2000. "Raising Academic Achievement for America's Youth: A Study of 20 Successful Programs." American Youth Policy Forum, Washington, D.C.

Kaiser Commission on Medicaid and the Uninsured. 2007. "The Uninsured: A Primer: Key Facts About Americans Without Health Insurance." Kaiser Family Foundation Report No. 7451-03. Kaiser Family Foundation, Washington, D.C.

Kandel, William. 2006. "Rural Meat Processing Industry Draws Hispanic Workers." *Amber Waves* 4 (3): 11–15.

Kandel, William, and David Brown, eds. 2006. *Population Change and Rural Society.* Dordrecht: Springer.

Kandel, William, and John Cromartie. 2004. "New Patterns of Hispanic Settlement in Rural America." Rural Development Research Report 99. U.S. Department of Agriculture, Washington, D.C.

Kandel, William, and Constance Newman. 2004. "Rural Hispanics: Employment and Residential Trends." *Amber Waves* (June): 38–45.

Kandel, William, and Emilio A. Parrado. 2005. "Restructuring of the US Meat Processing Industry and New Hispanic Migrant Destinations." *Population and Development Review* 31 (3): 447–71.

Kaplan, April. 1998. "Financial Resources for Child Care." *Welfare Information Network* 2 (6). http://www.financeproject.org/Publications/issuechild.htm.

Kavet, Thomas, Deborah Brighton, Douglas Hoffer, and Elaine McCrate. 1999. "Act 21 Research and Analysis in Support of the Livable Income Study Committee." Vermont State Legislature, Livable Income Study Committee. http://www.leg.state.vt.us/jfo/reports/1999-11%20Livable%20Income%20Study.pdf.

Kelly, E. Brooke. 2007. "Leaving and Losing Jobs: The Plight of Rural Low-Income Mothers." *Perspectives on Poverty, Policy, and Place* 4 (1): 4–6.

Kemple, James J., and Judith Scott-Clayton. 2004. *Career Academies: Impacts on Labor Market Outcomes and Educational Attainment.* New York: MDRC.

Kennedy, Sheela, and Larry Bumpass. 2008. "Cohabitation and Children's Living Arrangements: New Estimates from the United States." *Demographic Research* 19:1663–92.

Kessler, Ronald C., J. Blake Turner, and James S. House. 1988. "Effects of Unemployment on Health in a Community Survey: Main, Modifying and Mediating Effects." *Journal of Social Issues* 44:69–85.

Kilty, Keith M., and Elizabeth A. Segal. 2006. *The Promise of Welfare Reform: Political Rhetoric and the Reality of Poverty in the Twenty-First Century.* Binghamton, N.H.: Haworth Press.

Kim, Marlene. 2000. "Women Paid Low Wages: Who They Are and Where They Work." *Monthly Labor Review* 123 (9): 26–30.

Kimmel, Jean. 1998. "Child Care Costs as a Barrier to Employment for Single and Married Mothers." *Review of Economics and Statistics* 80 (2): 297–99.

Kingsley, G. Thomas, and Kathryn L. S. Pettit. 2003. "Concentrated Poverty: A Change in Course." Neighborhood Change in Urban America 2. Urban Institute, Washington, D.C.

Kirschner, Annabel. 2005. "Poverty in the Rural West." *Perspectives on Poverty, Policy, and Place* 3 (1): 406.

Kirschner, Annabel, E. Helen Berry, and Nina Glasgow. 2006. "The Changing Face of Rural America." In Kandel and Brown 2006, 53–74.

Kleiner, Brian, Mary Jo Nolin, and Chris Chapman. 2004. "Before- and After-School Care, Programs, and Activities of Children in Kindergarten Through Eighth Grade: 2001." National Center for Education Statistics (NCES) 2004-008. U.S. Department of Education, Washington, D.C.

Knapp, Tim. 1995. "Rust in the Wheatbelt: The Social Impacts of Industrial Decline in a Rural Kansas Community." *Sociological Inquiry* 65 (1): 47–66.

Kokko, Katja, and Lea Pulkkinen. 2000. "Aggression in Childhood and Long-Term Unemployment in Adulthood: A Cycle of Maladaptation and Some Protective Factors." *Developmental Psychology* 36:463–72.

Komarovsky, Mirra. 1940. *The Unemployed Man and His Family: The Effect of Unemployment upon the Status of the Man in Fifty-Nine Families.* New York: Dryden Press.

Korenman, Sanders, and David Newmark. 1991. "Does Marriage Really Make Men More Productive?" *Journal of Human Resources* 26 (2): 282–307.

Kress, Cathann. n.d. "Transforming the Lives of Youth: Why 4-H Matters." http://www .national4-hheadquarters.gov/library/transforming_youth_WI06.ppt.

Kurz, Demie. 1995. *For Richer, for Poorer: Mothers Confront Divorce.* New York: Routledge.

Kusel, Jonathan, and Louise Fortmann. 1991. *Well-Being in Forest-Dependent Communities.* Vol. 1, *Forest and Rangeland Resources Assessment Program.* Sacramento, Calif.: Forest and Rangeland Resources Assessment Program.

Kusmin, Lorin. 2007. "Rural Labor and Education: Nonmetro Employment and Unemployment." http://www.ers.usda.gov/Briefing/LaborAndEducation/ employment.htm.

———. 2009. "Rural America at a Glance: 2009 Edition." Economic Information Bulletin 59 (EIB-59). U.S. Department of Agriculture, Washington, D.C.

Lambert, Susan J. 2008. "Passing the Buck: Labor Flexibility Practices That Transfer Risk onto Hourly Workers." *Human Relations* 61 (9) 1203–27.

———. 2009. "Making a Difference for Hourly Employees." In *Work-Life Policies,* edited by Ann C. Crouter and Alan Booth, 169–95. Washington, D.C.: Urban Institute Press.

Lambrew, Jeanne M., and Jonathan Gruber. 2006. "Money and Mandates: Relative Effects of Key Policy Levers in Expanding Health Insurance Coverage to All Americans." *Inquiry* 43 (4): 333–44.

Landale, Nancy S., and R. S. Oropesa. 2007. "Hispanic Families: Stability and Change." *Annual Review of Sociology* 33:381–405.

Larson, Jeffrey H., Stephan M. Wilson, and Rochelle Beley. 1994. "The Impact of Job Insecurity on Marital and Family Relationships." *Family Relations* (43) 2: 138–43.

Lasley, Paul, F., Larry Leistritz, Linda M. Lobao, and Katherine Meyer. 1995. *Beyond the Amber Waves of Grain: An Examination of Social and Economic Restructuring in the Heartland.* Boulder, Colo.: Westview Press.

Laureau, Annette 2002. "Invisible Inequality: Social Class and Childrearing in Black and White Families." *American Sociological Review* 67 (5): 747–76.

Lee, M. A., Mark Harvey, and Allison Neustrom. 2002. "Local Labor Markets and Caseload Decline in Louisiana in the 1900s." *Rural Sociology* 67 (4): 556–77.

Lee, P., and D. Paxman. 1997. "Reinventing Public Health." *Annual Review of Public Health* 18:1–35.

Leslie, Ann. 2007. "YouthBuild USA: Youthful Offender Project Year I." http://www.youth build.org/atf/cf/%7B22B5F680-2AF9-4ED2-B948-40C4B32E6198%7D/Youthful OffenderProject1.pdf.

Leventhal, Tama, and Jeanne Brooks-Gunn. 2003. "Moving on Up: Neighborhood Effects on Children and Families." In Bornstein and Bradley 2003, 209–30.

Levy, Frank. 1998. *The New Dollars and Dreams: American Incomes and Economic Change.* New York: Russell Sage Foundation.

Lewis, Jane. 2001. "The Decline of the Male Breadwinner Model: Implications for Work and Care." *Social Politics* 2:152–69.

Lewis, Susan K., Catherine E. Ross, and John Mirowsky. 1999. "Establishing a Sense of Personal Control in the Transition to Adulthood." *Social Forces* 77:1573–99.

Lichter, Daniel T. 1989. "The Underemployment of American Rural Women: Prevalence, Trends, and Spatial Inequality." *Journal of Rural Studies* 5 (2): 199–208.

———. 1993. "Demographic Aspects of the Changing Rural Labor Force." In *Population Change and the Future of Rural America*, edited by Linda L. Swanson and David L. Brown, 136–50. Washington, D.C.: U.S. Department of Agriculture, Economic Research Service.

Lichter, Daniel T., Christine D. Batson, and J. Brian Brown. 2004. "Welfare Reform and Marriage Promotion: The Marital Expectations and Desires of Single and Cohabiting Mothers." *Social Service Review* 78:2–25.

Lichter, Daniel T., Gretchen T. Cornwell, and David J. Eggebeen. 1993. "Harvesting Human Capital: Family Structure and Education Among Rural Youth." *Rural Sociology* 58:53–75.

Lichter, Daniel T., and Janice A. Costanzo. 1987. "Nonmetropolitan Underemployment and Labor Force Composition." *Rural Sociology* 52:329–44.

Lichter, Daniel T., and M. Crowley. 2002. "Poverty in America: Beyond Welfare Reform." *Population Bulletin* 57 (2): 1–36.

Lichter, Daniel T., and David Eggebeen. 1993. "Rich Kids, Poor Kids: Changing Income Inequality Among American Children." *Social Forces* 71 (3): 761–80.

———. 1994. "The Effect of Parental Employment on Child Poverty." *Journal of Marriage and the Family* 56:633–45.

Lichter, Daniel T., and Deborah Roempke Graefe. 2001. "Finding a Mate? The Marital and Cohabitation Histories of Unwed Mothers." In *Out of Wedlock: Causes and Consequences of Nonmarital Fertility*, edited by Lawrence L. Wu and Barbara Wolfe, 317–43. New York: Russell Sage Foundation.

Lichter, Daniel T., and Rukmalie Jayakody. 2002. "Welfare Reform: How Do We Measure Success?" *Annual Review of Sociology* 28:117–41.

Lichter, Daniel T., and Leif Jensen. 2001. "Poverty and Welfare Among Rural Female-Headed Families Before and After PRWORA." *Rural America* 16 (3): 28–35.

———. 2002. "Rural America in Transition: Poverty and Welfare at the Turn of the Twenty-First Century." In Weber, Duncan, and Whitener 2002, 77–110.

Lichter, Daniel T., and Kenneth M. Johnson. 2006. "Emerging Rural Settlement Patterns and the Geographic Redistribution of America's New Immigrants." *Rural Sociology* 71:109–31.

———. 2007. "The Changing Spatial Concentration of America's Rural Poor Population." *Rural Sociology* 72 (3): 331–58.

Lichter, Daniel T., Kenneth M. Johnson, Richard N. Turner, and Allison Churilla. 2010. "Immigrant Incorporation and Fertility in New Hispanic Destinations." Paper presented at the annual meeting of the Population Association of America, Dallas, Tex.

Lichter, Daniel T., George C. Kephart, Diane K. McLaughlin, and David J. Landry. 1992. "Race and Retreat from Marriage: A Shortage of Marriageable Men?" *American Sociological Review* 57:781–99.

Lichter, Daniel T., and Diane K. McLaughlin. 1995. "Changing Economic Opportunities, Family Structure, and Poverty in Rural Areas." *Rural Sociology* 60:688–706.

Lichter, Daniel T., Diane K. McLaughlin, and Gretchen T. Cornwell. 1995. "Migration and the Loss of Human Resources in Rural Areas." In Beaulieu and Mulkey 1995, 235–56.

Lichter, Daniel T., Diane K. McLaughlin, and David C. Ribar. 2002. "Economic Restructuring and the Retreat from Marriage." *Social Science Research* 31:230–56.

Lichter, Daniel T., Domenico Parisi, Steven Michael Grice, and Michael C. Taquino. 2007a. "National Estimates of Racial Segregation in Rural and Small Town America." *Demography* 44:563–81.

———. 2007b. "Municipal Underbounding: Annexation and Racial Exclusion in Southern Small Towns." *Rural Sociology* 72:47–68.

Lichter, Daniel T., Domenico Parisi, Michael C. Taquino, and Brian Beaulieu. 2008. "Race and the Micro-scale Spatial Concentration of Poverty." *Cambridge Journal of Regions, Economy, and Society* 1 (1): 51–67.

Lichter, Daniel T., and Zhenchao Qian. 2004. "Marriage and Family in a Multiracial Society." In Farley and Haaga 2004, 169–200.

Lichter, Daniel T., Zhenchao Qian, and Martha Crowley. 2006. "Poverty and Economic Polarization Among Children in Racial Minority and Immigrant Families." In *Handbook of Families and Poverty*, edited by Russell D. Crane and Tim B. Heaton, 119–43. Thousand Oaks, Calif.: Russell Sage Foundation.

Lichter, Daniel T., Zhenchao Qian, and Leanna M. Mellott. 2006. "Marriage or Disolution? Union Transitions Among Poor Cohabitating Women." *Demography* 43 (2): 223–40.

Liebschutz, Sarah F. 2000. "Public Opinion, Political Leadership, and Welfare Reform." In *Managing Welfare Reform in Five States: The Challenge of Devolution*, edited by Sarah F. Liebschutz, 1–24. Albany: Rockefeller Institute Press.

Liem, Joan Huser, and G. Ramsay Liem. 1990. "Understanding the Individual and Family Effects of Unemployment." In *Stress Between Work and Family*, edited by John Eckenrode and Susan Gore, 175–204. New York: Plenum Press.

Lin, Nan, and Walter M. Ensel. 1989. "Life Stress and Health: Stressors and Resources." *American Sociological Review* 54:382–99.

Livingston, Joy, and Elaine McCrate. 1993. *Women and Economic Development in Vermont: A Study for the Governor's Commission on Women*. Montpelier, Vt.: Governor's Commission on the Status of Women.

Lobao, Linda M., Lawrence A. Brown, and Jon Moore. 2003. "Old Industrial Regions and the Political Economy of Development." In Falk, Schulman, and Tickamyer 2003, 3–30.

Lobao, Linda, and Gregory Hooks. 2003. "Public Employment, Welfare Transfers, and Economic Well-Being Across Local Populations: Does a Lean and Mean Government Benefit the Masses?" *Social Forces* 82 (2): 519–56.

Lobao, Linda, Gregory Hooks, and Ann Tickamyer, eds. 2007. *The Sociology of Spatial Inequality*. New York: SUNY Press.

Lobao, Linda M., and Paul Lasley. 1995. "Farm Restructuring and Crisis in the Heartland: An Introduction." In Lasley et al. 1995, 1–28.

Lobao, Linda, and Katherine Meyer. 1995. "Economic Decline, Gender, and Labor Flexibility in Family-Based Enterprises: The Case of Midwestern Farming in the 1980s." *Social Forces* 74 (2): 575–608.

———. 2001. "The Great Agricultural Transition: Crisis, Change, and Social Consequences of Twentieth Century US Farming." *Annual Review of Sociology* 27:103–24.

Lobao, Linda M., and Michael D. Schulman. 1991. "Farming Patterns, Rural Restructuring, and Poverty: A Comparative Regional Analysis." *Rural Sociology* 56 (5): 564–602.

Logan, J. 1996. "Rural America as a Symbol of American Values." *Rural Development Perspectives* 12 (1): 24–28.

Logan, J. R., and R. D. Alba. 1993. "Locational Returns to Human Capital: Minority Access to Suburban Community Resources." *Demography* 30 (2): 243–68.

Lombardi, Joan. 2003. *Time to Care: Redesigning Child Care to Promote Education, Support Families and Build Communities*. Philadelphia: Temple University Press.

Loprest, Pamela. 1999. "Families Who Left Welfare: Who Are They and How Are They Doing?" Urban Institute, Washington, D.C.

Lorenz, Frederick O., Rand D. Conger, Ruth Montague, and K. A. S. Wickrama. 1993. "Economic Conditions, Spouse Support, and Psychological Distress of Rural Husbands and Wives." *Rural Sociology* 58:247–68.

Ludwig, Jens, and Susan Mayer. 2006. "'Culture' and the Intergenerational Transmission of Poverty: The Prevention Paradox." *Future of Children* 16 (2): 175–96.

Luloff, A. E., and L. E. Swanson. 1995. "Community Agency and Disaffection: Enhancing Collective Resources." In Beaulieu and Mulkey 1995, 351–72.

MacDermid, Shelley M., and Chiung Ya Tang. 2006. "Flexibility and Control: Does One Necessarily Bring the Other?" In *Handbook of Families and Work: Interdisciplinary Perspectives,* edited by D. Russell Crane and E. Jeffrey Hill, 241 – 64. Lanham, Md.: University Press of America.

MacDonald, John, and Robert Moffitt. 1980. "The Uses of Tobit Analysis." *Review of Economics and Statistics* 62 (2): 318–21.

Macmillan, Ross, Barbara McMorris, and Candace Kruttschnitt. 2004. "Linked Lives: Stability and Change in Maternal Circumstances and Trajectories of Antisocial Behavior in Children." *Child Development* 75 (January–February): 205–20.

MacTavish, Katherine, and Sonya Salamon. 2003a. "Mobile Home Park on the Prairie: A New Rural Community Form." *Rural Sociology* 66 (4):487–506.

———. 2003b. "What Do Rural Families Look Like Today?" In Brown and Swanson 2003, 73–85.

Manning, Wendy D., and Susan Brown. 2006. "Children's Economic Well-Being in Married and Cohabiting Parent Families." *Journal of Marriage and the Family* 68 (2): 345–62.

Marotz-Baden, Ramona, Charles B. Hennon, and Timothy H. Brubaker, eds. 1988. *Families in Rural America: Stress, Adaptation, and Revitalization.* St. Paul, Minn.: National Council on Family Relations.

Marsteller, Jill A., Len M. Nichols, Adam Badawi, Bethany Kessler, Shruti Rajan, and Stephen Zuckerman. 1998. "Variations in the Uninsured: State and County Level Analyses." Urban Institute, Washington, D.C.

Martin, Molly. 2006. "Family Structure and Income Inequality in Families with Children, 1976 to 2000." *Demography* 43 (3): 421–45.

Massey, Douglas S., and Nancy Denton. 1993. *American Apartheid: Segregation and the Making of the Underclass.* Cambridge, Mass.: Harvard University Press.

Mayer, Susan E. 1997. *What Money Can't Buy: Family Income and Children's Life Chances.* Cambridge, Mass.: Harvard University Press.

McCall, Leslie. 2001. *Complex Inequality: Gender, Class, and Race in the New Economy.* New York: Routledge.

McCrate, Elaine. 2003. "Working Mothers in a Double Bind." Briefing paper 124. Economic Policy Institute, Washington, D.C.

———. 2005. "Flexible Hours, Workplace Authority, and Compensating Wage Differentials in the U.S." *Feminist Economics* 11 (1): 11–40.

———. Forthcoming. "Flexibility for Whom? Control over the Variability of Work Schedules." *Feminist Economics.*

McGinnis, J. Michael, Pamela Williams-Russo, and James R. Knickman. 2002. "The Case for More Active Policy Attention to Health Promotion." *Health Affairs* 2:78–93.

McGranahan, David A. 1999. "Natural Amenities Drive Population Change." Agricultural Economics Report No. AER781. USDA Economic Research Service, Washington, D.C.

———. 2003. "How People Make a Living in Rural America." In Brown and Swanson 2003, 135–51.

McLanahan, Sara. 2009. "Fragile Families and the Reproduction of Poverty." *Annals of the American Academy of Political and Social Science* 621 (1): 111–31.

McLanahan, Sara, Irwin Garfinkel, and Ronald B. Mincy. 2001. "Fragile Families, Welfare Reform, and Marriage." Policy Brief 10. Brookings Institute, Washington, D.C.

McLanahan, Sara, and Christine Percheski. 2008. "Family Structure and the Reproduction of Inequalities." *Annual Review of Sociology* 34:257–76.

McLanahan, Sara, and Gary Sandefur. 1994. *Growing up with a Single Parent: What Hurts, What Helps.* Cambridge, Mass.: Harvard University Press.

McLaughlin, Diane K. 2002. "Changing Income Inequality in Nonmetropolitan Counties, 1980 to 1990." *Rural Sociology* 67 (4): 512–33.

McLaughlin, Diane K., and Alisha J. Coleman-Jensen. 2008. "Nonstandard Employment in the Nonmetropolitan United States." *Rural Sociology* 73 (4): 631–59.

McLaughlin, Diane K., Erica L. Gardner, and Daniel T. Lichter. 1999. "Economic Restructuring and Changing Prevalence of Female-Headed Families in America." *Rural Sociology* 64 (3): 394–416.

McLaughlin, Diane K., Daniel T. Lichter, and Gail M. Johnston. 1993. "Some Women Marry Young: Transitions to First Marriage in Metropolitan and Nonmetropolitan Areas." *Journal of Marriage and the Family* 55:827–38.

McLaughlin, Diane K., and Laurie Perman. 1991. "Returns vs. Endowments in the Earnings Attainment Process for Metropolitan and Nonmetropolitan Men and Women." *Rural Sociology* 56:339–65.

McLeod, Jane D., and Michael J. Shanahan. 1996. "Trajectories of Poverty and Children's Mental Health." *Journal of Health and Social Behavior* 37:207–20.

McLoyd, Vonnie C. 1990. "The Impact of Economic Hardship on Black Families and Children: Psychological Distress, Parenting, and Socioemotional Development." *Child Development* 61 (2): 311–46.

———. 1998. "Socioeconomic Disadvantage and Child Development." *American Psychologist* 53:185–204.

McLoyd, Vonnie C., Toby Epstein Jayaratne, Rosario Ceballo, and Julio Borquez. 1994. "Unemployment and Work Interruption Among African American Single Mothers: Effects on Parenting and Adolescent Socioemotional Functioning." *Child Development* 65:562–89.

Mederer, Helen J. 1999. "Surviving the Demise of a Way of Life: Stress and Resilience in Northeastern Commercial Fishing Families." In *The Dynamics of Resilient Families,* edited by Hamilton I. McCubbin, Elizabeth A. Thompson, Anne I. Thompson, and Jo A. Futrell, 203–35. Thousand Oaks, Calif.: Sage.

Melby, Janet N., and Rand D. Conger. 2001. "The Iowa Family Interaction Rating Scales: Instrument Summary." In *Family Observational Coding Systems: Resources for Systematic Research,* edited by Patricia K. Kerig and Kristin M. Lindahl, 33–58. Mahwah, N.J.: Lawrence Erlbaum.

Meyer, Daniel R., and Maria Cancian. 1998. "Economic Well-Being Following an Exit from Aid to Families with Dependent Children." *Journal of Marriage and Family* 60:479–92.

Mezzacappa, Enrico. 2004. "Alerting, Orienting, and Executive Attention: Developmental Properties and Sociodemographic Correlates in an Epidemiological Sample of Young, Urban Children." *Child Development* 75:1373–86.

Miller, Kathleen, and Bruce Weber. 2003. "Persistent Poverty Across the Rural-Urban Continuum." RPRC Working Paper 03-01. Rural Policy Research Center, Columbia, Mo.

Mills, Bradford F., and Gautam Hazarika. 2003. "Do Single Mothers Face Greater Constraints to Workforce Participation in Non-metropolitan Areas?" *American Journal of Agricultural Economics* 85 (1): 143–61.

Mills, L., D. Weiss, S. Boston, I. Goodman, K. Mohrle, M. Minardi, Mills and Pardee Inc., and Goodman Research Group Inc. 2001. "Vermont Child Care: A Study of Wages, Credentials, Benefits, and Market Rates." Waterbury, Vt.: Child Care Services Division, Department of Social and Rehabilitation Services, State of Vermont, Waterbury, Vt.

Mirowsky, John, and Catherine E. Ross. 1998. "Education, Personal Control, Lifestyle and Health: A Human Capital Hypothesis." *Research on Aging* 20:415–49.

Mistry, Rashmita S., Elizabeth A. Vandewater, Aletha C. Huston, and Vonnie C. McLoyd. 2002. "Economic Well-Being and Children's Social Adjustment: The Role of Family Process in an Ethnically Diverse Low-Income Sample." *Child Development* 73:935–51.

Moffitt, Robert A. 2002. "From Welfare to Work: What the Evidence Shows." Policy Brief 13. Brookings Institution, Washington, D.C.

Moffitt, Robert A., and LaDonna A. Pavetti. 1999. "Time Limits." Paper prepared for the Conference on Labor Markets and Less Skilled Workers, Washington, D.C., sponsored by the Joint Center for Poverty Research.

Monheit, Alan C., and Jessica P. Vistnes. 2000. "Race/Ethnicity and Health Insurance Status: 1987 and 1996." *Medical Care Research Review* 57 (supp. 1): 11–35.

Moore, Kristin A., and Nancy O. Snyder. 1991. "Cognitive Attainment Among Firstborn Children of Adolescent Mothers." *American Sociological Review* 56 (5): 612–24.

Moore, R. M., III, ed. 2001. *The Hidden America: Social Problems in Rural America for the Twenty-First Century.*

Morgan, Jonathan Q., William Lambe, and Allan Freyer. 2009. "Homegrown Responses to Economic Uncertainty in Rural America." *Rural Realities* 3 (2): 1–15.

Morgen, Sandra, Joan Acker, Jill Weigt, and Lisa Gonzales. 2006. "Living Economic Restructuring at the Bottom: Welfare Restructuring and Low-Wage Work." In Kilty and Segal 2006, 81–94.

Moss, Philip, Harold Salzman, and Chis Tilly. 2005. "When Firms Restructure: Understanding Work-Life Outcomes." In *Work and Life Integration: Organizational, Cultural, and Individual Perspectives,* edited by Ellen Ernst Kossek and Susan J. Lambert, 127–50. Mahwah, N.J.: Lawrence Erlbaum.

Mulligan, Gail M., DeAnn Brimhall, Jerry West, and Christopher Chapman. 2005. "Child Care and Early Education Arrangements of Infants, Toddlers, and Preschoolers: 2001." National Center for Education Statistics, Washington, D.C.

Murata, Jo Ellen. 1994. "Family Stress, Social Support, Violence, and Sons' Behavior." *Western Journal of Nursing Research* 16:154–68.

Murdock, Steve H., and F. Larry Leistritz. 1988. *The Farm Financial Crisis: Socioeconomic Dimensions and Implications for Producers and Rural Areas.* Boulder, Colo.: Westview Press.

Murray, Charles. 1984. *Losing Ground: American Social Policy, 1950–1980.* New York: Basic Books.

Musick, Kelly, and Robert D. Mare. 2006. "Recent Trends in the Inheritance of Poverty and Family Structure." *Social Science Research* 35 (2): 471–99.

Myers, Scott M., and Donald W. Hastings. 1995. "Convergence of Rural-Urban Patterns of Nuptiality and Mortality: A Life Table Update." *Sociological Spectrum* 15:227–56.

Naftzger, Neil, Seth Kaufman, Jonathan Margolin, and Asma Ali. 2006. "Twenty-First Century Community Learning Centers (21st CCLC) Analytic Support for Evaluation and Program Monitoring: An Overview of the 21st CCLC Program: 2004–05." Learning Point Associates, Napierville, Ill.

Nathan, Richard, and Thomas Gais. 2001. "Federal and State Roles in Welfare: Is Devolution Working?" *Brookings Review* 19 (3): 25–29.

National Association of Child Care Resource and Referral Agencies (NACCRRA). 2009. "We CAN Do Better: 2009 Update: NACCRRA's Ranking of State Child Care Center Regulations and Oversight." National Association of Child Care Resource and Referral Agencies, Arlington, Va.

National Center on Addiction and Substance Abuse. 2000. "No Place to Hide: Substance Abuse in Mid-size Cities and Rural America." National Center on Addiction and Substance Abuse, New York.

National Child Care Information and Technical Assistance Center (NCCIC). 2009. "Child Care and Development Fund: Report of State and Territory Plans FY 2008–2009." U.S. Department of Health and Human Services, Washington, D.C.

National Education Association. 2007. "Rural Education." http://www.nea.org/rural/lacpa pers-rural.html.

National 4-H Headquarters. 2006. "2005 4-H Youth Development ES–237 Statistics." http:// www.national4-hheadquarters.gov/library/2005_ES–237_stats_6-06.pdf.

National Partnership for Women and Families. 2005. "At-Home Infant Care (AHIC): A Side-by-Side Comparison of Federal and State Initiatives." National Partnership for Women and Families, Washington, D.C.

National Research Council. 1998. *Protecting Youth at Work: Health, Safety, and Development of Working Children and Adolescents in the United States.* Washington, D.C.: National Academies Press.

National Women's Law Center. 2006. "Making Care Less Taxing: Improving State Child and Dependent Care Tax Provisions." National Women's Law Center, Washington, D.C.

Nelson, Margaret K. 1999a. "Between Paid and Unpaid Work: Gender Patterns in Supplemental Economic Activities Among White, Rural Families." *Gender and Society* 13 (4): 518–39.

———. 1999b. "Economic Restructuring, Gender, and Informal Work: A Case Study of a Rural County." *Rural Sociology* 64 (1): 18–42.

———. 2000. "Single Mothers and Social Support: The Commitment to and Retreat from Reciprocity." *Qualitative Sociology* 23 (3): 291–319.

———. 2005. *The Social Economy of Single Motherhood: Raising Children in Rural America.* New York: Routledge.

Nelson, Margaret K., and Joan Smith. 1998. "Economic Restructuring, Household Strategies, and Gender: A Case Study of a Rural Community." *Feminist Studies* 24:79–114.

———. 1999. *Working Hard and Making Do: Surviving in Small Town America.* Berkeley: University of California Press.

Neumark, David. 2004. *The Effects of School-to-Career Programs on Postsecondary Enrollment and Employment.* San Francisco: Public Policy Institute of California.

Newman, Katherine S., and Victor Tan Chen. 2007. "The Crisis of the Near Poor." *Chronicle of Higher Education* 54 (6): 48.

NICHD Early Child Care Research Network, ed. 2005. *Child Care and Child Development: Results from the NICHD Study of Early Child Care and Youth Development.* New York: Guilford Press.

Nock, Steven L. 2001. "The Marriages of Equally Dependent Spouses." *Journal of Family Issues* 22:755–75.

———. 2005. "Marriage as a Public Issue." *Future of Children* 15 (2): 13–32.

Nonn, Timothy. 2004. "Hitting Bottom: Homelessness, Poverty, and Masculinity." In *Men's Lives,* edited by Michael S. Kimmel and Michael A. Messner, 318–27. Boston: Pearson.

Nord, Mark. 2000. "Does It Cost Less to Live in Rural Areas? Evidence from New Data on Food Security and Hunger." *Rural Sociology* 65 (1): 104–25.

Norem, Rosalie Husinga, and Joan Blundall. 1988. "Farm Families and Marital Disruption During a Time of Crisis." In Marotz-Baden, Hennon, and Brubaker 1988, 21–31.

Oaxaca, Ronald. 1973. "Male-Female Wage Differentials in Urban Labor Markets." *International Economic Review* 14:693–709.

Oberhauser, Ann, and Anne-Marie Turnage. 1999. "A Coalfield Tapestry: Weaving the Socioeconomic Fabric of Women's Lives." In *Neither Separate nor Equal: Women, Race, and Class in the South,* edited by Barbara Ellen Smith, 109–22. Philadelphia: Temple University Press.

O'Brien, Ellen. 2003. "Employers' Benefits from Workers' Health Insurance." *Milbank Quarterly* 81 (1):5–43.

Office of Management and Budget (OMB). 2003. "Revised Definitions of Metropolitan Statistical Areas, New Definitions of Micropolitan Statistical Areas and Combined Statistical Areas, and Guidance on Uses of the Statistical Definitions of These Areas."

OMB Bulletin No. 03-04, June 6. Office of Management and Budget, Washington, D.C. http://www.whitehouse.gov/omb/bulletins/b03-04.html. Accessed July 24, 2008.

O'Hare, William P. 2007. "Rural Workers Would Benefit More than Urban Workers from Increase in the Federal Minimum Wage." Carsey Institute Fact Sheet 4. Carsey Institute, Durham, N.H.

O'Hare, William P., and Allison Churilla. 2008. "Rural Children Now Less Likely to Live in Married-Couple Families." Carsey Institute Fact Sheet 13. Carsey Institute, Durham, N.H.

O'Hare, William P., and Elizabeth Kneebone. 2007. "EITC Is Vital for Working-Poor Families in Rural America." Carsey Institute Fact Sheet 8. Carsey Institute, Durham, N.H.

O'Hare, William P., Wendy Manning, Meredith Porter, and Heidi Lyons. 2009. "Rural Children Are More Likely to Live in Cohabitating-Couple Households." Carsey Institute Policy Brief 14. Carsey Institute, Durham, N.H.

Oklahoma Institute for Child Advocacy and Arkansas Advocates for Children. 2004. *Rural Kids Count: Sharing the Stories and Statistics from Oklahoma and Arkansas.* Baltimore: Annie E. Casey Foundation.

Ono, Hiromo. 1998. "Husbands' and Wives' Resources and Marital Dissolution." *Journal of Marriage and the Family* 60 (3): 674–89.

———. 1999. "Historical Time and U.S. Marital Dissolution." *Social Forces* 77:969–99.

Ontai, Lenna, Yoshie Sano, Holly Hatton, and Katherine J. Conger. 2008. "Low-Income Rural Mothers' Perceptions of Parent Confidence: The Role of Family Health Problems and Partner Status." *Family Relations* 57 (3): 324–34.

Oppenheimer, Valerie K. 1997. "Women's Employment and the Gain to Marriage: The Specialization and Trading Model." *Annual Review of Sociology* 23:431–53.

Osgood, D. Wayne, and Jeff M. Chambers. 2003. "Community Correlates of Rural Youth Violence." *Juvenile Justice Bulletin* (May).

Parisi, Domenico, Deborah A. Harris, Steven Michael Grice, Michael Taquino, and Duane A. Gill. 2005. "Does the Work-First Initiative Make a Difference for Low Income People?" *Journal of Poverty* 9:65–81.

Parisi, Domenico, Diane McLaughlin, Steven Grice, and Michael Taquino. 2006. "Exiting TANF: Individual and Local Factors and Their Differential Influence Across Racial Groups." *Social Science Quarterly* 87 (1): 76–90.

Parisi, Domenico, Diane McLaughlin, Steven Grice, Michael Taquino, and Duane Gill. 2003. "TANF Participation Rates: Do Community Conditions Matter?" *Rural Sociology* 68 (4): 491–512.

Parisi, Domenico, Diane K. McLaughlin, Michael Taquino, Steven Michael Grice, and Neil R. White. 2002. "TANF/Welfare Decline and Community Context in the Rural South, 1997–2000." *Southern Rural Sociology* 18 (1): 154–85.

Parke, Ross D., Scott Coltrane, Sharon Duffy, Raymond Buriel, Jessica Dennis, Justina Powers, Sabine French, and Keith F. Widaman. 2005. "Economic Stress, Parenting, and Child Adjustment in Mexican American and European American Families." *Child Development* 75:1632–56.

Parrado, Emilio, and William Kandel. 2010. "Hispanic Population Growth and Rural Income Inequality." *Social Forces* 86:1421–50.

Partee, Glenda L. n.d. "Preparing Youth for Employment: Principles and Characteristics of Five Leading United States Youth Development Programs." Washington, D.C.: American Youth Policy Forum.

Partridge, Mark D., and Dan S. Rickman. 2005. "High Poverty Nonmetropolitan Counties in the United States: Can Economic Development Help?" *International Regional Science Review* 28:415–40.

———. 2006. *The Geography of American Poverty: Is There a Need for Place-Based Policies?* Kalamazoo, Mich.: W. E. Upjohn Institute for Employment Research.

Pavetti, LaDonna, and Gregory Acs. 2001. "Moving Up, Moving Out, or Going Nowhere? A Study of the Employment Patterns of Young Women and the Implications for Welfare Mothers." *Journal of Policy Analysis and Management* 20:721–36.

Pavetti, LaDonna, and Dan Bloom. 2001. "State Sanctions and Time Limits." In *The New World of Welfare,* edited by Rebecca M. Blank and Ron Haskins, 254–69. Washington, D.C.: Brookings Institution.

Peace and Justice Center. 1999. "The Vermont Job Gap Study, Phase 5: Basic Needs and a Livable Wage, 1998 Update." Peace and Justice Center, Burlington, Vt.

Pearlin, Leonard I., Elizabeth G. Menaghan, Morton A. Lieberman, and Joseph T. Mullan. 1981. "The Stress Process." *Journal of Health and Social Behavior* 22:337–56.

Perucci, Carolyn C., and Dena B. Targ. 1988. "Effects of a Plant Closing on Marriage and Family Life." In *Families and Economic Distress: Coping Strategies and Social Policy,* edited by Patricia Voydanoff and Linda C. Majika, 55–71. Beverly Hills, Calif.: Sage.

Peters, Victoria J., E. R. Oetting, and Ruth W. Edwards. 1992. "Drug Use in Rural Communities: An Epidemiology." In Edwards 1992, 9–30.

Philliber, Susan, Jackie Kaye, and Scott Herrling. 2001. *The National Evaluation of the Children's Aid Society Carrera-Model Program to Prevent Teen Pregnancy.* New York: Philliber Research Associates.

Pickering, Kathleen, Mark H. Harvey, Gene F. Summers, and David Mushinski. 2006. *Welfare Reform in Persistent Rural Poverty: Dreams, Disenchantment, and Diversity.* University Park: Pennsylvania State University Press.

Pines, Marion. 2000. *The 21st Century Challenge: Moving the Youth Public Agenda Forward.* Baltimore: Johns Hopkins University.

Porter, Michael E. 2004. "Competitiveness in Rural U.S. Regions: Learning and Research Agenda." http://www.nyecon.cornell.edu/downloads/research/Competitiveness_Rural_US.pdf.

Porter, Toni, and Shannon Kearns. 2006. "Family, Friends and Neighbor Care: Crib Notes on a Complex Issue." In *Perspectives on Family, Friend and Neighbor Child Care: Research, Programs and Policy,* edited by Rena Rice. New York: Bank Street College of Education.

Porterfield, Shirley L. 1998. "On the Precipice of Reform: Welfare Spell Durations for Rural, Female-Headed Families." *American Journal of Agricultural Economics* 80:994–99.

———. 2001. "Economic Vulnerability Among Rural Single-Mother Families." *American Journal of Agricultural Economics* 83 (5) :1302–11.

Posner, Jill K., and Deborah Lowe Vandell. 1994. "Low-Income Children's After-School Care: Are There Beneficial Effects of After-School Programs?" *Child Development* 65:440–56.

Presser, Harriet B. 1999. "Toward a 24-Hour Economy." *Science* 284 (5421): 1178–79.

———. 2000. "Nonstandard Work Schedules and Marital Instability." *Journal of Marriage and the Family* 62 (1): 93–110.

———. 2003. *Working in a 24/7 Economy: Challenges for American Families.* New York: Russell Sage Foundation.

Probst, Janice C., Charity G. Moore, Saundra H. Glover, and Michael G. Samuels. 2004. "Person and Place: The Compounding Effects of Race/Ethnicity and Rurality on Health." *American Journal of Public Health* 94:1695–1703.

Public/Private Ventures. 2002. "Serving High-Risk Youth: Lessons from Research and Programming." September 2002. http://www.hewlett.org/NR/rdonlyres/F936A6E2-5347-4ECD-966A-29E1EA2A991A/o/ServingHighRiskYouthLessonsFromResearchandProgramm.pdf.

Rank, Mark Robert. 2004. *One Nation, Underprivileged: Why American Poverty Affects Us All.* Oxford: Oxford University Press.

Rank, Mark Robert, and Thomas A. Hirschl. 1993. "The Link Between Population Density and Welfare Participation." *Demography* 30 (4): 607–22.

Ray, Raka. 2000. "Masculinity, Femininity, and Servitude: Domestic Workers in Calcutta in the Late Twentieth Century." *Feminist Studies* 26 (3): 691–718.

Reeb, Ben T., and Katherine J. Conger. 2009. "The Unique Effect of Paternal Depressive Symptoms on Adolescent Functioning: Associations with Gender and Father-Adolescent Relationship Closeness." *Journal of Family Psychology* 23 (5): 758–61.

Reeder, Richard, and Dennis Brown. 2005. "Recreation, Tourism, and Rural Well-Being." USDA Economic Research Service Report No. 7. http://www.ers.usda/gov/Publica tions/ERR7.

Reimers, Cordelia, and Pamela Stone. 2007. "Opting out Among College-Educated Women, 1982–2005: Trends and Explanations." Paper presented at the Annual Meeting of the American Sociological Association, August 11–14, New York.

Renzulli, Linda A., and Lorraine Evans. 2005. "School Choice, Charter Schools, and White Flight." *Social Problems* 52:398–418.

Reschke, Kathy L., Margaret M. Manoogian, Leslie N. Richards, Susan K. Walker, and Sharon B. Seiling. 2006. "Maternal Grandparents as Child Care Providers for Rural, Low-Income Mothers." *Journal of Children and Poverty* 12 (2): 159–74.

Reschke, Kathy L., and Susan K. Walker. 2006. "Mothers' Child Caregiving and Employment Commitments and Choices in the Context of Rural Poverty." *Affilia: Journal of Women and Social Work* 21 (3): 306–20.

Ricketts, Thomas C. 1999. *Rural Health in the United States.* New York: Oxford University Press.

Roberts, Brandon. 2006. "Area Poverty Effects on Local Health Care Costs: An Analysis of Mississippi." *Review of Policy Research* 23 (1): 223–33.

Robertson, Elizabeth B., Glen H. Elder Jr., and Martie L. Skinner. 1991. "The Costs and Benefits of Social Support in Families." *Journal of Marriage and Family* 53:403–16.

Rodgers, Yana van der Muellen. 2006. "A Primer on Wage Gap Decompositions in the Analysis of Labor Market Discrimination." In *Handbook on the Economics of Discrimination,* edited by William M. Rodgers III, 11–28. New Brunswick, N.J.: Edward Elgar.

Rogers, Stacy J., and Danelle D. DeBoer. 2001. "Changes in Wives' Income: Effects on Marital Happiness, Psychological Well-Being, and the Risk of Divorce." *Journal of Marriage and the Family* 63 (2): 458–72.

Roscigno, Vincent J. 1995. "The Social Embeddedness of Racial Educational Inequality: The Black-White Gap and the Impact of Racial and Local Political-Economic Contexts." *Research in Social Stratification and Mobility* 14:135–65.

Roscigno, Vincent J., Donald Tomaskovic-Devey, and Martha Crowley. 2006. "Education and the Inequalities of Place." *Social Forces* 84 (4): 2121–45.

Rosenbaum, Sara, Phyllis C. Borzai, and Vernon Smith. 2000. *Allowing Small Businesses and the Self-Employed to Buy Health Care Coverage Through Public Programs.* Washington, D.C.: Commonwealth Fund.

Rosenblatt, Paul. 1990. *Farming Is in Our Blood: Farm Families in Economic Crisis.* Ames: Iowa State University Press.

Rubin, Lillian Breslow. 1976. *Worlds of Pain: Life in the Working-Class Family.* New York: Basic Books.

Rural Families Data Center. 2004. "Strengthening Rural Families: America's Rural Children." Rural Families Data Center, Population Reference Bureau, Washington, D.C.

Rural Policy Research Institute. 1999. "Rural America and Welfare Reform: An Overview Assessment." P99-3. Rural Policy Research Institute, Columbia, Mo.

Rural Sociological Society Task Force on Persistent Rural Poverty. 1993. *Persistent Poverty in Rural America.* Boulder, Colo.: Westview Press.

Rutland Herald. 2002. "Closing Doors." August 16, A8.

Sampson, Robert J., and W. Byron Groves. 1989. "Community Structure and Crime: Testing Social-Disorganization Theory." *American Journal of Sociology* 94 (4): 774–802.

Sandefur, Gary D., Sara McLanahan, Roger A. Wojtkiewicz. 1992. "The Effects of Parental Marital Status During Adolescence on High School Graduation." *Social Forces* 71:103–21.

Sayer, Liana C., Phillip N. Cohen, and Lynne M. Casper. 2004. *Women, Men, and Work.* New York: Russell Sage Foundation.

Scaramella, Laura V., Sara L. Sohr-Preston, Kristen L. Callahan, and Scott P. Mirabile. 2008. "A Test of the Family Stress Model on Toddler-Aged Children's Adjustment Among Hurricane Katrina Impacted and Nonimpacted Low-Income Families." *Journal of Clinical Child and Adolescent Psychology* 37 (3): 530–41.

Scheer, Scott D., Lynne M. Borden, and Joseph F. Donnermeyer. 2000. "The Relationship Between Family Factors and Adolescent Substance Use in Rural, Suburban, and Urban Settings." *Journal of Child and Family Studies* 9 (1): 105–15.

Schodolaski, Vincent J. 1997. "Farm Workers Earn Less than in '76, Data Show." *Chicago Tribune,* April 12.

Scholz, John Karl. 1994. "The Earned Income Tax Credit: Participation, Compliance, and Antipoverty Effectiveness." *National Tax Journal* 47:63–87.

Schulman, Karen. 2000. "The High Cost of Child Care Puts Quality Care out of Reach for Many Families." Children's Defense Fund, Washington, D.C.

Schulman, Karen, and Helen Blank. 2008. "State Child Care Assistance Policies 2008: Too Little Progress for Children and Families." National Women's Law Center Issue Brief. National Women's Law Center, Washington, D.C.

Scrivener, Susan, Hendra Redcross, Cindy Richard, Dan Bloom, Charles Michalopoulos, and Johanna Walter. 2002. "WRP: Final Report on Vermont's Welfare Restructuring Project." Manpower Demonstration Research Corporation, New York.

Seccombe, Karen, and Cheryl Amey. 1995. "Playing by the Rules and Losing: Health Insurance and the Working Poor." *Journal of Health and Social Behavior* 36:168–81.

Seebach, Michele. 1992. "Small Towns Have a Rosy Image." *American Demographics* 14 (10): 19.

Seltzer, Judith A. 2000. "Families Formed Outside of Marriage." *Journal of Marriage and Family* 62 (4): 1247–68.

Shelton, Beth Anne. 1987. "Variations in Divorce Rates by Community Size: A Test of the Social Integration Hypothesis." *Journal of Marriage and the Family* 49 (4): 827–32.

Shelton, Beth Anne, and Daphne John. 1996. "The Division of Household Labor." *Annual Review of Sociology* 22 (1): 299–322.

Sherman, Jennifer. 2007. "Coping with Rural Poverty: Economic Survival and Moral Capital in Rural America." *Perspectives on Poverty, Policy, and Place* 4 (1): 7–10.

Shoffner, Sarah M. 1986. "Child Care in Rural Areas: Needs, Attitudes, and Preferences." *American Journal of Community Psychology* 14:521–39.

Simmons, Leigh Ann, Bonnie Braun, David W. Wright, and Scott R. Miller. 2007. "Human Capital, Social Support, and Economic Well-Being Among Rural, Low-Income Mothers: A Latent Growth Curve Analysis." *Journal of Family Economic Issues* 28:635–52.

Simons, Ronald L., and Associates. 1996. *Understanding Differences Between Divorced and Intact Families: Stress, Interaction, and Child Outcome.* Thousand Oaks, Calif.: Sage.

Skaptadottir, Unnur Dis. 2000. "Women Coping with Change in an Icelandic Fishing Community: A Case Study." *Women's Studies International Forum* 23 (3): 311–21.

Slack, Tim, and Leif Jensen. 2002. "Race, Ethnicity, and Underemployment in Nonmetropolitan America: A 30-Year Profile." *Rural Sociology* 67:208–33.

———. 2004. "Employment Adequacy in Extractive Industries: An Analysis of Underemployment, 1974–1998." *Society and Natural Resources* 17:129–46.

Smith, Kristin. 2006. "Rural Families Choose Home-Based Child Care for Their Preschool-Aged Children." Carsey Institute Policy Brief No. 3. Carsey Institute, Durham, N.H.

———. 2007. "Rural Women and Work." Carsey Institute Report on Rural America 4. Carsey Institute, Durham, N.H.

———. 2008. "Working Hard for the Money: Trends in Women's Employment, 1970–2007." Carsey Institute Report on Rural America No. 5. Carsey Institute, Durham, N.H.

———. 2009. "Increased Reliance on Wives as Breadwinners During the First Year of the Recession." Carsey Institute Issue Brief No. 9. Carsey Institute, Durham, N.H.

Smith, Kristin, and Kristi Gozjolko. 2010. "Low Income and Impoverished Families Pay More Disproportionately for Child Care." Carsey Institute Policy Brief No. 16. Carsey Institute, Durham, N.H.

Smith, Margot W., Richard A. Kreutzer, Lynn Goldman, Amy Casey-Paal, and Kenneth W. Kizer. 1996. "How Economic Demand Influenced Access to Medical Care for Hispanic Children." *Medical Care* 34:1135–48.

Smith, Suzanna, Steve Jacob, Michael Jepson, and Glenn Israel. 2003. "After the Florida Net Ban: The Impacts on Commercial Fishing Families." *Society and Natural Resources* 16:39–59.

Smith, Timothy, Anne Kleiner, Basmat Parsad, and Elizabeth Farris. 2003. Pre-kindergarten in U.S. Public Schools: 2000–2001: Statistical Analysis Report. U.S. Department of Education, Institute for Education Sciences, NCES, Washington, D.C.

Smith, William M., and Raymond T. Coward. 1981. "The Family in Rural Sociology: Images of the Future." In Coward and Smith 1981, 221–30.

Snyder, Anastasia R. 2006. "The Role of Contemporary Family Behaviors in Nonmarital Conception Outcomes of Nonmetro Women: Comments on Albrecht and Albrecht (2004)." *Rural Sociology* 71:155–63.

Snyder, Anastasia R., Susan L. Brown, and Erin P. Condo. 2004. "Residential Differences in Family Formation: The Significance of Cohabitation." *Rural Sociology* 69:235–60.

Snyder, Anastasia R., and Diane K. McLaughlin. 2004. "Female-Headed Families and Poverty in Rural America." *Rural Sociology* 69 (1): 127–49.

———. 2006. "Economic Well-Being and Cohabitation: Another Nonmetro Disadvantage?" *Journal of Family and Economic Issues* 27:562–82.

———. 2008. "Rural Youth Are More Likely to Be Idle." Carsey Institute Fact Sheet No. 11. Durham, N.H.: Carsey Institute, Durham, N.H.

Snyder, Anastasia R., Diane K. McLaughlin, and Jill Findeis. 2006. "Household Composition and Poverty Among Female-Headed Households with Children: Differences by Race and Residence." *Rural Sociology* 71:597–624.

Solantaus, Tytti, Jenni Leinonen, and Raija-Leena Punamäki. 2004. "Children's Mental Health in Times of Economic Recession: Replication and Extension of the Family Economic Stress Model in Finland." *Developmental Psychology* 40:412–29.

Sommer, Judith E., Robert A. Hoppe, Robert C. Greene, and Penelope J. Korb. 1998. "Structural and Financial Characteristics of U.S. Farms, 1995: 20th Annual Family Farm Report to Congress." Research Economics Division, Economic Research Service Agricultural Information Bulletin No. 746. U.S. Department of Agriculture, Washington, D.C.

South, Scott J. 1991. "Sociodemographic Differentials in Mate Selection Preferences." *Journal of Marriage and the Family* 53 (4): 928–40.

South, Scott J., and Eric P. Baumer. 2001. "Community Effects on the Resolution of Adolescent Premarital Pregnancy." *Journal of Family Issues* 22:1025–43.

Spoth, Richard, Catherine Goldberg, Tricia Neppl, Linda Trudeau, and Suhasini Ramisetty-Mikler. 2001. "Rural-Urban Differences in the Distribution of Parent-Reported Risk Factors for Substance Use Among Young Adolescents." *Journal of Substance Abuse* 13:609–23.

Stack, Carol. 1974. *All Our Kin.* New York: Harper and Row.

Stauber, Karl N. 2001. "Why Invest in Rural America—and How? A Critical Public Policy Question for the 21st Century." In *Exploring Policy Options for a New Rural America*, 9–29. Kansas City, Mo.: Center for the Study of Rural America.

Stolzenberg, Ross M. 1978. "Bringing the Boss Back in: Employer Size, Employee Schooling, and Socioeconomic Achievement." *American Sociological Review* 43 (6): 828–31.

Strom, Sara. 2003. "Unemployment and Families: A Review of Research." *Social Service Review* 77 (September 3): 399–430.

Strong, Debra A., Patricia Del Grosso, Andrew Burwick, Vinita Jethwani, and Michael Ponza. 2005. "Rural Research Needs and Data Sources for Selected Human Service Topics." http://aspe.hhs.gov/hsp/05/rural-data/.

Struthers, Cynthia B., and Janet L. Bokemeier. 2000. "Myths and Realities of Raising Children and Creating Family Life in a Rural County." *Journal of Family Issues* 21:17–46.

Sullivan, Teresa A. 1978. *Marginal Workers, Marginal Jobs: Underutilization of the U.S. Work Force.* Austin: University of Texas Press.

Swaim, Paul. 1990. "Rural Earnings Holding Steady in the Early 1990s." *Rural Conditions and Trends* 6 (1): 18–21.

Swanson, Linda L., and Margaret A. Butler. 1988. "Human Resource Base of Rural Econo-mies." In *Rural Economic Development in the 1980's: Prospects for the Future,* edited by David L. Brown, 159–79. Washington, D.C.: USDA Economic Research Service.

Swenson, Kendall. 2007. "Child Care Arrangements in Urban and Rural Areas." Paper pre-sented at the National Association for Welfare Research and Statistics 47th Annual Meeting, Charleston, W.V.

Swidler, Ann. 1986. "Culture in Action: Symbols and Strategies." *American Sociological Review* 51:273–86.

Task Force on Employment and Training for Court-Involved Youth. 2000. "Employment and Training for Court-Involved Youth." U.S. Department of Justice, Office of Justice and Delinquency Prevention, Washington, D.C.

Teachman, Jay D. 2002. "Stability Across Cohorts in Divorce Risk Factors." *Demography* 39 (2): 331–51.

Tekin, Erdal. 2005. "Child Care Subsidy Receipt, Employment, and Child Care Choice of Single Mothers." *Economic Letters* 89:1–6.

"Temporary Assistance for Needy Families—Closed Cases, Percent Distribution of TANF Closed-Case Families by Reason for Closure, October 2004–September 2005." 2008. U.S. Department of Health and Human Services, Washington, D.C.

Testa, Mark, Ann Marie Astone, Marilyn Krogh, and Kathryn M. Neckerman. 1989. "Employ-ment and Marriage Among Inner-City Fathers." *Annals of the American Academy of Political and Social Science* 501:79–91.

Thoits, Peggy A. 2006. "Personal Agency in the Stress Process." *Journal of Health and Social Behavior* 47:309–23.

Thomasson, Melissa A. 2000. "From Sickness to Health: The Twentieth-Century Develop-ment of the Demand for Health Insurance." *Journal of Economic History* 60 (2):504–8.

Thompson, Maxine S., Karl L. Entwisle, Doris R. Alexander. 1988. "Household Composition, Parental Expectations, and School Achievement." *Social Forces* 67:424–51.

Thornton, Arland, and Linda Young-DeMarco. 2001. "Four Decades of Trends in Attitudes Toward Family Issues in the United States: The 1960s Through the 1990s." *Journal of Marriage and the Family* 63:1009–37.

Tickamyer, Ann R., and Janet Bokemeier. 1988. "Sex Differences in Labor Market Experi-ences." *Rural Sociology* 53:166–89.

Tickamyer, Ann R., and Cynthia M. Duncan. 1990. "Poverty and Opportunity Structure in Rural America." *Annual Review of Sociology* 16:67–86.

Tickamyer, Ann R., and Debra A. Henderson. 2003. "Rural Women: New Roles for the New Century?" In Brown and Swanson 2003, 109–17. University Park: Pennsylvania State University Press.

Tickamyer, Ann R., Julie White, Barry Tadlock, and Debra Henderson. 2002. "Where All the Counties Are Above Average." In Weber, Duncan, and Whitener 2002, 231–54.

———. 2007. "The Spatial Politics of Public Policy: Devolution, Development, and Welfare Reform." In Lobao, Hooks, and Tickamyer 2007, 113–40.

Tickamyer, Ann R., and Theresa Wood. 2003. "The Social and Economic Context of Informal Work." In Falk, Schulman, and Tickamyer 2003, 394–418.

Tierney, Joseph P., Jean Baldwin Grossman, and Nancy L. Resch. 1995. *Making a Difference: An Impact Study of Big Brothers / Big Sisters.* Philadelphia: Public/Private Ventures.

Tigges, Leanne M., and Glenn V. Fuguitt. 2003. "Commuting: A Good Job Nearby?" In Brown and Swanson 2003, 166–76. University Park: Pennsylvania State University Press.

Tilly, Linda, Apreill Curtis Hartsfield, Lisa Parrish, Debra Miller, Valerie Salley, Linda O'Neal, Pam Brown, and Edwina Chappell. 2004. *The Rural South: Listening to Families in Alabama, Kentucky, and Tennessee.* Montgomery, Ala.: VOICES for Alabama's Children; Jeffersontown, Ky.: Kentucky Youth Advocates; Nashville, Tenn.: Tennessee Commission on Children and Youth.

Torgerson, David, and Karen Hamrick. 1999. "Global Conditions Hurting Rural Economy." *Rural Conditions and Trends* 9 (3): 7–11.

Torres, Rebecca M., E. Jeffrey Popke, and Holly M. Hapke. 2006. "The South's Silent Bargain: Rural Restructuring, Latino Labor and the Ambiguities of Migrant Experience." In *Latinos in the New South: Transformations of Place,* edited by Heather A. Smith and Owen J. Furuseth, 37–67. Burlington, Vt.: Ashgate.

Tout, Kathryn, Martha Zaslow, Tamara Halle, and Nicole Forry. 2009. "Issues for the Next Decade of Quality Rating and Improvement Systems." Office of Planning Research and Evaluation Issue Brief No. 3. Child Trends, Washington, D.C.

Uchitelle, Louis. 2006. *The Disposable American: Layoffs and Their Consequences.* New York: Alfred A. Knopf.

U.S. Census Bureau. 1990. U.S. Census Summary Tape Files 1 and 3.

———. 1999. *Statistical Abstract of the United States, 1999.* Washington, D.C.: U.S. Government Printing Office.

———. 2000. U.S. Census Summary Tape Files 1 and 3.

———. 2006. POV40: Age, Sex, Household Relationship by Region and Residence—Ratio of Income to Poverty Level: 2005. http://www.census.gov/hhes/www/cpstables/032010/pov/new40_000.htm.

———. 2009a. Table FG10: Family Groups: 2008. http://www.census.gov/population/www/socdemo/hh-fam/cps2008.html.

———. 2009b. Table C9: Children by Presence and Type of Parent(s), Race, and Hispanic Origin. http://www.census.gov/population/www/socdemo/hh-fam/cps2008.html.

———. 2010. POV41: Region, Division and Type of Residence—Poverty Status for All People, Family Members and Unrelated Individuals by Family Structure: 2009. http://www.census.gov/hhes/www/cpstables/032010/pov/new41_100_01.htm.

U.S. Department of Agriculture (USDA) Economic Research Service. 2007a. "Measuring Rurality." http://www.ers.usda.gov/Briefing/Rurality.

———. 2007b. "Rural Labor and Education: Nonmetro Employment and Unemployment."

U.S. Department of Commerce. Selected years. *County and City Data Book.* Washington, D.C.: U.S. Department of Commerce, Economics and Statistics Administration, Bureau of the Census.

U.S. Department of Education. 2010. "Twenty-First Century Community Learning Centers." http://www2.ed.gov/programs/21stcclc/index.html.

U.S. Department of Education, Institute of Education Sciences. 2003. "Prekindergarten in U.S. Public Schools: 2000–2001." Statistical Analysis Report. NCES 2003019. http://nces.ed.gov/surveys/frss/publications/2003019/index.asp?sectionID=9.

U.S. Department of Health and Human Services (U.S. DHHS). 2000. *Healthy People 2010: Understanding and Improving Health.* 2nd ed. Washington, D.C.: Office of Disease Prevention, U.S. Department of Health and Human Services.

————. 2004. "Head Start Program Fact Sheet 2004." http://www.acf.hhs.gov/programs/hsb/research/2004.htm.

————. 2005. *The National Survey of Children's Health 2003.* Rockville, Md.: U.S. Department of Health and Human Services.

————. 2007. "Child Care and Development Fund: Report of State and Territory Plans, FY 2006–2007." U.S. Child Care Bureau, Washington, D.C. http://nccic.acf.hhs.gov/pubs/stateplan2006-07/stateplan.pdf.

————. 2008. "Temporary Assistance for Needy Families—Closed Cases, Percent Distribution of TANF Closed-Case Families by Reaason for Closure, October 2004–September 2005." http://www.acf.hhs.gov/index.html.

————. 2009. "Child Care and Development Fund Report of State and Territory Plans, FY 2008–2009." U.S. Department of Health and Human Services, Administration for Children and Families, Administration for Children and Families, Office of Family Assistance, Washington, D.C.

U.S. Department of Labor. 1991. "What Work Requires of Schools: A SCANS Report for America 2000." http://wdr.doleta.gov/SCANS/whatwork/whatwork.pdf.

————. 2007. "What Is Job Corps?"

U.S. Department of Labor, Bureau of Labor Statistics. *See* Bureau of Labor Statistics.

U.S. Government Accountability Office (U.S. GAO). 2004. "Welfare Reform: Rural TANF Programs Have Developed Many Strategies to Address Rural Challenges." GAO-04-921. http://www.gao.gov/products/GAO-04-921.

Uttal, Lynet. 1999. "Using Kin for Child Care: Embedment in the Socioeconomic Networks of Extended Families." *Journal of Marriage and Family* 61 (4): 845–57.

Venkatesh, Sudhir Alladi. 2000. *American Project: The Rise and Fall of a Modern Ghetto.* Cambridge, Mass.: Harvard University Press.

Vias, Alexander C., and Peter B. Nelson. 2006. "Changing Livelihoods in Rural America." In Kandal and Brown 2006, 75–102.

Votruba-Drzal, Elizabeth, Rebekah Levine Coley, and P. Lindsay Chase-Lansdale. 2004. "Child Care and Low-Income Children's Development: Direct and Moderated Effects." *Child Development* 75 (1): 296–312.

Wald, Michael, and Tia Martinez. 2003. "Connected by 25: Improving the Life Chances of the Country's Most Vulnerable 14–24 Year Olds." http://www.hewlett.org/library/connected-by-25-improving-the-life-chances-of-the-country-s-most-vulnerable-youth.

Waldfogel, Jane. 1997. "The Effect of Children on Women's Wages." *American Sociological Review* 62:209–17.

Waldfogel, Jane, and Susan Mayer. 1999. "Male-Female Differences in the Low-Wage Labor Market." Harris School of Public Policy Studies Working Paper 9904.

Walker, Susan, and Kathy Reschke. 2004. "Child Care Use by Low-Income Families in Rural Areas: A Contemporary Look at the Influence of Women's Work and Partner Availability." *Journal of Children and Poverty* 102 (2): 149–67.

Waller, Maureen R. 2002. *My Baby's Father: Unmarried Parents and Paternal Responsibility.* Ithaca: Cornell University Press.

Ward, Sally, and Heather Turner. 2007. "Work and Welfare Strategies Among Single Mothers in Rural New England: The Role of Social Networks and Social Support." *Community Development* 38:43–58.

Watts, Michael, and David Goodman. 1997. "Agrarian Questions: Global Appetite, Local Metabolism: Nature, Culture, and Industry in *Fin-de-Siècle* Agro-food Systems." In *Globalising Food: Agrarian Questions and Global Restructuring,* edited by David Goodman and Michael Watts, 1–24. London: Routledge.

Weber, Bruce, Greg Duncan, and Leslie Whitener. 2002. *Rural Dimensions of Welfare Reform: Welfare, Food Assistance, and Poverty in Rural America.* Kalamazoo, Mich.: W. E. Upjohn Institute for Employment Research.

Weber, Bruce, Leif Jensen, Kathleen Miller, Jane Mosley, and Monica Fisher. 2005. "A Critical Review of Rural Poverty Literature: Is There Truly a Rural Effect?" *International Regional Science Review* 28:381–414.

Websdale, Neil. 1998. *Rural Woman Battering and the Justice System: An Ethnography.* Thousand Oaks, Calif.: Sage.

Weinberg, Daniel H. 1987. "Rural Pockets of Poverty." *Rural Sociology* 52:398–408.

Weisheit, Ralph A., and Joseph F. Donnermeyer. 2000. "Change and Continuity in Crime in Rural America." In *The Nature of Crime: Continuity and Change,* edited by Gary LaFree, 309–57. Washington, D.C.: U.S. Department of Justice, Office of Justice Programs, National Institute of Justice.

Weissman, Joel S., and Arnold M. Epstein. 1994. *Falling Through the Safety Net: Insurance Status and Access to Health.* Baltimore: Johns Hopkins University Press.

Wenglinsky, Harold. 1997. "How Money Matters: The Effect of School District Spending on Academic Achievement." *Sociology of Education* 70:221–37.

Westat (Preparer). 2001. *Survey of Income and Program Participation Users' Guide (Supplement to the Technical Documentation).* 3rd ed. Washington, D.C.: U.S. Department of Commerce, Economics and Statistics Administration, U.S. Census Bureau.

White, Lynn, and Stacy J. Rogers. 2000. "Economic Circumstances and Family Outcomes: A Review of the 1990s." *Journal of Marriage and the Family* 62 (4): 1035–51.

Whitener, Leslie A., and Tim Parker. 2007. "Policy Options for a Changing Rural America." *Amber Waves* 5:58–65.

Whitener, Leslie, Bruce A. Weber, and Greg J. Duncan. 2001. "Reforming Welfare: Implications for Rural America." *Rural America* 16:3.

White House Task Force for Disadvantaged Youth. 2003. "White House Task Force for Disadvantaged Youth Final Report." White House Task Force, Washington, D.C.

Wiley, Angela R., Henriette Buur Warren, and Dale S. Montanelli. 2002. "Shelter in a Time of Storm: Parenting in Poor Rural African American Communities." *Family Relations* 51 (3): 265–73.

Wilkinson, Kenneth P. 1984. "Rurality and Patterns of Social Disruption." *Rural Sociology* 49 (1): 23–36.

———. 2000. *The Community in Rural America.* Middleton, Wis.: Social Ecology Press.

Williams, Joan C., and Holly Cohen Cooper. 2004. "The Public Policy of Motherhood." *Journal of Social Issues* 60 (4): 849–65.

Williams, Shannon T., Katherine J. Conger, and Shelley Blozis. 2007. "The Development of Interpersonal Aggression During Adolescence: The Importance of Parents, Siblings, and Family Economic." *Child Development* 78:1526–42.

Wilson, William Julius. 1987. *The Truly Disadvantaged: The Inner City, the Underclass, and Public Policy.* Chicago: University of Chicago Press.

———. 1996. *When Work Disappears: The World of the New Urban Poor.* New York: Vintage Books.

Wolfe, Barbara, and Scott Scrivner. 2004. "Child Care Use and Parental Desire to Switch Care Type Among a Low-Income Population." *Journal of Family and Economic Issues* 25 (2): 139–62.

Wolfe, Barbara, Nathan Tefft. 2006. "Childhood Interventions That May Lead to Increased Economic Growth." *La Follette Policy Report* 16 (2): 1–2, 8–14.

Wright, Elisabeth. 2003. "Finding Resources to Support Rural Out-of-School Time Initiatives." Strategy Brief 4 (1). Finance Project, Washington, D.C.

YouthBuild USA. n.d. History. http://www.youthbuild.org/site/c.htIRI3PIKoG/b.1240601/k.C3BC/History.htm.

Zhou, Jiping, and Shengming Tang. 2000. "Breadwinner Status and Gender Ideologies of Men and Women Regarding Family Roles." *Sociological Perspectives* 43 (1): 29–43.

Zill, Nicholas. 1996. "Family Change and Student Achievement: What We Have Learned, What It Means for Schools." In *Family-School Links: How Do They Affect Educational*

Outcomes?, edited by Alan Booth and Judith F. Dunn, 139–74. Hillsdale, N.J.: Lawrence Erlbaum.

Ziller, Erika C., Andrew F. Coburn, Stephenie L. Loux, Catherine Hoffman, and Timothy D. McBride. 2003. "Health Insurance Coverage in Rural America." Kaiser Family Foundation, Washington, D.C.

Zuñiga, Victor, and Rubén Hernández-León, eds. 2005. *New Destinations: Mexican Immigration in the United States.* New York: Russell Sage Foundation.

Contributors

Kristin E. Smith is a family demographer at the Carsey Institute and Research Assistant Professor of Sociology at the University of New Hampshire. Her research explores women's labor force participation, wives as breadwinners, and work and family policy. Her research has been published in academic journals, including *Demography, Monthly Labor Review,* and *Family Relations,* and has also been reported in the *New York Times,* the *Los Angeles Times,* the *Washington Post,* the *Boston Globe,* and numerous online and local media outlets, and she has appeared on National Public Radio.

Ann R. Tickamyer is Professor of Rural Sociology and Head of the Department of Agricultural Economics and Rural Sociology at the Pennsylvania State University. She is a past president of the Rural Sociological Society and a past editor of *Rural Sociology.* Her research focuses on rural poverty and inequality, gender, work, and development, and social welfare provision in the United States and Indonesia. Her work is published in leading journals, and she is the co-editor of two books, *Communities of Work: Rural Restructuring in Local and Global Contexts* and *The Sociology of Spatial Inequality.*

Cynthia D. Anderson is Associate Professor of Sociology and Director of Graduate Studies at Ohio University. Her research focuses on inequality, low-wage labor markets, the working poor, and critical theory. In additional to quantitative modeling of the working poor, she is pursuing an NSF-funded qualitative research agenda that examines the role of community colleges in advancing women in science and engineering. Some of her publication outlets include *Rural Sociology, Gender and Society,* and the *Review of Regional Studies.*

Guangqing Chi is Assistant Professor of Sociology and Coordinator of the Computational and Spatial Analysis Laboratory within the Department of Sociology, and Research Scientist at the Social Science Research Center at Mississippi State University. His program of research seeks to examine the interactions between human population and the built and natural environment upon which we all depend. In 2007, he received the Walter E. Terrie Award from the Southern Demographic Association for his development of spatial regression models for small-area population forecasting.

Alisha J. Coleman-Jensen is a Social Science Analyst at USDA Economic Research Service, where her research focuses on the measurement and determinants of food insecurity. Her research also examines the relationship between work characteristics and household food insecurity, preferences for and outcomes of nonstandard work arrangements across gender and residence, and work and educational outcomes for rural youth.

Katherine Jewsbury Conger is Associate Professor in the Department of Human and Community Development at the University of California–Davis and Director of the Family Research Group. Her program of research focuses on the antecedents, correlates, and consequences of economic stress on family functioning and individual well-being. During the past twenty years, her research has been supported by grants from NIMH, NIDA, and NICHD as well as UCD and has been published in numerous book chapters and journal articles.

Nicole D. Forry is a Senior Research Scientist in the Early Childhood Program Area of Child Trends in Washington, D.C. Her research interests include child care subsidies, tax credits, child care decision making, disparities in children's developmental outcomes, and predictors and measurements of quality in center- and home-based early care and education settings.

Deborah Roempke Graefe is a Social Demographer at the Population Research Institute at Penn State University. Her research focuses on family life course transitions in diverse contexts and government policy pertaining to the well-being of family members. She has researched family health issues extensively, and her research also focuses on welfare reform and family demographic processes, including migration and family formation among immigrants and low-income women. Her work has been published in several books and journals, such as *Demography,* the *Journal of Family Issues,* and the *Journal of Policy Analysis and Management.*

Steven Michael Grice is an Associate Research Professor and Associate Director of the National Strategic Planning and Analysis Research Center (nSPARC) at Mississippi State University. His research interests are in the areas of education, workforce and community development, and welfare policy. His work appears in technical reports, policy briefs, and journals such as *Demography, Rural Sociology,* the *Social Science Quarterly,* the *Journal of Poverty,* and *Society and Natural Resources.*

Andrew B. Hahn is a Professor with the Heller School for Social Policy and Management at Brandeis University. He is the newly appointed director of the Sillerman Center for the Advancement of Philanthropy in the Heller School. A leading expert on youth development for international donors, multinational corporations, and American foundations, Hahn teaches courses on policy implementation, evaluation research, youth policy, community building, and other subjects.

Debra A. Henderson is an Associate Professor of Sociology and Presidential Teacher at Ohio University and a Faculty Fellow at the Voinovich Center for Leadership and Public Affairs. Her research interests are rural poverty, intersectionality, and the impact of structural inequality on culturally diverse families.

Eric B. Jensen is a demographer in the Net International Migration Branch of the U.S. Census Bureau, where his research focuses on estimates of international migration. His other research interests include new immigrant destinations, farm labor policy, and rural economic restructuring.

Leif Jensen is Professor of Rural Sociology and Demography at the Pennsylvania State University. His research interests are in social stratification, with emphasis on poverty, employment hardship, and informal work; demography, with special attention to migration and immigration; and international development, with a focus on children and youth.

Marlene Lee is a Senior Research Associate at the Population Reference Bureau, where her work includes analyses of well-being, the science and engineering workforce, and dissemination of research on population aging. She holds degrees in comparative literature, public policy analysis, and sociology, with concentrations in family demography and community development. She has previously been on the faculty of the University of Wisconsin–Madison and Louisiana State University, and has served as an Associate Director in the U.S. Peace Corps.

Daniel T. Lichter is the Ferris Family Professor in the Departments of Policy Analysis and Management and Sociology at Cornell University. His research focuses on changing patterns of poverty and racial inequality among rural families and children. He is currently studying patterns of immigrant adaptation in the United States, especially among Hispanics in new rural destinations. His paper with David L. Brown on "Rural America in an Urban Society: Changing Spatial and Social Boundaries" appears in the 2011 volume of the *Annual Review of Sociology*. Lichter is President of the Rural Sociological Society and President-Elect of the Population Association of America.

Elaine McCrate has a joint appointment in Economics and Women's Studies at the University of Vermont. Her most recent research concerns race and gender differences in job control, including such issues as scheduling, monitoring, decision making, and workplace punishment. Her work has appeared in *Feminist Economics, Industrial Relations,* and other journals.

Diane K. McLaughlin is Professor of Rural Sociology and Demography at the Pennsylvania State University. Her research examines the influence of economic and demographic change on income inequality, poverty, female-headed families and well-being, and rural youth educational, occupational, and residential aspirations and attainment. She has published in *Rural Sociology,* the *American Sociological Review,* and elsewhere.

Margaret K. Nelson is the A. Barton Hepburn Professor of Sociology at Middlebury College. Her research focuses on the survival strategies of rural families and parental attitudes towards monitoring children. She is the author of several books, of which the two most recent are *The Social Economy of Single Motherhood: Raising Children in Rural America* and *Parenting Out of Control: Anxious Families in Uncertain Times.*

Domenico "Mimmo" Parisi is Professor of Sociology and Director of the National Strategic Planning and Analysis Research Center (nSPARC) at Mississippi State University. The major thrust of his research is in the area of workforce, economic, business, and community development. Using place as a major conceptual and analytical framework, his research has contributed to the general field of sociology by providing insight into the factors that promote or thwart community development. His work has appeared in technical reports, book chapters, policy briefs, and journals such as *Demography, Rural Sociology,* the *Social Science Quarterly, Society and Natural Resources, Community Development Society,* and the *Journal of Poverty.*

Liliokanaio Peaslee is an Assistant Professor in the Department of Political Science at James Madison University. She teaches in the department's undergraduate Public Policy and Administration major and in the Master of Public Administration program, including courses in policy analysis, education policy, social welfare, American government, local policy, and applied state policy research. Her research includes work on youth development, community policing, civic engagement, and university-community partnerships.

Jed Pressgrove is the Technical Writer of the National Strategic Planning and Analysis Research Center (nSPARC) at Mississippi State University. His main research interests are racial residential segregation, sociology of religion, and media analysis. His work has appeared in *Community Development* and *Southern Rural Sociology.*

Jennifer Sherman is Assistant Professor of Sociology at Washington State University. Her research focuses on poverty, family, gender, and cultural discourses, particularly in rural communities. She is the author of *Those Who Work, Those Who Don't: Poverty, Morality, and Family in Rural America,* and has published articles in *Social Problems, Social Forces,* and elsewhere.

Anastasia Snyder is an Associate Professor in the Department of Human Development and Family Science at Ohio State University. Her research focuses on adolescent and youth development, family demography, and the transition to adulthood. She has published several book chapters and journal articles in *Rural Sociology,* the *Journal of Family and Economic Issues,* and elsewhere.

Susan K. Walker is Associate Professor in the Family, Youth, and Community program area, Department of Curriculum and Instruction, University of Minnesota. Her research, policy, and program development work centers on intersections of context and caregiving as they impact the lives of children and families. Her current research explores parents' use of technology, integration of technology into educational strategies for parents, and the evaluation of online platforms for parent learning and development.

Chih-Yuan Weng is Assistant Professor in the Department of Sociology at Fu Jen Catholic University in Taiwan. His research in progress examines, on the micro level, the prospective psychosocial pathways through which earlier life experiences might affect subsequent health and well-being among adolescents, and, on the macro level, the structural-ecological correlates of spatial disparities in working poor and mortality rates.

Index